1051

1051

by

Millard E. Hileman
and
Paul Fridlund

WORDS WORTH PRESS
Walla Walla, Washington

Copyright © 1992 by Millard E. Hileman and Paul Fridlund

All rights reserved

No part of this book may be reproduced in any form or by any electronic or mechanical means, including information storage or retrieval systems, without permission in writing from the authors or the publisher, except by a reviewer who may quote brief passages in a review.

Published by
Words Worth Press
P.O. Box 247
Walla Walla, WA 99362

First Edition

Library of Congress Card Number:
92-080080

ISBN 0-915214-26-1

To the humble people of
the Philippine Islands
who risked their lives
that others might live.

"Greater love has no man than this,
that he lay down his life for his friends."

— John 15:13

Foreword

The Apostle Peter speaks of the promise of "joy inexpressible and full of glory." Having worked closely with the authors in writing this book, I am keenly aware that life holds, for some of us, pain and sorrow which likewise is inexpressible, and full of man's inhumanity to man. I am convinced the printed word can never fully relate the fear, the frustrations, and the anger that have so deeply scarred every man who has been forced to endure the humiliation of being a prisoner of war. At the same time I marvel at the strength and resiliency of the human mind and body as those same men have been enabled upon liberation to assume their rightful roles as citizens, husbands, and fathers.

It has been my privilege not only to be married to one of those men for almost forty-six years, but also to be friends with many of them. I have been witness to the misunderstanding and prejudice many of them have known, but I have also been witness to the unique bond of friendship and trust that continues to exist among them even as the bitterness of their prison experiences gradually fades into the past. They are men who have known each other under the most dire circumstances imaginable, so they can afford now to be totally honest with one another, unabashedly revealing their weaknesses as well as their strengths.

I deeply treasure a comment made by one of them at a reunion.

"A lot of us," he said, "have done things we are not very proud of, but Millard is one guy who never lost his sense of integrity."

That sense of integrity has remained the standard of his life and has been the guiding rule for determining the content of this book. *1051* relates one man's experience, but in a sense it reflects the despair, the determination, and the faith that is inherent in the experiences of all who survived the atrocity and brutality of being a prisoner of war.

My prayer is that each of them may yet receive the promise of joy inexpressible.

Bea Hileman

ACKNOWLEDGMENTS

I want to express my personal gratitude to the four men who, along with myself, are the only known survivors of the Clark Field contingent of the old 698th Ordnance. The input of Charlie Johnson, Homer Boren, Arthur Standlee, and Grover Bump has given credence to my own recollections of the early weeks of the war in the Philippines, and their willingness to share has been a motivating factor in recording this story.

The pictures of me and PeeWee Standlee taken in the barracks at Clark Field were, with others, carried through the entire Bataan Death March and various prison camps by Grover Bump. Considering the never-ending efforts of the Japanese guards to destroy or pilfer all personal effects, saving the pictures was a rare accomplishment.

I want to give special thanks to Leland Montgomery of San Diego, a fellow prisoner on the *Nissyo Maru*. He ferreted out the information from the book *Silent Victory* by Clay Blair, Jr., that gave us the details of the submarine attack on the convoy which included our prison ship.

I am indebted to Dr. Paul Ashton for his encouragement when dealing with memories was difficult, and for his willingness to share material from his book *Bataan Diary*.

My coauthor, Paul Fridlund, deserves special mention, not only for his initial interest and zeal in convincing me this story should be written, but for his continued enthusiasm and expertise as he sifted through reams of material in his quest for accuracy in organizing and relating the events here recorded. I shall be forever grateful to him for that, and for the friendship which has developed between us.

Last, but certainly not least, I owe a special debt of gratitude to my beloved wife Bea for the hundreds of hours she spent editing, restructuring sentences and paragraphs, correcting punctuation and grammar. Her diplomacy and tact have been a continuing inspiration for me. She played a vital role in seeing the book to completion.

Millard E. Hileman

INTRODUCTION

1051 An insignificant number printed on white cardboard and pressed against the chest of a prisoner of war. Despite armed Japanese guards and the bright sunlight of August 6, 1944, his angry eyes bored into the lens of the photographer's camera. A week earlier he had tried to kill a man, smashing his head repeatedly into the steel deck of a transport ship in a fight for a piece of ice. Now he was beginning a year of slave labor in the Yawata Steel Mills in Japan. He felt isolated and forgotten, and hate alone sustained his will to survive the man-made hell which controlled every aspect of his existence.

To survive he ate weevil-infested rice, smelly whale meat, and a pet cat. He washed another man's dirty socks for cigarettes. During his imprisonment he lost his self-esteem, and as number 1051, he lost his personal identity. His name faded into insignificance, and as time passed, so did his number. Like most others, he was stripped of everything except his will to survive.

The first time I saw Millard Hileman was just after my family moved to Benson Avenue in 1956. I can remember Hileman standing at the back door of his concrete block house which looked like a fort to a six-year-old boy who lived at the other end of the alley. He wore khaki pants and shirt, his hair was cut in a flattop, and he stared with piercing eyes.

Somewhere I had been warned about the former prisoner of war, perhaps unfairly. When I heard people talk about him, they spoke with a sense of awe and uncertainty. I was sure from their tone his wartime service had involved a kind of dark, sinister experience. On my block every youngster's father had been in the service, but their World War II experiences were not like Hileman's. My little-boy instincts warned me to avoid him.

While home on leave four months after the war ended, Hileman sat down at a typewriter in his parents' empty basement. Alone, except for the punching bag he had hung from the heavy beams earlier that week, he spent hours at the keys of the black Royal. In thirty-two pages of single-spaced type, he recorded the events surrounding his escape from Bataan which had begun on April 9, 1942. When he finished he put the story away.

Working hard to adjust to civilian life and concentrating on raising his family of three daughters, it was not until thirty-seven years later that he began to delve into the events that had haunted his life for more than a quarter century.

He took out the account he had written in 1945 and began writing a narrative of his experience, expanding the original and continuing from where it left off.

Hileman had kept in contact with some friends who had shared his experience, and he found others who confirmed dates and remembered experiences.

In 1983 I was writing a local history of Prosser, Washington, during World War II. In the course of my research, I learned more about the events that had scared a six-year-old boy. I made contact with Hileman, arranged an interview, and paid him a visit. When that book was published, it included a short summary of Hileman's experience as a prisoner of war in Asia. It was not, however, enough to satisfy my curiosity, but only piqued my interest. I had to find out more, so I contacted him again, and together we began this book. I wanted to journey into hell without going there, and he would be my guide.

Hileman's experiences, and scars, are forever branded in his memory. He vividly recalls the details of his imprisonment and strongly feels the harsh reality of his ordeal needs no embellishment.

Hileman remembers, and according to his wife, his stories have remained unchanged since their marriage forty-five years ago.

Hileman's narrative is the basis for several chapters in this book. The rest of his story was put together through tapes, interviews, and correspondence.

When the first draft was completed, Hileman's wife, Bea, joined us. She has been actively involved in the editing and emending of this book through several drafts. Together we have reconstructed Hileman's experience from his escape from Bataan in the Philippines through his liberation four years later in Japan.

During his escape from Bataan in 1942, Hileman wondered which of the seven men who fled together would be the first to die and who would be the last.

Now fifty years later, only Millard Hileman, prisoner of war number 1051, remains to tell this story, and he tells it with openness, candor, and honesty. He tells it to preserve the memory of lost friends, to give witness to the horror they all experienced, and to give testimony of his own personal struggle to survive. He shares his story so others might better understand the American prisoner of war experience in Asia.

1051 is the true story of his remarkable journey through World War II.

Paul Fridlund

Nobody believes
the stories we tell.

Oh, yes, even today . . .
I remember them well.

Homer Boren
1984

Chapter One

Surrender was not something I had seriously considered during the months following the attack on Clark Field. Even with our subsequent withdrawal into Bataan, and knowing we could not withstand the Japanese onslaught there indefinitely, the thought of becoming a prisoner of war had been remote. Yet here we were, trudging slowly southward toward the surrender point at Mariveles. Word had been passed on to us the previous evening that the official surrender would be effective at 6:00 A.M. It was April 9, 1942.

I was part of a twelve-man demolition team which had stayed behind when the rest of the 698th Ordnance left earlier in the morning to join the surrendering forces. Now we, too, had fulfilled our last act of war, and as we walked silently along, the acrid smell of gunpowder and cordite cut through the air. Black smoke rose from the burning ammunition dump which had supplied defensive positions along the west coast of the Bataan Peninsula. Our mission had been accomplished, and all that remained for us now was to join the others.

Sherdie Allin and four other men from the demolition team were already some distance ahead of us. Sergeants Wally Kinder and Forrest Henderson walked together, followed closely by George Wicks, Bill Main, and Orlo Heinzman. Paul Vacher and I trailed behind. Vacher and I had been close friends since shortly after high school when we had been in the same CCC camp in California. In the years since then we had shared all kinds of experiences, yet nothing before compared to the prospects we faced as we walked down the road toward the surrender point at Mariveles. We were not alone, however. Hundreds of other weary Americans and Filipinos, with dazed and frightened expressions, plodded down the road.

Throughout the night there had been much activity on the road, and now with the morning hours, traffic had increased. Overloaded buses, packed with Filipino soldiers and civilians, worked their way through the crowd. Even the tops of the buses were packed with people, mattresses, burlap bags crammed with personal effects, and bicycles.

American trucks carrying demoralized soldiers stopped now and then to pick up others. Supplies and equipment were thrown out to make room for passengers, and discarded boxes lay scattered along the road. Some had burst open when they were tossed from passing trucks, scattering their contents like garbage. A barefoot Filipino was pushing a wheelbarrow piled high with discarded supplies. On one side of the road a group of soldiers struggled to push their truck out of the mud. A seemingly endless parade of people, ghostlike with a coat of powdery gray dust, shuffled silently past jeeps and trucks which had been abandoned. Step by step, I was becoming a part of this strange procession.

"Down! Get down! Jap planes!" someone shouted from behind.

Instinctively I dived headfirst into the ditch. Machine-gun bullets pelted the ground as three Japanese planes strafed the congested road. Nine antipersonnel bombs exploded, one after the other. The painful cries of the wounded were muffled as the dive bombers came roaring in for another pass, this time firing machine guns and 20mm cannons. One of the shells exploded with a dull thud between Vacher and me in the ditch. The concussion shook the ground, but neither of us was hit.

"What the hell's going on here?" Vacher shouted in anger. "Son of a bitch! Is this what a goddamned Jap surrender is?"

Vacher pounded his fist into his musette bag and staggered to his feet. He turned toward me, and I could see the slimy, brown muck that covered the front of his fatigue jacket. His eyes were red and glazed as he tried to rub the debris from them with his grimy hands. I could hear the wounded around me screaming for help while others lay motionless, casualties of a campaign that had officially ended hours earlier. I shook with rage at the viciousness of the attack.

"How come those shitheads are shooting at us now?"

I cursed them with every breath as I began to scrape the mud off myself. Then I heard Orlo's high-pitched voice as it pierced through the noisy confusion.

"Those goddamn sons of bitches won't shoot at me again, unless I have a chance to shoot back," he shouted defiantly as he waved his long arms. "Let's get out of here. To hell with going to Mariveles!"

"Orlo, that's a damn good idea," Sergeant Kinder said.

All of us shared Orlo's frustration, and from the hostile glare in Kinder's piercing brown eyes, I knew he was serious about escape.

"Come on, let's go talk it over," Kinder said.

The six of us followed Kinder up a dusty trail that wound its way through the brush and trees. I was excited with anticipation by the time we reached a clearing next to a small stream. During the rainy season it would become an impassable torrent, but now it was reduced to a small trickle meandering around large boulders in the streambed. In the distance, and obscured by the dense undergrowth, we could still hear the activity on the road. The only other sounds were the trickling water and bees working in the nearby flowers.

Kinder reached down and turned a rock, exposing its flat side. He sat down, and the rest of us gathered around him. I joined Vacher and Orlo as we squatted together on the ground.

Kinder was a small, wiry man with a natural military bearing and an air of confidence that had set him apart. We were not drawn to him because he outranked us, but rather because he had already demonstrated his leadership skills. He had been on detached duty before the invasion, but had been ordered back to Clark Field just before the evacuation on Christmas Day. Kinder had been put in charge when the demolition crew from the 698th was ordered to destroy the stores of bombs and gasoline left behind when the air base was evacuated.

I had been amazed at the desolation we left at Clark Field that day. Kinder directed us as we set the fuses to destroy the thousands of tons of bombs stored in five giant igloo magazines. As we sought an efficient method of destroying the gasoline that had been stored in piles of fifty-gallon drums, Kinder suggested firing tracer bullets at random into them. Almost a million gallons of aviation fuel was burned, keeping it from getting into the hands of the Japanese.

I had wondered if anyone in the history of warfare had ever witnessed such damage and desolation as those explosions had caused. From seven kilometers away we had watched the boiling pillars of smoke and eruptions of the great igloo magazines as they belched dust and debris to heights of probably seven or eight thousand feet. Even from that distance we would have been blown into the ditch by the concussion had we not hung onto the trucks for dear life. Kinder's efficiency and clear thinking had earned my respect, and the respect of others.

Now, with the impulsive act of escape being suggested, we looked to him for guidance.

An eerie silence fell over us as we huddled together in this secluded spot. I could hear the trucks and buses on the road, and voices speaking both English and the native Tagalog drifted up the ravine. They seemed farther away now, as if our world had changed and we were part of a different reality. Finally Kinder looked up, pushed back his battered campaign hat, and butted his Camel on the toe of his shoe.

"You know, the Japs are crazy as hell, and being a prisoner of war in their place of business isn't going to be any goddamn picnic," he said in an even, clear voice. "I don't think there's anything in the *Articles of War* that says we have to surrender, especially now that we've completed our last assignment."

Kinder paused as the impact of his words began to sink in. I was not yet sure I wanted to risk my life trying to escape, but at the same time, the very thought of escape gave me a thrill I had not known since we had withdrawn into Bataan.

"Wally, what the hell are the *Articles of War?*" Orlo asked.

I had only a vague idea about what they were, but would never have asked a question that exposed my ignorance, especially in front of Vacher.

Kinder explained the *Articles of War* covered a soldier's conduct during surrender and imprisonment. If escape was a violation, he said we might be court-martialed after the war. I certainly had no desire to face a court-martial, so I welcomed Kinder's caution.

"Before we make a decision, let's make sure it's okay," he said. "You guys stay put. I think Lieutenant Ulak may still be at the quartermaster, and if he is, I want a signed note from him giving us his authorization."

I trusted Kinder, and if getting Ulak's permission was important to him, it was important to me.

Kinder returned an hour later and said Lieutenant Ulak was gone, but he had talked to a colonel from the quartermaster unit who had signed a note giving us his authorization for the escape. He also had given Kinder a warning. If we were caught, he said, the Japanese would accuse us of espionage, and that would likely mean execution.

Listening to Kinder's report, I knew escape was a deadly business, but by then I was eager for the chance to try to outwit the Japanese.

Eyes traveled from man to man as Kinder asked each one what he wanted to do. I harbored certain fears, but had no doubt about my response.

"What the hell. Let's get going," I said when my turn came. My decision, like those of the other six, was for escape. We would take our chances in the jungle rather than in a Japanese prison camp.

Having decided to flee, we faced another crucial decision. Would we carry guns? The quartermaster colonel had warned Kinder the Japanese would execute us if we were caught with arms. Despite the risks, we chose to carry our weapons so we could defend ourselves.

Throughout the day I had experienced a full gamut of emotions. I had felt fear, excitement, loneliness, sadness, confusion, and anger. Now, with six others, I had decided to escape, and the decision gave me a sense of exhilaration. I looked at Vacher.

"Hileman, you're okay," he said with a confident smile of approval.

Chapter Two

"You ought to see the road now," Kinder said after our unanimous decision. "There are even more trucks and buses. I can't imagine where everyone is coming from, and just about everyone is carrying a white flag."

White flags. Somehow that was an unexpected, and depressing, affirmation of our defeat.

"Let's see what's going on," Orlo said excitedly to me.

Leaving the others, we climbed a small hill, sat down on the hard-packed dirt, lit a cigarette, and watched the road. It was congested with buses, trucks, and Filipino soldiers, the whole scene seeming to blend together in a confused mass of humanity. The procession stretched in both directions along the road, and sure enough, many men carried white flags. As we watched the melancholy scene, we suddenly heard the familiar scream of dive bombers. Again, three planes opened up with machine guns, riddling the crowded road as nine antipersonnel bombs fell. The battle for Bataan was over, yet Japanese pilots seemed to delight in using human beings for target practice. A renewed hatred for the Japanese strengthened my resolve to escape.

We waited a few minutes before leaving the hill and walking down to the road. We could not see any Americans, but wounded and dead

Filipinos were everywhere. The sight of scattered supplies, brightly colored clothing, and mass confusion was overshadowed by the splotches of blood that still poured from fresh wounds, seeming almost to sparkle in the bright sunlight. Men with torn limbs called for help. Filipino medics, ill equipped and few in number, offered whatever comfort they could. Chaos, panic, and bewilderment showed in their dark brown eyes as I stared in stunned silence at the agony and suffering all around us.

"What kind of bastards would do such a thing?" I said.

I spotted a pair of Japanese binoculars in the ditch, probably an American soldier's souvenir discarded in fear. I picked them up and hung them around my neck.

"Hey, Hileman, want a Lucky?" Orlo said as he tossed me a pack. He had found an unopened carton and stuffed the remaining packs in his musette bag. We could see a wide variety of articles and equipment along the road as we turned to go back to the others.

Everyone was gathered around Kinder who was drawing a map of the Bataan Peninsula in the dust. I had appreciated his caution when we made our decision to flee, and now I was drawn to his thoroughness in planning our escape. As Orlo and I joined the others, Kinder was discussing what we would need for a trip through the jungle.

"Somebody's got to be in charge," he said.

Without hesitation we chose him, and he agreed his leadership could be replaced by a majority vote. Kinder discussed discipline, saying there would be no room for dissension.

"If there's a disagreement, I'll have the final say. If anyone still disagrees, we'll divide the supplies and that man can leave immediately."

"What the hell supplies are you talking about?" Orlo asked.

We had only our guns, some ammunition, and the clothes we were wearing. Some of us had musette bags, mess kits, and cigarettes, but otherwise we were unprepared for any kind of journey. Sergeant Henderson took a small notebook from his pocket, and we began suggesting things we would need. Kinder insisted on giving equal priority to food and medical supplies. I had not thought about the need for medicine, but quickly realized Kinder was right. Malaria, dengue fever, and even dysentery could be fatal on the trail.

As we listed our needs, I noticed Orlo had disappeared. Impulsive and always curious to know what was going on around him, he had apparently gone back to the road. When he returned, he tossed me a small, watch-size compass he had found.

"Here, Hileman. This'll keep you from getting lost," he said.

Orlo showed us some of his other finds, including more cigarettes, a thousand-tablet bottle of quinine, two Army blankets, and several capsules of chlorine.

Following Orlo's example, we made several trips to the road where an unbelievable variety of supplies and equipment had been dropped or discarded. We found sulfapyrazine, bandages, iodine, more blankets, shelter halves, canteens, mess equipment, clothing, and ammunition. Orlo found a sack of rice and seventeen cans of salmon.

I suddenly sensed the irony of having fought a campaign with dire shortages of both food and medicine, and now, on the day of surrender, finding ourselves with a surplus. We worked until midafternoon as Kinder and Henderson inventoried our acquisitions. After looking over the accumulated booty, Kinder said one more trip was necessary. We would be walking long distances in tropical jungles and needed foot protection. We would have to bathe our feet and change our socks frequently. Kinder sent Wicks and Vacher to the road for socks, and they returned with several pairs for each man.

"Hey, why don't we fill those damn socks with rice?" Orlo suggested in the casual, offhanded way I had learned to expect from him.

His suggestion made sense, not only because it was a good way to carry rice, but it allowed each of us to carry our own rations. If we became separated, that could be important. I reached into the sack of rice and filled my socks.

We spent several hours gathering supplies. Although he was inexperienced in jungle living, Kinder's leadership was already proving to be practical. We would not be fleeing pell-mell into the jungle, but instead were purposely preparing for a journey through it. The hours passed quickly, and it was almost 3:00 P.M. by the time we finished.

A branch snapped on the far side of the stream, and we all turned to see a curious Filipino emerging from the brush. Kinder had talked about the natives as we planned our escape, pointing out most Filipinos hated the Japanese. He emphasized we would be fugitives in a foreign land, and without support and help from the Filipino people, would have little chance of survival.

"Hello, Joe." Kinder extended his hand to the Filipino. "I'm Sergeant Kinder."

"I am Arturo Espirito, sir. I am a journalist from Manila. My family and I came to Bataan when the Japanese occupied the city."

Arturo told us about his flight into Bataan with his wife, Juanita, and their four children. He said thousands of Filipino civilians had taken refuge behind American lines in Bataan. Arturo said his family had been wealthy in Manila, but now was reduced to living in a small camp upstream in the trees.

He showed great interest in our plans to escape, but he also perceived our inexperience and began quizzing us about jungle survival.

"How about food?" he asked. "How do you plan to eat?"

"Well, we've got rice and fish, Joe," Orlo said. "How's that for a start?"

"Rice and fish are very good, sir, but first you must know how to cook the rice. How about the days when you are too close to the Japanese to light a fire?"

I could see the Filipino's insight into our inexperience had offended Orlo, but fortunately Kinder stepped in.

"We don't know a damn thing about cooking rice, Arturo," Kinder said. "We'd be much obliged if you'd give us some help."

"You will all come to my camp and eat with us," Arturo said as he smiled at Orlo. "We have plenty, and my wife can show you how to cook rice."

"Thank you," Kinder said.

Arturo gave us directions and said to come in an hour. It had been a long day, and we were all hungry. We welcomed the invitation.

"Somebody should stay here and guard this stuff," Kinder said as we prepared to leave. We had collected a substantial store of valuable supplies which could be easily ransacked or stolen.

"I'll stay," Wicks said, "but make sure you bring some food when you come back."

I was glad Wicks volunteered because I, for one, wanted to see the Filipino's camp. Jumping from boulder to boulder, we crossed the stream and followed a dirt trail. The sound of children's voices came through the trees, and just as we spotted the camp, a young boy came running to meet us.

"Hello, sir. I am Ernesto, and I am my father's oldest son."

He appeared to be about twelve years old, wearing shorts and a GI undershirt and an old army belt that hung loosely around his waist. A wooden scabbard attached to it caught my eye. It contained a bolo, the machete considered the universal tool of the Filipino people. I had seen them used to cut through the jungle, cut firewood, and cut cogan grass for their thatched roofs. They also were used to butcher pigs, carabao, and chickens.

"I've got to find one of those," Orlo said to Ernesto in admiration. Like myself, he had recognized the usefulness of such a tool.

As we talked with Ernesto, his sister Consuelo and brother Rudy came to join us. The children led us into the camp where the youngest child, Loling, was holding a string tightly in her hand. On the other end of it a giant bamboo beetle flew and tugged in a vain attempt to win its freedom. Ernesto proudly told us he had caught the big insect and his mother would cook it in boiling grease when Loling no longer played with it.

"You mean you eat those bugs?" Orlo asked.

"Yes, sir, and the grubs too. They are very good, sir."

While we talked with Arturo and the children, a slim, beautiful woman with dark oval eyes and skin of Polynesian texture came from the grass hut and introduced herself.

"I am Juanita. I am happy my husband invited you to eat with us."

It was apparent she was a strong woman who had been able to maintain a family life under extremely adverse conditions, and her demeanor indicated she was very much devoted to her husband.

We noticed none of the family was wearing shoes.

"We brought our shoes with us from Manila," Arturo said, "but if we have to escape in a hurry through the mountains, we need to be prepared to go without shoes. It is good to have tough feet."

"I will teach you to cook rice," Juanita said in a soft, accented voice as she turned to the fire.

Earlier that day we had decided Bill Main would be our cook, so he went with her to the fire. With one graceful motion, Juanita pulled the back hem of her skirt between her legs and tucked it in at her waist, modestly covering her legs as she rested her buttocks just above the ground in what was called a dobie squat.

"Now, you listen, Beel," she said. "You must remember to always wash the rice. Washing removes the weevils."

I watched her as she carefully showed Main how to steam the rice over an open fire, controlling the hot coals so it would neither cook too fast nor burn. Juanita also described the proper way to prepare foods that grew wild in the jungle, such as bananas, banana blossoms, and bamboo shoots.

I ate the meal of rice, fish, and mangoes with relish, and then reached for the pack of Luckies Orlo had given me earlier. It was almost empty as I pulled one out, tapped it on my wrist, and lit it with a burning coal. Arturo kept talking, sharing his knowledge with us. We knew little about jungle survival, and he told us many things that would be useful. I was grateful for our chance meeting.

In the flickering light of the fire, I realized I had never met upper-class Filipinos before. Around Clark Field, young Filipinos from nearby barrios had been our bunk boys. They had polished our boots, taken care of our laundry, and made our beds. Others worked on the post grooming horses, pulling kitchen duty, and doing many other menial jobs for low wages. Most of the women I had seen around the barrios were uneducated and were content to live under very simple, almost primitive, conditions. During my five months of peacetime duty, I had learned to like the Filipinos, and had learned to admire their self-sufficiency and simple ways. Now, in the presence of the Espiritos, I realized there was another kind of Filipino. Both Arturo and Juanita were college-educated people who had worked for the largest newspaper in Manila. They had been accustomed to a much higher standard of living. I admired their ability to adapt to the harsh conditions of their jungle camp.

Following the dark trail, we arrived back at our store of supplies and found Wicks sleeping. Main gave him the promised rice and some small fish.

"This goddamned rice doesn't have any salt on it," Wicks said.

"Of course not," Main said with a smile. "Don't you know salt ruins rice when it's put in the water before cooking? Salt goes on after the rice is cooked."

Main had learned to cook rice like the Filipinos, and I realized he would be a vital asset to us.

"I'm going back to the road to see if I can find one of those damn bolos," Orlo said.

In a few moments, I heard him running back up the trail.

"There's goddamn Japs all over down there!" he said in a breathless whisper.

Alarmed, I listened carefully as he caught his breath and corrected himself.

"Well, not all over, but I did see a car with a Jap officer in back."

We knew the time to leave had arrived. I picked up my musette bag, carrying my share of the supplies. I could hear horses on the road. During the retreat into Bataan, starving American and Filipino soldiers had eaten all the American 26th Cavalry's horses and mules. The horses we heard now could only belong to the Japanese cavalry.

"Let's get out of here," Kinder said quietly.

As we started moving into the dark jungle, something Arturo had said came back to me. It seemed to justify the decision to escape.

"I have kept in contact with friends in Manila, and the atrocities there have been horrible. One thing you can count on, all Americans in Japanese hands will be treated badly. They care nothing for human life," he had said.

"No matter how it turns out for you, you will be much better off than if you surrender to the Japanese."

Chapter Three

We began to move quietly into the jungle. In the darkness I stumbled over rocks and exposed tree roots, and the underbrush seemed to reach out and grab my equipment. The moon was rising, but little light penetrated the dense canopy of trees. I was grateful for the darkness which provided a sense of security as we moved slowly along one of numerous trails that crisscrossed the peninsula. The trail broke into a small clearing, and Kinder called a halt.

"We're far enough from the road. Let's get some sleep and take off first thing in the morning," he said.

I spread my canvas shelter half on the ground and wrapped myself in a blanket. I had found both articles on the road and was glad for the warmth they provided in the chilly evening air. The vastness of the stars seemed to swallow me as doubts and fears filled my mind. Night had always been difficult for me when I faced the unknown, and now it seemed a thousand things could go wrong. The jungle shadows appeared sinister in the moonlight, as if some unforeseen evil were lurking just out of sight.

My mind went back to a night from my youth. After my father lost his business during the Great Depression, he took our family to the

Santa Clara Valley to pick fruit. On the first night away from home we stayed in a cheap cabin in an auto court. It had seemed like a great adventure when we left Riverside, but as darkness fell I was filled with apprehension. While the rest of my family slept, I was gripped by a dread of the unknown, and the feeling remained until sunrise.

Now, in the jungles of Bataan, I suddenly felt the same kind of doubt and apprehension. Absorbed in my personal thoughts, I was gazing at the star-studded sky when Vacher lit a cigarette.

"Hey, what the hell are you doing? Trying to get us all killed?"

"Take it easy," Vacher said in a calm voice. "Hell, there's no one around to see it."

He took a deep drag, and the orange glow seemed unusually bright in the darkness. I could hear a Japanese tank rumbling in the distance, but realized it was useless to press the point.

I knew Vacher well, and in the darkness of the jungle night I thought about our long friendship, sensing again that in so many ways he was the man I could never be. His physical prowess never ceased to amaze me. Of French descent, he stood five feet ten inches tall and weighed about two hundred pounds. I had always envied his natural, God-given physique. He possessed a strength most men only dreamed of having, and he was as strong mentally as he was physically. I had been a B student in high school, but when Vacher introduced me to classical music, literature, philosophy, and history, my intellectual curiosity began to develop and I became an avid reader. As I grew intellectually I was able to discuss, and occasionally debate, issues with him. His broad knowledge both impressed and challenged me.

"Hileman, you've got to read that book," Vacher had said as we sat in a restaurant together one night in 1939.

During the previous week he had been reading Hitler's *Mein Kampf*. The waitress emptied the ashtray and poured another cup of coffee.

"That son of a bitch Hitler is nuts," he said.

He went on to muse how forces beyond anyone's control were sweeping the world into war, and he predicted the United States would eventually join the struggle. In 1939 I knew little about Hitler, but Vacher filled me in on the *führer's* views of racial superiority and his hatred for Jews.

I found Vacher's criticism ironic since Nietzsche's theory of might is right seemed to be his own philosophy of life. Vacher accepted his own unusual physical and mental strength as nature's way of making him superior to others. Despite his arrogance, I drew heavily from his strength and intelligence, and we were close friends.

Vacher was already working at the American Potash and Chemical plant in Trona, California, when I got a job there in February of 1941. Orlo Heinzman, a lanky, easygoing man from Canton, Illinois, had been sharing living quarters with Vacher, and I moved in with them. Shortly after my arrival in Trona, the union went on strike. Almost broke, and under the pressure of having to make car payments, I drove into Los Angeles to check on my draft status and learned I would be called in a few months.

"Hell, why don't we all enlist right now?" Orlo had impulsively suggested when I gave them the news.

We pooled our money, bought a tank of gas, and drove to the recruiting station in Los Angeles the next day. The sergeant there, a veteran who had served in the Philippines, told us about sandy beaches, easy duty, and beautiful girls. He recommended Air Corps Ordnance, the branch of the Air Corps that handled ammunition, arms, and bombs. He made no mention of tense relations between the United States and Japan or the danger they posed. He painted an attractive verbal picture, and we all eagerly enlisted.

A few weeks later we arrived in Manila where we learned we had been assigned to duty at Clark Field, about sixty miles north. Transported there by truck, we stopped in front of an L-shaped, white, single-story barracks which was raised about three feet off the ground, a precaution against the torrential rains. The first sergeant stood on the screened porch, leaning against the entry as the new recruits scrambled into formation. It was obvious he had been drinking. I soon learned Sergeant John O'Conner was seldom sober. Duty in the Philippines and alcohol, for some soldiers, were inseparable entities.

"My name is O'Conner, and I'm the first sergeant of this outfit, so listen good, you jerks." The old soldier pushed back his campaign hat.

"One thing I will not tolerate in this outfit or on these premises is any drinking during working hours. What you do on your own time is up to you, but remember this: you had better be goddamn ready to answer roll call in the morning or I'll have your asses." O'Conner steadied himself against the post as he spoke.

My attention was broken when I noticed the sergeant's left eye wandering up and down as he talked. It was difficult to concentrate on anything but the bloodshot eye.

"That eye looks like a piss hole in the snow," Vacher said afterward.

"You're in the ordnance now, and this is a working outfit," O'Conner continued. "We're going to work your asses off here. We'll work you until the sweat drips right off your balls. You'll load ammo; you'll unload ammo. You'll load and unload bombs until you can't stand the sight of the bastards. You'll learn to handle the fuses for those bombs, a piece of equipment so delicate it will go off in your hands if you so much as fart while you're holding it.

"Now, as for military courtesy, we just don't have too much of that in the ordnance. You'll salute the old man first thing in the morning, and you don't pay any attention to the son of a bitch for the rest of the day. You'll be taking your orders from me!" O'Conner turned and staggered into the barracks.

Despite O'Conner's warning, I found service at Clark Field was, in reality, the easy duty the recruiter had promised. It was an eight-to-five job with interesting work and little harassment. I was assigned to the shop, a metal building about half a mile from the barracks, near the far end of the main runway. I helped rebuild and repair both fixed and flexible aircraft machine guns, link ammunition, and modify many types of outdated bombs. In addition, I drove one of the bomb service trucks.

In the barracks I became friends with others who had shipped over with me on the USS *President Pierce*. It became our habit to gather in the open area under the barracks porch after work each day where we mixed gin, grapefruit juice, and ice in a galvanized bucket. Seated on orange crates salvaged from the PX and using a large packing crate as a table, each of us helped himself by dipping his canteen cup into the bucket. We sipped the cool refreshment and talked about everything from the war in Europe to the girls at the Star Bar in Angeles. We seemed to engage in a never-ending argument about the time difference between San Francisco and Manila, and we never did reach a consensus. The evening bull sessions gave us a deep sense of camaraderie and cemented our relationships.

As we became more closely acquainted, I found there were others, like myself, who were eager to experience whatever the tropical islands had to offer. I remembered the promises of the recruiting sergeant who had talked about sandy beaches and beautiful girls, and I had enjoyed visiting the barrios near Clark Field. So when Sherdie Allin got permission to use three bomb service trucks one Saturday, about twelve of us set out for whatever excitement we could find.

With plenty of fried chicken, Coca Cola, and beer from the post exchange, we headed north toward Lingayan Gulf. At Aguilar we stopped in front of a large, gray stone church that attracted our attention. A broken sidewalk led to steps cradled between two stone banisters of early Spanish design. Vacher tried the latch and found it unlocked. The big wooden door squeaked as it slowly swung open. From the foyer we went through a second door and stood in awe as we gazed down the long, narrow sanctuary to an altar, flanked on either side with ornate seats resembling thrones. There were sufficient pews to seat several hundred people.

"Good morning, gentlemen. Is there something I can do for you?"

The words echoed through the old, empty church. We looked up to see an old priest standing on the balcony. Dressed in a heavy brown robe with a rope sash, he reminded me of Friar Tuck in the story *Robin Hood*.

"You men will come up," he said. "You are always welcome in this house."

Vacher's eyes were fixed on the priest as he started up the stairs without a word, the rest of us following. He had been raised Catholic and seemed to be at ease in the old church. I was grateful he was along.

"What is your name, young man?" the priest asked.

"Corporal Vacher, sir, of the Six ninety-eighth Ordnance from Clark Field."

Vacher had often voiced contempt for religion, but when he stood face-to-face with that parish priest, I sensed his deeply ingrained respect for what the old man represented.

"Well, Corporal, I certainly want to meet all of your men. I am Father Dominic Madera. I only wish I had some food to share with you, but today the cupboard is empty. I might ask you, though, to share some wine with me."

The priest led us to his study. The room was bare except for an old oak roll-top desk, a swivel chair with a worn leather cushion, and a wooden bench along the wall. We seated ourselves on the bench, on three folding chairs, and on the floor. Through an open door I could see the priest's meager living quarters with a single bed and a small wooden table with a matching straight chair.

Father Madera handed each of us a small glass, and opened a dusty, earthen jug of dark wine. It tasted like the wine Vacher and I drank in California when we had tapped the keg belonging to his father. As we slowly sipped the aged wine, Father Madera told us about himself. He had come from Europe before the United States took control of the Philippines in 1898. For over four decades the seventy-seven-year-old priest had lived in Aguilar and ministered to the people in the parish there.

After a brief tour of the old church, Father Madera gave us his blessing and sent us on our way.

We drove on to a park at Lingayan Gulf, a beautiful bay with clear water and sandy beaches. As we unloaded our picnic supplies, we heard girls' voices through the trees. A group of young Filipino women was having a picnic, and they invited us to join them. Women in the Philippines seldom drank alcohol, so we left the beer in the truck, content to drink Coca Cola. We shared lunch together, and several of us went swimming in the gulf.

It was late afternoon when we left the girls, climbed in the bomb service trucks, and headed back to Clark Field. As we passed through Aguilar I recalled the hospitality of the old priest.

"He's sure a great old guy," I said to Vacher.

"My God, he's been here for more than forty years. That's what I call dedication."

We were still talking about the good day when ahead of us I saw Boren's truck pulled off the side of the road, his passengers looking under the hood.

"What's the problem, Homer?" I asked as I pulled up beside them.

"We got a busted fan belt. This is sure a helluva place for that damned thing to give out. I'll have all hell to pay if I leave this truck out here. The Filipinos will have it stripped and the parts all over the country by tomorrow."

"Hey," I said. "Someplace along here this morning I saw an old GMC truck by a shed. S'pose we can find it?"

Leaving the rest of the men with the stalled truck, and with the warm beer left unopened at the park, Boren and I took off on the little-traveled road. We had gone only a short distance when we spotted the truck and walked over to examine it. Sure enough, there was a worn, but usable, fan belt. We were considering helping ourselves to it when an old Filipino came from his hut beyond the shed.

"Hi, Joe," Boren said. "We were wondering if we could buy this fan belt."

Apparently sensing our immediate need, the old man said he would sell it for five pesos.

"Five pesos!" I said. "You think we're nuts? That damned belt is worn out."

"I sell it for three pesos."

"Hell, we can buy a new one for that."

"Okay, okay, Joe, I sell it to you for one peso fifty centavos."

"Sold," Boren said.

Driving back to the stalled truck, Boren and I laughed as we realized the Filipino custom of price dickering had so easily become a part of our own habit.

"Hell," Boren said, "next thing you know we'll be dobie citizens."

It had been a good day, one in which I had begun to experience the wonder of the Philippines and its people.

Birds began singing as I lay, still awake, in the predawn darkness of Bataan. Their cheerful music seemed only to emphasize the heavy breathing of my six sleeping companions. My mind continued to go over the experiences of prewar life in the Philippines, and I wondered why we had not been more alert to the growing tensions between Japan and the United States. It had all seemed so peaceful and idyllic then.

Sunday, December 7, the day before the war broke out, was one of those seemingly perfect days. For several weeks Sherdie Allin and I had been visiting the surrounding barrios, getting acquainted with the Filipinos and observing their way of life. We had particularly enjoyed the times we spent in Sapang Batu, familiarly known to the soldiers as Sloppy Bottom. It was there we met Mose Robinson, a black American whose stories of Army service in the Philippines in the early 1900s intrigued us. We became friends with the old man and with his two daughters who lived with him.

On that particular Sunday we had gone to the post exchange to get beer for Mose and lunches for ourselves and the girls. We had enjoyed an all-day outing along the banks of the Bamban River, a clear stream that flowed from the jungle-covered Zambales Mountains.

The day had been fun, and as we returned to Sapang Batu the smell of cooking fires and open sewage lingered in the cool evening breeze. Pigs, chickens, and children ran among the huts, and behind the huts long-horned black water buffalo, called carabao, stared blankly. These beasts of burden spent their lives toiling in the rice paddies. When age sapped their strength, carabao flesh was cooked, and the hides became shoes, belts, and other apparel.

Barrio life was relaxed, and it held a strong appeal for both Sherdie and me. So after we walked the girls home and continued on our way to Clark Field, we began discussing the possibility of shacking up with the two sisters. Filipino women took good care of soldiers who cohabited with them in the barrios, and most Filipino parents seemed to accept the arrangement. We knew Mose Robinson liked us, and it was something for us to consider.

It was dark when we passed the complacent military policeman stationed at the gate and walked to our barracks. As I fell into my bunk and pulled the mosquito bar around my bed that night, I did not care whether I ever returned to the United States. Life was good, and I was happy. The Philippines was a strange, wonderful world, and I was finding my place in it. I understood why old soldiers called duty there the Army's best kept secret. I had drifted off to sleep that night unaware that all hell would break loose in the morning.

Chapter Four

"Let's get going."

Kinder's voice signaled an abrupt end to my reverie. I had slept little, if any, but I was quickly alert to the immediate situation and was eager to face my first day on the trail.

Fearing a fire would attract too much attention, we ate a cold, but relatively hearty, breakfast. We shared a gallon can of corned beef hash Kinder had brought back from the quartermaster. When we finished, Main meticulously scrubbed the can with sand from the nearby stream. He would save it, with its cover, for a rice pot.

As we prepared to leave we did not have a final destination in mind. Our sole purpose was to get out of Bataan, and we knew we had to go north. Our first goal was the Pilar-Bagac Road which crossed the Bataan Peninsula from east to west. According to a military map Kinder had picked up at the quartermaster, it was twelve kilometers to the road. He estimated the trip would take us from two to three days. We knew the Japanese would be making extensive use of the Pilar-Bagac Road, however, and crossing would be hazardous. Before leaving, Kinder went over the trail rules one more time.

"Stay in single file, keep the talking down to a whisper, and don't follow the man in front of you too closely. Remember, no shooting unless someone fires at you first."

As I reached down for my pack I heard someone running through the brush and breaking branches as though he were being pursued. I grabbed my rifle and looked at Vacher. He hurriedly pumped a round into the chamber of his rifle.

"Hold it," Kinder whispered. "If there is going to be any killing, let's do it quietly."

Tensions were relieved when an American emerged from the brush. It took only a second for us to recognize him. It was Alva Carpenter, six foot four, two hundred fifty pounds, a Colt .45 in a holster on his belt, a bandolier of ammunition over his shoulder, and a Springfield rifle slung across his back. He wore tattered blue fatigues and an officer's hat he had picked up somewhere.

"Hey, Kinder, I want to go with you guys," he hollered when he saw us. I had no idea how he found us or how he knew what we were up to. I was sure, however, we all shared the same thought: how could we take him along, yet how could we leave him behind? He had nothing to contribute and was totally unprepared to travel with us.

Carpenter had been a member of the 698th Ordnance with us at Clark Field and on Bataan. A pathetic sort of character from the East Coast, he had related many stories of time spent in various prisons. His favorite expression was, "I hate cops." He had not been blessed with a particularly high IQ, and we did not think he could be trusted.

Our distrust stemmed mainly from the night on Bataan when some of us had been playing poker in the quartermaster tent. Carpenter had lifted the tent flap and stared at us with a silly grin on his face. He had pulled the pin on a hand grenade, tossed it on the blanket where we were playing, and laughed fiendishly as we scattered. The grenade had been defused, but to him it was a great joke as he scooped up the pot and walked away.

"I don't want that dumb son of a bitch following me," Vacher whispered to me as Carpenter approached our group.

"Okay, Carpenter, you can follow behind," Kinder said reluctantly.

Heavy jungle, mountain streams, and steep ravines covered the Bataan Peninsula, and we found travel difficult. Vines and briers caught our equipment, scratched our hands and faces, and made every step difficult. Like the others, I repeatedly slipped and fell. After about two hours on the trail, Carpenter stumbled over a large rock.

"Son of a bitchin' rock. To hell with it," he shouted.

He angrily lifted the enormous weight over his head and heaved it down the hill. Everyone stopped as the boulder crashed its way through the hillside brush. With Japanese soldiers in the area, it was vital to be as quiet as possible. None of us said a word as Carpenter caught up with us. Each of us realized his flagrant act could have resulted in death for all of us.

Vacher walked wordlessly past me, raised his rifle, and pumped another cartridge into the chamber. Carpenter reached for his pistol, but stopped when Vacher shoved the rifle into his stomach.

"Carpenter, don't reach for that," Vacher said. "Turn around right now, start back down the hill, and don't look back. If you do, I'll shoot you."

Carpenter turned and walked down the trail. We watched as he disappeared in the dense jungle without even a backward glance.

We descended the gentle slope of a hill and were relieved to find a small, cool stream. Kinder called a halt, and we soaked our feet, rested, and smoked a cigarette.

During the morning's travel we had crossed several military trails that offered easier walking, but Kinder had insisted that following such trails would be too dangerous.

"Wally, the Japs are too busy doing other things to patrol these damn trails," Orlo said during the rest break.

I was surprised at how quickly, and sharply, Kinder responded.

"Orlo, if you don't like the way I run things, you know the choices. You can leave right now, or you can get together and choose another leader and I'll leave."

That ended the discussion, and none of us challenged any of Kinder's decisions again.

"Let's go," he said.

Ahead was another steep hill, and we fought rocks, brush, thorns, and heat all afternoon, making little progress. With approaching darkness, we found an overhang and decided to spend the night beneath its protection.

Still nervous about Japanese patrols, Kinder said there would be no fire, which meant no rice for supper. Main started to divide two cans of salmon.

"Bullshit, Bill. We didn't eat anything at noon and we've had a hell of a day," Vacher said. "I'm hungry."

It was obvious Main was intimidated by Vacher and did not know how to respond, but Kinder quickly took control of the situation. He walked over to Main, picked up a can of salmon as though he were reading the label, looked up, pushed back his campaign hat, and turned to Vacher.

"Vacher, you know the rules. Main is in charge of the food, and that's the way it's going to be."

"If I want it," Vacher said, "I'll damn well take it. I'm the biggest man here, and I need a bigger ration."

I knew Vacher's physical strength and temper could be a threat to Kinder's authority.

"I know you're the biggest one here." Kinder looked straight into Vacher's eyes. "I also know there are six of us and one of you. If we decide you should take your pack and your lousy two or three cans of salmon and leave, that's exactly what you'll do. If anyone wants to join Vacher, just stand up and leave with him."

I listened in stunned silence. I had never known anyone to confront Vacher like that. After a minute that seemed like an eternity, Orlo jumped up.

"Who wants to split some fish?" he asked.

Vacher's face had a set expression as he sat down and looked at Kinder.

"Okay, Wally. I'll give your way a try."

I was relieved Kinder and Orlo had dispelled a dangerous situation and Vacher had realized an important fact. He needed us more than we needed him.

We ate our salmon in silence, smoked a cigarette, and lay down as darkness settled around us. It had been a day of rough traveling, and we had not come far. Through Kinder, we had learned an important lesson. The group came first. Both Carpenter's irresponsibility and Vacher's selfishness had threatened our unity, and both problems had been solved. When Orlo had wanted to use the trails, Kinder had firmly asserted his leadership. I felt a sense of relief knowing Kinder had things under control.

Chapter Five

Waking before sunrise, Kinder suggested we travel until we reached a secluded place with water. Then we would stop, cook some rice, and quickly move on. An hour later we found a clear mountain stream that wound its way down the mountain slope under a canopy of trees. I watched Main wash the rice and use his fingers to measure the water in the cooking can. We climbed to a bench overlooking the stream where Vacher and I kept an eye on the trail while Main cooked rice for the first time. We ate quietly and departed.

As we pushed deeper into the jungle, it became a constant struggle to get through the dense underbrush. At times I had to crawl through thick, thorny vegetation that snagged my gear, tore my shirt, and cut into my flesh. Climbing the side of a steep ravine, the underbrush became so thick the only way we could keep contact with one another was by sound. Frustrated, I kept pulling myself through. Ahead, I could hear Orlo cursing the underbrush, apparently reaching the end of his patience.

"I'll never use this damn thing anyway," Orlo cried out in a loud voice.

With that he threw his rifle down the hillside. It dislodged rocks as it crashed through the brush, and I froze. Kinder called us together on a rock overhang.

"Orlo, that was a stupid damned thing to do. Remember what happened to Carpenter."

Orlo's action was no less irresponsible, and Kinder warned us he would not tolerate any more tantrums like the one with Orlo's rifle.

"Orlo, you might need that rifle in a fight, and if the noise had alerted a Jap patrol, they'd shoot all of us, not just you."

"Sorry, Wally. I wasn't thinking too good."

We reached the top and moved down the other side where a stream flowed into a crystal clear pool. I scrubbed my feet and socks, and washed the blood from my scratched arms and face. In this serene tropical setting, the tensions created by Orlo's action seemed to disappear. By the time we finished refreshing ourselves in the cooling water, we were teasing him about not having a rifle to defend himself.

We each smoked a cigarette, and somewhat rested, started up the other side. The steep canyon wall made progress slow, and it was night when we reached the top. Main cooked some rice and split a can of fish. Sleep came quickly to our tired bodies.

The arduous journey through the jungle continued for the next two days. Considering the time we had been on the trail, we felt we should have been out of the province. Unaware of how little progress we were making, we moved along a ridge line, crossed it, and found a remote mountain trail. Orlo spotted a telephone wire, the type used at artillery observation posts, and we followed it into an open area. After our time under the canopy of jungle trees, the sun in the clearing seemed especially bright.

The view was spectacular. Looking west we could see the China Sea, and on the east was Manila Bay. After five days in the jungle, I sat down with the others on that mountaintop, soaking up the view. It was then I fully realized how small the Bataan Peninsula really was. Only ten to twelve miles wide and twenty-five miles long, it had seemed much larger during the fighting.

Scanning the dense jungle with my binoculars, I saw small dust clouds to the north. They were rising from the Pilar-Bagac Road, our first goal. It was still five or six kilometers away, but the presence of Japanese trucks passing in and out of the trees confirmed the sighting.

As we surveyed the scene from our mountain perch, small birds began diving at us, pulling out of their dives within inches of our faces. Their wings made a peculiar whirring noise that sounded like a bullet in flight, and Vacher immediately dubbed them bullet birds. The jungle was a hostile world, and now it seemed even the birds were against us.

It was there, high on that as yet unknown mountain, that I experienced extreme loneliness. I thought about home, wondering if I had been reported missing in action, and whether the story of Bataan was even in the newspapers back home. For the first time, I realized I might be a fugitive for years. My mother was a worrier, and I wondered if she could endure the stress. For a moment, I wished I had surrendered. At least then, I thought, I could contact my family and let them know I was all right. Covering my face with my hands, I longed to be anywhere other than on that damned mountain. New doubts about the wisdom of escape enveloped me.

My inner thoughts and fears were sharply interrupted by the sound of machine-gun fire in the distance, followed by a Japanese knee mortar. Any doubts I had quickly vanished as I flushed with hatred for the Japanese. I speculated Japanese soldiers were shooting at a fugitive American or Filipino, but I had no way of knowing.

Silently we resumed our journey up the trail. The telephone wire ran along the path, and we followed it to a deserted artillery observation post on the mountaintop. I spotted a square cement marker near the trail and kicked the dirt off its surface. It was a survey marker apparently placed there years earlier by some U.S. government agency. To my surprise, we had climbed Mount Bataan, an elevation of 4,700 feet.

Kinder checked his map and announced we had averaged just over one kilometer a day. We were only six kilometers from where we started at Km 188. After my initial disbelief, I was totally disheartened.

"Hey, look at it this way," Orlo said. "Here we are on the highest point in the Mariveles Mountains. From now on, it's all downhill."

Orlo always saw the humorous, positive aspect in a discouraging situation and instinctively said the right thing at the right time. I broke out in laughter, as did the others.

We poked around the observation post, a collection of sandbags and trenches. From empty Carnation milk cans and cigarette butts, we determined it had been an American post. The former occupants had left little behind, but Orlo and Main collected cigarette butts while the rest of us examined the area. The butts were damp, but Orlo planned to break them open, empty the tobacco into his mess kit, and dry it over a fire. All of us smoked, so tobacco was important.

Descending the mountain, we reached the Pantingan River in the late afternoon. We had planned to cross the Pilar-Bagac Road at the point where the Pantingan flowed under it. We camped that night in a ravine about three hundred meters from the river. Extra caution was necessary in the lower elevations.

In the morning we filled our canteens. Although the water was crystal clear, we added chlorine as a precaution against amoebic dysentery. The last can of fish complemented our rice breakfast, leaving only rice in our food supply.

We planned to follow the Pantingan River, but Kinder advised that because we were so near the road we should move at a distance from the riverbank. We waded across the river and found a seemingly little-used path. As the river disappeared from sight behind us, Kinder, in the lead, held up his hand and we stopped. He knelt down to check the ashes in an abandoned campfire. He quickly jerked his hand back from the still-hot coals, and we realized someone had camped very near us the night before. We had heard nothing, so we assumed it was one person, most likely an American or Filipino.

The jungle was so dense along the Pantingan River that only glimpses of the water could be seen through the foliage. Then ascending a hill, we had our first clear view of the river since crossing it. George Wicks pointed as he whispered to Kinder and Henderson. He had spotted someone across the river, and we all ducked down into the high grass. It was a Filipino, walking in the opposite direction, carrying a white flag on a long pole. We silently watched as he passed and moved out of sight.

The Filipino's presence raised new questions for us. Were there Japanese in the area? Did the white flag mean he had crossed the road? We had been hearing the faint sounds of traffic all morning. We continued on.

Main had suggested cooking an extra pot of rice that morning in case we reached a place where cooking was impossible. As I ate my ration of cold rice for supper, I realized how prudent his suggestion had been.

After spending the night in a dry camp, we started our eighth day.

It was Friday, April 17. We hit the trail without breakfast, and I soon began to feel weak from hunger. The hunger and the weakness that accompanied it alarmed me. Throughout the Bataan Campaign, we had eaten reduced rations, and it had been difficult to function well under such conditions. Now hunger was affecting our physical and mental health, and I knew we had to have food.

"Let's eat," Kinder whispered without any advance warning.

Main had been experimenting with different kinds of wood in an effort to find one which created little smoke or odor, so we felt safe as he built a fire and cooked a pot of rice. When we had eaten, he gave us some bad news.

"We're almost out of rice. If I stretch it, we have enough for two small meals, but we've got to find more soon."

"Damn it all, we just have to move farther down into the valley. That means a bigger chance of getting our asses shot off, but we might be able to find something to eat," Kinder said.

We decided to travel the trails leading out of the jungle and into the lower elevations. Hunger was beginning to control our actions.

Cautiously following a well-used trail, Kinder spotted a burlap bag and stopped. We watched him lift the bag with his rifle and carefully empty its contents on the ground. To our amazement, eleven cans fell out. The Japanese labels pictured salmon.

Hunger had forced us to move into the lower elevations, and now it determined our behavior. Laughing and slapping each other on the back, we made no attempt to keep quiet. We were famished men who had found food, and our elation made us careless.

Moving off the trail, Kinder handed a can of salmon to each of us. We ate ravenously, even wiping the remaining oil from the cans with our fingers. Then Vacher produced a pack of Camels and passed out cigarettes. With a good meal and a good cigarette, we all felt better.

We were near the Pilar-Bagac Road, and it was time to inspect it. Throughout the morning we had been hearing trucks on the road, and as we moved out of the hills, we had heard voices, Japanese voices. From our vantage point we could see trucks moving in a steady procession, and we realized crossing would be difficult and dangerous. After eight tough days on the trail, we had reached our first goal, the Pilar-Bagac Road.

CHAPTER SIX

"We'll cross at dusk," Kinder said as we huddled in the brush. "I'm going down to see what's happening on the road. I'll be back before dark."

I rested my head on my pack and dozed in the afternoon heat. Vacher lay next to me, Wicks and Henderson sat talking quietly, Main kept rearranging his pack, and Orlo went to look around.

"Hey, look who I found," he said on his return. Standing beside Orlo was a young Filipino, nineteen or twenty years old.

"I am a Philippine Scout, Joe, in the Forty-fifth Infantry. I am also wanting to cross the road."

He spoke both English and Tagalog, the national dialect of the Philippines. Thinking we would eventually need a translator, we welcomed him.

Main had been fidgeting with his equipment ever since we stopped and seemed nervous.

"I'm going to get a look at that road for myself," he said finally. Cautious by nature, he apparently wanted to personally assess the situation.

"We shouldn't have too much trouble, although there's Jap cavalry riding guard on the road," he said on his return. He estimated the cavalrymen were separated at quarter-mile intervals. Approaching one another, the guards met and then proceeded with their backs to each other. That would be the time to cross. Main said the traffic was light.

Kinder returned with the same assessment and even more encouraging news.

"I think the cavalry is leaving. It looks good to me," he said.

"We'll cross one at a time. Henderson, you'll go first, then Wicks, myself, and the Filipino. Hileman, you follow the Filipino, then Vacher, Orlo, and Main. Main, I want you to keep an eye on the road from this side and send the others over when it's clear."

Kinder said each of us was to signal after crossing. In case of any danger, we were to motion for the others to stay put, and if we became separated, those who remained behind would be on their own.

At dusk Main crawled to a hiding spot next to the road. When he saw it was clear, he signaled and Henderson ran across. After looking both ways, Henderson, in turn, signaled the all clear. Main passed the message to Wicks who then crossed. Kinder followed, and then the Filipino. Darkness was moving in as I crawled to the road for my turn. I watched Main for a signal, since from his vantage point he was the only one who could see the signals from the other side of the road.

"Something's wrong," he whispered as he crawled over to me. "I can't see any Japs, but the Filipino gave me the hold signal."

"Damn it, Bill. If there aren't any Japs, what could be wrong?"

We went back to Orlo and Vacher, and together decided it was too dark for the crossing. We would try again in the morning.

We crawled back into the underbrush, ate some cold rice, and bedded down. As Main, Vacher, and Orlo slept, I lay awake in the darkness, thinking about the separation. What had happened? I knew Main was cautious, but I did not think he was a coward. What could have happened to Kinder's plan? Then suddenly the answer came to me.

In the Philippines, hand signals were opposite from those we used in the United States. The Filipino had wanted me to cross and had given Main a pushing signal, the reverse of the American beckon to come. I was furious, thinking to myself it was a stupid mistake. I wanted to wake Main and slap him across the face, but curbed the impulse and eventually drifted off to sleep.

Later that night I was startled from my sleep by a clanging sound. Instantly I was wide awake with all my senses tuned into the dark world around me. I crawled over and silently woke the others. Huddled together in the darkness, we carefully listened, finally determining the Japanese had set up a camp just down the road. We did not change our plan to cross at daybreak, but we knew extra caution would be required.

In the early light Main left us and crawled back to the road. From his hiding place, he watched Japanese cavalry moving up the road towards Pilar. The procession seemed to be unending, so we decided to retreat and attempt to cross another time.

The separation from Kinder, Wicks, and Henderson was especially disturbing for me. Ever since the first day when Vacher had confronted Main over a can of fish, the relationship between them had been tense. Kinder had been a moderating influence between them, and now he was gone.

I was certain none of us was capable of assuming Kinder's leadership role. I would miss him and the others, but survival meant moving without them. Perhaps we would catch up with them later. For now, crossing the road safely was our most important concern.

Chapter Seven

I told the others my theory about the mix-up in hand signals, and even before Main had a chance to respond, Vacher jumped on him.

"What happened, Main? Did you see a wild chicken?"

Main bore the insult in silence, but I noticed his face pale at the realization of his mistake and at Vacher's unnecessary insult.

"Let's go east," I said to break the silence. I did not know whether crossing would be easier somewhere else, but some kind of decision was needed. The others agreed, and I took the lead as we crept through the brush, found an old trail, and headed towards Pilar. An hour later we left the trail and moved up a small stream to eat.

Main tested the wind. It was blowing away from the road, so he built a small fire and cooked the last of our rice. We were out of food again.

We discussed several options. We could make another attempt to cross the road that evening, but even if successful, that would require traveling at top speed the next day without food. We had already noticed signs of malnutrition and exhaustion, and our bodily functions had changed. We had been going four or five days without a bowel movement, and Orlo said he had not had one since fleeing nine days earlier.

"Hell, I'm not worried," he said to me with a wry smile. "Nature takes care of everything."

I had had only two bowel movements during the nine days on the run, and the small amount of waste I passed concerned me, but then I had not eaten much. The frequency of urination, however, had increased dramatically. I woke two or three times a night to relieve myself, and it seemed as though one of us was always stopping to urinate as we moved down the trails.

We decided we had to find food before crossing the Pilar-Bagac Road, and we knew the crossing had to be made soon. April was a hot, dry month in the Philippines, but in May the rainy season would begin. We had to be out of Bataan before the rains started because traveling in the rain and mud in our weakened condition would be life threatening.

Main suggested returning to an abandoned Japanese campsite we had passed the night before where he had seen some rice scattered on the ground. We turned back, found all the rice we could carry, and even some salt, the first we had seen since leaving Km 188.

Throughout the afternoon we scrounged the abandoned camp, a typical Japanese bivouac area. In the U.S. Army, meals were cooked in central areas for many men, but in the Japanese army individual soldiers cooked their own meals. Ashes from many small fires had been left at the campsite. I found piles of empty cans that had contained fruit, juice, vegetables, milk, and fish. All were American brands, undoubtedly part of the food supply left behind when our troops had withdrawn into Bataan. During the withdrawal I had seen empty trucks moving into the peninsula, a costly oversight since they could have hauled food.

Kicking at the cans in frustration, I thought about a trip I had made back to the evacuated Clark Field on New Year's Eve. During the withdrawal into Bataan, tail fins, which were necessary to stabilize bombs as they fell towards their targets, had been left behind. Without fins, the bombs carried into Bataan were useless, so the demolition crew had taken three bomb service trucks and trailers and returned to get them.

In the moonlight the deserted airfield was a cold, ghostly place, much like a cemetery at night. We found the metal fins and quickly loaded two trailers. Then we drove to the quartermaster warehouse at

Fort Stotsenburg where cases of food remained stacked to the ceiling. We had loaded more than fifty cases of canned milk and several cases of strawberry preserves and vegetables on the empty trailer. When we returned to Bataan, the captain ordered us to turn it over to the quartermaster. We never saw any of it again.

Now I realized the full impact of the mistake our leaders had made as I looked at all the empty cans strewn about this abandoned Japanese camp. During the campaign on Bataan, we had eaten skimpy rations, often without meat or vegetables. We had even cooked the weevil-infested oats intended to feed the horses. I could see now that while we had been starving on Bataan, the Japanese had been dining on the food reserves left behind by poor planning on the part of our officers.

Convinced all we would find in the abandoned camp was rice and salt, we prepared to leave, but first we had to find Orlo. He had been gone an hour, so we began searching and found a trail leading to another section of the camp. Leaving Main and Vacher behind, I followed it up a hill and spotted a small building in a grove of mango trees. I unslung my rifle, slowly climbed the steps, and moved towards the open door.

"Hileman, I'm down here."

I saw Orlo crawling around under the building, stuffing a cloth bag with cigarette butts that had been dropped between the slats of the bamboo floor.

"I know we've got to eat, but we got to smoke too, don't we?"

Smoking was important to all of us, and our supply of cigarettes was low. That day I had been nursing a Chesterfield, lighting it and putting it out after a few puffs. Orlo had been rolling salvaged tobacco in Japanese propaganda paper, and Main had been experimenting with dried leaves. For the past few days Main had often lagged behind us as we traveled. We could hear him coughing and gagging as he tried out possible tobacco substitutes. Vacher, somehow, managed to have a seemingly endless supply of Camels, a circumstance which irritated me more and more. I had opened my last pack of Chesterfields, a brand I had rejected in peacetime. Vacher always had my favorite, Camels, and as far as I could tell, he had not even cut down on his tobacco consumption.

Orlo finished collecting butts under the building, and with the replenishment of our rice, salt, and tobacco, we had supplies for the next few days.

We returned to the trail we had been following earlier. The heat, and the stress of living hand-to-mouth behind enemy lines, was beginning to get to me. I lagged behind, sulking in my misery and fuming over Vacher's Camels.

When I caught up with the others, they were preparing camp. We could hear Japanese voices, trucks, and occasionally the clatter of horses' hooves on the cobblestone road. Vigilance was important, but so was eating. When Main started the fire, I noticed he used a bolo he had found in the abandoned Japanese camp.

The bolo's usefulness was demonstrated that evening. On a hillside, Main found a muddy spot with a small water seepage. Using the bolo, he dug a hole and lined it with rocks. The crudely fashioned cistern filled in a short time, providing us with a good supply of drinking water. I had not seen that done before and grudgingly conceded to myself that Main was a capable outdoorsman.

To celebrate finding the salt, Main cooked an extra portion of rice. While it steamed, he and I helped Orlo tear up cigarette butts and empty the tobacco into his mess kit for drying. As we worked, Vacher lit another Camel. The simple act did not seem to bother Main or Orlo, but flaunting my favorite brand angered me. I took out my Chesterfields, lit one, and then in personal defiance to Vacher, offered cigarettes to Main and Orlo. They declined.

With a satisfying supper and some rest, my morale picked up and I slept soundly that night.

A tree sheltered us from the gentle rain that was falling when I opened my eyes the next morning. It was Sunday, April 19, our tenth day on the trail. Extreme hot weather had drained our energy, so the cooling rain was a welcome relief, but it also served as a warning.

"It looks like we might be in for an early rainy season," Main said.

I sleepily nodded my agreement.

"Let's go see if we can find some mangoes," Vacher said to me after a plain rice breakfast.

We started up the narrow trail that followed a small stream. I reflected on a change in our attitudes towards using trails as we walked. When we first fled we had abandoned the trails and hacked our way through the jungle to avoid being near the Japanese. Now, ten days later, we were walking up a well-worn trail, knowing there were hundreds of Japanese soldiers in the surrounding area. Suddenly Vacher froze.

"I smell smoke," he whispered.

Main had doused our fire earlier, so someone else was in the area. We proceeded cautiously until the smell of smoke stopped us again. We hid on the hillside and listened. There was no noise, but we could see bluish smoke rising lazily from the streambed.

"What do you think?" Vacher whispered.

"I don't know. It could be a couple Filipinos, or it could be Japs. Let's rush the bastards. If they're Filipinos, no harm done. If they're Japs, so what? We'll have the drop on them." I was surprised at my own words, but for some reason I craved action. I actually found myself hoping it was Japanese soldiers who would resist.

As a safety precaution when we were following the trails, we did not carry cartridges in the chambers of our rifles. Now Vacher and I quietly pumped a round into our Springfields. We decided to rush whoever was there, Vacher going to the left of the tree that stood between us and the fire, and me to the right. Crawling on our stomachs, we inched our way to the large mango tree. With rifles at the ready, we jumped up and charged around the tree.

"Do not shoot, Joe!" a frightened, young Filipino cried. "I am a Scout. I am your friend, sir."

During the Bataan campaign, Philippine Scouts had served alongside the Americans. I was shaking from the aborted plan to attack as I faced the terrified Filipino boy who looked about seventeen. The thin, dark-skinned youngster had been bandaging his infected thumb. It had swollen to three times its normal size.

"What happened to your thumb?" I asked.

"I cut it with my bolo, sir, and I think it is very sick."

"What's your name, Joe?" Vacher asked.

"Maxmillian, sir. I am from the Fifty-seventh Infantry, and I am your friend."

"You come with us, and we'll fix that up for you," I said after examining the infected thumb. "We've got medicine and a friend who can help you." Main considered himself the camp doctor as well as the chief cook.

"You got any food?" I asked. The Filipino said he had not eaten any rice for three days, but he did have some beans.

As we walked back to our camp site, Maxmillian told us how he had become stranded in the jungle. When his company retreated, he said, he got lost behind Japanese lines. He had done all right until he cut his thumb.

Main whistled when he saw the thumb, but determined the boy did not have any fever or signs of blood poisoning. He cleaned the pus from the cut and poured alcohol over it.

Max insisted we should cook the beans he brought. We had already decided to spend the day resting before we attempted another crossing, so Main put the beans in water to soak. He decided to make soup for supper, and Max suggested we add sliced green mangoes.

With the beans soaking and the promise of a good supper, we sat around questioning Max all afternoon. He said he had seen Japanese soldiers once or twice, and he had watched them move along a trail at the foot of the hill where he had hidden. He had seen no other Americans, and that pleased me because I knew too many Americans in the jungle would draw attention, but I also had another reason.

In our escape plan, we had vowed we would not jeopardize the safety of Filipino people living in the provinces. We feared, however, that some fugitive Americans would take undue advantage of the native people and damage the reputations of all Americans. Kinder had given high priority to using diplomacy and kindness with the Filipinos, and everyone had agreed with his judgement.

"Hey, I'm going to put the beans on to cook," Main said as he looked at me. "Why don't you see if you can find some mangoes."

Vacher and I left camp in search of the green mangoes Max had suggested adding to the soup. When we were out of sight, Vacher pulled a new pack of Camels from his pocket.

"Don't you ever run out of those things?" I asked in irritation.

"Oh, I've got a few left," Vacher said. "Cigarettes are pretty important to me, especially when I don't have coffee. In fact, without coffee, I feel the need for a good cigarette even more. You know, I think things like that are probably more important to me than the average guy."

"What the hell kind of logic is that?"

Vacher struck the pack against his hand so one would rise from the pack.

"Here, have a Camel. You've earned it."

I had not earned a cigarette any more than the others, and I resented Vacher's arrogance.

"No thanks. I still have a few Chesterfields left, and when they're gone I may just quit." I did not want charity from Vacher and only wished I could make my cigarettes last longer than his so he would have to beg from me. I knew, though, Vacher would have smokes long after mine were gone.

We found the mangoes and returned to camp. Main tossed a knife to Vacher and told him to slice them for the soup.

"Hell, Main, slice them yourself. I'm not the cook," Vacher said.

They began arguing, and Vacher's ears turned red and his face flushed. I had become aware of the increasing tension between the two, so I quickly intervened.

"Give me the knife. I'll slice them." I grabbed the knife and began cutting the green fruit. The argument ended, at least for the time being, but I knew the conflict between Vacher and Main would erupt again. Vacher's arrogant personality and Main's overcautious attitude would never mix well.

"Max, these look like lima beans," Main said as he poured the beans into the soup.

"They are beluga beans that grow wild in the jungle," Max said. "They grow on vines that climb trees."

I wondered how many beluga vines we had unwittingly passed during our escape. This was useful information, and I became more convinced that running into the Filipino was a fortunate break. We needed him. I had noticed, though, that the argument between Main and Vacher had disturbed him, and I vowed to myself I would keep the others from scaring Max into leaving.

"Soup should be ready in about an hour," Main mumbled.

His habit of muttering to himself rather than speaking directly to us was a cause of irritation to both Vacher and me.

"An hour?" Vacher said. "Come on, Main. It doesn't take vegetables an hour to cook."

"You can have yours right now," Main said sarcastically.

"Don't be a smart ass, Bill."

Vacher fell quiet, and when Main let the soup cook a few extra minutes, I noticed he said nothing.

"Soup's on," Main finally said. "Come and get it before I throw it out."

"Man, oh man, Bill, that looks good," Vacher said as Main poured the soup over rice. He set the servings out and each of us chose a ration. Main took the last serving, in compliance with our unwritten rule that whoever dished up the food had last choice. I had noticed Main's portion was usually smaller.

Vacher grabbed the first mess kit and dug into the hot concoction. His face froze, his lips puckered, and he quickly spit the whole mouthful out.

"What the hell you trying to feed us?" Vacher said as he stared at Max. "If you guys can eat this shit, then you can eat anything."

Vacher waited for me to taste the soup. Even in my state of hunger, I spit the bitter concoction on the ground. Main, Orlo, and Max did the same.

"I do not know, sir. We ate cooked mangoes when I was with the Fifty-seventh Infantry, and they were good cooked with beans," Max said apologetically.

I picked the green mangoes out of my mess kit and ate the rest. The taste was bitter, but I needed the nourishment of the beans and rice. In the future, though, I would think twice about Max's suggestions.

The next day broke clear and hot, a good day for travel. We decided to attempt another crossing that evening and moved quietly towards the Pilar-Bagac Road. With my binoculars I could see Japanese cavalry, trucks, construction equipment, and tanks. The tanks, with their massive firepower, especially worried me. We crawled back from the road, discussed the situation, and decided to move farther east and wait until morning.

Although surrounded by Japanese activity, we became less cautious. The Japanese were busy with a multitude of tasks like taking care of horses, equipment repair, and other noisy, smelly jobs that would camouflage the smoke from a cooking fire. As long as we stayed out of sight, we felt relatively safe.

At dusk we moved to a deserted clearing where Main dished out some cold rice.

"Where's Orlo?" Main asked when he noticed his absence.

"Who knows?" Vacher said. "He left just as we started to eat."

We continued eating, wondering about Orlo's disappearance. Soon we heard him coming up the trail, proudly displaying a sock filled with cigarette butts and two small mesh bags of Japanese hardtack. I had already learned the Japanese crackers were pretty good when I was hungry. Orlo handed some to each of us.

    I studied Orlo for a moment. Generous by nature, he shared what he had, including the hardtack. Vacher, Main, and I had changed during our ten days on the trail, but Orlo was the same man I had known before the war. The three of us yammered at each other, but Orlo did not argue or fuss. I thought we could all learn a lesson from him.

    The Japanese were still moving troops and equipment east towards Pilar when we awoke the next morning, so we pulled back again. Two more days passed before the time seemed right. It was early afternoon when we finally found a promising spot. The location offered an unobstructed view of the road in both directions. I scanned the cobblestone road with my binoculars for twenty minutes. During that time I saw two Japanese trucks, but no foot soldiers or cavalry. There was nothing questionable in sight except a small shack a short distance away. A Japanese flag fluttered in the gentle breeze, but the shack appeared deserted. When we had first discussed crossing four days earlier, we felt the safest way would be to crawl under a bridge, but now, on this seemingly deserted stretch of road, that would not be necessary.

    Across the road I could see a four-foot, woven-wire fence stretched between two poles like a fishnet. We would have to scale the fence and proceed under the cover of darkness. The moon would be bright enough to light the way. We moved back, excited about the prospects of crossing that night. We ate some cold rice, smoked a cigarette and relaxed, all except Orlo. He had wandered off again.

    Seated on a log, I surveyed the scene around me. We were in the lowlands near Manila Bay, and just over a kilometer way I could see Mt. Sumat. Some of the heaviest fighting had taken place there, and the Japanese had made their final breakthrough at that point. We had seen foxholes and shell craters that littered the ground. Some of the large trees bore the scars of artillery bombardment, while smaller trees were twisted and torn. Black ash from recent fires covered the area.

    "Where's Orlo?" I asked Main.

    "He's gone to look around."

    "He better be back when we get ready or we'll have to go without him," I said with some concern.

Kinder, Wicks, Henderson, and the Filipino had crossed the road safely four days earlier. It seemed almost inconceivable to me the rest of us had been trying to cross ever since then. I was determined to cross that night, with or without Orlo. Realizing all too well he easily lost track of time when on one of his scavenger hunts, I decided to find him before it was too late.

I followed his footprints on the dusty trail to a point where it intersected an old path leading through the underbrush and they were no longer visible. I continued on, and ten minutes up the trail I found a cave in an embankment. From the ashes and debris, I knew it had been used recently, probably by Japanese soldiers during the fight for Bataan. There were no cigarette butts on the ground, and I supposed Orlo had probably stopped at the cave and cleaned up the butts. I poked around the cave, and continued up the trail, but soon realized trying to find Orlo was a vain task. I sat down on an old tree trunk and rolled a cigarette.

I was ready to return to the others when I heard a commotion in the brush. The noise seemed to be coming towards me, so I jumped behind the log and stretched out to hide. Peeking between the branches, I saw Orlo come tearing out of the brush, swinging and waving his hands frantically in the air and at his face. I could see he was being chased by something. I jumped to my feet and Orlo stopped, but the swarm of jungle bees did not. Orlo began running again, this time with me trailing behind. The bees shifted their attention to me. I managed to keep them from my face, but my arms and hands felt the painful stings of the insects that were larger and more ferocious than the bumblebees I remembered in California. Running, swatting, and crashing through the brush, Orlo reached the others with me on his heels. Both of us had been stung many times. With one eye swollen shut and the other a mere slit, Orlo was unrecognizable. My hands began to swell from the painful stings.

"Bill, don't people die from beestings?" I asked Main.

"Sure. In the States more people die from beestings than rattlesnake bites," Main said with a sadistic smile. "But if you think you're on your deathbed, what about Orlo? You look good compared to him."

I soon realized my life was not in danger, and neither was Orlo's, but the pain lingered.

"Just sit there and take it easy," Vacher said as he pulled a pack of

Camels from his pocket. "You'll be okay."

He lit one and then did the unexpected. Although he ignored Main and Max, he handed a cigarette to both Orlo and me. We settled down, smoked the cigarettes, and soon found humor in our misery. The pain subsided, but not the grotesque swelling.

Twilight settled over the foothills of Bataan and shadows grew longer, casting eerie images through the gigantic trees that bore the scars of war. With the exception of an occasional truck, we heard no movement on the Pilar-Bagac Road. Now, as we crept to a vantage point, I was elated at the sight of no guards, no trucks, no horses, and no tanks. We could cross safely. I felt the blood pulsating in my temples as the sudden thrill of adventure swept over me. This, indeed, was the place to cross, and now was the time.

Chapter Eight

"Okay, let's get the hell out of here," Vacher said quietly as he jumped to his feet.

Single file, with Max in the rear, we moved to the bottom of the hill where open ground spread for a hundred meters to the Pilar-Bagac Road. Next to the road was a ditch deep enough to conceal us from passing vehicles. On the other side, a second ditch ran along the only transportation link across the Bataan Peninsula. Beyond the second ditch was the woven-wire fence.

We discussed the crossing in whispers, deciding to run to the first ditch, one at a time, and wait until everything was clear. We would cross the road together, hide in the second ditch, and then climb over the wire-mesh fence.

Vacher crossed the open area first, running low as he raced to the first ditch. Main, Max, Orlo, and I followed in turn. Lying in the ditch, the deep silence seemed to press in on me.

"Let's go," Vacher whispered after waiting several minutes.

Crouching low, we ran across the road and dived into the second ditch, pausing briefly to listen for any sounds of the enemy.

We jumped up together, ran to the fence, and began climbing the wire mesh. It squeaked with each step like someone jumping on rusty bed springs. If there was anyone within hearing range, we had surely sounded the alarm. Dropping quickly to the ground, we landed at the edge of a deep canal about three meters wide. Wanting to stay dry, we moved east along the water barrier, looking for a way to cross.

"There's a foot bridge," Vacher whispered.

Silently scurrying across in single file, we found ourselves in a grove of trees with no underbrush. We moved through the trees and started down a narrow road. Ahead, I thought I saw a small shack with a light.

"Let's see what it is," I whispered to Vacher as we neared the light.

"Shut up," Vacher whispered. "That's a goddamn tank."

He was right, and for a moment I had visions of the tank chasing me through the jungle with guns blazing. However, we were able to creep past without disturbing the crew. Main, who had brought up the rear, said he had seen a tent where a bunch of drunk Japanese soldiers were playing cards.

Maintaining strict silence, we headed north away from the Pilar-Bagac Road, wanting to put as much distance as possible between it and ourselves.

We entered a bamboo thicket. Penetrating the thicket was difficult, but we stumbled through, occasionally stepping on dry pieces of bamboo. The snapping bamboo sounded like rifle shots, a clear warning to anyone within hearing range. In his excitement, Max fell two or three times. With each fall he hurt his thumb and moaned, not loudly, but loud enough to be heard by anyone nearby. The noise of Max's groans, like the snapping bamboo, alarmed me. My eyes kept darting around as I heard noises, mostly in my imagination. Like the others, I knew it was time to stop, listen, and rest. We huddled together and collected our thoughts for a few moments. With the immediate danger past, we listened gratefully to the absolute stillness of the jungle. Then a dog barked in the distance, the first I had heard in months. Hungry soldiers had eaten the dogs behind our lines on Bataan early in the campaign. The barking was evidence of a nearby barrio.

The first sliver of moonlight rose over the hill as we rested. Again, with Vacher in the lead, we continued on, moving among the shadows of large trees. Moonlight filtering through the trees played tricks with our vision as we moved from darkness into bright moonlight, and back into darkness. Tensely, we continued moving forward with Main bringing up the rear.

A loud crash shattered the silence, and I froze, awaiting any clue to the source of the noise.

"Goddamn!"

I heard the cursing of a muffled voice and knew it was Main. I ran back towards him.

"I think I broke my leg," he whispered. He struggled to his feet, and both of us were relieved that he was able to walk. Pain and wounded pride were his only problems.

Main had stumbled over a discarded ammunition box. When I stepped back after helping him, I lost my footing and fell into a pile of empty tin cans. The cans clanged and crashed in the darkness as I struggled to get to my feet.

"Hey, you guys, cool it," Vacher said as he ran up. "You sound like you're loose in a tin can factory. You want to get us all shot?"

The cans continued to clatter as I climbed out of the pile. For a few moments we listened for anyone who might have heard the racket, but silence mercifully engulfed us and we continued on in the darkness. We found still more discarded Japanese boxes, some containing ammunition and others hardtack, the little crackers in small mesh bags. We gathered as much hardtack as we could carry.

The sound of rippling water guided us to a river, and each of us, in turn, waded across with only the moon to guide our steps. On the other side we faced another obstacle.

A sheer bluff rose above the riverbank, and in the increasing darkness, we had trouble finding a place where we could get through or over the rock wall that imprisoned us. Main finally found a spot that, during the rainy season, would become a rocky funnel of rushing water. Now, however, it was dry, and the gully was covered with a dense growth of brush that would provide something to hold on to while we attempted to climb the steep cliff. It was a risky venture in the darkness, but we could not wait for daylight. If sighted, we would be pinned against the rock wall.

I tied my mesh sacks of biscuits together, draped them around my neck, and grabbed a bush. Carefully I pulled myself up one slow step at a time. One of the hardtack sacks snagged on a bush and tore, and the biscuits tumbled down the cliff, bouncing off rocks and landing on the creek bed. I managed to grab the other sack, put the string in my mouth, and continue climbing with clenched teeth. I could hear the grunts, curses, and heavy breathing of the others as we continued moving upward. By now the moon had disappeared behind the trees, and we were climbing in total darkness.

I could hear whispers above me as I pulled myself up to a narrow ledge about three feet wide and eight feet long. The others were crowded together on the ledge, hardly leaving room for me to join them.

Looking down from the narrow ledge, I could barely see the creek about twenty meters below, bubbling and churning as it swept over large boulders. From the ledge we could not see a clear path in any direction, so stranded in the darkness, we decided to wait until daylight before going any farther.

"I have a surprise for you," Max said as he reached into his burlap sack and pulled out two bottles of wine. He had found them in a box where Main had fallen.

"I do not drink the wine, but I think my American friends will like it so I bring it."

He handed a bottle to Vacher who pulled the cork on the first bottle, raised it to his nose, and took a sniff.

"Hey, this is good stuff," he said with conviction.

He took a swig and passed the bottle to me. Sitting precariously on that narrow ledge, the petty disagreements of the past few days were forgotten, and for the time being, at least, I was again aware of the bond of friendship which had brought us together.

"Here, you guys, have a Camel," Vacher said. He passed a cigarette to each of us. "This is my last pack, and we might as well kill it here. I can't think of a better place."

He tossed the crumpled pack over the cliff and opened the second bottle of wine.

"Smoke, drink, and be merry, for tomorrow you may die," Vacher said as he paraphrased an old cliche. "Don't ever say old Vacher didn't share his last smoke with you."

I smiled to myself as I took a deep drag on the Camel and stared into the darkness of Bataan. In the past Vacher and I had shared cars, double dated, lived together, and sometimes shared our last dollar. Now as we shared wine and cigarettes on that cliff in Bataan, I again sensed the friendship we had experienced then. I dozed off, remembering better days with Vacher.

"Watch out, you're going to fall."

I felt a hand grab my shirt and pull me back. Startled, I realized I had almost fallen off the ledge, and then turned to see Orlo beaming down at me.

"Hileman, you're lucky I never sleep."

It was a small act, one hardly worth noticing, but Orlo had probably saved my life. The commotion woke the others.

"Let's get out of here," Orlo said as he gazed down the cliff at the tree-covered valley.

The night before, Vacher had assumed leadership, but now it was daylight and Orlo took charge.

"This bluff's not so tough," he said. "I got the route all figured out before you guys even woke up."

I doubted that.

"Listen, wise guy, just show us the way, and we'll decide how well you figured it out," Vacher said.

"That's okay with me," Orlo answered as he started moving along the sheer rock wall.

I watched closely as Orlo inched ahead, carefully moving over a rounded face in the stone and disappearing into a hidden vertical crevice. Moments later he leaned out and gave the okay sign with his index finger and thumb. One by one we followed, with me bringing up the rear. By the time I reached the crevice, Orlo had already climbed to the top. The crevice had widened near the top, providing an easy trail to the rim of the bluff.

After scaling the cliff, I was sure Orlo had not known where he was going when he had said, "This bluff's not so tough." Orlo's way of doing things was simply to charge ahead and trust in success at least fifty percent of the time. I delighted in his impulsiveness, even when it resulted in near disaster, as it had the previous day when we both got the hell stung out of us by the jungle bees.

We moved quickly away from the crest and into the trees. We found a secluded stream, and Main fixed some rice while we considered our next step. We could move into the lowlands where travel would be easier and food more available, or remain in the foothills where travel would be difficult but safer. With rice and Max's beluga beans, we decided we had ample food for a safer journey through the higher elevations.

While the rice boiled, I went to the stream to shave. I had only one blade, and it had become duller with each use. Several times I had tried to sharpen it on rocks without success, and I knew the day was coming when even a painful shave would be impossible.

Covering our trail and cooking fire, we moved in a northwesterly direction. With minimal underbrush, we were able to make good time and soon reached a well-used trail. It was evident that someone had been using the trail, and when we saw the prints of hobnail boots we knew it was the Japanese.

"Let's get the hell out of here," Main said with concern. "These tracks are fresh!"

When we had put some distance between ourselves and the trail, I asked Main about the footprints.

"Bill, how do you know those tracks were made this morning?"

"Hileman, when you've done as much hunting as I have, you just learn certain things," Main said in a matter-of-fact voice. In the United States, Main had been an avid hunter as well as an expert gunsmith.

"But how did you know those tracks were so fresh?" I impatiently asked again.

"Well, there were deer tracks on that trail too, and in places they were blotted out by the boot tracks. I also saw deer droppings, still soft and fresh. So the Japs must have used the trail just before we came along."

Main's ability to read tracks had convinced me, and I was eager to move out.

We entered an area with several deserted farms. The residents had probably evacuated them during the fighting and had left behind, among other things, their gardens. We gorged ourselves on tomatoes, string beans, okra, and even a few ears of sweet corn.

Late in the afternoon, as we approached another seemingly deserted farmhouse, we spotted a soldier sitting on the porch, the first American we had seen since our escape.

After greeting him, I asked if there were any Japanese in the area. He said there had been several patrols in the past few days.

"I think they've been picking up their dead and moving out some equipment. Looks like some pretty heavy fighting took place here.

"It's pretty quiet now," he said. "I'm going to sit out the rest of the war right here. That should only be a couple of months, but if it takes longer, I've got enough rice to last me two years."

"Hey, Jack," Orlo blurted out, using the name he often used to address strangers, "how about telling us where that rice is?"

"Listen, smart-ass, my name isn't Jack, and I'm more interested in saving my butt than yours. Why don't you and your friends get the hell out of here?"

Orlo had not intended to create a confrontation, but Vacher quickly took offense. He handed his rifle to me and walked over to the porch. He grabbed the man's shirt, jerked him to his feet, and forced him to look eye-to-eye on his tiptoes.

"Now, Buster, there's a little difference between someone calling you Jack and you calling someone a smart-ass," Vacher said. "We don't want your damn rice, but I'll tell you one thing, if we did you'd tell me where it is right now. I don't give a damn what your name is, but this man's name is Orlo Heinzman and I'd like you to remember that."

Vacher dropped the man and grabbed his rifle from me.

"Let's get out of here before I lose my temper," he said.

I glanced at Main who had known Vacher only a few weeks, but had seen, in that time, the explosive nature of his temper. Earlier, when we had been alone, Main had brought up the Carpenter incident.

"You know, someday someone is going to kill Vacher," Main had commented.

I had chosen not to discuss it with him. Now, as the man on the porch regained his composure, Main walked over and introduced himself. He began a conversation, mostly to show his opposition to Vacher's outburst. The man's attitude changed.

"I'm Robin Oakes from the 803rd Engineers. Hey, I've got plenty of rice. I found almost half a ton at a deserted Jap headquarters, but I don't have any matches."

Main produced two valuable matches, and then gave the man a suggestion.

"As long as you stay in one place, you can keep your fire alive by covering a burning piece of wood with ashes at night," Main said. "Then just by blowing on it, you'll have fire in the morning."

Main continued talking with Oakes and learned that large numbers of Japanese had been in the area. They posed little threat, however, as long as we were careful to avoid them. The incident with Vacher was soon forgotten.

"Come on, Orlo. I'll get you guys enough rice to last you a while," Oakes said as we prepared to move on.

I sat down and waited. Vacher had remained silent after the confrontation, and I wondered if Main's diplomacy with the stranger had intimidated him.

Orlo and Oakes returned in about half an hour with enough rice to last a week. Because it was getting late, we decided to spend the night before moving on in the morning. Main started supper.

Our new acquaintance had been stationed at Clark Field with the engineers. I recalled that when the 803rd had arrived at Clark, I had considered them pushy easterners from New York and New Jersey, but at the Pilar airstrip during our withdrawal into Bataan, I had seen them handle heavy equipment with one hand while firing their rifles at Japanese dive bombers with the other. They had defiantly shouted obscenities at the enemy as bullets and bombs riddled the runway. I had grudgingly learned to respect the engineers. That evening I learned more about Oakes and was interested in his reason for being alone.

"Close quarters breeds nothing but contempt among friends," he said. "I escaped with some good friends from the 803rd, guys I grew up with. I don't want to grow to hate them, so I separated from them."

The words cut deeply into my mind. I had already seen the contempt Vacher and Main had for each other, and at times I had been aggravated with both of them. Yet I was not ready to face the solitary existence sought by Oakes. His words made me aware of the potential explosiveness of our situation.

"Hope you make it, Oakes," Orlo said as we left in the morning. "See you in the States in a few months."

CHAPTER NINE

I had seen Vacher shaving that morning in the stream by Robin Oakes's shack. Wearing only his GI undershorts, the change in his physical appearance was apparent. The broad chest and strong thighs I had admired and envied had lost their muscular bulk and tone. I was disturbed by my friend's deteriorating physique.

Then I turned to myself. My once strong legs were thin with knobby knees, showing the effects of hard travel and poor diet. Leaving camp that morning, I looked at Orlo and realized that he, too, had lost weight, making his Ichabod Crane appearance even more pronounced. Only Main seemed to retain his weight, yet I was certain he was not cheating when he cooked. Main was an enigma: quiet, timid, and fastidious, yet somehow better equipped than the rest of us for the rigors of life on the run.

As we headed north, I wondered how long we could maintain adequate strength. I shared my concerns with the others when we stopped for a cigarette. The sudden awareness of our physical conditions made us realize it was necessary to increase our rations to three meals a day and larger portions. We were in an inhabited area now, and getting food should be easier.

With our food supply replenished at Oakes's camp, we decided to move through the hills, and that error in judgment was soon apparent. In three days, we had eaten all of Max's beluga beans and about half of the rice.

During one break Vacher and I sat away from the others and talked. Since leaving Oakes's shack we had moved deeper into the jungle, but now, sensing everyone's weakness and irritability, we discussed the advisability of leaving the mountains. The suggestion had been made several times, but Main had been adamant in his desire to stay in the hills.

"Do you suppose Main is just plain scared?" Vacher asked. "I don't think he'll ever leave these damn hills if we don't force the issue. Between you and me, I'd just as soon he stayed here. Being around him is like being tied to an old woman."

Vacher continued his gripes. He was bothered by the way Main washed the rice, the way he mumbled to himself, and the way he worked at adjusting his mirror to just the right angle while shaving. Vacher even resented the fact that Main still had a small bar of soap.

I was not surprised by Vacher's comments. In fact, I suspected Vacher had been looking for reasons to split with Main.

"We started together, and that may have been a mistake, but for now, let's stick together," I said. "We'll just tell Bill it's time to leave the hills. I think he'll come along."

I knew Orlo and Max would join Vacher and me, and Main could stay in the hills by himself or go with us.

"I'll talk to him," I said, "but in the meantime watch your temper around him. I think our diet is starting to affect us all. To tell the truth, some of the things you do bother me."

"Like what?" Vacher snapped back. "Tell me what you don't like, and maybe I'll change. Then again, maybe I won't."

I kept quiet, knowing anything I said would only aggravate him. Main finished cooking the rice and brought the pot over to Vacher and me.

"Sit down, Bill," I said. "We need to talk about a couple of things."

As Main sat down on a log, we heard a branch crack across the stream. I grabbed my rifle.

"Sounds like we've got company," I whispered to the others.

Motionless, we watched the small trail that led to the stream. A middle-aged, weather-beaten Filipino wearing a tattered uniform walked out from among the trees and studied the stream for a crossing spot. Waiting long enough to make sure the man was alone, I stood up.

"Hey, over here, Joe," I called. "We are friends. You don't need to be afraid."

For a few moments the Filipino studied us before slowly wading across the stream.

"What's your name, Joe?" Vacher asked.

"My name is Julio Galanza. I am a Philippine Scout, sir, from the Twenty-sixth Cavalry."

The Filipino eyed us suspiciously when he spotted Max.

"Who is he?" he asked. "Why is he with you?"

I sensed mistrust in Galanza's voice. I told him about meeting Max and caring for his sore thumb and that he had been traveling with us since. Then I related Max's story about being cut off from the 57th Infantry.

"I do not think that he is from the Scouts," Galanza said. "If he was a Scout, he would have a uniform."

That thought had occurred to us, but Max had said a civilian gave him clothes during his escape, and we had believed him.

"Oh, hell, Pop," Vacher said. "He's just a kid. He's okay."

Galanza seemed to like Vacher's reference to his age. He smiled, but then frowned as he gave us a warning.

"He is very young, yes," he said. "I do not think he was a Scout. I think he lies to you. He will wait for you to send him into a barrio to buy rice, and then he will not come back with your money."

Pop, as we immediately started calling Galanza, called in Tagalog to Max who ran over. They talked a few minutes, with Pop asking questions and Max answering in short sentences.

"I do not like him," Pop said to us. "I think he lies."

Dumbfounded, Max listened in embarrassment, unable to defend himself against the older man. I, for one, still believed Max's story.

Pop went on to tell us about himself. He had been stationed at Fort Stotsenburg and had lived in Barrio Margot, next to Clark Field, with his wife and five children. Like us, he had chosen to escape into the hills rather than surrender, and he was on his way home.

I asked Pop if we could travel with him. We were lost, knowing only that we were heading north. Besides, if we went with Pop, I would not have to confront Main about leaving.

Pop reluctantly agreed to guide us on condition that he would be in charge. The Filipino immediately took on an air of authority. With his agreement to lead us into Pampanga Province, he seemed to assume he was fully responsible for our welfare. We finished our rice and continued moving north.

On the trail Pop and Max got into an argument. Max wanted to go into the lowlands and get some food for supper. Pop insisted we stay in the hills. They argued in Tagalog, so we understood little of what was said, but it was apparent Pop won. Max sulked all afternoon.

I sensed the old Filipino knew where he was, unlike the rest of us. Meeting Pop was our good fortune, and I found opportunities to talk to the others about keeping him happy. We needed an experienced guide.

Occasionally during the next two days, I offered Pop the use of my compass. He ignored it, traveling instead by sight. He would climb a hill, spot a familiar landmark, and head in that direction. Sometimes we would not see the landmark again for hours, but we always seemed to arrive at the intended place. Pop's fast-paced walk was almost too much for us, and at times we were forced to ask him to slow down. Although considerably older than any of us, Pop was in good physical condition and obviously better acclimated to trail life than we were.

At breakfast the next morning, Main used what was left of our rice supply. More than once we reminded Pop that we needed to get more rice.

"Never mind," he kept saying. "You will not starve."

The four of us and Max followed Pop all day as he led us through the foothills to a trail leading toward the lowlands. Just before dusk, he called a halt, walked to the top of a small knoll, and surveyed the countryside before calling me over.

"See, look closely and you can see a barrio," Pop said as he pointed north. I could see only stacks of dry cogan grass and a few trees. With my binoculars, however, I finally saw two small thatched roofs which blended into the dry terrain. Pop and I rejoined the others.

We decided to send Max into the barrio for food. Pop agreed, as long as we gave Max no more than five pesos. He said that should be enough to buy eggs and two *gantas* of rice, about twelve cups. Orlo suggested giving Max more money, but the old man objected. Max took off while we rested in a thicket along the trail. Half an hour later he returned with no food. Vacher went out to meet him.

"The whole barrio is sick with malaria, sir," he said to Vacher. "We will give them some quinine, and they will sell us some food."

Pop objected, doubting Max had even gone into the barrio, but we prevailed. Main doled out about two hundred quinine tablets, and Max left again. Darkness settled over us as Main built a small fire. Max returned a short time later carrying two sacks. Relieved that he had apparently honored our trust, we grabbed the bags and looked inside. One contained two *gantas* of rice and five packs of black cigarettes. He said the cost was nine pesos per *ganta,* and the cigarettes were fifty centavos per pack.

Max had five small crabs in the second sack. Pop told us the freshwater crabs lived in the mountain streams, and anyone could easily catch them, but Max said an old woman had given him the crabs. If we wanted them, the price was four and one half pesos. With the quinine and five pesos he had already paid, Max said he needed another ten pesos to pay for everything. Pop became angry when Orlo gave the ten pesos to Max.

"Never mind, Pop," Vacher said. "Hell, there's a war going on, and things are bound to be higher than you remember them."

"Mr. Vacher, I told you that boy was not good for us," Pop said. "You will find out I am right. You wait."

"Yeah, Pop, we'll wait, but when it comes to food and cigarettes, what the hell's a few pesos?"

We waited for Max's return, and waited, and waited. Max did not come back.

"I told you he would steal your money," Pop kept repeating as the hours passed. "I told you he would cheat you. Now you be sorry."

Pop woke us at first light, and a few minutes later Orlo disappeared.

"Hey, any of you seen Orlo?" Main asked as he started a fire.

"He was here when I woke up, but I haven't seen him since," I said. "Do you suppose he went into the barrio?"

"Sure as hell, that's where he is," Vacher said as he walked up from the stream. "You know, before we get out of here, that curious bastard's going to get us all killed."

As we talked Orlo came up the trail holding a bag of rice, two packs of cigarettes, some rice cakes resembling pancakes, and some hot rice wrapped in a banana leaf.

"You know what?" Orlo said. "That little son of a bitch really gave us the shaft last night. I got all this for less than five pesos. Can you believe it? I thought he was our friend."

Pop grinned triumphantly as Orlo continued. Orlo said he had found the old lady who sold Max the food and cigarettes for twenty quinine tablets, and she had not seen him since.

"I hope that sore thumb of his drops off," Orlo said.

I could see he had trusted Max and felt betrayed.

"I am not surprised," Pop said. "I do not think he was ever a Scout."

I had learned an important lesson. Not every Filipino could be trusted, no matter how friendly he appeared. Pop had been grumpy, but now I realized he was on our side. His authoritarian attitude was difficult at times, but he had earned my trust.

Chapter Ten

More and more, the four of us recognized our need for outside help. We had figured Max could be of service, and he had betrayed us. Now we were trusting our fate to a cranky old Filipino with a know-it-all attitude. We had little choice. We were lost, were untrained for the rigors of jungle life, and were deteriorating both physically and mentally. We needed help, and Pop was the only one who could provide it.

Pop assured us that Mt. Arayat and the Plains of Pampanga would be visible after two or three hours of walking. The promise of a familiar landmark gave us a new sense of security. I knew pilots had used Mt. Arayat as a beacon when landing planes at Clark Field. The east-west runway had lined up between Mt. Arayat and Mt. Pinatubo.

We silently followed Pop along a seldom-used trail leading through the dense trees. Orlo seemed particularly quiet, and I assumed his silence was related to the incident with Max.

Late that morning Pop halted us at the top of a small knoll and pointed into the distance. I stared, almost disbelieving. There was Mt. Arayat, standing high above the Plains of Pampanga like a silent sentinel. Even with an altitude of only 3,000 feet, it was the only mountain in the sprawling flat plain, and it dominated the landscape.

Looking across the plain, I remembered an old Filipino legend I had heard in Sapang Batu before the war. According to the story, Mt. Arayat had once been in the Mariveles Mountains surrounded by many taller peaks. The other peaks ridiculed the little mountain, so Mt. Arayat left and moved into the Plains of Pampanga where it was the only mountain for miles around. The tale had seemed childish when I first heard it, but now the story touched me with its emotional impact.

Mt. Arayat represented a milepost in our escape from Bataan and all the terrible memories I had of our time there. I thought back to the events that had brought me to this place. In Bataan I had endured adversity, hunger, and fatigue. I had seen death and destruction, and finally surrender. We had fled into the jungle, literally cutting our way through at times. Now all the experiences of the last nineteen days seemed to flood over me: the long treks up and down hills, the numerous streams we had forded, the dangerous climbs up sheer bluffs, the close encounters with the Japanese, and the gnawing hunger that had seemed to follow every step. Conflict had arisen between individuals in our group several times. Now, as I stared at the first familiar landmark we had seen, tears ran down my gaunt cheeks. Mt. Arayat seemed to symbolize a new beginning and possibly an end to the hell we had fled. I began laughing, and then turned to Main and slapped him on the back.

"Bill, for the first time since we left kilometer one eighty-eight, I feel like we have a chance of making it. It's all downhill from here."

In the back of my mind I had never really expected to get out of Bataan alive, but I had, and I was ecstatic with the accomplishment. For the first time I had a real sense of optimism.

Main did not seem to share my enthusiasm, maintaining his fear and distrust of inhabited areas. His preference for the sanctuary of the mountains, even though food there was hard to find, had been obvious all along. As I looked at Main, I realized how different we were from one another. He would have been content to hide in the hills like a hermit. I liked people around me, and my social nature craved companionship.

Pop squatted down and used a stick to draw a map in the dust. I could see his route went in a straight line to Fort Stotsenburg. Under favorable conditions we could make the trip in three days. We would be leaving the hills behind us, and Pop strongly advised that we travel at night and sleep during the day. The Japanese occupied the rich food-producing province of Pampanga now, and staying out of sight was vital.

Pop suggested we go with him to Fort Stotsenburg, saying he knew where he could hide us. We made no commitment. When we moved on, I lagged behind Pop, talking individually with Vacher, Main, and Orlo. We all agreed Pop had been a great help to us, but the time to leave him was coming. His offer of sanctuary was tempting, but each of us felt strongly it would be better if we did not go with him. He had his own family, and the additional strain of caring for us might be too much. We were grateful to the old Filipino even though his assumed sense of responsibility had constantly irritated us. Separation was important for Pop's sake as well as our own.

Although we had decided to travel at night, we were too exhausted that first night to move into the plains. We needed rest.

For the first time since fleeing Bataan, we encountered swarms of mosquitos that night, and sleep was difficult. Without mosquito netting, I tried to hide under my canvas shelter half, but the effort was futile. Within minutes my skin was covered with welts. Mosquitoes bit my face, shoulders, back, stomach, and even my feet. I tossed and turned all night.

The mosquitos disappeared at dawn, and I fell asleep, only to be wakened early by Pop. I could sense his concern and nervousness. The openness of the Plains of Pampanga would add greatly to the hazards of movement.

Vacher and Main started arguing about breakfast. Main felt we should not build a fire, but Vacher wanted cooked rice.

"Listen, Vach, we're too damn close to the Japs to take a chance," Main said. "I heard a bugle this morning before I got up."

"Damn it, I've told you before, my name isn't Vach, even to my friends, and I don't put you in that category. I'm building a fire to cook some rice, and if you don't like it, Billy Boy, you can get the hell out of here."

Pop and I listened in silence. I agreed with Vacher, feeling that since we were near houses, the smoke would draw no special attention. I was sure no one was aware of our presence in the area.

Vacher built the fire, and Main grudgingly fixed the rice. In this case Vacher proved might is right. All but Orlo ate.

"Where is Mr. Heinzman?" Pop asked after breakfast.

"Who the hell knows," I said. "If there's a barrio near, that's probably where he is."

We waited more than an hour before Orlo came running up the trail. His flushed face was evidence of his nervousness and excitement. Breathless, he sat down and told us about his early morning experience.

Just over a kilometer from our camp was a barrio consisting of only a small number of grass and bamboo huts. Orlo said he had approached the barrio cautiously, and just before he had reached the shacks, he had gone down into a ravine where he had temporarily lost sight of the barrio. When he had crawled up the embankment and peered over the top, barking dogs ran from under the huts, defending the barrio against an apparent threat from the opposite direction. Orlo's hand trembled as he lit one of the brown cigarettes.

"I saw about thirty Japs come marching into the barrio," he said, "and they were armed to the teeth." The patrol carried rifles, sidearms, two light machine guns, and small mortars. Orlo said he had not known whether to run or stay put. He had feared that his running would have caused the dogs to bark, alerting the Japanese. So he had decided to hide and crawled into some tall grass.

Orlo had watched the patrol fan out, separating into small groups. Some approached huts, while others guarded strategic locations. All were armed and appeared ready for some kind of action.

An old Filipino had appeared in the door of a hut and talked to the Japanese commander. The officer yelled to his men who charged immediately into the shacks. For half an hour, the Japanese soldiers searched the barrio. Finding nothing, they left, and Orlo remained hidden for some time.

"I had to find out what was going on," Orlo continued, "so I sneaked into the barrio and called to the old man. When he spotted me, he jumped to the ground and grabbed me by the shirt.

"'Please, sir, they are looking for some Americans carrying guns. You will surely be killed if you stay here,' the old man said."

He then told Orlo the Japanese were looking for four heavily armed Americans traveling with a Filipino.

He said everyone in the whole area knew about us.

"Let's get the hell out of here," Orlo said.

His story shook me. The heavily armed patrol was looking for us.

We had been reported, and I felt it was probably Max. Whoever it was, it did not matter now. What did matter was the Japanese knew about us, and they were searching for us. The familiarity of Mt. Arayat and the Plains of Pampanga no longer offered any comfort to me. We were not just fugitives now: we were hunted fugitives. Our escape from Bataan had been a gamble, and the price of poker had just gone up.

Chapter Eleven

"Mr. Heinzman, you will get us all killed!" Pop exploded. "You must not leave camp without telling me where you are going and when you will be back. You are no good, and I do not want you with us anymore."

Vacher and I tried to reason with the furious old man, arguing Orlo's trip had been a fortunate break because now we knew someone had told the Japanese about us. Pop could not understand our logic. It seemed to me that he was so dedicated to our safety he wanted to control every move we made.

"He's getting worse every day," Vacher whispered to me. "I think it's time we parted company."

Pop continued ranting and raving about Orlo's visit, and Vacher finally had enough.

"Pop, it's time for us to leave you."

"Hell, no, I will not leave you. The Japs would catch you before night," Pop shot back. "You know how the Japs found out about you? It was Max. I told you Max was no good, but you did not believe me. Now you know he turned you in."

Pop's accusations disturbed me. As far as I knew, no one else had seen us on the trail, except Robin Oakes. Unless Oakes had been captured and tortured, he would not have betrayed us. I agreed with Pop that it had to have been Max who we had befriended and trusted.

Pop grumbled all day, and none of us got our much-needed rest. Between discovering a Japanese patrol was looking for us and learning the full scope of our mistake with Max, we were all on edge. When we set out that night, we were tired.

Shortly after sunset, the moon rose in the east, and we made good time until it disappeared behind the Zambales Mountains. We traveled through rice paddies and passed numerous small shacks, occasionally rousting dogs that barked at us as we stumbled through the darkness. Past the dogs and shacks, Pop led us up a stream. He thought it was the Culo River which flowed along the highway leading to Olongapo. If his calculations were correct, we were close to Layac Junction, near the town of Dinalupihan. During the withdrawal into Bataan, U.S. and Philippine forces had fought to keep the bridge spanning the Culo River open. The loss of that bridge would have caused American and Filipino soldiers on the front lines to have been cut off from the rest of us on Bataan. Now it was a hub of Japanese activity and filled with great peril for us.

Dawn breaks quickly in the tropics, so when the sky began to lighten Pop scanned the area for a safe hiding place. He spotted a dry wash across the river. A drainage during the rainy season, the wash was overgrown with vines and offered excellent cover. We waded through the knee-deep river, its sandy bottom providing an easy crossing, and then concealed ourselves among the bushes in the dry wash.

Main pulled some guava wood from his pack. The dry wood burned hot with no telltale smoke. More and more, he realized that satisfying our hunger had to be tempered with caution. Soon he had rice boiling gently in the corned beef hash can he had been using since the first day.

As we rested and waited for the rice, I examined my shoes. There was a hole in the sole of the right one, and the rocky trails had bruised my foot.

I was considering ways to repair my shoe when the sudden, shrill blast of a bugle echoed off the hillside. It was close.

"What the hell?" Vacher whispered.

Main jerked the burning wood from the fire, but he left the rice pot on the hot coals. Pop and I crawled up the ledge and peeked over.

There, less than half a kilometer away, were fifty or sixty horses tethered to a long rope stretched between two large trees. When I looked through my binoculars, the horses seemed graphically close. Japanese soldiers and Filipino grooms moved among the horses carrying hay and water, and in the morning stillness I could hear their voices.

Pop and I scooted back down the slope to warn the others. Main covered the fire with dirt, but the double portion of rice was all ready cooked. We would have enough for two meals. Main was clearly worried, and I wondered if he regretted leaving the safety of the hills.

As we ate we decided to remain hidden in the dry wash. Every ten minutes or so one of us crawled up the bank to check on the Japanese. From our hiding place we could hear traffic, moving equipment, and voices. Most of the Japanese and Filipinos were smoking cigarettes while caring for the horses, so we reasoned it was safe to smoke in our hiding place.

The day was extremely hot, and we drowsed away the morning hours trying to get some needed sleep. A sudden splash jarred me awake. It came from behind us where the dry wash entered the Culo River. Orlo jumped up, motioned for us to stay put, and crawled down the ravine.

"Hey, you guys want a laugh?" he whispered when he returned a few minutes later. "There's two Japs down there, naked as jaybirds, taking a bath. Their guns and clothes are on the bank not ten feet from where I was hiding."

Impulsively Vacher, Orlo, and I began to make plans to kill the soldiers and steal their money, but as we prepared to leave, Pop jumped in our way.

"There is nothing to be gained," Pop said. "We do not need the money. Then why do you do it?"

"Listen, old man," Vacher began, his neck turning red with anger.

"You listen, Vacher," Main broke in, "and hear me through. I know you think I'm chicken when it comes to violence. Okay, maybe I am, I don't know, but I'll tell you one thing, Pop's right!"

We listened to Main, surprised at the strength and conviction of his words, qualities none of us had known he possessed.

"For God's sake, let's not take any unnecessary chances and blow it now," he said. "We've come a long way together, and it hasn't been easy. Let's just cool it for the rest of the day and walk out of here tonight in one piece."

Main's hand trembled as he lit a cigarette and sat down.

"What do you think, Hileman?" Vacher said.

"They're probably right. We were about ready to go off the deep end."

The two Japanese soldiers went on their way, never suspecting their fate had been the subject of discussion only a few meters away. Main's outburst may have prevented a catastrophe for us. Had anything gone wrong with our plan, the Japanese would have hunted us down without mercy.

We ate the rest of our cold rice that evening, then began moving farther into farmlands, crossing both wet and dry rice paddies. With the darkness and the unevenness of the terrain, each of us fell once or more into the water-filled ditches. I was wet and cold, and my bones ached as stiffness set in. I thought about the meager diet we had had for the past four months and realized my physical endurance had dropped dramatically in just the past few days. Fortunately, we still had quinine and none of us suffered from malaria.

Late that night when we entered a sugarcane field, I broke off a piece and chewed the pulp. Its sweetness somehow made me aware of the simple things I missed so much: a bar of soap, a sharp razor, a cup of coffee, even salt. And, oh, how I longed for a bottle of ice-cold Coca Cola. These were all things I had so readily taken for granted during peacetime, but now saw as the luxuries of another time.

In a thoughtful attitude, I wandered ahead of the others. Suddenly, just in front of me, two headlights appeared as a car sped down a paved road. I ducked down, realizing we had reached the highway to Olongapo, the last hurdle in our escape from Bataan. We crossed the road quickly and sat in a ditch, delirious with joy. Bataan Province was behind us. We were in Pampanga, a province that, in our minds, symbolized peace and tranquility. We began laughing and slapping each other on the back, as if we did not have a care in the world. Pop watched silently.

When dogs began barking at us, we realized we were at the edge of a small barrio. The night sky that had hidden the huts was fading, and in ten minutes it would be daylight. We had to do something, and fast. We put our heads down and ran right through the barrio, and as we did, dogs barked and chickens squawked. On the other side we crossed a stream and proceeded up a bank into a cane field. We stopped and remained completely still as we listened. The dogs were still barking, and we could hear Filipino voices, but no Japanese.

I reached into my pocket and pulled out the scratch pad on which I had been keeping track of the days. It was Wednesday, April 29, our twentieth day on the run.

We stayed in the cane field only long enough to catch our breath and to be certain we were not being pursued. Then Pop moved us farther into the foothills for the day. Main built a fire while Pop gathered banana blossoms, hearts from young banana trees, and wild *gobi*, a tuberous plant covered with hairlike roots. When peeled, *gobi* resembled potatoes. Main even added a little salt, a carefully hoarded luxury. I thought the mixture tasted bland, but it was more substantial than plain rice and a welcome change.

Pop lay down and fell into a deep sleep. For days he had sacrificed sleep to keep an eye on his inexperienced American friends. We had become his personal responsibility.

While he slept, the four of us talked about splitting with the old man. He was but a day's walk from his home and family at Fort Stotsenburg. With Bataan behind us, we were eager to find a place to settle before the rainy season began. We decided to discuss the split with Pop that night.

When he was ready to move us out after supper, we told him we planned to spend the night there. We encouraged him to leave, but he resisted all our arguments. Vacher lost his temper and hollered at the old man.

"Listen, Pop, we're going to spend the night right here. Why the hell don't you just head for home? We'll be just fine."

Pop seemed surprised at the outburst, but maintained his authoritarian attitude.

"Corporal Vacher," he said, addressing Vacher by his rank for the first time, "you must remember I am the one to be in charge."

I could see a confrontation brewing, so I broke in.

"Pop, we want what's best for you, and right now that means getting back to your family. We really do want you to go."

Tears filled the old man's eyes, and I realized the depth of Pop's assumed responsibility and how much he cared for us.

"You know the Japs have a description of us," I said. "It is best for all of us if we separate now. You stay with us until tomorrow, and then you will leave."

When we woke early the next morning, I had cramps in my lower abdomen and a shakiness I had not noticed before. Still, we set out, and an hour later we reached the Gumain River.

Winding its way from the mountains near Mt. Pinatubo, the river separated Pampanga and Zambales Provinces. At the place we chose to cross, it appeared quiet and serene. Pop told us that farther north the Gumain River ran through a deep gorge where it traversed huge boulders, cataracts, and rapids. The river was peaceful now, but during the rainy season it would turn into a raging torrent, rolling stones the size of washtubs and making it virtually impossible to cross. It was still the dry season, however, so with the others I held my clothing, rifle, ammunition, and pack over my head and waded across the river. Even then I found the water was swift and shoulder deep in places.

A steep wall of rock faced us on the other side. Moving upstream, Pop located a deep cut in the rock. Its wide entry narrowed as we went farther into it, and travel became difficult. In some places, water had carved natural steps in the rocks. In others, we had to remove rifle slings, tie them together, and use them as a rope to pull one another up the crevasse. It took all morning to reach the top.

"I sure as hell can't keep this up much longer on just rice," Vacher said as he collapsed next to me. "I need some meat and eggs."

Pausing just long enough to catch our breath, we again shouldered our packs and continued up the hill ahead of us. I was amazed at the altitude we had gained since leaving the river. When we reached the crest, I could see the rich, fertile Plains of Pampanga, looking like an enormous truck garden with acres and acres of cane fields, rice paddies, and other crops. Some of the cane fields were brown, some black. It was harvest season, and some fields had been burned before mechanical harvesters cut the sweet stalks. The others would be harvested by hand, producing a superior sugar.

Through my binoculars I could see dozens of grass huts resembling haystacks. I saw carabao, the draft animal of the Philippines, moving back and forth in the paddies and fields. On the surface, I could not see anything that indicated life had been disturbed by the Japanese invasion.

"I wonder how long it'll be?" I mumbled to no one in particular.

"How long will what be?" Orlo asked.

I turned to see him lighting a poorly rolled cigarette.

"Good God, Orlo, haven't you learned how to roll a cigarette yet?"

"Doesn't look like it, but what do you mean, you wonder how long it will be?"

"I guess I wonder how long it'll be before the damn Japs are out of the P.I.," I said quietly.

I sat back in silence, gazing out at the striking beauty before me. I could see Mt. Arayat to the northeast and Mt. Pinatubo to the north. Somewhere between the two, I knew Pop's family was waiting for him at Fort Stotsenburg. It was time for us to part.

For several days Pop had guided, advised, and helped us. Even yet he wanted us to go with him, but we continued to reject his offer.

"This is it, Pop," Vacher said. "We will always be grateful for what you've done for us."

The old man sadly threw his meager belongings over his shoulder and moved down the trail alone, never looking back. He soon dropped out of sight and was gone.

"You know, he's a hell of an old guy," Vacher said.

Right or wrong, we had decided to find our own way now.

Chapter Twelve

We shouldered our packs, and quietly turned back to the trail. A herd of goats had appeared while we were watching Pop set off toward Fort Stotsenburg, and now as they moved closer we were certain they were domestic. That meant there were people living nearby.

Moving up a low hill, we peered cautiously over the top and spotted several small bamboo and sawali huts scattered among the trees. We squatted down and watched. Dogs barked, children squealed as they played, and chickens, hunting for insects, strutted and scratched between the huts. For fifteen minutes we surveyed the scene, passing the binoculars from one to another to be certain we had not missed anything. We saw only three adults, two women washing clothes in a small creek and a man plowing a field with a carabao. Everything looked peaceful.

What little rice we had left would not last long, and even the cautious Main conceded it was time to go into the barrio. We reasoned that if we could buy a good supply of food, we could spend a week resting and regaining our strength somewhere in the nearby hills. Our reduced rations during the campaign on Bataan, followed by three weeks on the run with only meager rations of plain rice, had affected our health in several ways. Orlo was showing symptoms of scurvy or pellagra. His hands had dried out, and rough, dead skin covered his knuckles. All of us suffered from the dobie itch, a symptom of pellagra. Rashes had formed on our legs, and our scrotums had swelled. Orlo had shown us the painful red swelling on his scrotum. His case was the worst. Main's shoes had never fit well, and now many blisters, some infected, covered his feet.

Gravely aware of our need for food, we decided two of us would go into the barrio, and the other two would remain behind just in case something went wrong. Orlo said he wanted to go because he knew a little Tagalog. Vacher and I wanted to remain behind, so Main accompanied Orlo. He stashed his rifle in the brush before starting down the trail. We watched them move across a small ravine toward a hut that stood somewhat separated from others in the barrio.

From the shade of a tree I watched our two companions through my binoculars. They appeared relaxed, laughing and joking as though they had not a care in the world. It looked as though Orlo was coaching Main on how to act in the secluded barrio. Vehicle access to the barrio was limited to one road, and while we watched our friends approach the hut, I also kept a cautious eye on the road.

An old man and woman came down the steps to greet them. Orlo did the talking, apparently trying to communicate in the native dialect, but he had to resort to hand signals.

"Hey, look at that," Vacher said as he handed the binoculars to me. "The old lady is going back into the house for something."

She came out with two glasses of water. Orlo and Main drank deeply and handed the glasses back, and then Orlo pointed at a chicken and made an oval with his thumb and finger. She went back into the house and returned with a basket. She handed Orlo a towel, and he began picking eggs from the basket, putting them in the towel. When they finished counting eggs, they put their packs down next to the three-step ladder and followed the old couple inside.

We waited several minutes, but they did not come out.

"You know what?" Vacher said. "That old couple invited those bastards inside for a meal. They're going to be one up on us."

In the midday heat, Vacher and I became hotter, sweatier, and more irritated as we sat on the hill and waited.

"I've had enough of this shit," I finally said. "Let's go into the barrio."

We chose a different path than the others had taken. We picked up our equipment, including Main's rifle, and moved around to the far end of the barrio. Unshaven and carrying three rifles, sidearms, and extra bandoliers of ammunition, I'm sure we had a rough, threatening appearance.

As we emerged from a bamboo thicket near one of the huts, we startled three young children who spotted us, screamed, and ran inside. Vacher and I listened as the children, chattering like excited monkeys, told their story. Moving back into the bushes, we could hear an adult asking the children questions.

Moments later a man and a woman, followed by six children, climbed single file down the short ladder from their house. The oldest child was in his teens, the youngest still in its mother's arms. I wondered what they would think of us, two unshaven Americans wearing ragged clothes and carrying enough guns and ammunition to start a small war.

The Filipinos did not see us until we stood up. The children ran behind their father, a short, medium-built man who appeared to be in his early forties. I sensed the children's fear, mixed with curiosity, as they peeked around their father, looking at us with saucerlike eyes.

"Are you American soldiers?" the man asked.

I nodded and we introduced ourselves.

"I am Dr. Pineda, and this is my wife." He pointed to the attractive lady behind him who appeared too young to have so many children.

"Are these your children?" I asked.

"Oh, yes, and one more besides," Dr. Pineda said with a smile. "Ernesto, my oldest son, is staying now in Barrio Pio with his grandfather."

"Where is Barrio Pio?" Vacher asked.

I knew he was not really interested in the barrio, but we had decided earlier to lead the Filipinos into conversation without revealing too much about ourselves.

Dr. Pineda pointed eastward toward Mt. Arayat. "Do you see that white dome? That is the big church in Barrio Pio."

He told us the church, the largest in the area, had been built by a Spanish plantation owner many years earlier, and that his son was staying near the church.

The doctor spoke to his wife in Tagalog, and then turned back to us.

"She will cook you some rice. I know you are hungry. While she is cooking, we will decide where you will spend the night."

Vacher and I sat on wooden blocks in the dirt yard, and the doctor told us about himself. He had worked for the U.S. government as a charity doctor in Porac, a town about eight kilometers beyond Barrio Pio. For a fixed monthly income, he had treated people who could not afford medical care. When the war came, he had lost his house, furniture, and clinic in Porac. The Japanese had taken his medical supplies and equipment, ransacked his office, and frozen his bank account. The family had been forced into living in this small barrio, Pasbul, where the doctor's father had once homesteaded.

Now the doctor owned the land, which he farmed. He employed Negritos to do most of the work. He said this particular Negrito tribe had close ties to the Pineda family. Some of them lived in the barrio all year round, while others came only at harvesttime to help with the rice, sugarcane, and pineapple. Even during peacetime, Dr. Pineda and his family had come to the barrio every year to supervise the harvest.

I could hear Mrs. Pineda giving instructions to the children inside the house. A young boy ran to get some freshly chopped wood for the fire, and soon I smelled smoke. The Pineda house, like other Filipino houses, had an open fire pit next to an outside wall so the smoke could go out through the window openings that ran the length of the room.

Dr. Pineda wanted to know all about us, our escape, and our physical conditions.

"I can tell that you are very weak. Your diet has not been good," he said. "You will stay with us until you are rested and feel strong again."

Dogs began barking, and we turned to see a Negrito leading a carabao down the narrow, dirt street in front of the house. Believed to have been the first settlers in the Philippines, Negritos were true pygmies. The word *Negrito* means little black. I did not consider myself very tall at five feet, seven inches, yet I seemed to tower over the small men who averaged less than five feet in height. Living deep in the jungles, most Negritos subsisted on rice, wild fruit, roots, and certain kinds of insects and small game. They would come down from the hills to help harvest rice, receive payment in rice, and then return to the jungle. Negritos were savage fighters whose primary weapon was the bow and arrow. They had designed a steel arrowhead specifically for killing Japanese soldiers. These arrows had a special collar with barbs. The first set of barbs curved away from the head so that the shaft entered the flesh for several inches. A second set of barbs slanted the other direction, stopping the arrow from passing through the body. Thus lodged, only a surgeon's skill could remove the arrow. Fortunately for us, Negritos were pro-American.

"I will send my son Salvadore to get your friends," Dr. Pineda said. "They will want to eat also."

I wondered if they would be up to a second meal. Salvadore started back up the dusty street as Dr. Pineda's wife called through the kitchen window.

"My wife feels very ashamed that she cannot speak English," he said. "She says that you must come in now and eat."

The doctor's soft voice and easy smile had the reassuring quality of compassion and understanding expected from a doctor.

We laid our packs on the ground before climbing up the three wooden steps leading into the Pineda house. We kept our guns, however, because they were our only protection in an emergency. A low table, perhaps eight or ten inches high, stood in the center of the room. There were five settings, one for the doctor and each of his four American guests. Women and children rarely ate with the men when guests were present. Mrs. Pineda had placed two huge bowls of rice, some fried fish, and steamed eggplant on the table.

I mentioned I thought Orlo and Main had already eaten.

"They will eat again when they arrive at my house," Dr. Pineda said.

Sitting cross-legged on the bamboo floor, Vacher and I began eating as Dr. Pineda told us more about the barrio and his family. The Pineda children, and others from the barrio, had gathered to watch us. They peered through the door, sat in the open window frames, and squatted on the floor across the room from us. To the curious, chattering little boys and girls, we seemed to be objects of great interest.

Dr. Pineda began discussing the Japanese military and relating what had occurred after Bataan fell. We had heard nothing about the events that followed the American surrender. During our rugged three-week journey through the jungle, we had often wondered what had become of our friends from the 698th who surrendered.

Numbly, Vacher and I listened as our host told us about a forced march out of Bataan. Along the sixty-five-mile route, hundreds of Americans and Filipinos had been overcome by heat, lack of food, and thirst. He said many Filipino civilians had risked their lives to give food and water to the prisoners, some of whom were reduced to crawling along the road. Those who had fallen out were systematically executed, and the road had been littered with the bloated corpses of American and Filipino soldiers.

"The bastards," I said.

"Yes, Mr. Hileman. The Japanese were very cruel on the march. Many people died."

CHAPTER THIRTEEN

"No matter how it turns out for you, you will be much better off than if you surrender to the Japanese," Arturo Espirito had warned us when we started our escape from Bataan three weeks earlier. "One thing you can count on, all Americans in Japanese hands will be treated badly. They care nothing for human life."

Now, as Dr. Pineda talked about the march of prisoners, I knew the Filipino journalist had been right. I thought about Sherdie Allin, Homer Boren, Charlie Johnson, Peewee Standlee, Harold Hall, and my other friends from the 698th. I especially worried about Grover Bump. During the December 8 attack on Clark Field, aviation fuel drums had been strafed, sending a deadly flow of fire that critically burned him. Still in fragile condition, he had rejoined us just before the surrender. The more the doctor told us about the march, the more I feared for my friends. I could not comprehend the full impact of the account, but the thought of my friends undergoing such extreme brutality created a mixed emotion of horror, anger, and compassion deep within me.

"When the Americans return, I can go back to Porac," Dr. Pineda said after his shocking account of the forced march. He said he wanted to resume his practice, educate his children, and enjoy a peacetime life.

As he spoke I sensed his deep faith in the United States. Dr. Pineda viewed the Japanese occupation as temporary, and his confidence never seemed to waver.

In the months that followed, I found most Filipino people shared Dr. Pineda's sentiments. "When the Americans return," became a phrase that served as an emotional cornerstone for both Filipinos and American fugitives. Even when their personal survival was in jeopardy, the Filipinos never expressed any doubts about the ultimate outcome of the war.

Dr. Pineda began telling us about local people who had organized as guerrillas. He said some were receiving orders from Americans, a factor that bothered me. I wondered who these Americans were and how they had organized so quickly. According to Dr. Pineda, American officers were dividing the islands into sectors of military resistance. I knew some soldiers had been cut off during the withdrawal into Bataan and that others had deserted. Whoever these Americans were, I felt uneasy about them.

Barking dogs interrupted our conversation, and when Vacher and I heard voices, we instinctively grabbed our rifles and took positions near the window.

"Do not be afraid," Dr. Pineda said in a reassuring calm voice. "There is no danger now. That is my son, Salvadore, returning with your friends."

Peering through the window, I saw Orlo and Main walking up the barrio street surrounded by dogs and children and accompanied by two Negritos. The Negritos attracted my attention. Despite their small size, the little black men presented a hostile appearance. They carried long bows, arrows in native quivers, and bolos in wooden scabbards attached to crude belts. I was glad they liked Americans.

Children giggled as Orlo laughed and talked to them in a mixture of English and Tagalog. His charisma with the children reminded me of the *Pied Piper* story of my youth. As I watched Orlo, I realized it had been only ten months since the three of us had arrived in the Philippines. My mind raced back to the day when Orlo, Vacher, and I were about to arrive in the Philippines. I remembered our conversation on the fantail of the USS *President Pierce* as the ship moved through the San Bernardino Straits.

"Orlo, where do you think we'll be a year from now?" I had asked.

Orlo had remained silent, gazing thoughtfully into the dark water. He seemed oblivious to the spectacular world around him. The blue sky, lush green coastline, and deep violet ocean radiated in the balmy tropical afternoon sun, but Orlo's mind seemed to be somewhere else.

"What are you thinking about, Orlo?" I had persisted.

After a long pause, Orlo had looked up at me with piercing eyes, his face flushed with concern, and his voice subdued with an inner fear.

"Hileman, a year from now I'll be dead. They're going to bury me over here. Don't ask me how I know, but I'm never going home."

His eyes seemed to look right through me as he spoke. His words were out of character, and they made Vacher and me uncomfortable. We had changed the subject.

Now it seemed like a lifetime had passed, and there had been nothing but war.

Main and Orlo joined us at the table. We talked and laughed as we shared the excitement of being in a home where people showed genuine interest in our welfare.

"You will eat now," Dr. Pineda said to Orlo and Main.

They proceeded to eat a full meal, despite having already eaten. They did not want to offend the doctor or his wife.

When they finished, Dr. Pineda offered us American cigarettes. Using a pair of tongs, his daughter picked a hot coal from the fire and brought it to each of us for a light. I took a deep drag and leaned back, enjoying the luxury of a good cigarette after a satisfying meal.

"Where will you go now?" the doctor asked.

"Well, I know one thing, we've got to rest for a couple of days," Orlo answered quickly. "Then maybe we'll head north and try to make connections with the guys we got separated from."

"I have an unused house," Dr. Pineda said. "You are welcome to use it."

We gratefully accepted the doctor's offer. Then, in a serious voice, he cautioned us.

"I think that you should plan on more than two days to rest. In my opinion, you are more tired than you think. You will find now that you have stopped and are not under such a strain, you will have a physical letdown.

"While you rest perhaps we can find shoes for you. Americans are not used to traveling barefoot, and your shoes are worn out. Barefoot walking is okay for Filipinos, but not Americans."

I was relieved when he made that suggestion because by now my second shoe was about to give out.

Dr. Pineda asked if we had anything in which to carry rice, and Orlo produced a cloth bag that had been partially filled by his other host. The doctor spoke to one of his children in Tagalog, and the child immediately fetched two one-pound coffee cans filled with white rice from the storage area. Dr. Pineda poured the rice into Orlo's sack, and Orlo reached in his pocket for some money.

"You will not pay me," Dr. Pineda said as he held up his hand. "We are to help one another in this time of need.

"Come now, you will follow me." He got up from the table, strapped a bolo around his waist, and put on his straw hat.

We thanked Mrs. Pineda for the meal, picked up the gear we had dropped by the step, and followed the doctor up the barrio street. At the end, he turned right onto a well-worn trail. We followed him down a slight hill to the creek which we crossed. The trail continued into a dense thicket of trees where we came to a thatch-roofed shack. It was well hidden and no more than one hundred meters from the stream.

"You will make yourselves at home here," the doctor said.

He turned and walked back down the trail, leaving us alone.

We climbed the four ladderlike steps leading into the elevated shack, placed our packs on the bamboo-slatted floor, and sat down. The shack's remote location pleased us, though we were somewhat uneasy about not being able to see the barrio to determine who might be in the area.

Resting in the secluded shack, I realized what a welcome, but unexpected, turn of events the day had brought. I found it hard to believe all that had happened since we sent Pop on his way that morning.

Orlo had been in an uncharacteristically quiet mood while we had eaten at the Pineda house, and his manner continued now in this shack. Without a word he reached into his pack, pulled out his ragged Army blanket, and draped it over his shoulders. When he began shivering, I immediately recognized the onset of a malaria chill.

I had seen others suffering from malaria on Bataan, although the 698th had maintained enough quinine to prevent malarial attacks during the fighting. It had been to our advantage that the fighting had taken place during the dry season. Now, however, the rainy season was approaching, and frequent showers would create stagnant pools which would become breeding grounds for mosquitoes. Now I realized Max's betrayal had created another serious problem for us. The few remaining quinine tablets we had not given to Max had been consumed on the trail. There were none left for Orlo or for the rest of us.

Orlo's teeth began to chatter, and his face revealed the growing tenseness of his body. Knowing a raging fever would follow, I went to find Dr. Pineda who gave me a small amount of quinine.

"I do not have enough to do Mr. Heinzman much good," he said.

The doctor said that to be effective, large doses were needed at the beginning of treatment, and then the dosage should be tapered off. If it were not enough to help, the doctor would brew some herbal tea called *dita*.

The coolness of the early evening was refreshing as I returned to the shack and gave the quinine to Orlo. Wrapping the remnant of my old Army blanket around myself, I looked forward to the next day. It would be May 1, and I was sure it would mark the beginning of a new life for us.

Chapter Fourteen

Bright sunshine streamed through the window opening of the shack as I wiped the sleep from my eyes. I heard the happy chatter of the Pineda children, and looking out, could see Salvadore and his brothers and sisters coming up the trail ahead of their father. Dr. Pineda's bolo swung from side to side as he walked, and his straw hat rested on his head at a jaunty angle. The giggling children scurried up the steps and entered the hut.

Since our arrival in the Philippines, none of us had been affected by any of the diseases so prevalent in the tropics, but that night had been rough for Orlo. When his chills subsided, a raging fever had descended over him. His semiconscious babbling, twisting, and turning had wakened me several times, and Main had stayed up with him, wiping his forehead with a cloth soaked in cold water. In his delirium Orlo had cursed Main who patiently continued caring for him. Main said the fever had dropped about midnight when Orlo fell into a deep sleep.

"Man, am I glad to see you." Orlo's voice was weak as he looked up at Dr. Pineda through glazed eyes.

"Mr. Heinzman, you have malaria. You will be very weak until the fever leaves you completely. Mr. Main will fix you something to eat."

"I don't want anything right now," Orlo said. "I think I'll hold off on the food for a while, if you don't mind."

Orlo's words startled me because up to now we had been eating everything we could find. Dr. Pineda said that malaria victims often lose their appetite and sometimes needed to be forced to eat. Later that day Orlo ate a soft-boiled egg, even though he complained it had a fishy taste.

Main continued giving Orlo the few quinine tablets Dr. Pineda brought, but they did little good. That afternoon Orlo had more chills, and we all knew fever would follow.

To complicate matters, Vacher developed diarrhea which made us aware of a double problem: the sickness itself and the acute shortage of paper. During our escape out of Bataan, we had used leaves, grass, or Japanese propaganda leaflets to keep ourselves clean. Now, with a severe case of diarrhea and the soreness that accompanied it, Vacher's temper grew short. Main and I tried to avoid antagonizing him, but his chronic griping began to wear on our nerves. I thought he was smoking too much and told him so.

"Where the hell are you getting all those cigarettes?" I asked.

"Hileman, shut your damn mouth before I jam my thumb in your eye and drag you down to the creek."

I said nothing more, but his constant smoking continued to gnaw at me. I presumed he had bummed the cigarettes from Dr. Pineda, and that bothered me. We still had tobacco scrounged from cigarette butts in the Japanese camp site, and as my temper festered, I reached into my bag and grabbed a pinch of loose tobacco. I started to roll a cigarette in a scrap of paper, but my hands trembled with anger, and I finally crumpled up my wasted effort and flung it out the door.

"What's the matter, Hileman? You're shaking like you've got the chills. Here, have a cigarette. There are four packs on the shelf above the window. Dr. Pineda brought them for us last night."

I felt ashamed for my thoughts, and at the same time, began to realize how frayed our nerves had become. I knew I should apologize, but I did not. Lack of sleep, shortage of food, physical exhaustion, and close quarters were beginning to tear at our nerves. I feared we would soon be at each other's throats, but I was not about to play the part of peacemaker with men who were aggravating me.

Main continued to nurse Orlo, wiping his forehead with a damp cloth and encouraging him to eat. Once when Main took a break, Orlo yelled at him.

"Hey, Main, get off your ass and get me a damp cloth." Main patiently brought the cloth to him.

Later that afternoon I felt a chill and wrapped my tattered blanket around my shoulders. I recognized the symptoms of malaria, and knew I, too, would soon need Main's help.

Dr. Pineda came that evening to examine Orlo, and then checked me.

"You will all be here for a few days," the doctor said. "Tomorrow I will go to Porac to see if I can find some quinine. If I can't, I'll have to use some native medicine."

My chill left in an hour, and I tried to eat. Main had prepared some duck eggs, but they smelled like fish and I could not get them down. I also tried some rice, but my appetite was gone. I felt a sudden flush of heat surging through my body, threw my blanket down, and lay down on the floor of the shack. I tossed and turned on the floor for several hours, going in and out of a strange world of delirious dreams. I dreamed about a large pit filled with cracked ice and cold bottles of Coca Cola. Each bottle dripped with tiny beads of icy sweat. In my dream I kept reaching for the bottles, but they were always just beyond my grasp.

When I woke, Main brought me a drink of water and wiped my forehead with a wet cloth. Still in a daze, I felt only contempt for him, angered that he felt so good while I suffered. I looked across the room at Vacher, hoping he would get sick from all the brown Filipino cigarettes he had smoked and that he would get malaria, too. In my delirium, with hate filling my thoughts, I drifted back to sleep.

It was still dark when my fever broke. I awoke and staggered outside where Main was sitting by the fire smoking a hand-rolled cigarette.

"How are you feeling?" Main asked. "You sure raised a lot of hell for a while."

"I've still got a headache, but I feel a lot better. You got any cold rice?"

"I can beat that all to hell if you're interested. I've got a new pot on the coals."

Since our arrival in Pasbul, Main had learned to cook in native clay pots, and the old hash can had been discarded. I reached into the clay pot and scooped out some of the hot rice. I also got some of the crisp, browned rice from the side of the pot, which tasted better to me than the fluffy, white rice. Filipinos called the burnt rice *bungee*. I ate a few bites and put my spoon down.

"What time is it?"

"Around four, I guess," Main said as he looked up at the morning sky.

He said Vacher had made several trips to the latrine area in the past couple hours.

"Boy, is he in a rough mood. He told me he's not passing anything except blood and mucus. Doesn't sound too good."

With Vacher's diarrhea and both Orlo and me in the throes of malaria, we knew we were in for a rough time. Then I shared another concern. If the Japanese overran the barrio, we would be shot on sight, and Dr. Pineda and the other Filipinos would be punished. I suggested moving at the first opportunity, and Main agreed. We decided to talk to Dr. Pineda about it.

Birds began chirping as the eastern sky turned a bright pink. A new day had begun.

"It must be going to rain," Main said. "This is the first time I've seen those colors in the sky this time of day."

I cringed with jealous contempt at hearing yet another of Main's skills. He was a gunsmith, camp doctor, jungle cook, and now a goddamn weatherman.

Vacher and Orlo joined us at the fire. Main dished up the rice and slices of eggplant he had laid over the rice to steam. Orlo said he was hungry.

"Don't give me any of that damn eggplant," he added.

I forced down a little of each, although I, too, disliked the tasteless vegetable. Vacher sat in the corner and ate two helpings of rice. Main grumbled, saying each man should get an equal share.

"I'm a big man with a big appetite," Vacher said as he shrugged his shoulders. Main turned away in disgust.

Vacher continued his runs to the latrine area, complaining that he was not passing anything. All he got for his efforts was cramps and a lot of straining.

I had been constipated for a week, but that morning I felt some action in my bowels and headed for the latrine area. As I ran through the bushes, I discovered three piles of runny feces. Uncovered, they were already attracting the large green flies that constantly swarmed through the jungle seeking out places to lay their eggs. Momentarily I felt embarrassed, as though I had been caught spying on Vacher, but quickly my mood turned to uncontrolled anger. My first thought was to grab my Colt .45 and force Vacher to clean it up, but as I sat down on a log to gather my thoughts, my temper cooled. I grabbed the bolo and covered the mess myself, but I needed to figure out a way to handle the problem. I decided to confront Vacher when we were alone.

Back at the shack, I felt another malarial chill and did not say anything to Vacher. Soon I was cowering in the corner as the raging fever returned in all its fury.

"Hileman! You sniveling bastard," Vacher screamed as he charged through the door. "What sort of animal are you anyway? You get your kicks sniffing out other people's shit?"

I shrugged and turned towards the wall, trying to ignore Vacher.

"Don't turn your back on me, you bastard."

Vacher grabbed my shirt and pulled me to my feet. My head throbbed.

"Leave him alone!" Main shouted at Vacher. "Can't you see he's in no condition to defend himself?"

"And I'm in no mood to take any shit from you either," Vacher said. "Shut your fucking mouth before you get yourself killed."

Main took a step backwards, but in a firm, steady voice, he warned Vacher that someday he would face a situation he could not handle with his fists.

"Like what, Billy Boy?"

"Like the way you handled Carpenter," Main replied. "A thirty-caliber slug in the guts, that's what I mean. That seems to be the only language you understand."

"You mean by you?" A flushed, red color crept up Vacher's neck. "You chicken-shit bastard, you haven't got the guts to stick a gun in my ribs and pull the trigger."

I had no idea covering Vacher's waste would lead to such a confrontation, but I knew Main had hidden strength and realized, for the first time, that Main could pull the trigger on Vacher. A gunsmith and hunter in civilian life, Main would use his gun if backed into a corner.

Vacher released me, and I fell to the floor. At that moment I felt sorrow for all of us and for the people we had become. We had deteriorated into a state where murder was a real possibility. I had contemplated forcing Vacher at gunpoint to cover his feces. Now Main was probably thinking about shooting Vacher, and Vacher was mad enough to kill both of us.

Then as suddenly as the flare-up had started, it was over. Vacher stood, looking ashamedly toward the floor.

"I was going to clean up my mess," he said. "Hell, I'm not stupid. I was going to cover it up. That's how I knew someone had snooped on me."

"You're all acting like a bunch of kids," Orlo said when things quieted down. "Just relax. Everything will work out."

During the day Orlo seemed to improve, and he even ate without complaint, but that night he developed diarrhea. Now he had both malaria and dysentery, a dangerous combination.

Dr. Pineda's oldest son, fifteen-year-old Ernie, had visited us earlier that day after returning from his grandfather's house in Barrio Pio. He brought three cans of Carnation condensed milk, but the welcome treat posed a dilemma for us. How would we use the milk? If we decided to split it, how would we divide three cans evenly four ways?

We discussed the best way to use the milk. I wanted to pour it over the rice along with some sugar, the way my mother had fixed rice back home. The others thought that was a stupid way to eat rice. Vacher wanted to use the milk to make gravy, but Main reminded him that would require some kind of cooking fat which we did not have. We agreed to use some of the canned milk to make rice pudding, though Orlo complained that rice pudding was no good without raisins.

Ernie returned a second time that day and brought some duck eggs. I commented that I hoped the ducks had not been eating fish.

"No, sir, Mr. Hileman," Ernie said. "My grandfather's ducks cannot find the fish."

I doubted Ernie's words, but welcomed the gift.

"I will be the one to bring you food while you are here," Ernie said. "Even when we move you to the river, I will be the one to carry food to you."

This news took me by surprise. Main and I had talked about moving, and now it was apparent the Filipinos had also been discussing our situation. Realizing that made it easier for us to talk to Dr. Pineda about it.

That evening Dr. Pineda came from Porac carrying a burlap bag. Carefully he pulled out a bottle of quinine, six more cans of condensed milk, four packs of brown cigarettes, and a paper bag filled with Picadura tobacco, the high-quality, fine-cut native tobacco most Filipinos smoked. He also brought a small roll of slick paper for rolling cigarettes, the quality of which was not much better than the propaganda leaflets we had used on Bataan.

Dr. Pineda examined me, diagnosed malaria, and put me on a quinine ration.

"I hope Mr. Vacher and Mr. Main do not get malaria," he said. "Quinine is very difficult to buy in the barrio. The price is very dear."

Dr. Pineda related the latest news. The Japanese had a garrison of fifty or more soldiers in Porac who were attached to the main garrison at San Fernando, the provincial capital of Pampanga Province. For the time being they were preoccupied with Hukbalahaps, communist guerrillas who had fought the Filipino constabulary before the war. Currently the Huks were fighting the Japanese, and Dr. Pineda felt we had nothing to fear from them.

The Japanese in Porac were aware, however, of various reports about Americans rumored to be hiding in the hills. This deeply concerned me, and so did the fact that so many Filipinos knew we were hiding in Barrio Pasbul. Since we had arrived at Dr. Pineda's house, it seemed strangers dropped by daily to welcome us. Sometimes in groups, and sometimes alone, they always said they were cousins, uncles, nephews, or brothers-in-law of someone they thought we should know. We had known since Orlo's visit to the small barrio back on the trail that the Japanese had a good description of us, and that only heightened my anxiety. They would undoubtedly come looking for us soon, and we were in no condition to either fight or run.

Thinking about our situation, I was apprehensive. The Japanese would view us, the four heavily armed Americans, as a menace in the area. In their eyes we were not fugitives, but armed and dangerous guerrillas. It would be only a matter of time until a reward would be offered for our capture.

I thought about my three companions. I knew Main wanted to go deeper into the hills and hide out, taking no chances whatsoever.

Vacher seemed to be concerned primarily with being near a good supply of food, coffee, and cigarettes. I was sure he was ready to fight the Japanese if the need arose. Orlo agreed with me that the best plan was to stay on the move. I had already decided if our differences ever split us up I wanted to pair up with Orlo. He was easy to live with, and we shared the philosophy of constant movement.

Over the next few days we repeatedly heard rumors about Japanese patrols, particularly to the southeast near Del Carmen and Florida Blanca. The Japanese were looking primarily for Huks, but were on the alert for any Americans they might find.

On the heels of his bout with dysentery, malaria hit Vacher hard. For two days he huddled in a corner. He did not talk, eat, or even complain about not having coffee. Dr. Pineda put him on quinine along with Orlo and me. A stranger in Porac had given the doctor a bottle with one hundred quinine tablets, saying specifically they were for us. The man's compassionate generosity touched me, but it also alarmed me that so many Filipinos in the area knew about us.

The next day, about noon, a Filipino runner came into Barrio Pasbul, warning Dr. Pineda that a Japanese patrol was already near Barrio Pio and that it might come on to Pasbul. The doctor ran to our shack and told us it was time to move. He would take us to a secluded spot along the Gumain River.

Chapter Fifteen

*D*r. Pineda instructed us to gather our meager belongings. "The Negritos will carry your supplies," he said. "You are very weak, and the trail will be very difficult for you." Orlo and Vacher were both suffering from the debilitating effects of dysentery, and all three of us were experiencing the chills and fever that accompanied malaria. Despite our weakened conditions, however, it was necessary that we move deeper into the jungle.

It was a strange-appearing procession that started down the trail into the Gumain River Canyon. The Negritos were in the lead, all shouldering rifles and carrying our packs. Of the four of us who followed, only Main had any energy and interest in where we were going. The rest of us were too sick and weak to care. Bringing up the rear were Dr. Pineda, his son Ernie, and his brother Sylvestre.

It began to rain, and in just minutes we were all soaked from the steady downpour. Dispositions quickly became as dank and cold as our rain-drenched bodies. We had to stop several times as dysentery repeatedly forced Orlo and Vacher to seek the privacy of the jungle.

"I will give Mr. Vacher and Mr. Heinzman an enema when we reach our destination," Dr. Pineda said.

Silently, I wondered if Vacher would let Dr. Pineda proceed with such a treatment.

In about an hour we reached the Gumain River. I took off my shoes for the crossing, and noting how easily the Filipinos and Negritos walked barefoot, left them off as we continued north along the muddy jungle trail. I soon learned my feet were not toughened as theirs were, and with sharp rocks bruising my feet, I put my shoes back on. They were so wet and muddy that when we crossed the zigzag river six or seven more times, I no longer bothered to remove them.

My mood began to sour when, in addition to the pain of walking and the misery of the drenching rain, I began to feel the surging pain of abdominal cramps. As my physical discomfort increased, my mental faculties seemed to fall in tune with it. Anger and resentment festered in my mind, and I wondered how we had allowed these primitive people to assume control of our lives. I began to doubt the report of the Japanese patrol, convinced that this trek through the wet jungle was the Filipinos' way of getting rid of us. Once in the jungle, I thought, they would desert us, and we would wait hopelessly for help and supplies that would never come. As my irrational thoughts continued, I was certain we were going to die in the jungle, and no one would ever know what happened to us.

My cramps were becoming more acute, and when I sneezed I was aware of a warm liquid running down my leg. The sneeze had broken loose my cramping bowels, and now the uncontrolled feces added humiliation to my physical discomfort. My emotional and physical state seemed only to heighten my mistrust of the Filipinos. I had faced hardship and tough times before, but I had never experienced a day such as this. I felt a malarial chill and told Dr. Pineda.

"Mr. Hileman, you will be okay now," the doctor reassured me. "We are very near our destination."

The painful cramps and my uncontrollable bowels continued their rampage against decency. The warm liquid ran down my legs and into my shoes. I got my blanket from one of the Negritos and wrapped it around myself in an effort to hide my humiliation.

The rain continued, and darkness fell early in the jungle canyon. The Negritos, using torches now to lead the way, finally stopped under an overhanging cliff along the riverbank. Dr. Pineda referred to the area as the cave. Directly across the river, near a little stream which emptied into the Gumain, a small hut had been specially constructed for us. Four bamboo poles had been driven into the ground, providing the framework for the sawali siding which enclosed the shack on three sides. The front was open. A thatched roof covered the lean-to, and a slatted floor about two feet above the ground would serve as our sleeping area.

The Negritos unloaded the supplies they had carried through the canyon. There were clay pots for cooking, a sack of rice, and a small can of salt. In addition, there were several cans of condensed milk, some papayas and bananas, Picadura tobacco, and a few matches. Each of us had a tattered blanket and a canvas shelter half. The shelter halves were worn and had been punctured by thorns on the way out of Bataan, but they would help during the rain.

As the Negritos gathered wood and built a fire, Dr. Pineda suggested that Main should start cooking some rice. With the fire snapping, Dr. Pineda brewed some guava leaf tea which he said was for the promised enemas. I was surprised when after treating Vacher and Orlo, he turned to me. Too weak to resist, I surrendered to the same ordeal. Then Dr. Pineda said we were to drink the medicinal tea, and nothing else, for the next two days.

"I'll try anything," Vacher said.

I was wholly surprised by the submissive attitude of Vacher who, for the past few weeks, had been in an uncooperative, argumentative mood. I took a morbid pleasure in Vacher's weakness and delighted in the thought that he was without coffee or good cigarettes like his favorite Camels. Vacher, as well as Orlo and I, had been reduced to a feeble specimen of manhood. Dysentery and malaria were great equalizers.

Then I looked at Main, still a picture of good health. During the journey to the river encampment he had been in good spirits, whistling and mumbling to himself as he walked along. He had been wanting to find a remote location to live out the war, and now, it seemed, he had. I resented Main's good health and secretly hoped he, too, would become ill. At the same time I realized how important his well-being was to the rest of us. He could care for us, something we could not do for ourselves.

I felt a sense of relief when the Filipinos and Negritos finally departed. During the trek they had constantly given us much unsolicited advice about jungle survival and had directed every move we made. As I watched the blazing torches disappear down the trail I settled back with a sigh of relief. It was good to be alone.

The tensions and pressures of the day lessened as the four of us started eating our supper. Like Vacher and Orlo, I had trouble getting the rice down, although I did enjoy a ripe banana. Only Main seemed to have a normal appetite. After our meal Main took the rice pot down to the river and washed it with sand.

I watched the moon disappear behind a cloud. Shrouded in darkness, I could hear the river's rippling water. It gave the night a tranquil atmosphere, and I felt at peace. Although I was weak and still covered with filth, life seemed worthwhile again.

Vacher lifted a hot coal, lit a brown Filipino cigarette, and passed the coal to me. He gazed into the fire, letting the smoke curl around his head.

"Well, are you guys ready to start living like natives?" he said. "It'll be different, but I'm ready for it. I'm tired of having the Filipinos and Negritos play nursemaid for us."

I agreed with Vacher, and then expressed the thoughts which had been festering in my mind all afternoon.

"You know, I'll bet those damn Filipinos brought us up here just to get rid of us. They don't want us in their hair in case the Japs show up. And you know what? Once the rainy season starts and the river rises, there'll be no way out of this damned canyon. They won't be back, and we won't be able to leave. They just wanted to get us out of that damn barrio. I'll bet the Japs will never even visit that piddlyassed little barrio."

"Hileman, there are times when you just gripe the hell out of me," Main said. "Dr. Pineda knows what he's doing, and you'd better learn to trust him. We're sitting here in a strange land, sicker than hell, and all you can do is shoot your damn mouth off about the only people who can help us."

I listened silently as Main continued with unusual force in his voice.

"Think about it," he said. "If the Japs found us in that barrio, they'd kill all the Filipinos and Negritos, including the kids. It's as simple as that, so keep your damn mouth shut."

I wanted to argue with Main, but knew in my heart he was probably right.

Vacher took a drink of tea from his canteen and quickly spit it out.

"I can't drink this shit!" he said. "Main, give me some of that water you use for cooking."

"You'd better drink it," Main said. "I've been drinking my guava leaf tea, and I'm not sick. You're the one who said we were starting to live like natives, so you'd better get at it. You might even have to learn to live without coffee before we're out of this mess."

"Don't push your luck, Billy Boy. As sick as I am, I can still put you on your ass with one hand tied behind my back."

Main quietly got up and went to relieve himself in the bushes before going to bed. When the four of us stretched out on the bamboo floor we realized how small the lean-to was. It was adequate only for sleeping and for protection from the rain, but not suitable for any other activity.

Sleep came slowly for me as my old nighttime fears dominated my thinking. I thought about being sick and dying in this remote jungle location. I hated being at the mercy of the Filipinos, but my destiny seemed to be in their hands. I was still certain they had deserted us and knew we could not survive without them.

I listened to Main's snoring, wondering why it always seemed that the person who snored was the first to fall asleep. Vacher tossed and turned, and Orlo mumbled in his restless sleep.

My abdominal cramps surged, and I rushed to the latrine area. Vacher and Orlo each made several trips during the night. Only Main slept soundly.

Rain was pouring down on the small hut, and I had to move several times to avoid the water that dripped through the new roof. Eventually the cogan grass would swell and stop the leaks, but for now it was dripping everywhere. Lightning flashed in the sky, and thunder boomed off the canyon walls. Doubts continued to haunt my thoughts as I drifted into a restless sleep.

Chapter Sixteen

Orlo was still sleeping when I awoke the next morning. From his labored breathing and occasional wheezing, I knew he was very sick. Main and Vacher were outside warming themselves by the fire. For a few minutes I lay there thinking about our situation. The isolated shack was a poor place for Orlo. He needed medical attention, and I was convinced Dr. Pineda had deserted us. I wondered about taking him to a Japanese hospital, but when I put myself in Orlo's place, I knew I would rather die in this remote jungle than surrender. We would keep Orlo warm and dry the best we could, but there was nothing more we could do.

I joined the other two at the fire. Main had cooked rice and broken two duck eggs into it, his way of evenly dividing the needed protein. I was hungry and quickly began eating, but Vacher took one look at his breakfast, jumped to his feet, and rushed to the latrine with the bolo. His dysentery was still out of control.

"I'll sure be glad when he's back on his feet," Main said. "I'd rather have him bitching about not having coffee and enough food than the way he is now."

I nodded in agreement.

"Just a lot of bloody mucus," Vacher said when he returned. "I'll sure as hell be glad when I can squeeze out a normal turd again."

He picked up his mess kit, started eating, and then put it down.

"The longer I chew this shit, the bigger it gets," he said. "To hell with it."

Vacher went back into the shack and lay down.

"Bill, do you think the Pinedas will be back?" I asked.

"Sure, they'll come back, and when they do, the doctor will stick another enema tube up your ass. How come you're so anxious, anyway?"

I stared at the fire in silence. I had forgotten about the enemas until Main spouted off, and now my resentment toward his good health resurfaced. It seemed Main thrived on preparing guava leaf tea and nursing everyone else. I wished again he would get sick, but then realized that would threaten all of us. I needed to get my thoughts in order and decided to take a walk.

I had not gone far when my knees became shaky, so I sat down on a large rock that had been warmed by the morning sun. The secluded canyon brought me a sense of inner peace, and I wondered if I might not be the first white man to have ever seen its pristine beauty. I thought about the trail I had just traversed. I had lost sight of it several times as I crossed large boulders along the streambed, but then I would find it again as I continued through the underbrush.

For some time I continued to bask in the beautiful canyon. Then I noticed my shoes, and my attention turned to the more pragmatic issues of my existence. For the past two weeks, I had been covering the holes in the soles with a variety of materials. I had used banana leaves, scraps from cardboard boxes, or anything else that seemed appropriate for insoles. Nothing seemed to work, and the shoes were too worn out for repair. I knew I would have to start going barefoot sooner or later. We had asked the Filipinos about new shoes and been told none were available in the barrios. I had been walking around camp barefoot for the past few days, and my feet had toughened somewhat, but I knew they were not ready for traveling over the rocky trails. Still, I would have to get used to being barefoot before too long. I reached down, pulled my shoes off, tied the strings together, and hurled them across the river into the dense underbrush. For a moment I felt good about my deliberate action, but then I started walking.

I continued up the canyon, carefully stepping on smooth rocks.

When I waded in the water, the slick rocks caused my feet to slip and smash painfully against the stony bottom. I made little progress before I was aware of a dull pain in my feet. Realizing I was already suffering from stone bruises, I turned and started back to camp. I was joined by two Negritos on the trail who kept laughing and pointing at my tender, bare feet. They even imitated my way of gingerly stepping from stone to stone. Eventually, the three of us reached a spot directly across the river from our secluded camp.

One of the Negritos pointed to my rifle, wanting to trade some bananas and papayas for it. When I shook my head in denial, he grabbed for it. I stepped back, pulled back the bolt, and shoved a cartridge into the chamber, an action the primitive man readily understood. He smiled broadly and began talking in his native dialect. I understood the native word *baboy*, which meant pig, and realized he wanted to trade a pig for my rifle. Again the answer was no. They both smiled and handed me some fruit as I turned to cross the river.

Back at the fire, I told Main about my encounter with the Negritos. He suggested it might be a good idea to trade a rifle for a pig, but I was not ready to part with mine, and I doubted Main would give his in trade.

The conversation switched to our interest in the Negritos. There had been Negritos at Clark Field, but these were entirely different. These Negritos had rarely seen an American. Although most worked for Dr. Pineda, they remained primitive jungle people, living day to day. Dr. Pineda's brother, Silvestre, had told us about the local Negritos.

They were a nomadic tribe who came down from the mountains at harvesttime. The men, women, children, and dogs all came. Dr. Pineda paid them in rice, salt, and sometimes a little sugar at the end of each day. Each evening they cooked all the rice from their day's work, no matter how much they had received. They ate it all, then spent the rest of the evening smoking, belching, and patting their stomachs in satisfaction, as though they would never have another hungry day in their lives.

The Negritos appeared to be a happy, carefree people, but they lived with constant health problems. Sometimes Dr. Pineda was able to help them, but mostly they were on their own. When the harvest was finished at Dr. Pineda's, they returned to their primitive nomadic life in the jungle. Some seasons they found abundant wild fruit, grubs, and vegetables. Other times food was scarce, and they subsisted on sweet potatoes called kamotes and starchy gobi roots.

As we talked, Main noticed my feet.

"What happened to your shoes?" he asked. "Did you throw them away?"

"Yeah. One of these days we'll all be without shoes, and I figured the sooner I get my feet toughened up, the better off I'll be."

"Well, you're a big boy, and you can do what you want, but I think I'll keep mine."

His response came as no surprise. Main kept everything, always anticipating a future need. He seemed to think people who did not save things were careless, and I was sure I had been placed in that category. The subject was dropped.

"You know, Orlo's not doing well at all," he said. "He won't eat, and without eating, he's not going to last long. Besides, the rain soaked him good last night, and he's got a cold that could turn to pneumonia. I hope Dr. Pineda shows up soon. If he doesn't, somebody will have to walk to the barrio and get him."

I did not answer. I was still sure the Filipinos would not return, and with my feet already suffering painful bruises, I had no intention of making a trip through the river canyon.

The clouds turned darker in the afternoon. The weather was changing, and soon the nightly display of thunder and lightning would be followed by constant, heavy rain. Main finished preparing the evening meal, rice with some duck eggs and steamed eggplant. Then he went over and helped Orlo to the fire.

"I got to go!" Orlo said.

Main and I grabbed his arms and helped him to the latrine area. His thin frame startled me. He had lost the flesh from his buttocks, and there appeared to be only loose skin hanging over his hip bones. For the first time, I feared for Orlo's life. We returned to the fire and Main gave him some guava leaf tea. He drank it without complaint and wanted to lie down again.

Vacher ate a small portion of rice and joined Orlo in the lean-to. As Main and I continued talking we saw two Negritos approaching us from the river. One carried what appeared to be a homemade shotgun. The two little black men joined us at the fire. Laughing and chattering in their native dialect, they were apparently amused by Main's method of building a fire. One of them picked up the bamboo blowpipe Main used to start fires and began blowing on the coals, causing the fire to burst into flames. Main had carefully placed the coals under the rice pot, and I saw a frown on his face when the Negrito pulled the coals out and rearranged them. One of them took the lid off the cooking pot and looked pleased to see some rice left. He looked up and rubbed his stomach. Main struck a deal. His former gunsmith experience had roused his curiosity, and he wanted to see the homemade shotgun. The Negrito understood, handed the gun to Main, pulled a banana leaf from his G-string, and piled the rice on it. The Negritos ate heartily while Main examined the gun.

The experienced gunsmith pulled a large nail used to hold the barrel in a firing position. He broke the gun down and removed a Super X twelve-gauge shell from the chamber.

"Unbelievable," he said. "I can't see how they keep from killing themselves when they fire this damn thing."

Main handed the gun back to its owner and praised the workmanship.

The little black man's toothless smile showed his pleasure at earning an American's respect.

"*Paultic,*" he said as he patted the gun. It was the Negrito word for the homemade gun. They finished the rice and left.

"They'll be back," I predicted. "I'll bet we see them tomorrow, and the day after that, until we get tired of them, and next time they'll bring their friends."

Thinking of the probable future visits, we felt certain there would be no problem as long as we had rice to share. We wondered, however, what they might do if they found the rice pot empty.

I limped on sore feet as I walked to the latrine area and back to my sleeping mat. I rubbed the bruises and vowed at the same time to continue walking until my feet were tough enough to travel anywhere. I was determined to walk farther up the river the next morning and still farther the day after that. Getting my feet in good condition would be my top priority.

When I walked up the river in the morning, I went almost a kilometer farther than I had the day before. By the time I turned around, my feet burned as though I had been walking on a bed of coals, and it was difficult to fight back the tears. When I reached camp, bloody cuts covered my feet, and my soles were like one giant stone bruise. I sat down by the fire.

Main was quietly smoking a cigarette and gazing into the distance. I knew he had something on his mind.

"Orlo's in bad shape," he finally said. "We've got to get Dr. Pineda up here right away. One of us is going to have to walk to the barrio and get him."

"Bill, I don't have any shoes, and my feet are a mess. I can't make it."

"Well, I don't know who else is going. Vacher sure can't make it, and Orlo's practically on his death bed. That leaves you."

"Me? I can't make it."

Main seemed to ignore my words. "I can't go," he said. "Someone's got to stay here and take care of Orlo and Vacher."

"Main, can't you understand plain English? I can't make it with these damn feet. You go into the barrio, and I'll take care of Orlo and Paul.

"Don't worry. There aren't any Japs in the barrio. That's what you're afraid of, isn't it?" I said, digging into Main's perceived weakness. I got up and left before he could answer.

Back in the lean-to, I admitted to myself that throwing my shoes away had probably been a stupid mistake. If my feet were in better shape, I would be glad to go for the doctor. Then, I thought, I could just keep going, leaving my cantankerous companions and the Filipinos behind. I was tired of everyone.

Orlo lay motionless on the ground nearby, and I walked over to him, knelt down, and spoke. There was no response. I was certain he was awake, and I wondered if he had heard my argument with Main. I spoke again, and again there was no answer. He rolled over, looked up at me with wet, sad eyes, and tried to blink away the tears. I felt a terrible hollowness in the pit of my stomach as I realized Orlo had heard every word. Silently and guiltily, I returned to the fire and sat down on a log.

I was filled with hatred, not for my companions now, but for myself. I wondered what it would be like if Kinder were still with us. Would his leadership have held us together? None of us had been prepared for the sickness, hunger, and emotional strain that had taken over our lives. I looked ahead to the day when all of us would be healthy and things would be better.

I began reflecting on my own behavior. What I saw disgusted me, and the urge to leave the others grew strong within me. Orlo had always been the one who relieved tensions by turning adversity into lightheartedness, and now I had let him down when he needed me. I buried my face in my hands and began crying as, with bitter remorse, I tried to sort out the events leading to the argument.

In the obviously strained silence between Main and me, I heard only the ripple of the river. Suddenly I knew there was only one solution. For my own peace of mind and to regain Orlo's respect, I would walk to the barrio, no matter what it took. Even if I had to crawl, I would get there. Maybe the Negritos could help me.

The Negritos! I could not understand how we had not thought of them before. They could take a message to Dr. Pineda. Just as the thought passed through my mind, I heard someone across the river and recognized Ernie's voice talking with Main. Wrapped as I was in my own self-pity, I had not even noticed Main's absence. Now it seemed apparent he had started for help after all and met Ernie on the trail.

As Main and Ernie approached the fire, Vacher joined us. Ernie had brought rice, Picadura tobacco, some sugar, several quinine tablets, a bamboo tube filled with chicken soup, and some duck eggs. We inspected the new supplies, then sat back as Ernie told us the latest news.

Dr. Pineda had been in Porac for the past two days, but had returned to his family at Pasbul that morning. The Japanese had questioned him about fugitive Americans living near the barrio. They had warned him any Filipinos who helped Americans would be punished. Apparently there were other Americans in the area too, and the Japanese were pressuring local Filipinos for information.

I asked Ernie if any Japanese patrols had visited Barrio Pasbul.

"No, sir, they have not yet come that far."

"Then let me go back to the barrio with you so I can talk with your father about Orlo."

"That is not a good idea, Mr. Hileman," Ernie said. "My father is afraid some of the people might be talking with the Japanese. He would not like it if you came to our barrio. Even today, when I brought the food to you, I had to be careful no one saw me. I pretended I was going to Barrio Pio to see my grandfather, and then circled back to the trail that led me to the river."

"But, Ernie," I said, "your father must know the condition of Mr.

Heinzman. He—"

"No!" Ernie interrupted me in midsentence. "I have been told to tell you to stay hidden. It is very important that no one sees you."

"Don't worry, Ernie," Main said. "We'll stay right here."

I dropped my plan. Ernie did not leave until late afternoon, saying he wanted to arrive home after dark so no one would see him enter the barrio.

Black clouds filled the afternoon sky, and I knew it would be another wet night. I had let Orlo down, but nothing could change that now. The long hours slipped into darkness.

Chapter Seventeen

Orlo perked up somewhat after eating the soup Ernie brought, but as the days passed, he quit eating. The three of us saved our eggs for him, but we could find no way to make him eat. He drifted in and out of delirium and became too weak to get up from his mat. I helped Main bathe him, but his bowels discharged where he lay, and he was never really clean. For the most part, Orlo bore his pain in silence.

Vacher's dysentery hung on, and the intermittent malarial chills and fever took their toll on the man who had prided himself on his physical strength. He managed, however, to retain his quick wit, which had become a strange mixture of humor, anger, and sarcasm.

"I knew that damned Filipino tea wasn't any good," he said when the guava leaf brew was gone. "It just makes you piss more, and a jug of wine would have done the same thing."

Still determined to get my feet in condition for travel, I continued to walk every day. It became increasingly difficult to muster the ambition to get out of camp, and each day the distance I walked became shorter. Lethargy set in.

I gave up the effort to keep the calendar I had started on our flight from Bataan. Time became a blur in our jungle hideaway and seemed to have no meaning, except possibly to prolong our agony.

Main still showed no signs of either dysentery or malaria. In camp, he whistled in a monotone that irritated both Vacher and me. When he was not whistling, he muttered to himself. In the morning, when he bathed in the river, he sang "Danny Boy" in his rich tenor voice. It seemed to be the only song he sang, another irritation for Vacher and me. Though physically unchanged, Main was beginning to show signs of stress. When Orlo screamed at him for help, he often grimaced or sometimes ignored the demanding plea. Yet if Vacher or I made a move to help Orlo, Main quickly jumped up and took care of him. He jealously guarded his position as camp cook and nursemaid. He seemed to want, or need, the rest of us to depend upon him.

It seemed earlier each day when the dark gray clouds unleashed their incessant downpour. The oppressive dampness pressed in from all sides, and the trees dripped day and night. The four of us lost all sense of time, not knowing if it was still May or if it was now June.

Orlo ranted at night during his malarial fevers, but fell into a passive, listless existence during the day. He did not eat, except an occasional banana left by the Negritos who continued stopping at the camp to check the rice pot. He developed an insatiable craving for water, however, and when we tried to keep him from drinking too much he exploded into raging tantrums, completely uncharacteristic of the healthy, even-tempered Orlo we had known. His condition continued to worsen.

"If Orlo gets pneumonia, that will be the end," Main said to me one day. He had remained optimistic about Orlo's chances of recovery, but now his hope was waning.

One morning the melodious strains of "Danny Boy" woke Vacher and me as the song reverberated through the sun-drenched confines of the Gumain Canyon. I listened to Main sing, wondering if it bothered Vacher. I soon found out.

"I'm sick and tired of that damn song," Vacher said. "I'm going to let him know just how sick of it I am!" Although weakened by illness and hoarse with a cold, Vacher bounded from his mat and grabbed his shoes.

"Hell, Vacher, let him sing. At least it's better than his damned mumbling and whistling."

"Yeah, I guess you're right," Vacher agreed. "Anyway, he gives us a variety of things to bitch about. Singing in the morning with his bath. Hell, I can't even remember the last time I had a bath. And right after his bath, he'll trot off into the bushes muttering that he sure hopes he has a successful bowel movement. I wish he'd get a good case of the GIs along with malaria. Then he'd sing a different tune."

The wish seemed to trigger a reaction in Vacher's own intestinal system as he grabbed the bolo and ran toward the latrine area.

That afternoon as the rain began its monotonous pounding on the cogan grass roof, I saw Ernie and Salvadore coming across the river. Ernie unpacked some welcome food. Our supplies were low because Main had been cooking extra rice for the daily visits from the Negritos.

"Only today the Japanese came to the barrio to talk with my father," Ernie said. "We had to be careful that they did not see us leave to come to you."

Ernie said his father and uncle would visit us very soon, perhaps the next day, to discuss moving us to a different location. The news thrilled me. I was sick of the Gumain River Canyon and asked where we would be going. Ernie either did not know or had been instructed not to say.

As the two young Pinedas left, I asked what day it was. Ernie said he did not know for sure, but he thought it was May 31. We had been on the river for almost a month, but it seemed so much longer.

Vacher, Main, and I huddled next to the fire under our shelter halves as the rain fell. We talked about the future with renewed excitement. Vacher and I wanted to find a place where we could make our own life, away from the dominance of the Filipinos. Main did not comment, but I suspected he would prefer hiding in the jungle until the war ended.

Main said he would miss the Gumain River because it reminded him of the place in California where he and a miner named Ned, and Ned's mule Jennifer, had worked a mine in Seneca. Main's Old Ned stories had been the one source of entertainment we had all enjoyed since fleeing Bataan.

According to Main, he and Old Ned never had to set the alarm in the morning. At 6 A.M. sharp, Jennifer would back up to the door and kick until someone came out to feed her. The mule earned her oats by pulling a small cart loaded with ore from the mine shaft to a sluice box. If he had made any money at the mine, Main never mentioned it.

Most of his stories concerned Old Ned and his trips to the local tavern where Ned usually got so drunk Main had to carry him out. Then he would whistle for Jennifer, and the mule would come running to carry Ned back to camp. Jennifer always sensed when Ned was in trouble and needed her help, Main said. During the workday, however, Jennifer would bite Ned or kick at him if he turned his back. The stories helped break the monotony of the pounding rain.

Two days after the Pineda boys' visit, Ernie returned with his father and Sylvestre. We eagerly greeted the doctor, anxious for him to examine Orlo. The patient was lying under a canvas cover Main had constructed by driving four stakes in the ground and tying a corner of Orlo's shelter half to each stake. During the rain, it kept him dry. When the sun broke through the clouds, it shaded him. Orlo was wrapped in a light blanket that Ernie had brought on his last visit.

Dr. Pineda questioned Orlo, and then returned to talk with Main.

"You know, Mr. Main, Mr. Heinzman's malaria and dysentery are no worse than Mr. Vacher's or Mr. Hileman's, but if he gets pneumonia, he will not live. You must keep him warm and dry." Then he added something even more disturbing. "Mr. Heinzman has lost his will to live.

"We will leave now," the doctor said. "If we have no problems with the Japanese, someone will be back in a day or two with more supplies for you. You must not worry. We will not forget you."

His last statement seemed to be aimed at me. When we were alone again, I looked at my companions and thought about the sorry lot we had become. Orlo was gravely ill, Vacher had not improved, and my own health was shaky, although I was sure my feet were tough enough now for the walk into the barrio if necessary. Only Main remained in good health.

The next few days passed quietly. Each day the afternoon sky grew black and the clouds released their relentless rain. Every day Negritos stopped to clean out the rice pot, no longer waiting for an invitation. They regularly tried to trade for our rifles, but we consistently refused. I worried they would steal them, but Main did not.

"Don't worry," he said. "They're our friends. As long as we feed them we don't have anything to fear."

I was not convinced.

Vacher complained about his dysentery cramps and the soreness around his rectal area. He said it was impossible for him to have a bowel movement without tearing a scablike material off his anus. It seemed his graphic descriptions were usually given in conversation at meal time.

Ernie visited camp once or twice, bringing the promised supplies. He said the doctor was getting ready to move us, but he did not know any details.

Since the rainy season had begun, I had marked places along the river to measure the rising water level. Each day I checked my markers and could see an increase in the flow. I kept working at the conditioning of my sore feet, although malaria and dysentery continued to sap my strength.

Main kept trying, with little success, to get Orlo to eat. When the Negritos stopped each day, they brought bananas, pointed at Orlo, and rubbed their stomachs. I realized they understood malaria and felt sympathy for the sick American.

I was sleeping soundly on the morning of Sunday, June 14, 1942, when Main shook my shoulder and woke me.

"Orlo has pneumonia," he said with concern.

The words fell on me like a ton of cement. I had expected it, but somehow had refused to believe it would happen. Now, I looked over at Orlo and was sure death was not far away.

I waded across the river and waited along the trail, knowing the Negritos would pass by. When two of them came down the path carrying baskets of bananas and papayas, I brought them across the river into camp where, with some effort, Main and I got the message across: we needed Dr. Pineda. The Negritos left, apparently pleased we had turned to them for help.

Dr. Pineda arrived the next evening and gave Orlo some herbal tea and chicken soup. That was all he could do.

Orlo Heinzman died sometime in the early morning hours of June 16, 1942.

Chapter Eighteen

Staring at the wasted body of my friend, it seemed great fountains of grief and guilt were being poured upon me, drenching my very soul. I knew I would never again enjoy Orlo's impulsiveness or his laughter, and I would miss him terribly. I had a strong compulsion to run away and never look back.

With head bowed, I crossed the river and began walking towards Pasbul. I rounded a corner in the trail, and finding myself completely away from the others, I was no longer able to hold back my feelings. I sat down on a log and began to cry. I was lonely, sick, hungry, and wanted only to escape from the somber world in which I was trapped.

Even as I wept I heard voices coming toward me on the trail. It was Dr. Pineda, Ernie, Sylvestre, and several Negritos. I found it difficult to identify them through my misty eyes.

Dr. Pineda came to me and put both his hands on my shoulders.

"We are aware that Mr. Heinzman died last night. We have come to prepare the body for burial."

I did not understand how they could have known, but it did not matter. I gazed at the doctor through my tears, unable to respond, but grateful he was there.

I remained behind as the Filipinos and Negritos moved on to the camp, and as I sat there my mind went back to the day almost a year earlier when Orlo, Vacher, and I were about to arrive in the Philippines. I remembered our conversation on the fantail of the USS *President Pierce* as the ship moved through the San Bernardino Straits. Orlo's premonition came back to me.

"Hileman, a year from now I'll be dead," Orlo had said. "They're going to bury me over here. Don't ask me how I know, but I'm never going home."

Now his words bore into my soul, making his death seem all the more haunting. He lay dead under a sheet of canvas deep in the Gumain River Canyon, a casualty of war who had foreseen his own death.

Time and time again during the escape from Bataan, I had wondered which of us would be the first to die and who would be the last. I did not know what had become of Forrest Henderson, George Wicks, and Wally Kinder, but Orlo's death made me wonder if they were alive or dead. My mind was filled with thoughts of them all as I finally stood up and returned to camp.

Dr. Pineda and Sylvestre were talking with Main, and the Negritos were nonchalantly emptying the rice pot. I approached Vacher who sat alone, and I noted how thin and feeble he looked.

"Hileman, I can't believe Orlo's gone." His voice was weak and shaken. "My God, I guess I never realized how bad he was. Hell, he wasn't any sicker than the rest of us. He just didn't want to live anymore."

I listened silently as Vacher continued talking.

"You know what? I look back over the last two weeks, and I'm not even sure I spoke to him. If I had taken more interest in his condition, he might have made it."

Tears streamed down Vacher's gaunt cheeks, and his voice choked. I had never seen Vacher's emotional vulnerability before, and it added to my depression.

I told Vacher about the day Main had asked me to walk into the barrio and I had refused because I had no shoes.

"See what I mean?" Vacher said. "This is the first I knew you didn't have any shoes. I've been feeling so damned sorry for myself I didn't bother to give any of you a second thought. I'm a no good son of a bitch. I knew Orlo longer than any of you, and I sat here on my dead ass and let him die."

It was difficult for me to listen to Vacher put himself down. It was so totally out of character. Suddenly my longtime friend appeared weak, and I wanted to find an appropriate response. I searched for reassuring words that did not seem to come.

"Vacher, there wasn't anything any of us could have done for him," I finally said. "Orlo had it in his mind he was going to die over here. You know that. Remember what he said when we came through the San Bernardino Straits the day before we got into Manila? You remember, I know you do. I even remember what you said to him, and when you laughed Orlo said he didn't think you were very damn funny."

"Sure, I remember what I said," Vacher shot back. "I said, 'Come on, Orlo, don't give me that shit. I've known you too long to believe something like that.' But if you think I laughed at the poor guy, you've got another think coming."

The spell seemed to be broken. I did not argue, but smiled to myself as I recalled Vacher's laughter. Now his self-defense seemed reassuring to me. He was his stubborn, cantankerous self again.

The Negritos began digging a grave in the rain-soaked soil near the riverbank. Dr. Pineda and Sylvestre were preparing Orlo's body for burial. Sensing the need to do something, I went to help the Negritos. Most of the work was being done by young boys, sons of two of the older men who had stopped by the camp several times. I had not seen the boys before, but Ernie said their names were Felix and Sundai. They were not particularly industrious and wanted to quit digging several times, but Dr. Pineda patiently urged them on. It was late afternoon before the hole was deep enough.

Orlo's body was sewn into his shelter half, but as Dr. Pineda and Sylvestre placed it near the grave the Negritos quickly became agitated and began speaking harshly to the doctor. A disagreement followed, and I watched in bewilderment as the doctor seemed to back down. The two boys reached down, picked up Orlo's body, and turned it around. Dr. Pineda smiled as he walked over to us.

"The Negritos say that because they were the ones to do the digging, they will be the ones to position the body and place it in the grave."

One of them produced a small bag with several articles in it, including rice cookies, toes of garlic, coconut shells, some small seashells, a flask of oil, and other items.

"They say Mr. Heinzman will have a Negrito funeral," Dr. Pineda said. "This means he must be buried with his head upstream so he will be in the good graces of the spirits. With the head upstream, the evil spirits will be afraid to molest the body, and Mr. Heinzman will be allowed to rest in peace."

Dr. Pineda continued to describe the primitive ritual. After the burial the Negritos would put cookies in the coconut shells and place them near the grave where the spirits would find them and be happy food was left for them.

"Just before we place Mr. Heinzman in the ground they will heat some oil in one of the shells," the doctor said. "They will open the canvas and rub hot oil on his forehead. Then they will scatter garlic in the grave as they cover the body with dirt. When the grave is filled, they will light flares from oil-soaked rags and place them near the cookies so the spirits can see the food."

The Negrito ritual seemed strange and filled with superstition, but under the circumstances, we had no choice in allowing them to carry out the tribal custom.

The rain continued falling, and everyone was drenched. I wondered about Orlo's relatives. He had a sister in California, but beyond that, I knew nothing about his family. Would they ever know what happened?

As the Negritos finished their ritualistic preparations, Dr. Pineda brought relief to the primitive atmosphere by reading from a prayer book. Vacher, Main, and I bowed our heads sorrowfully while he led us in prayer. As the Negritos lowered Orlo into the wet grave, a weight of heavy grief and sorrow swept over me. The dismal surroundings and the unusual circumstances of burial combined to make the day one of the blackest of my life.

Once the grave was filled, the Negritos lit torches and headed up river to their primitive camp. The Filipinos remained behind.

"We will come for you late tomorrow," Dr. Pineda said. "You will be ready when we arrive. It will be a hard trip because it must be made after darkness falls."

The doctor did not mention where he was taking us, and we did not ask. I did not care as long as it was away from the Gumain River Canyon. I had basked for brief moments in its tropical beauty, but for the most part it had been a place of dreary existence marked by sickness and conflict. I watched the torches disappear in the rainy darkness as the Filipinos returned to Barrio Pasbul. This would be my last night in the Gumain Canyon, and the thought of leaving gave me a sense of relief.

Now, only Orlo would remain in the tropical canyon.

Chapter Nineteen

The morning broke cool and clear, a striking contrast to the previous dark day when Orlo was buried. Sunlight pierced through the trees, casting warm rays of light on the new grave just beyond the camp. Somehow, Orlo's death seemed like a dream from the distant past, not a reality of the previous day. I wondered if his death would have had less impact on a nicer day. I was not sure, but the nagging pain and sorrow lingered as Main and I went through his effects. We saved his old, worn blanket, the light blanket Ernie brought, and his mess gear, though Vacher would have preferred to keep nothing around to remind him of Orlo. Despite the welcome morning sun, the hours dragged as we waited for the Pinedas. Forced to remain near Orlo's grave, our muffled conversations centered around the loss of our friend.

Vacher and I continued making frequent runs to the latrine area, unable to control our bowels. In addition, Vacher came down with a chill about noon, and would undoubtedly be in the throes of a malaria attack when the Filipinos came for us.

Dark rain clouds had filled the late afternoon sky by the time Dr. Pineda, Sylvestre, Ernie, and some Negrito helpers made their way to our camp.

"It will be a hard trip for both of you," Dr. Pineda said as he looked at Vacher and me. "The Negritos will help you if you cannot make it yourself."

Dr. Pineda said we would walk to Barrio Pasbul where a bullcart waited. From there we would be taken to Barrio Pio where we had seen the dome of the old Spanish church. Dr. Pineda told us an American civilian, Joe Cheesman, was living near Barrio Pio.

The Filipinos had timed our departure from the Gumain Canyon so we would arrive in Pasbul after dark. Japanese patrols had been active in Porac and Pio during the past few days and extreme caution was necessary. When we rode in the bullcart, the Filipinos would cover us with straw to conceal us from any Japanese patrols we might encounter along the way. A shiver ran down my spine as I imagined a Japanese guard jabbing his bayonet into the straw, but I quickly put that thought out of my mind. At the moment I wanted only to leave the river. I really did not have a voice in the matter anyway, and had resigned myself to trusting the Filipinos one more time.

We started across the river just before the sun disappeared behind the trees to the west. Negritos carried the small canvas bags holding all our worldly possessions, and both the Negritos and Filipinos carried torches that would light the way when darkness fell.

My body was weakened by dysentery, but I felt good about my feet. I had spent time conditioning them, and my efforts seemed to be paying off. I felt little discomfort as I moved down the trail, but I realized months of conditioning would yet be necessary before I could walk easily over any terrain. I would know in the morning how well I had prepared my feet.

Darkness settled over the river canyon, and the torches were lit. The light rain became one of the torrential rains that had been falling every night. Vacher slipped and fell, and I stubbed my bare toe on a rock. Dysentery plagued both of us, and we had to stop frequently to relieve ourselves.

As we moved under the dark trees, I thought about my changing situation and realized it was hazardous at best. I also worried about my health and appearance. If captured by the Japanese in such a decrepit, filthy condition, I would be embarrassed. My self-image had become distasteful, and I vowed to make getting well my top priority.

I watched Dr. Pineda ahead of me and regretted any mistrust I had felt toward him. I knew now the doctor and other Filipinos were doing all they could for us. They had taken many risks, and I wondered if I would have done the same for them. The answering thought brought a sense of shame and embarrassment. Filipinos caught caring for us would be tortured and possibly executed. Even their families were at risk. I felt a deep appreciation for what they were doing.

Minutes seemed like hours as we plodded through the dreariness of the stormy night. When we stopped to rest, we sat numbly in a daze waiting for the word to continue. Main, as expected, was handling the trip well. He seemed to have complete immunity from the diseases which had plagued Vacher and me and had killed Heinzman. Main and Sylvestre talked as they trailed behind us.

In the flickering torchlight my mind turned back to Orlo, deserted now in that isolated canyon, and I felt an overwhelming sadness at the thought of his being buried so far from anyone who cared for him. The same deep sense of guilt I had experienced the day before swept over me as I remembered how little I had done for him. Then in a deliberate effort to protect myself from my debilitating emotions, I put Orlo out of my mind.

I turned and looked at Vacher. He had fallen several times, and each time a Negrito had helped him to his feet. He had not uttered a word, and his breathing was labored. Vacher's aggressive manner may have caused friction when he was well, but I preferred that to seeing him reduced to weakness, dependent on little black men half his size.

With my mind on Vacher, I stumbled over a rock and fell into the river. I lay there a moment, allowing myself to wallow in self-pity, hoping the cold Gumain River would swallow me up or at least help cleanse my filthy body. Vacher reached down and pulled me up.

"Get your damn hands off me!" I shouted. "I can take care of myself."

Vacher let go, and I fell back into the water with a splash.

"Okay," he said. "I was just trying to help."

As I struggled to my feet I felt warm liquid running down my leg. My bowels were out of control, and for a moment I stood shaking in the cold water. A Negrito waited for me to move on. My toe throbbed in pain, but I was determined to show no sign of weakness, especially around Vacher. Anger moved my feet one deliberate step at a time.

The hours, like the rain, seemed to be unending. Then, without realizing it, we were starting up the hill into Pasbul. I kept slipping and sliding as I worked my way up the hill in the darkness. A Negrito behind me carried a torch, and by its light I glanced down at my cold, numb feet. I could see blood oozing between my toes.

Looking up, I realized we had reached the first huts of the barrio. I had walked the entire distance barefoot, and though I could feel the pain in my feet, I was filled with a great sense of accomplishment. I felt superior to my two companions who had needed shoes.

A two-wheeled bullcart waited at the top of the hill. The Negritos tossed our meager belongings into it, and the three of us climbed into the primitive vehicle. I could feel the stickiness of my pants as I lay down and was overwhelmingly aware of the filth of my body. A stranger led the carabao as the cart carried us into Barrio Pasbul. In the flickering torchlight, I recognized the small shacks and Dr. Pineda's house in the distance. The cart stopped at Dr. Pineda's, and the Filipinos covered us with straw.

How ridiculous that seemed to me. A cart of straw moving down an isolated road in the middle of the night would not fool the Japanese, especially in light of recent reports. They were still searching for the four heavily armed Americans who had been reported in the area in April. I remembered Max and muttered to myself, "The traitorous little son of a bitch." The thought of Japanese bayonets plunging into the straw weighed heavily on my mind, and then I inhaled the stench of musty straw and almost choked.

"You must not make noise," someone whispered. "Please, do not talk or cough."

"Hey, pip-squeak, what the hell do you want us to do, choke to death quietly?" Vacher said.

Despite his poor physical condition, Vacher's tongue was still capable of sharpness and sarcasm. I wanted to laugh at Vacher's retort, but instead my guts wrenched and I felt filth oozing inside my trousers. I was eager now to get moving and cared little whether there would be Japanese soldiers on the trail.

Waiting in the darkness, I checked my feet with trembling fingers, afraid of what I might find. My worst thoughts were confirmed as I felt the gashes and blood from my barefoot journey. It would take time for my feet to heal.

The Filipinos talked in subdued tones as the cart started down the trail leading to Barrio Pio. I did not recognize the voices and realized the Pinedas had stayed behind in Pasbul. I wondered if we should trust these strangers. The squeaky cart rocked, rolled, and bumped over the narrow, rutted road. I quit trying to control my bowels as dysentery continued its rampage. I shivered with a malarial chill and wrapped myself in my old blanket.

Any concept of time or distance was lost as we lay buried in the straw, and I began to worry about our destination. What if these unfamiliar Filipinos were after the reward offered by the Japanese? They could easily bypass Barrio Pio and take us directly to the Japanese garrison in Porac. I quietly slipped five cartridges into my Springfield. Vacher heard the sound and asked what I was doing.

"Hell," he whispered. "I loaded my gun before we left the river, and I'll use the son of a bitch if these people try anything funny."

"What about you, Bill?" I asked. "What do you think?"

"He's been asleep for an hour," Vacher said. "I'll tell you one thing about old Bill, though. He keeps his rifle loaded all the time. You didn't know that, did you? He's scared to death of the Japs, but if he gets backed into a corner, he'll use it."

The cart stopped, and the Filipino driver uncovered us. In the torchlight he introduced himself.

"Sir, I am Alberto Luna, and I am the cousin of Dr. Pineda. We are now beside the Porac River. I am the one who will take you across." Then he pointed to his two companions. "These are my younger brothers."

Luna lit another torch, and I looked around. I had no idea where we were, except it was off the beaten path.

"Do not worry about the light, sir," Luna said. "The Japanese do not patrol the roads this late at night. I think they are frightened when it gets dark.

"We will leave the bullcart on this side of the river," he said. "You will ride the carabao across. You are very sick, and it will be better that way."

Luna said we would spend the night in a small shack across the river. In the morning, we would move on to the Jordan house.

"Who are the Jordans?" Vacher asked. "Sounds like an American name."

"No, sir, they are only half American." Mr. Jordan had come to the Philippines during the Spanish-American War, Luna said. He had since died, but his wife lived with their two sons and three daughters. Until we found a place of our own, we would stay at the Jordan farm.

The carabao was unhitched, and I was the first to cross with one of Luna's brothers leading the animal. I sat astride the animal's back with one hand behind me grasping the tail. Luna said I would not fall if I held its tail tightly, which I did. Safely across, I waited for Main and Vacher. My body shook with a malarial chill, and I pulled my blanket around my shoulders. When my two companions arrived, the Filipinos led the three of us up the narrow trail to a small bamboo hut built on stilts.

The Lunas started a fire, and I huddled close to the flames, soaking up the warmth. I could see the first trace of morning light in the east, and the thought of sunlight was comforting. Yet even as I anticipated its warming rays I realized my chills would be followed by a raging fever, and I would fall into the torment of dreams and delirium. My dream of a pit filled with ice and Coca Cola would return. It was always the same, and in my dream, I could never quite reach the cold bottles.

Exhausted, I went into the shack and lay down.

Chapter Twenty

I felt the coolness of a damp cloth on my forehead and slowly opened my watery eyes. After a long moment, I recognized Bill Main.

"You must be hungry," he said with a relaxed smile. "How about some rice?"

I continued staring through glazed eyes, studying the thatched roof of the hut. Suddenly I realized I was in an unfamiliar place, and I was confused.

"Bill, where the hell are we?"

"This is the shack where they brought us when we crossed the river," Main said. "That was two days ago."

The last thing I remembered was sitting next to the fire. Now, according to Main, two days had passed, and I felt uneasy.

"What the hell's been going on?"

"Well, Vacher went back with the Jordan girls a little while ago. He wanted to see where they live," Main said. "They want us to come up to their house just as soon as you can walk."

I did not know anyone named Jordan, but I let Main's words pass for the moment. He handed me a bowl of steaming rice with a soft-boiled egg on top and a papaya. I ate with relish while Main told me the Jordan girls brought the papaya on their first visit. It seemed I had missed a lot during the past two days.

When I had eaten, I tried to stand, but fell backward as Main grabbed my arm.

"You're not as strong as you think," he said.

Regaining my balance, I realized I was wearing blue denim shorts I had never seen before.

"Where did these shorts come from?" I asked. Main said the Jordan sisters brought them. Then I realized I was clean.

"Bill, did you give me a bath?"

"Nope," he said, and his smile seemed to have a note of teasing in it. "Nina and Nieves did that. You should have been awake. See what you miss when you sleep for two days."

I felt myself turning red with embarrassment, and Main broke into laughter.

"Who in the hell are Nina and Nieves?"

Main told me they were the daughters of Mrs. Jordan who lived on a nearby farm, and the family had agreed to provide a place for us to live. Vacher had gone with them to check out the new living quarters.

"At least that's what he said. When Vacher saw that youngest sister, I couldn't hold him here. He had all kinds of excuses to go home with her. It's amazing what a little feminine company can do. Old Vach was feeling good this morning."

Main's attitude had surely changed. Whatever had happened while I was unconsious had improved the spirits of my companions.

He eagerly told me about the Jordan sisters. Nieves was about thirty, and Nina was three or four years younger. Both were beautiful, he said.

"Bill, knock off the bullshit," I said. "I don't believe a damn word you're telling me. Where's Vacher?"

"I told you. He left here an hour or two ago with the Jordan girls. They're the ones who cleaned you up. If you don't believe me, check out the strange underwear on that pink, clean ass of yours."

It was true. I was wearing strange, clean underwear under my new denim shorts. I changed the subject, and Main walked outside to the fire.

Following him, I sat down on a small bench and tried to sort out the events of the past two days. Vacher had been sick for weeks, but now, according to Main, he felt fine. On the Gumain River, Vacher never left camp. Now he was off with a couple women, and I felt left out. As I considered these new developments, my guts suddenly wrenched and I ran into the bushes. My problems were not over yet.

"What's for supper?" I asked when I returned to the fire.

"Rice and pish, Joe," Main answered with a sarcastic imitation of the Filipino way of talking. Even as he spoke, a Filipino came running up the trail.

"The *Hapon* are in the barrio, sir!" he said, using the idiomatic term for the Japanese. Fighting to regain his breath, the Filipino continued, "You will go quick and hide on the mountain. Where is Mr. Vacher?"

The Filipino's familiarity with our names surprised me.

Main's carefree mood turned somber as if a dark cloud had fallen on him. The Filipino told us to gather our belongings and leave quickly while he ran to warn the Jordans and Vacher.

I was certainly in no shape to run. I was weak from fever, but Main scurried around camp, dousing the fire and gathering our meager belongings. In just moments we started up the hill.

I knew I could not go far. If someone had reported us, I was in real trouble. If not, I did not want to expend my energy. Main carried Vacher's pack as we moved out with everything, including all the weapons except Vacher's rifle, which he had carried with him when he left camp.

We had gone less than half a kilometer when I tired.

"I'm not going any farther," I said. "I doubt if there's any Japs in the barrio. It's just another damn Filipino rumor. They're always imagining some kind of crap."

Main did not reply as we sat down. In hushed tones, he suggested we might have to spend the night there, even though it would undoubtedly rain. The idea irritated me, but my thoughts were interrupted by voices drifting up the hill from the direction of our shack. We listened carefully before recognizing a few words of Tagalog. Both of us felt a sense of relief.

"Mr. Main. Mr. Hileman," someone called. "It is okay now. The *Hapon*, they did not come to the barrio."

The rain began pouring down as Main and I turned back to the shack, and I began to shiver. I was angry with the Filipinos, feeling they were a poor source of information.

At the shack Vacher was sitting on a log smoking a cigarette and eating a guava.

"Where the hell have you been?"

His nonchalant manner irked me.

"Same place you've been, Vacher," Main answered. "Hiding."

I went to the fire pit and tried blowing on the coals, not wanting anything to do with the argument that seemed to be brewing between the other two.

"Here, you guys want some guavas?" Vacher reached into a small cloth bag. "They're good for what ails you. The seeds will change the consistency of those runny turds you've been leaving all over the place."

He took a long drag from his brown dobie cigarette and looked up at Main.

"If you think I was hiding from those slant-eyed sons of a bitches, Billy Boy, then you've got another think coming," he said. "When that guy came up there hollering 'Japs in the barrio,' Mrs. Jordan told me they wouldn't come that far. She says they're afraid of guerrillas and won't leave the well-traveled roads. The way I figure it, she knows a hell of a lot more about it than some jittery Filipino kid. So I just grabbed my rifle and headed back down here. In case of a showdown, I figured we'd be better off together than split up. More firepower."

"Vacher, you're full of bullshit," Main said. "With an attitude like that, you're going to get your ass shot off, but what I don't like is you'll probably get mine shot off too."

He reminded Vacher the Japanese had been searching for four heavily armed Americans ever since Max stole the quinine back in April. Main had wanted then to retreat deeper into the hills, and he still felt that would be the safest course of action.

"Listen, Billy Boy, you just go ahead and bury yourself in the goddamned mountains. As far as I'm concerned the quicker the better," Vacher said. "I'll even help you pack."

I thought Vacher's statement about boldly coming back down the trail with his rifle slung over his shoulder was designed to irritate Main. If so, it had achieved its desired effect, and I felt a need to step in.

"You guys are both wrong," I said. "We'd be nuts to go back in the hills with malaria season just starting. Where would we get quinine? And food would be hell to find. Let's not do something stupid."

I criticized Vacher's openly walking on the trail when we had been warned of a patrol, agreeing with Main on that point. I resented both of them for the moment, but was not ready or willing to go off on my own. Not yet, anyway. I was still very weak from the malaria, and I huddled next to the fire, trying to get warm and dry. As I shivered in my cold, damp blanket, I knew I needed them, despite my irritation with their habits.

Main sliced an eggplant and laid the pieces over the rice steaming in the pot. Shivering and feeling sorry for myself, I was staring into the fire when I suddenly realized the other two were eating. No one had said a word for some time, and no one had asked me if I was hungry. *Greedy bastards*, I thought to myself. My chills passed, and the fever returned. I went into the shack and fell asleep.

It was dark when I awoke, and the shack was empty. Outside, I joined Main at the fire.

"Where's Vacher?"

"Who the hell knows?" Main said. "He took a crap about an hour ago and then came back for his gun and left. He didn't say a word after you popped off."

"You think he went back to the Jordan's place?" I asked.

"No. He went the other way. He said something about going upriver to see if he can find where this Cheesman family lives."

Joe Cheesman, the head of the household, had been a copra broker before the war. He had operated a small rice mill and owned a poultry farm. He also had worked for the U.S. government as a veterinarian when an anthrax epidemic killed many carabao on Luzon. The law had required their bodies be burned, and Cheesman had supervised the cremations. Now Cheesman and his family, like many others, were hiding from the Japanese.

"When are we going to move in with the Jordans?" I asked.

"I don't know," Main said, "but from what the girls said yesterday, they'll be an interesting family to be around. One of their brothers is a Huk who lost a finger when a Jap soldier shot him in the hand. Everyone calls him Three-Fingered Jack."

The girls had said little about the other brother Rufino, who was younger and apparently did not live at home. Main continued talking, telling me about Nieves, a pretty *mestiza* with long black hair that hung to her waist. I sensed he was strongly attracted to this American-Filipino girl.

Feminine voices woke me in the morning, and getting to my feet I looked out the door. Gathered around the fire, Main and Vacher sat talking to two women. They saw me standing in the doorway.

"Hey, buddy, want a cup of Java?"

Vacher handed me a coconut shell filled with hot coffee.

"Hileman, you finally get to meet the Jordan sisters. This one is Nina," Vacher said. "The other good-looking gal is Nieves. They met you when you were flat on your back. They're the ones who made you presentable."

Embarrassed, I tried to ignore the last remark.

"Where did you get the coffee, from the Jordans?" I asked Vacher.

"Nope. I've been over at Cheesman's. It's not too far from here. I even got a pack of Luckies from Old Joe."

Vacher said he had also met Cheesman's wife, Loring, and son, Roy.

"Nice people. You'll like them," he said.

Main was cooking rice, and near him I spotted something resembling pancakes. Nina said they were *bibinka,* made from rice flour and baked in a special clay platter.

"Very good, Mr. Hileman," she said. "You will like, no?"

"Yes, I'm sure I will like them." Nina placed the *bibinka* on a banana leaf for me, along with some brown sugar and shredded coconut for topping. As we ate, the girls sat on the ladder leading into the hut, obviously pleased at our enjoyment of the food.

As I ate my breakfast I was struck by the complications the two girls posed. I was the odd man. Vacher had been spending time with Nina, and Main had raved on and on about Neives. I realized the girls had come that morning to move us to the farm, but I suddenly felt my going would be like trying to add a fifth spoke to a four-spoked wheel. I was uncomfortable with my changing situation, and yet felt there was no other choice.

CHAPTER TWENTY-ONE

We ate the *bibinka* with great relish, appreciating the welcome change from our usual bland morning meal. When we finished, Nina and Nieves gathered the small bowls and utensils and carefully placed them in a cardboard carton. We picked up our guns, packs, and other equipment, including the binoculars and compass I had carried out of Bataan. Nieves balanced the carton of utensils on her head and walked ahead of us. I marvelled at her straight, sure posture. Her head did not move, but her supple body swung along at a lively gait.

The trail was new to me, and I was struck by its serenity. Underbrush separated it from the Porac River which it followed. A fence on the other side marked off the Jordan property. The trail itself was well worn, but without the ruts which were characteristic of bullcart trails. The secluded trail was apparently used only by people who walked to or from the Jordan farm.

As we walked along, Nieves told us about the farm. It was twenty hectares, which I calculated to be about fifty acres, a large farm by Filipino standards. I knew there were guava trees and wondered what other crops the Jordans grew. When we had walked about two kilometers, Nieves pointed to the house. Unlike most Filipino homes, it was constructed from lumber. Between the house and road was a building that appeared from its high windows to have an upper story. Nieves called it a barn and toolshed. The description surprised me. I had not heard the words *barn* and *toolshed* since leaving the United States. The girls' American heritage was apparent, and I became curious about their deceased father.

Nieves said we would live in the barn. That bothered me, not because it was an inadequate shelter, but because it was so near the road. The sisters led us into the twenty-by-thirty-foot building. A stairway led to a loft, where I immediately determined I did not want to sleep. Rust had eaten through the sheet metal roof, and in a few places pieces hung loosely. It would be noisy when it rained or when the wind blew. The noise would drown out the sound of barking dogs, and we depended on dogs to warn us when Japanese patrols came into the area.

"Please, come in and eat," Mrs. Jordan said in perfect English as she came from the house. "You will be safe here. The Japanese patrols do not leave the main roads."

I hoped she was right, remembering Kinder's advice during the escape.

"Never stay in one place too long. Keep on the move or too many people will get to know you, and pretty soon some son of a bitch will turn you in."

I remembered something else he had said.

"Don't ever stay anywhere that has only one door, or at least be sure there's a window you can jump out of."

Kinder had other advice, like listening for the sound of rattling equipment or the hobnailed boots Japanese soldiers wore on patrol. I missed his sound advice and stabilizing influence and still hoped he would come wandering into camp one day.

On the way to the house Nieves pointed to the well with towels neatly hung on one side. We could bathe there, she said. In a low voice I told Main I preferred bathing in the river.

"The river makes a bend back aways and heads south," Main said. "You can go to the river if you want to, but it might be a pretty long walk."

Despite my malaria, I ate heartily. Mrs. Jordan's meal was the best I had eaten in the six weeks since we had arrived at Dr. Pineda's house in Barrio Pasbul. While we were still enjoying the American-style hospitality, it began to rain, and we were drenched as we walked back to the barn.

In our new surroundings, I was in a reflective mood that night. Vacher and I had been in the Philippines a full year. We did not know what the next few weeks would bring, but we did know the rainy season was at its peak with its endless hours of dark, dreary days. The roar of rain on the metal roof reminded me of our days at Clark Field. We had found it almost impossible there to visit when the rain pounded on the roof and we had to shout to be heard. I had never fully adjusted to the incessant pounding on the roof of the barracks, and I was not sure how I would handle it now in the Jordan barn.

The illnesses that had plagued Vacher and me on the Gumain River continued to torment us. I fell into the every-other-day cycle of malarial chills and fever, and my dysentery continued to flare up. Vacher's cramps and uncontrollable bowels kept him in bad spirits. Only Main seemed to feel good all the time, and one day I asked him why he never got sick.

"Well, I guess I must take better care of myself than you guys do."

His sarcastic answer made me immediately angry. I wondered if he had a secret supply of quinine, and I was jealous of his always having a little bar of soap. Now with his developing romance with Nieves, he had a girl to take care of him, and I was sure their interest in one another would mean my own care would be neglected. More and more, such suspicions festered in my mind. During my malarial fevers, I passed in and out of restless sleep with vivid dreams and unwittingly scratched at the mosquito bites that covered my exposed body. I vowed to regain my health and leave.

During the first week at the Jordans, Main nursed me day and night, sometimes having to force me to swallow the quinine tablets. In my saner moments, I was ashamed of my attitude toward him.

Dr. Pineda visited us, bringing more quinine and administering large doses of the medicine to Vacher and me, along with the dreaded enemas of guava leaf tea. I tried to walk a little each day to toughen my feet, but the effort seemed to sap all my strength. In the evening Mrs. Jordan rubbed hot coconut oil on my sore feet and wrapped them in banana leaves. I had little confidence in the treatment, but enjoyed the motherly concern. I longed for the day when my health would return and my feet would be tough enough to travel.

I lost track of the days. One evening when Nieves came to the barn with an arm load of fresh corn from the garden, I asked her if she knew the date. It was June 27. We had been at the farm more than a week, and I noted the date on the makeshift calendar I had started keeping again after Orlo's death.

It had been only eleven days since we had buried Orlo, yet it seemed so much longer. I had not thought of him for the past few days, and that realization surprised me. Perhaps, I thought, it was because Kinder had been occupying my thoughts. I rationalized that with Orlo's death and burial, there was a finality to his being gone. With Kinder the separation had seemed temporary, and I still hoped he would reappear at any time, ready to assume his leadership role.

"Come and get it before I throw it out," Main said.

I snapped back to the present, eager to have my share of the roasted ears of corn. Main had left the husks on and roasted the ears in the hot coals. He had also cooked soft-boiled eggs. I broke my eggs over my rice so I could eat the mixture with my fingers, a Filipino custom we had adopted and liked. When the rice stuck to our fingers, we rinsed them in the bowl of water Main always set out at mealtime.

Since we had been taking the quinine Dr. Pineda brought, both Vacher and I were feeling better. I was still battling dysentery, but my appetite had returned. I was aware, however, of the abnormal silence which had become a regular accompaniment to our mealtimes. We never seemed to talk anymore, but on this night I had something to discuss with my companions. I finished my last ear of corn and broke the silence.

"Something's been on my mind. How much longer are we going to stay here? I'm ready to leave."

Main and Vacher looked at me in surprise.

"I just don't want to stay here any longer," I said. "This is no damn good. The Japs know we're in the area."

"You're probably right," Vacher said. "I'm ready to move, but let's give it some thought before we make up our minds."

Main listened silently. I sensed he had something to say, and finally, as he dished some more rice, he spoke.

"Last night when I was up at the house talking with Nieves and her mother, Three-Fingered Jack and Rufino came home." Main had talked with the two Jordan brothers late into the night. "According to them, they've got this area pretty well organized. They say the Huks are well armed and the Japs in Porac are scared to death of them."

"Bill, those people are Hukbalahaps," I interrupted. "They're a bunch of damned communists. Hell, about half of them are Chinese. Don't you remember at Clark they kept telling us about the Huks? They may be anti-Jap, but they're also anti-American. Sure, they probably want us to join them, but I don't want any part of their activities."

Main said no more to us, finished his rice, and left.

Vacher and I walked up the hill to the wire fence where we sat down on a pile of posts. Vacher pulled a pack of Luckies from his pocket, a gift from Joe Cheesman. He offered one to me, and I carefully tapped it on the back of my left hand as Vacher struck a match, lit his own cigarette, and then held the match for me. I inhaled deeply, savoring the luxury of an American cigarette. For the moment, we were communicating like friends.

"I'm glad you broke the ice back there," Vacher finally said. "I've been thinking about what we should do ever since we got here. I know I don't like it here one goddamn bit. Just too dangerous."

"Vacher, I'm leaving tomorrow. I think the Jordans will be glad to get rid of us. They're nice people, but it must be frightening as hell to have us around. I'm going back to Pasbul in the morning. I want to do a little nosing around, and I want to see if I can make it without shoes."

"Yeah, you're sure one up on Bill and me with your feet," Vacher said. "My shoes are shot, and I haven't gone barefoot since I was ten years old. I guess I'll go over to Cheesman's and see if Joe can come up with some shoes for me."

We figured Main would remain with the Jordans, but would perhaps join us when we found a place to stay. Vacher and I crawled through the wire fence, picked some guavas, and returned to the barn.

"I saw you guys up there talking," Main said when we returned. "Did you make any decisions?"

"I'm leaving in the morning, and Paul's going over to Cheesman's for a couple of days," I said.

Main said he wanted to stay behind until he decided what to do.

Going inside the barn, I gathered my belongings and prepared to leave at first light. Then I joined the other two around the fire. Darkness had settled over us as we sat quietly together discussing our separation. Despite the increased bickering that had taken place, there remained a close bond of friendship between us. The thought of leaving them seemed strange, yet I was sure I was ready to strike out on my own.

Something in me had changed. Throughout my life I had been dependent on the strength of others, seldom taking the initiative to act on my own. Even when the friction between Main and Vacher had seemed intolerable, I had felt a need to remain with them. Now I was ready to act independently and vowed to myself I would be my own person from that time forward. I did not want to let Filipinos control my life, and I felt I no longer needed the support of Vacher and Main.

We talked late into the night while rain pounded on the tin roof over our heads. We contemplated our future for a while, and then Main told some of the Old Ned stories, which always brightened the long, quiet hours. It had been weeks since I had so enjoyed the camaraderie we shared that night.

I drifted off to sleep, thinking about my decision. We were vulnerable here to Japanese attack, and our presence threatened the lives of the Jordan women. I was eager to leave at dawn.

Chapter Twenty-two

Early the next morning I left alone and headed down the trail towards Pasbul. Wearing a straw hat Nieves had given me, I moved along at a brisk pace and began whistling as a feeling of freedom crept over me. The rain had cleansed the countryside, and on this day the sun broke over the horizon like a brilliant yellow ball. I passed by the bullcart road we had traveled on our way to the Jordan farm. Nearing a dry wash, I found a well-worn trail. I was not familiar with the area, but I knew Pasbul was not far and recognized some of the landmarks. In the distance I could see the Del Carmen Sugar Central's tall smokestack, which Dr. Pineda had pointed out from Pasbul. Then I spotted traffic moving along the road which connected Porac and Florida Blanca. The vehicles were Japanese, and I felt a kind of thrill looking down on them from the remote trail. It gave me a sense of superiority, something I had not experienced since the war began.

The trail was smooth, damp, and cool, an easy surface for walking, and going barefoot, Filipino style, gave me a feeling of confidence. The dampness, however, meant there would be no dust clouds to give evidence of Japanese maneuvers. On the way out of Bataan, we had been able to spot dust clouds long before we reached the Pilar-Bagac Road. I was glad I still had my binoculars and made periodic checks whenever I was in sight of the road.

The pastoral beauty of Pampanga Province was reassuring in the morning sun, and I felt at peace with my conscience. I knew my decision to get out on my own, at least for the time being, was right.

Reaching some high ground, I sat down and looked out at a danger-filled world. I scanned the Plains of Pampanga with my binoculars and relished a new sense of freedom. Being alone that morning was very important to me, and I was sure I could outsmart the Japanese if the need arose. I reached into my pocket, grabbed a pinch of tobacco, and rolled a cigarette. Using one of my few matches, I lit the cigarette and inhaled deeply.

Suddenly the peaceful solitude was shattered by the sound of a truck horn. I jumped into the tall cogan grass and quickly scanned the countryside with my binoculars. I saw nothing and heard only the silence of the morning. At the same time, I knew the horn had to be Japanese, and it was nearby.

When I cautiously looked again toward the Del Carmen sugar mill, I saw a small truck parked on the bullcart road not more than a half kilometer away. The door was open, and I could see a driver sitting behind the wheel, his rifle propped against the windshield. It looked as though he might be waiting for someone. Then there was another blast from the horn. I stifled a sneeze and checked my own rifle, sliding the bolt back just enough to see that a cartridge was in the chamber. I slid the bolt home quietly and set the safety.

Voices broke the silence, and movement in the cane field on the other side of the road attracted my attention. Moments later six Japanese soldiers emerged from the field and climbed into the truck. I could hear them talking with the driver. Over the noise of the motor, they seemed excited as they started down the road towards Pasbul. I watched them disappear into a depression in the road, and soon the motor noise faded out. My own plans to go to Pasbul were momentarily delayed.

I continued scanning the countryside, content to lay low until the truck returned. I knew the road dead-ended in Pasbul, and sooner or later, the Japanese would have to return.

As I lay there quietly considering the possibilities, the roar of an aircraft engine split the air. I heard it backfire as the motor was coaxed into an even rhythm and imagined the blue smoke pouring out of the manifold with each choking cough. Through my binoculars, I spotted the blue puffs of smoke and remembered the Americans had built a small airfield at Del Carmen. Through the grass where I lay hidden, I could see a Japanese plane start down the runway.

For weeks we had been seeing Japanese planes in the air, most of them apparently on training exercises. With one plane towing a target for the others to shoot, the bursts of machine-gun fire could be heard for quite a distance. Vacher, Main, and I had supposed the planes came from Clark Field. We had not worried about being seen, knowing that from the air it was nearly impossible to spot anyone in the jungle terrain. Now, in this more open area, I found myself near a hidden Japanese airstrip. As the plane soared into the air, I rolled gently into the deeper grass, pulling it over myself. I watched with an inner excitement as two more planes took off. When the third one rose into the air, the first two circled back and all three headed southeast in the direction of Nichols Field in Manila.

Once again all was quiet. I rolled back to the trail for another look and continued waiting for the Japanese truck to return. In accordance with my thoughts, it appeared on the road a few minutes later. I heard the motor first, then spotted the truck as it emerged from the depression in the road. I carefully counted the soldiers. Seven. The same number I had seen going into the barrio earlier were returning. It was safe now to move on towards Pasbul.

I waited a few minutes after the truck passed and then resumed my journey. Heavy, dark clouds had begun to block out the bright sunlight. It would rain soon, and I knew I had to find shelter.

I followed the trail, keeping a wary eye on the road below. Fifteen minutes later I spotted a small hut beside the trail, knelt down, and surveyed the scene. A Filipino woman outside the hut pounded unhulled rice, called *palay*, in a large stone container, the method used by natives to separate the hulls from rice. As she pounded the *palay*, a man emerged from the shack and climbed down the ladder steps. From my vantage point, he looked like a Negrito. They talked for a moment, and then he started up the trail. I whistled, and the woman motioned for me to come down to the shack.

"Who are you?" she asked.

"Millard Hileman."

"I have heard of you," she said. "Where are your companions?"

Her response was surprising, not only because she had heard about me, but because she spoke perfect English.

She introduced herself as Carmen and said the Negrito's name was Serappio. I asked if Serappio was his first or last name. Smiling at my naivete, Carmen explained Negritos had only one name. Serappio was her husband, she said, and she was a refugee who had fled Manila before the Japanese occupation. I did not question her further, but I was extremely curious about this Filipino woman from the city who was living out the war as the wife of a primitive Negrito man.

Serappio returned, and the two began talking in a native dialect. I heard the word *Americano* and knew they were talking about me.

"Do you know the Pinedas?" I asked.

Carmen said they tended Dr. Pineda's kamote field. I understood then how she knew so much about me and my companions. She went into the shack and returned with a glass of water, the glass sparkling with cleanliness.

Carmen turned to Serappio and spoke in an authoritative manner. Without saying a word, he took the bow that had been hanging on the side of the house, along with a quiver containing several arrows of typical Negrito design. He hung the quiver over his shoulder and started up the hill.

Carmen invited me inside the hut where she had rice steaming over a bed of coals. We began talking, and in a few minutes Serappio joined us, carrying a squawking chicken. He hung the bow and quiver back in their place on the wall, and Carmen handed him a coconut shell. Serappio cut the chicken's throat with his bolo, allowing the blood to drain into the shell. I had seen this same procedure at the Jordan farm. The blood was saved and cooked separately. I had found it difficult at first to eat the cooked blood, but recognized its nutritional value and had learned to enjoy the native delicacy. Carmen carefully prepared all parts of the chicken. I had already learned to eat the head, feet, and even boiled legs because Main had acquired the Filipino habit of wasting nothing edible.

"I cook it all except the feathers and asshole," he had said.

When the chicken was cooked, Carmen spread it out on a fresh banana leaf from which we all ate. I ate heartily.

Serappio spoke to me in a steady stream of dialect, none of which I understood. The lack of understanding did not seem to bother him, however, and Carmen interpreted the essential points. I tried to talk with the Negrito in English mixed with a few Tagalog words. The response was a friendly, toothless grin. When we finished the meal, Carmen spread mats on the split bamboo floor.

"We will rest now," she said. I lay down for the traditional siesta, but did not sleep.

When they awoke, Carmen and Sarappio began talking, and from the few words I understood, I knew they were discussing the Japanese. I asked Carmen if they had seen the patrol that morning. She said it had been coming to Pasbul once a week.

Then she added some disturbing information. She said the Japanese had been pressing Dr. Pineda for information about four fugitive Americans. The Japanese had burned Dr. Pineda's office in Porac and taken his medical supplies, but, she quickly added, the doctor had not given them any information.

I wondered if they had burned his office recently, or if Carmen referred to an earlier time when the Japanese soldiers had passed through Porac on their way into Bataan. I did not ask. The news was disturbing, however, as I realized the Japanese connected Dr. Pineda with four Americans presumed to be in the area. I wanted more than ever to see the doctor, to learn for myself what had been happening and to ascertain just how much danger we posed to him and his family. My earlier mistrust had changed to grateful admiration for all he had done.

It was late afternoon when I prepared to leave the Serappio house. It had started to rain, and the darkening sky gave the impression night was about to fall. I thanked my benefactors and continued my walk toward Pasbul, a journey just over three kilometers. I was soaked by the time I reached the barrio.

I recognized the crude dirt street running through the barrio as the road we had seen when the four of us had come over the hill after leaving Pop about two months earlier. At its extreme north end, where the trail started down into the Gumain River canyon, a second dirt road branched off to the east and converged with the trail I was following.

In the rain the street was deserted, and I cautiously approached the few scattered shacks on the eastern fringe of the barrio. I saw a bareheaded man in front of one of the sawali huts. A fence made from three-by-five-foot sawali panels surrounded the thatched structure. Vines covered the roof, and as I came nearer, I could see they were heavy with squash. Children, oblivious to the drenching rain, played on a pile of boulders behind the hut. The man in front appeared to be about forty years old, and I did not recognize him. He looked up as I walked toward him.

"Are you one of the three Americans who now live near Barrio Pio?" he asked. He had chosen his words carefully, and I studied him in silence.

"Are you Mr. Vacher?" he asked.

I looked directly at him and shook my head. For the moment, I wanted to let the stranger do all the talking.

"My name is Malleri, Benito Malleri," he said. "I am a friend of Dr. Pineda."

"Where is Dr. Pineda now?" I asked. "I need to talk with him."

"Dr. Pineda is in Porac with his family. The Japanese have asked him to stay in town for a few days." After a pause, Malleri added, "I think they are trying to make Dr. Pineda tell them where the Americans are now hiding, the ones who were first hiding on the Gumain River."

I sat down on the porch and rolled a cigarette. Malleri's eyes darted back and forth, giving the impression he wanted to avoid any direct eye contact.

"Do you live in Pasbul, Mr. Malleri?"

"No, sir. Not all the time, sir. Just some of the time. Sometimes I work at the sugar central for the Japanese. I think you are one of the Americans who arrived in Pasbul from Bataan. Is that correct?"

"I have been to Pasbul once, but I am not living here," I said. "I now live a very long way from Pasbul."

I did not want to give Malleri any more information than was necessary. I was not sure I could trust him, especially since learning he worked for the Japanese. I had not given my name, and he had mentioned only Vacher. I was puzzled by Malleri's familiarity with my friend.

"Joe, you are very wet. You will come inside and get dry."

The Filipino continued to grin with a smile that seemed to be a fixed part of his face. I remained reluctant to divulge my identity, so Malleri called me Joe, a common practice among the Filipino people.

"You will stay with us tonight, Joe. I have another house here in the barrio where you can sleep."

Cautiously, I climbed the four-step ladder leading into Malleri's house. It was larger than I expected. In one corner of the room, a woman sat in a small rocking chair nursing a baby. She smiled at me.

"This is my wife, sir, and this is my little baby boy, Renaldo," Malleri said. "The ones outside are my children also. I have five counting this one, one girl and four boys."

I sat down on a small stool near the cooking fire, and Malleri and his wife began talking in dialect. Although uncomfortable with the Filipino, I decided to accept his invitation to spend the night.

Malleri joined me next to the fire and began telling me about work at the Del Carmen Sugar Central. He said he had a good job there before the war. Since the Japanese occupation he was employed only part time, and he did not know from one day to the next whether the mill would operate. The Japanese had fired the former manager who had worked at the mill for more than ten years. He had been replaced by a patron, a Filipino who chose to cooperate with the Japanese.

"The sugar mill is not running good, and everything is becoming broken, sir," Malleri said. "I am not liking the crew that is now operating the mill."

Malleri's story seemed straight, but I did not wholly trust the shifty-eyed Filipino with the constant grin.

Mrs. Malleri put a meal out on banana leaves which she had spread on the bamboo floor. The quality of the food surprised me, especially the poached fish. She had also prepared vegetable soup cooked in chicken broth that we drank from coconut shells. With the feeling of satisfaction a good meal brings, I leaned back, studied my host, and enjoyed one of his brown dobie cigarettes.

Darkness had fallen, and mosquitoes were buzzing around my ears when Malleri stood and beckoned for me to follow. Using a torch to light the way, he led me down a winding trail to a little hut. Malleri climbed the three-step ladder, and I followed. He lit a crude oil lamp made from a tin can, coconut oil, and a floating wick. It hung from a post in the center of the room. Malleri sat down on one of the wooden benches along the wall and motioned for me to do the same.

"Are you Mr. Vacher?" he asked again. "I have heard one of my friends in the town talk of Mr. Vacher."

I responded that I was not Mr. Vacher and continued to ignore the fact I knew Vacher. Then in a casual manner, I introduced myself.

"Ah, yes, Mr. Hileman." His eyes continued darting back and

forth. "You would like to live here with us? We can let you have this place, and we will bring you food."

I wondered what the Filipino had on his mind and did not have to wait long.

"I think if we do that, there is a way the United States will repay us," Malleri said. "Is that not correct?"

Malleri wanted a voucher which could be redeemed after the war. The opportunistic Filipino persisted.

"What is it, the paper the American soldier will sign to pay for food and keep, so we can be paid after the war? Is it a voucher?"

Malleri had done his homework. I tried to change the subject by asking if there were any other Americans in the area.

"Only some civilians, sir," he said. "I am knowing Mr. Joe Cheesman for many years. He has lived by the sugar central near Del Carmen in Barrio Salu. I think he is now living in the mountains with his family."

"Are there American soldiers who are paying Filipino people to care for them during the Japanese occupation?" I asked.

"Oh, yes, many. There is even a camp in the mountains near Dinalupihan where two American brothers who are civilians from Lubao give food and shelter to many Americans who have escaped from Bataan. I think their name is Fassoth."

My distrust faded as I realized Malleri was simply an opportunist trying to make money off the U.S. government. I did not see any particular harm in what he was doing, but I was not ready to sign a voucher. Trying to look into Malleri's shifting eyes, I said I was too tired to discuss the matter. We would talk again in the morning.

Malleri grabbed a couple of dry sticks and put them into the sand-filled firebox used for cooking. Blowing on a smoldering stick, he brought them into a low flame and told me the smoke would keep the mosquitoes away. He said good night and left.

I lay down, wrapped my feet in my old blanket and pulled my ragged shelter half around my shoulders. The worn covers would help keep the mosquitoes off me. I folded one arm under my head and contemplated the day. I had run into a Japanese patrol, discovered a hidden airstrip, eaten with the Serappios, learned more about Dr. Pineda, and met Benito Malleri. Most important, I had struck out, barefoot and alone, and made my way to Barrio Pasbul.

Chapter Twenty-three

Alone in the little hut, I indulged in fantasy, imagining the Japanese patrol I had seen had been searching for me. I pictured myself with a Browning Automatic Rifle instead of my old Springfield. How satisfying it would have been to spray the cane field and the Japanese with the automatic weapon. It would have been like shooting fish in a rain barrel, as Vacher would say. Perhaps I would have another chance.

My thoughts turned to Malleri who seemed to be some kind of a con man trying to take advantage of the U.S. government. I was sure there were men everywhere like Malleri, eager to exploit situations such as the one in which I was caught, yet I might need him and was not ready to break contact with the scheming Filipino.

Tired, I drifted into a restless sleep frequently interrupted by barking dogs. Voices woke me at dawn, and looking out the window opening, I saw Malleri and his children coming down the trail.

He greeted me and offered a welcome breakfast of rice and two boiled eggs wrapped in banana leaves. He asked if I had slept well, and I assured him the mosquitoes had not been a problem. I had been up several times during the night to rearrange the fire so it would create smoke, and the wind had risen somewhat. The two elements had kept the pests away.

A cramp surged through my abdomen, reminding me I had not escaped my dysentery when I left the Jordan farm. I went outside to relieve myself, rejoined Malleri, and asked again about Dr. Pineda.

"I do not think Dr. Pineda will be coming back soon. He is having trouble in the town."

Malleri seemed pleased with Dr. Pineda's problems, as if the situation would afford him opportunity to get an upper hand before the doctor returned. As we talked he fumbled with something in his pocket, finally producing a small piece of paper and a pencil. He extended it to me, but I ignored the offer.

"Why will you not sign this paper so you will be assured of proper food and shelter while you are in Pasbul?"

"Because, Mr. Malleri, I am not certain I will stay in Pasbul. Right now I'm interested in talking with the doctor. I need medicine, and I want to make sure the Japanese are not mistreating him or his family."

My words seemed to shake Malleri. He obviously wanted my signature before the doctor returned.

"What sort of trouble is Dr. Pineda having, Benito?" I asked. "Is he under house arrest in Porac?"

Malleri did not understand the term *house arrest,* so I asked if the doctor was being punished.

"I am not sure what they have done to him, sir. I have heard that the Japanese are very interested in finding four Americans who have been living in the area for several weeks. They said they will continue to send patrols into the barrios until the Americans are captured and placed on trial."

I could get no information of value from Malleri. Perhaps he would loosen up if I signed the paper, but I could not shake my feeling of mistrust. Malleri seemed like a chronic liar who would say or do anything to press his own advantage.

Once again violent cramps forced me to run outside, and when I returned, Malleri was gone. The food, however, had been left. Although dysentery continued to plague me, my appetite was good, and as I scooped up some rice I began to wonder about my malaria. Quinine had been scarce, and sooner or later the intermittent fevers and chills would return.

Alone, I wandered down to the creek to wash, but no matter how

I tried my face never felt clean. My only razor blade had become dull, and I had quit shaving when we were camped along the Gumain River. Main had painstakingly honed his blades against the inside of a drinking glass Nieves had given him. I could have asked him to sharpen mine, but I felt the request would have been seen as a sign of weakness. I had been so annoyed with his whistling and muttering to himself as he worked that I had vowed to let my beard grow rather than ask him for help. Now it was scruffy and unkempt and never felt clean.

I waited in Malleri's shack for an hour, but when my host did not return I gathered my belongings and headed towards Barrio Pio. The morning air was cool and clean in the bright sunlight, but rain clouds were already forming on the horizon. I reached the Serappio hut and found no one, but just as I was about to go on, Carmen rounded the trail carrying a basket of laundry on her head. She greeted me and asked if I had eaten.

"I have had breakfast and do not feel hungry, Carmen. Thanks anyway."

I was surprised by my response because when I did not have malaria I was always hungry.

"Where is Serappio this morning?"

"Serappio might come back in a few minutes, or he might not come back even in a week," she said with a shrug. "Sometimes he goes to visit his people in the mountains."

Carmen began hanging the wet clothes over a sawali fence. Then she turned to me.

"I think we should wash your clothes because they are very soiled," she said.

"No, Carmen, I am in a hurry because I want to find Dr. Pineda. I would not have time for them to dry."

"I do not think you are in a very big hurry." She looked directly at me. "I think you are embarrassed because you do not have extra clothing to wear while I am cleaning yours. If that is the reason, then I will find something of Serappio's you can wear while your clothes are drying."

The only clothing I had seen Negrito men wear were G-strings, and I had a fleeting vision of the consequences of being caught in the Negrito's hut wearing one of those. He might take one of those arrows designed to kill Japanese and put it through me. I thanked Carmen for the offer and restated my reasons for leaving. She seemed satisfied as she offered me some rice and leftover chicken to take with me. I left with a promise to return. It was raining.

Dark brown mud oozed between my toes as I walked, and soon I was soaking wet. Sharp rocks tore the skin on my toes, and my feet became painful and raw. My hip began to cramp as numbness crept down my lower legs and into my feet. The hip cramps and the numbness were something new. I had not experienced anything like them, and suddenly I felt very tired. I became unsteady, stumbling as I followed the familiar trail. My body began to chill, and I sensed the onslaught of a malarial attack. I forced myself to go on, knowing I would be unable to continue if I stopped.

Time and again I fell headlong into the mud. I cut my face, and mud caked my beard and hair. The pain in my hips became almost unbearable, and I sat down. I was ready to give up and let the pain and sickness take over. I was discovering, for the first time, that within myself there was a will to live and a will to die. If the will to die became stronger, then dying would be the easy choice. Living required strength, courage, and willpower.

After a short rest, I pulled myself to my feet and wiped the mixture of sweat, blood, and mud from my face. I mumbled incoherently, sensing I resembled a mentally deranged idiot turned loose in the wild.

"I'm going to shoot the first Jap son of a bitch I see," I said to myself. "Those bastards are the reason I'm here."

I thought about the previous morning and the opportunity I had then to shoot the Japanese soldiers. I could not understand why I had not done so. Any who might have survived would have thought twice before heading out into the tullies again, I reasoned.

Pain surged from my foot when I cut myself on another rock, and I watched my blood ooze into the mud. I took another step and fell. Enraged, I began cursing the Japanese, the Filipinos, and even Main and Vacher for not being there to share my misery. Again I rose to my feet as the fever burned through my weary body.

Approaching the river, I knew the crossing would be difficult. I started down the steep bank, grasping the wet vines to keep from falling. As I groped my way across the stream, I fell into the cold water several times. I was too drenched to be aware of the torrential rain which pounded down on me. My vision blurred, and everything became a gray haze. I kept pushing onward, saying to myself, "I can't quit. I won't stop." Then a feeling of peace settled over me, and I lost consciousness.

A cool, damp cloth on my forehead woke me, and I looked up to see the smiling face and rich brown eyes of Nieves Jordan. I looked for the trail and river, but then realized I was in the Jordan barn.

"How did I get here?" I asked. "And where are Bill and Paul?"

Nieves dug deeply as she cleaned the wound on my forehead.

"You are okay now, Mr. Hileman. Beel is outside preparing supper. Mr. Vacher is at the home of Joe Cheesman. He was there all night, I think.

"My brother Jack and José Montemayor brought you here," she said. "They found you on the trail. They do not think you had been there very long. José is very strong and he carried you here about an hour ago. You are once again very clean because we gave you a bath."

Despite my burning fever, I smiled at her last remark. I no longer cared who bathed me. It felt so good just to lie down and feel clean, my modesty did not matter.

I glanced over at the fire pit where Main was cooking, accompanied by the low, soft whistling that seemed so much a part of his character. In an attitude of amusement, I thought Main would make a great Filipino, and I was convinced he and Nieves made a good couple.

Main had taken my rifle and pistol apart and cleaned them. Parts were still laid out on a clean rag, and there was a small bottle of solvent and some light gun oil next to it.

"Where the hell did the gun oil come from, Bill?"

"From Nieves. She knows where Jack and José keep their supplies."

I dozed off again, and when I woke Nieves was gone. Both Main and Vacher were sitting on a box in the barn, smoking American cigarettes and talking.

"Hey, Vacher, where have you been?" I said. "You missed all the fun of seeing me carried in here and getting a bath."

Vacher grinned and handed me a coconut shell. "Here, how about a cup of real American coffee?" he said.

I savored the aroma of the rare treat before sipping it.

"Wow, this is the real McCoy. Where did you get it?"

Vacher quietly handed me a Lucky Strike, took a long drag on his, and looked at me with a smile. He was good company when things were going well for him, and this was apparently such a day.

"Hileman, let me tell you, you've got to meet Joe Cheesman. He's really something." Vacher went on to tell about Cheesman and Loring, his latest of several wives.

"He told me he'd had so many wives he'd actually lost track," Vacher said in amusement, "but then he told me he wasn't really married to them all. He said Loring was really his wife. She's part Chinese, and she sure takes good care of Old Joe.

"They have a son, Roy, good-looking kid and smart as hell. He's really talented. While I sat there with them he drew a couple of pictures of me and I couldn't believe how good the shading was. He plays a hell of a guitar too, and sings. Mostly he likes western music, probably because Joe came from Texas. He does a good job on popular music too. He sang 'Deep Purple,' and I swear he sounded like Bing Crosby.

"They seem to have everything they need," Vacher said. Loring Cheesman bought supplies for the family in Porac and Florida Blanca.

"You should see the stuff that gal carries back on her head," Vacher said. "Joe told me he thinks the Japs know who she is and have just chosen not to follow her. Hell, I think she's just too damn smart for the dumb bastards."

An American colonel had authorized Cheesman to organize a guerrilla unit, and he wanted the three of us to join him. He had already signed up a couple of other Americans I did not know, Hugh McCoy and Pierce Wade.

"Joe's especially interested in Bill because of his knowledge of small arms."

I saw Main grimace when Vacher mentioned his name as a possible guerrilla.

"Personally, I think Joe is about fifty percent bullshit," Vacher said. "But you guys will like the old boy. I've never met anyone who knows more about the Philippines than he does. I don't want to live too close to him, though. One of these days the Japs are going to follow Loring home, and when they do I want to be somewhere else."

Vacher continued talking about the Cheesmans as we ate our meal, taunting Main about joining the guerrilla unit. It was very apparent the old tensions were flaring up again. The scornful remarks continued in the days that followed, and in the close confines of the

Jordan barn the personality conflict festered.

I talked to Vacher about moving, and we decided to leave together. Main had Nieves to help him and would get along well without us. The shack Benito Malleri had offered me seemed like a good place, and when I suggested moving there Vacher agreed. We set out to find Malleri.

The opportunistic Filipino greeted us with his perpetual grin. His darting eyes flitted even more as he agreed to let us live in his shack. He pressed a voucher at us, but for the moment we procrastinated in signing. Nonetheless, we moved into the new quarters in Barrio Pasbul.

Chapter Twenty-four

I'm going to Cheesman's and see if I can talk the old boy out of some coffee," Vacher said about two weeks after we moved into Malleri's shack.

There had been constant rain for several days, but now the sun had broken through the heavy clouds, bathing the countryside in warm sunshine. With the welcome change in weather, I walked down to the stream.

I sat on a warm rock daydreaming as I soaked my feet in the cool water. Suddenly I was jolted back to reality by the sound of footsteps. I grabbed my rifle and wheeled around to see a beautiful girl looking down the trail at me. Her fair skin and fine features suggested she might be of Spanish descent. About nineteen years old, she seemed tall compared to the petite Jordan sisters. She smiled, revealing deep dimples and beautiful white teeth.

"My name is Isabel Montemayor, and I live in Barrio Pio," she said. "I am living in the big house by the church with the white dome."

"You startled me," I said. "I am Mr. Hileman, Millard Hileman. I, I mean we, my friend and I, are living in Barrio Pasbul. We are living in a house that belongs to Mr. Malleri. Do you know him?"

A sense of self-consciousness came over me as I spoke with this lovely young woman who had such an apparent air of self-confidence.

"Yes, Mr. Hileman, I know who you are, and I also know the name of your friend, Mr. Vacher. Nieves and Nina Jordan have already told me about all of you. They even told me when it is August sixth you will be having a birthday, and you will be twenty-eight years old. Is that correct?"

"I had not thought about it, but you're right, I will be having a birthday."

"I know that today is August fourth, which means your birthday will be Thursday because that is the day of August sixth. Now, I think you are wondering why I came to see you today. It is because I want to bake you a birthday cake. Will that be okay, Mr. Hileman?"

I was stunned at her offer. Why would this girl I had never seen before want to bake a cake for me?

Then a thought bolted through my mind. Main and Vacher, through their relationships with Nieves and Nina, had recognized my feeling of being the odd man and had conspired with the Jordan sisters to find a girl for me. Isabel's coming to the river to meet me was their idea. I was angry. If and when I wanted female companionship, I would find my own girl. At present I had no desire to have a woman complicating my life. On the other hand it was most pleasant, even somewhat exciting, to be approached by this beautiful, confident-appearing, young woman.

Ever since I had arrived in the Philippines, I had been told how well foreign blood mixed with that of the native people. Now as I looked at Isabel I was convinced the theory was certainly true in her case. Her olive complexion and fine features were a strong contrast to most of the darker, coarser natives. Her sparkling eyes especially caught my attention.

"Do you want me to call you Mr. Hileman, or would you prefer it if I call you Mee-lard?"

She pronounced my name with a heavy accent on the *ee* in the first syllable, and I decided not to correct her. I liked the way she said Mee-lard.

"Okay, Mee-lard, I think I like that name," she said.

Isabel kept talking, but I hardly heard a word she said. I was preoccupied with just gazing at this attractive, young Filipina who had walked into my life. I looked down at her tiny bare feet, and my eyes continued upward over two shapely brown legs. She wore a short dress that exposed two smooth, dimpled knees and a hint of what I imagined were two well-shaped thighs. Above her low-cut, summer print dress, I admired the tawny brownness of her shoulders. When I had first seen her approaching, her long, wavy black hair had fallen forward over her right shoulder and cascaded down the front of her slim body. When she reached me, she had tossed her head back and let her hair fall to her waist. If she was trying to get my attention, she most certainly had succeeded. I realized she had been doing all the talking since she arrived, and I made a conscious effort to make it a two-way conversation.

"Mee-lard, tell me about your home back in the United States," she said. "Are you very rich?"

Typical of a general Filipino attitude, she thought all Americans were wealthy.

I ignored the question and invited her to sit with me on the warm rock. She sat behind me, and when I inadvertently leaned back against her knee I jerked forward. She gently reached out and pulled me back. Glancing back at her, I was struck by the contrast between her and the Filipino women around Clark Field before the war. The smell of cheap cosmetics so prevalent among them was absent. Her fresh, natural beauty made me realize how long it had been since I had been around a girl like her.

Although it was the rainy season, sunshine continued to warm the day. I felt good about a lot of things, but especially about meeting Isabel and the way she made me feel. The war, with its pain and devastation, seemed far away, and even though my fugitive status was a constant threat, for the moment I was at peace with myself and the world around me.

We talked about our families, schools, and hopes for the future. Isabel said she wanted to go to Manila, enter college, and become a teacher. She had not quite completed high school in Porac when the war interrupted her educational plans.

She told me about her brother, José. When I had fallen unconscious on the trail during my malarial attack, it was he who had picked me up and carried me to the Jordan farm. Isabel said José and Jack Jordan had been on their way to meet the Hukbalahaps when they found me. She hated the Huks and was deeply concerned for her brother.

"I do not believe in the people fighting guerrilla warfare," she said. "It can only make the Japanese angry with the people. I think we should be patient and wait for the Americans to return." She expressed her faith, and that of her people, in the return of General MacArthur and the American army.

"Too much guerrilla activity from untrained soldiers can only cause more harm than good," she said.

This was the first time I had heard a Filipino question the validity of the guerrillas.

"Mee-lard, I know my brother and Jack Jordan will be asking you to join the Huks. Do you think you would be interested in doing that?"

"No. We were told at Clark Field the Huks are communists, and we should not go to any of their meetings." I had heard about the Huk headquarters near Mt. Arayat.

"I'm glad," Isabel said. "They will not do good for the Filipino people. They will only make the Japanese come into the barrios and harm the people."

I sensed her deep concern over the guerrilla situation and began to question the wisdom of guerrilla operations. Isabel's words, and her concerns, would remain with me. She was young, but like other Filipino women I had met, she was wise and had a deep inner strength.

It was late afternoon when we realized how long we had been talking. It had been a long time since I had been so at ease around anyone, and for the time being I forgot the anger I had experienced around Main and Vacher. Nor did I sense any of the distrust or suspicion I had known with most of the Filipinos I had met.

I could smell the fragrance of Isabel's hair as I slipped my right arm around her waist and entwined my fingers in the long tresses cascading down her back. She smiled and gently pressed her body against me. I leaned forward to kiss her, but was interrupted by the sound of footsteps on the trail. Isabel quickly pushed herself away, and we looked up to see Ernie Pineda grinning down at us from the bank.

"It is okay, Ernie," Isabel laughed. "I am just now ready to go."

Ernie joined me, and Isabel walked up the trail.

My eyes followed her admiringly, and I became aware that in one afternoon this young girl had won my heart.

Meeting her had rekindled my hatred for the Japanese. If they learned about her friendship with me, she might be punished, and I found myself wanting to protect her. She had suddenly become the first real ray of sunshine in an otherwise gloomy existence.

"Damn the Japs," I muttered to myself as I thought about Isabel's safety.

"Are you talking to me, Mr. Hileman?" Ernie asked.

"No, Ernie, I guess I was just talking to myself." I turned and smiled at the young boy with a real sense of gratitude and friendship.

Chapter Twenty-five

Rain pounded against the cogan grass roof of Benito Malleri's shack on the morning of August 6. I rubbed the sleep from my eyes and looked over at Vacher.

"Hey, happy birthday," he said. "Get your ass out of bed and look alive, boy. This is your big day."

Since splitting with Main, Vacher and I seemed to have regained our old camaraderie. Both of us had been busy. Vacher had spent time with Nina and with Joe Cheesman who seemed to keep him supplied with coffee and an occasional good cigarette. I had been spending time with Isabel since meeting her two days earlier.

"When I told Joe you were going to have a birthday cake today, the old bastard gave me some coffee," Vacher said. "He told me to tell you it was a birthday present."

It seemed much longer than two days since I had met Isabel at the creek. She had come by the shack the morning after our meeting, eager to make plans for the birthday party. Wanting me to feel special, she suggested she could wash my clothes before the party. I was struck by her generosity, but was somewhat embarrassed by the boldness of the young Filipino girl. I had introduced her to Vacher, and together we decided to invite Main and the Jordan girls over for cake. Isabel said she had some wheat flour stored in a jar and that the cake would be very good.

"Hileman, I think I've known just about every girl you've ever had anything to do with, and in my opinion, this one rates pretty damn high," Vacher had said when she left. "It looks like you've remembered everything I taught you about judging women."

"Listen, Vacher, don't go taking all the credit for my good taste. Hell! I didn't find her anyway, she found me."

I wondered again as I made that statement whether the Jordan sisters, or even Vacher and Main, had arranged the meeting.

I thought now about Ernie Pineda's interruption as I was about to kiss Isabel. When Ernie spoke, Isabel had let her arms slip from my neck. Now I remembered she had grabbed my left hand and held it tightly, twisting my class ring around my finger. I had worn the ring since 1932, my senior year at Riverside Polytechnic High School. As Isabel twisted the ring in her fingers, she had smiled and looked coyly up at me.

Vacher poured a cup of hot coffee and offered me a Lucky Strike, another gift from Joe Cheesman. We basked in the luxury of American coffee and cigarettes.

"My God, I'm hungry for some good music," he said. His comment sent my mind racing back to our days in California. Vacher had lived in Mrs. Freeman's boardinghouse where we often sat together and listened to a late-night program of classical music. He had been able to name the musical renditions before the announcer identified them, and it had bothered me that he knew the music and I did not.

The rain let up, and Vacher went for a walk. While he was gone, Isabel came to the shack with a beautiful chocolate cake. She carried a small package in a woven basket on her head. She handed the package to me.

"Happy birthday, Mee-lard," she smiled.

I started to unwrap the package and then stopped. "Should I wait until the others are here?"

"No, you will look at my present now before the others come," she said.

With excitement dancing in her eyes, Isabel watched me unwrap a new pair of shorts. Tan in color, they looked like military issue.

"Where in the world did you find these?" I took them to another part of the shack to change. "Are they GI shorts?"

"Yes, but I think from the Japanese, except that I am not sure," she replied. "My cousin got them for me in Guagua, and they might be from Japan."

Dressed in my Japanese shorts, I slipped my arm around Isabel's shoulders and gave her a quick kiss on the cheek. She smiled and took my left hand, again twisting the class ring on my finger.

"Do you like my ring?" I asked.

"Oh, yes, I like the ring. I have never had one like that."

"Would you like to have it?"

"Yes, Mee-lard, I think I would like that very much, but you must not give it to me now."

"Why not?"

"Because before you do that you must be very sure you like me."

I paused at the seriousness of her response. In the decade since my graduation, the ring had lost its meaning, but if I gave it to Isabel, it would gain new significance. I slipped the ring off and put it on her middle finger.

"It will fit there better," I said. "Your hand is so small you might lose it."

"Oh, no! I will not lose it ever."

She leaned close, and I bent to kiss her. Once again I was interrupted by a sudden sound, and looked up to see Ernie Pineda running up the trail. For the second time the young Filipino boy had frustrated my attempt to kiss Isabel.

"Mr. Hileman! Mr. Hileman!" Ernie shouted. "We have just heard that the Japanese are coming to the barrio."

"Which barrio?"

"I think they will come to Barrio Pio first, and maybe they will come to Pasbul. I do not know."

I calmly listened to Ernie. I always tried to mask my fear when dealing with Filipinos, but on this occasion the calmness was genuine and I was not worried. I knew communist guerrillas had moved into the area and would alert everyone in the vicinity if a Japanese patrol were coming our way.

The guerrillas had arrived in Pasbul a few days earlier. The Hukbalahaps, or Huks as they were commonly called, were an outgrowth of the Philippine Communist Party. They had been anti-

American and anti-Commonwealth, but when the war broke out they had become anti-Japanese. José Montemayor, Isabel's brother, had said the Huks wanted Americans, including Vacher and me, to join their ranks. I suspected they had ulterior motives for wanting us in their organization.

Now, in the shack at Pasbul, my apparent indifference to the news of another Japanese patrol seemed to disappoint Ernie, but his disappointment was soon forgotten. The boy had spotted my ring on Isabel's finger.

"Mr. Hileman, you give Isabel your ring!" he said.

I was sure the whole area would know in a matter of hours.

Vacher came whistling up the trail. He had been visiting the Huks near the barrio gate and knew about the Japanese activity. According to the Huks, the Japanese had moved two truckloads of riflemen into Porac. That meant patrols in the area would increase.

"With this news you can bet Nieves has moved Bill farther up the trail and has him hidden," Vacher said.

I was sure he was right.

"Are you afraid?" I asked Isabel.

"No, not now." Her brother had told her the guerrillas were very strong in the area, and the Japanese were afraid of them. He had said the patrols would not come until they got reinforcements. Those reinforcements had apparently arrived, but it would still be a few days before they came as far as Pasbul. Isabel was well informed.

"Look, Mr. Vacher," Ernie said with a big grin. "Mr. Hileman give Isabel his ring."

"Good boy, Ernie." Vacher patted the boy on the back. "I need to know about such things so I can keep up on what's going on. We'll have to keep an eye on Mr. Hileman."

"If I want to give her my ring, it's none of your damn business," I said in a tone reflecting my embarrassment. Vacher fell quiet, while Ernie seemed hurt. I changed the subject, thanking Ernie for keeping his eyes open and informing us about the Japanese. The tension eased.

Vacher had seen the Pinedas loading a bullcart as he went through the barrio that morning. Ernie said they were moving back to Porac because his father did not want his family around the Huks. The doctor had warned his son to make his visit with us brief, so after sharing his news, Ernie left.

Isabel scurried around the shack, cleaning up and making preparations for the birthday party. I was skeptical, however, sure the news of Japanese activity would discourage the cautious Main from coming. We waited long past the time Main, Nieves, and Nina were to join us before Vacher started the coffee.

While the coffee was brewing, we went outside where Isabel asked many questions about my family. She had already quizzed Vacher about my schooling, our long friendship, and about former girlfriends.

"Mee-lard, why you give me your gold ring, and you never give it to some other girl in the USA?" she asked. "You don't like another girl there so good?"

As I searched for a suitable answer Vacher announced the coffee was ready. I knew, however, that she would ask again.

We went back into the shack, and as Isabel rummaged through her basket for a knife to cut the cake, she impulsively handed me a small, silver spoon.

"I give you this spoon, Mee-lard, so you will think about me when you use it. Do not ever lose it. Okay?"

Isabel and Vacher sang "Happy Birthday" before we ate the delicious sweet cake, a special treat for Vacher and me. Afterwards we both kissed Isabel on the cheek, and she faked embarrassment. Then I told her about a Hileman family custom.

"Well, you kids, everybody has to kiss the cook," my father would say whenever we had eaten everything on the table. My mother always squealed a little when my father kissed her, and then my brother and I took our turns. Isabel giggled when I told her about the family fun.

I felt the onset of a chill as Isabel prepared to leave that afternoon and knew a malarial fever would follow. Sensing my discomfort, she promised to bring some quinine the next day.

I waited calmly for the attack. I had been through so many I knew now just what to expect. The chills would be followed by fever that night and I would suffer, but the attacks had fallen into a regular every-other-day pattern, so I knew I would feel better soon. I lay down on my mat and wrapped both Vacher's blanket and mine around me.

I awoke weak from the raging fever and found that Vacher had brewed some coffee and cooked some rice. He broke two eggs over the rice, a favorite breakfast for both of us. The fever had cut my appetite, but I managed to finish the meal. Assured I was feeling better, Vacher left to visit Joe Cheesman.

Two Chinese Huks came by the shack during the morning, found me weak from malaria, and offered to find some quinine. I confidently waved them off, knowing I had a supply coming. The Huks had butchered a carabao and said they would have a hearty soup that evening. They invited me to come to their kitchen and share it.

It was nearly noon when Isabel arrived with fifteen quinine tablets. She had walked into Porac to get them from Dr. Pineda.

"Have you seen Vacher?" I asked.

"Yes. I told Mr. Vacher that I would bring the quinine to you. He understood I want to be the one to come with the medicine. I think he is a very good friend for you, Mee-lard. I like your friends. Many times I wish I had known Mr. Heinzman."

Her sensitivity and compassion continued to impress me, and I found myself wishing she would put her hand on my brow as she had the day before with the onset of the malarial chill.

I sat on the rung of the ladder with Isabel leaning against my knees. I ran my fingers through the shiny black hair that cascaded over her shoulder.

"Hey, you guys, hold it right there. I want a picture of that."

We all laughed at Vacher's gentle teasing as he walked up the trail.

"Now, you be sure to take your medicine, Mee-lard," Isabel said as she prepared to leave. "I will check on you so you do not forget."

She turned to Vacher.

"Mr. Vacher, yet today did you see Mr. Main and Nieves?"

"Nope, haven't seen them. Joe and I have been busy making plans to form a guerrilla band."

I cringed at the thought of the hotheaded French-American and the eccentric old man planning together to form a guerrilla unit.

When Isabel was gone, Vacher pulled out a paper bag with some dobie cigarettes in it. He lit one and handed it to me.

"Pretty sharp little gal," he said. "You'd damn well better hang on to her."

"If I'm going to hang on to her, I better quit thinking about the guerrillas. She's dead set against them. She even wants her brother to quit the Huks."

"I can't blame her," Vacher said. "Those Chinks and Filipino kids have about the same finesse as a shittin' bull."

I told Vacher about the Huk invitation to have stew that night.

"Well, they're not all bad," he said. "Guess I'll go up to their cook shack and hang around a while."

"Bring me some stew," I said. "I think I can handle a little tonight."

Vacher returned in less than a hour carrying steamed rice wrapped in a banana leaf and an MJB coffee can filled with hot stew. I ate with relish and fell asleep immediately. The malaria of the previous night had left me weak and exhausted.

Chapter Twenty-six

I could smell coffee brewing when I woke the next morning and was grateful to Joe Cheesman for the birthday gift. Vacher had cooked some rice and steamed eggs, and I ate, knowing it was important to eat when I could because the fever would return that afternoon. As we ate Vacher and I talked.

"Malleri asked me if we'd like to buy a horse from him and make *tapa*," Vacher said. *Tapa* was the Tagalog word for dried meat. "He said he'd sell us one for fifty pesos, and we could sign a voucher for it."

"That's a damned good idea, but be sure the voucher includes the salt and vinegar we need to cure the meat."

After Vacher left to find Malleri, Jack Jordan and José Montemayor, Isabel's brother, stopped at the hut. I had not met them before, but it was they who had found me unconscious on the trail and carried me to the Jordan farm.

I noticed now that José had his sister's good looks. He had been a high school athlete and eagerly told me about his baseball experiences. He said he was a pitcher with a good fastball.

"I always strike almost everyone out," he said.

When José finished talking about baseball, I thanked him for his help on the trail.

"You were very, very sick, Mr. Hileman," José said. "I think you would not be here if I did not come to you that day."

"You're probably right, José. I don't know how to thank you."

"Oh, it is okay," José replied. "I know that my sister likes you, and for that only I am liking to help you."

José had been eyeing my forty-five-caliber Colt in the worn holster hanging from a peg in the corner of the room.

"Do you have a pistol?"

José shook his head.

"Take it down and hand it to me," I said, "but do not take it from the holster."

I gently pulled the gun out, removed the clip, and checked the chamber before handing it to José to examine.

"Would you like to have a gun like that someday?" I asked.

"Oh, yes sir, it is my desire to have a gun like that, but it is so many pesos I cannot buy one. I am so sorry."

"Well, José, I think I'll just give you this one."

As soon as the words came out, I questioned the wisdom of my generosity. How would I explain such a thing to Isabel? I could not ask José to return it, however, so I let it pass, hoping he would not tell his sister where he got the gun.

José and Jack told me that there were twenty Huks in Pasbul, and a hundred fifty more would arrive the next day.

"Would you not like to join the Huks, Mr. Hileman?" José asked.

Isabel had forewarned me they would ask me to become a part of their organization, so I was prepared for the suggestion. At one time I had thought about fighting as a guerrilla, but joining the communist Huks was a commitment I was unwilling to make.

"Maybe someday, but right now I'm not feeling very good."

I was careful to make no commitment, but neither did I want to antagonize the two young Filipinos.

The thought of one hundred fifty more Huks in the barrio created an air of uncertainty. I thought about leaving the area, remembering that Dr. Pineda left when the first ones had come. The doctor preferred living in Porac where the Japanese were in control rather than subject his family to the presence of the Huks.

With José proudly carrying his new Colt pistol, he and Jack left the shack for Pasbul. A few minutes later Vacher came in and said he had made a deal with Malleri, and we could make *tapa*. Malleri would bring a horse from Del Carmen in the morning and had agreed to supply the salt and vinegar. By making and storing jerky for future use, we could begin to take control of our food situation. The plan appealed to both of us.

Malleri came up the trail the next morning with a small horse which was led behind the shack where Vacher shot it with his pistol. They cut its throat and hoisted it up on a tree limb with a light rope. Vacher borrowed Malleri's bolo and gutted the horse. He skinned it and handed the pelt to Malleri.

The Filipino, who had brought a neighbor to witness the signing, presented a voucher with the terms of sale.

"What about the salt and vinegar?" I asked.

Malleri said he would go to his house and get it. Vacher and I signed the voucher, and Malleri left.

No sooner had we begun to cut the meat into thin strips than big greenish-blue flies made their appearance and hovered over the carcass. I covered the meat with leaves, but that did not seem to discourage the pests.

"Go up to Malleri's shack and tell that son of a bitch to hurry before this meat goes bad," Vacher said anxiously.

I went to Malleri's house and found it empty. I asked a neighbor if he had seen Benito.

"No, sir," the neighbor said. "There are Japanese on the way to the barrio, and Benito said he must go to Del Carmen to be with his family."

I stood for a moment in stunned disbelief. Then, realizing we had been deceived by the Filipino, I surged with anger and ran down the barrio street to see if I could catch up with Malleri, but he was gone. I recognized one of the Huks and asked if he had seen Mr. Malleri.

"Yes," the Huk said. "He was riding one of his horses when he left."

I asked a young boy if he knew how to make *tapa* and if he knew where we could get some salt and vinegar.

"But, sir," he said, "with the war we do not have salt and vinegar."

Furious, I started back to our shack, knowing Vacher would share my anger.

"Let's go to Del Carmen and get the bastard!" Vacher shouted in disgust.

He jammed Malleri's bolo into the ground and cursed the Filipino unmercifully.

"What about the Japs? Are they on their way to Pasbul?" he asked.

"No, but do you know what they told me in the barrio?"

"Shit no," Vacher said. "How the hell would I know? I wasn't with you."

I was prepared for Vacher's outburst and ignored it as I continued.

"They told me that the Japanese are afraid to come to Pasbul now because the Huks have more men coming in the morning. They say they will kill any Japs who come here."

Vacher's attention returned to the butchered horse.

"Well, shit," he said. "I'm not going to stand here with my thumb up my ass and let all this meat rot. Let's roast the liver."

We cut some green sticks, sliced the liver in strips, and roasted them over a cooking fire. Then we buried the already rotting carcass.

Over the next few days, my malaria was brought under control, thanks to the quinine Isabel brought from Porac. When I regained my strength, Vacher suggested I should meet Joe Cheesman.

He had talked a lot about Cheesman, but my malaria had kept me close to the shack and I had not yet met the old American. I looked forward to the meeting as we started toward the Porac River, crossed it, and came to a fork in the trail. Turning north would take us to the Jordan farm, but Vacher turned south. A short distance from the river we came to the shack where the Cheesman family was hiding out.

"There's the old bastard, stretched out sound asleep on his hammock," Vacher said.

I could see a slight, lean American on the rattan hammock suspended between two trees behind the shack. An old brown dog slept underneath the hammock. Vacher nudged Cheesman on the rump with his toe.

"Vacher, you son of a bitch!"

He sat upright and stared at us. "Don't you know you can get yourself killed sneaking up on a fellow like that? You're lucky as hell I didn't grab that bolo over there and castrate you right on the spot."

"Listen, you old fart, all you do is sleep," Vacher grinned. "That's a hell of a way to pull guard if you ask me."

"Well, ain't nobody asking you, and I wasn't asleep. I was just resting my eyes." Cheesman stretched and scratched his ribs. "Anyway, ain't no shittin' Jap going to sneak up on me and catch me asleep. I can smell those slant-eyed bastards a couple of kilometers down the trail. Who's this?"

"This is Hileman, the guy I was telling you about."

"That's what I figured. He wants to join the guerrillas, huh?"

"Shit, I don't know," Vacher said. "You'll have to ask him. I've learned to speak for myself only."

Cheesman offered us Lucky Strikes as an attractive woman came from the house. I was introduced to Loring. She seemed much too young to be Cheesman's wife, but Vacher had prepared me for the age difference between them.

"Where's that kid of yours?" Vacher asked. "I want Hileman to meet him."

I had heard a lot from Vacher about Roy Cheesman who was talented in both music and art. His father called, and the boy came from the shack and joined us.

"Would you like to see my drawings?" he asked.

I nodded, and he ran back into the house to get his scrapbook, which was filled with pencil drawings. The detail and shading were amazingly well done, and I agreed with Vacher that he was unusually gifted. I was especially impressed with the two portraits of Vacher. He had captured the attitude of self-pride which so characterized him.

"When this goddamn war is over, he's going to get some education and be a real artist," his father said proudly.

Loring served coffee and a sweet coconut-sugar confection, and Joe continued giving us Lucky Strikes. As we smoked he talked about himself, his businesses before the war, and about life under the Japanese occupation. We visited until late afternoon.

Before we left he showed us an organizational chart for his proposed guerrilla unit. It included the names of two other Americans living in the area, Hugh McCoy and Pierce Wade. His intent in showing it was to impress and recruit me, but, thinking of Isabel's statements about guerrillas, I let it pass without comment.

As August 1942 drew to a close, I asked Vacher if I could borrow his Parker 51 fountain pen to mark my calendar. By my calculations, it had been three weeks since my birthday, and five since we had left Main. I figured it was Thursday, August 27. I returned the pen to

Vacher who stuck it in the sawali siding next to his sleeping mat.

We were awakened several times that night by dogs barking in the barrio, but with the large force of Huks moving into Pasbul, we dismissed the barking as normal.

The sky was just turning light when I awoke from a restless sleep. I lay on my mat hearing only Vacher's rhythmic breathing and the chirping of birds. Suddenly, with no warning, an explosion shattered the predawn quiet. I immediately recognized the sound of a Japanese knee mortar, followed by twenty-five-caliber machine-gun fire which sounded like ripping canvas. Rifles returned the fire. The Japanese had ambushed the Huks, and a pitched battle was taking place, apparently at the barrio entrance.

I jumped up, grabbed my rifle, and threw my new shorts and some eating utensils into a burlap bag. We habitually slept in our clothes as an emergency precaution. My feet had become toughened, so I was not concerned about shoes. Vacher jumped into his old shoes and grabbed his rifle. We dove out the back window and slid down the bank to the creek.

We could hear rifle shots, mortar explosions, and lots of yelling, both in Japanese and Tagalog. We had to get out of Pasbul and fast. Homeless and with nowhere else to go, we headed toward Main's shack in Pio.

"You know, I feel kind of shitty crawling back to old Bill," Vacher said. "How about you?"

"Hell no. When you get shot out of your house, any old port will do."

I was surprised to find myself looking forward to seeing Main. Ernie had told us he was living in the shack by the river where the Filipinos had taken us the night they moved us from the Gumain Canyon. When we arrived there, I was struck by the improvements Main and the Filipinos had made on the shack. The hut was empty, so Vacher and I sat on the porch and waited for Main's return.

"You know what?" Vacher said. "I'll bet my back pay Bill's gone into the hills. Nieves probably hid him in some cozy hideaway when they heard about the ambush in Pasbul this morning."

Main returned that evening, and for the first time in five weeks the three of us were back together. We had many things to talk about that night, not only the Japanese attack and events of that day, but of the weeks we had been separated.

As we talked, I readily pictured Main hiding in the hills that morning while Vacher and I had sat exposed on the steps of the hut. His consistent fear and his cautious nature were irritating, but I could not help but envy and admire the practical way he had assumed control of his situation. He described the lean-to he and Nieves had built for an emergency hiding place. It was well hidden and was complete with a thatched roof and emergency supplies.

Vacher and I had barely escaped with our lives that day while Main had confidently spent a quiet day hiding with his girl. Now, despite our differences and the friction of the past, the three of us were together again.

Chapter Twenty-seven

Rain. Unremitting rain poured from heavy clouds which blackened the August sky. Its incessancy cast a chill over everything.

Confined to the small shack, the earlier frictions soon returned, and the three of us grated constantly on one another's nerves. More and more, we grew apart as the walls of the shack closed in on us. The stimulating conversations that had cemented the relationship between Vacher and me were again a thing of the past. Talk now was generally limited to criticism of one another's personal habits. Vacher and Main bickered constantly, and at times I was as irritating to them as they were to each other. I found Vacher overbearing and Main's fastidiousness irritating. I hated the constant friction and wanted to leave, but did not know where to go. Perhaps, I thought, I could go north in search of Kinder, Henderson, and Wicks. Foot travel during the rainy season was hazardous, however, so I was forced to remain confined in the loathsome shack. The hut provided shelter from the rain, but the weather imprisoned us, adding daily to our hostility towards each other. We planted a garden in an effort to overcome the boredom and frustration, but the rains washed it away. Nothing we did was sufficient to alleviate the growing tension. We found ourselves in a miserable situation, even though our basic needs were met.

Filipinos continued bringing us food, so we did not suffer the hollow pains of hunger. The diet was strictly Filipino, however, and we had grown tired of it. It consisted primarily of rice, eggplant, kamotes, and other local vegetables. The Filipinos brought us snails, crabs, and small fish they caught in the creek. We scalded the snails, broke off the end of the shell, and sucked out the insides. The small crabs were scalded and cracked, and the uncleaned fish were roasted whole over the campfire. We ate the heads, tails, bones, and all with rice. Occasionally the Filipinos brought corn, and we buried the unshucked ears in coals and roasted them. It was good, but I always wished I could coat the ears with butter. Our diet was nourishing, but monotonously bland.

Whenever short breaks in the weather permitted, we had a steady parade of Filipino visitors. One, Carling Fejardo, seemed to have taken a special interest in us. A slender, good-looking young man, Fejardo constantly asked questions about what we were doing and our future plans. He appeared to be friendly, but seemed to be keeping unusually close tabs on us. He never talked about his work, except that it was somewhere outside Barrio Pio.

Rare sunny days also allowed opportunity for us to visit the girls who had become so important in our lives. Isabel's mother feared the Japanese and worried about the consequences of my visits. I needed Isabel's company, however, so it was a great relief when Mrs. Montemayor accepted me and greeted my visits with a smile. Her old Spanish house, although in a state of deterioration, fascinated me. Its original stateliness was still evident, and it was easy to imagine its beauty fifty or sixty years earlier. I especially enjoyed the courtyard where Isabel and I spent hours talking. Stone walls formed three sides of the enclosure, the fourth side led into the house. Ornamental trees and shrubs flourished, and vines climbed up lattices. Across from the kitchen, near the courtyard gate, were two stone benches. It was here that we sat in quiet conversation.

I asked once about Isabel's father and was told only, "He's been gone a long time." The time was not right to press for more information.

Visits with Isabel were the one bright spot in my life. She gave me purpose and a will and always seemed to understand my needs. When I was down, she lifted me up with a smile. She was the one person with whom I could share my innermost feelings, especially those concerning my relationship with Main and Vacher. After my visits with Isabel I dreaded going back to the black cooking pot, the musty hut, and the constant bickering.

I knew Main and Vacher bickered when I was gone, and when I returned the three of us bickered. On days when the sun broke through, our moods improved somewhat, and occasionally we sat on the porch and listened to Main's stories of Old Ned. I still enjoyed them. Then the rain would return, darkness would close in from all sides, and our hateful relationship would resume.

From August through November, the relationship grew steadily worse. For all three of us, it was a sad, depressing time. Our monotonous existence and close quarters made life together almost unbearable. There were a few occasions, however, when we were able to sense a hint of the former camaraderie. On evening visits to the Jordan house, we gathered under the old guava tree and sang. A favorite song was the Hawaiian ballad, "I Want To Go Back To My Little Grass Shack." We would sing it and laugh because we were already living in a little grass shack. On those evenings we cut up worn automobile tires lying around, set them on fire when the mosquitoes came out, and continued our singing around the flames. Vacher and I taught Main the words to "Deep Purple" and "Stardust," but we especially enjoyed his rich tenor voice when he sang "San Antonio Rose."

Throughout those late months of 1942, Vacher and I went through periods of malaria and dysentery. Staying clean was a problem, as all we had for bathing was water heated in a small bucket. We continued to resent Main who never seemed to get sick and took such obvious pride in the soap and new razor blades Nieves brought him.

My beard became scraggly, and lice moved in. While Vacher and I visited one day at Cheesman's, Loring's brother who was a barber was there. He sharpened up his razor and gave me a good shave and haircut. I felt like a new man and could hardly wait to see Isabel who had been pleading with me to get rid of my beard.

As the tension and conflicts increased among the three of us during those months, we learned of another factor which added to our stress. Japanese patrols had begun actively searching for fugitive Americans in the area, and we had to depend on the Filipinos to keep us posted. It had been necessary several times to grab up our possessions, throw them into a sack, and run to the hillside shelter Main and Neives had built. Sometimes we spent the night there, wet, cold, and miserable.

"I have heard, sir," a breathless Alberto Luna warned us one day, "the *Hapon* are leaving Porac and will take the back trail to Pasbul. You must hide."

We gathered our belongings and moved up the hill to the hidden shelter. Luna returned to the barrio, but came again later that afternoon.

"The *Hapon* are now returning from Barrio Pasbul, sir. I am thinking they are now going up our trail." He said twelve soldiers had been in Pasbul. Luna joined Vacher and Main in the shelter, and I stationed myself at a vantage point overlooking the river.

As I rolled a cigarette, I caught some movement out of the corner of my eye. I adjusted my binoculars and saw five Japanese soldiers emerge from the brush, move up the trail, and then turn north just before they reached the shack where we were living.

The soldiers wore steel helmets, which struck me as unusual. I had seen them only with cloth hats, and I wondered what the change in uniform meant. I also wondered about the other seven who Luna said had been in Pasbul. I watched them go on up the trail, laughing and talking among themselves, giving the appearance they were on a casual walk. When they were out of sight, I ran to the hidden shelter, told the others about them, and returned to my vantage point.

An hour later, the five soldiers came back, crossed the river, and disappeared.

"It will be okay now," Luna said. "They will return to Porac."

During the next few weeks, Japanese patrols passed near our shack several times, but it was well hidden and they never found it. I often lay in the brush watching the patrols go by, and then waited for their return. The muddy, isolated terrain made patrols miserable for the Japanese soldiers, but it also made it possible for us to avoid capture. We learned to be extremely careful about footprints, noise, and smoke from our cooking fires. As long as the torrential rains fell, the patrols did not come, but when the seasonal rains began to abate in October, Japanese patrols came frequently to both Pio and Pasbul.

Gradually I learned more about the increase of Japanese patrols in the area. Colonel Yashima, the commander of the Japanese secret police stationed in San Fernando, was dedicated to capturing Americans who were still on the loose. Filipino collaborators had given him the names and approximate locations of most of the American fugitives in Pampanga Province, including Vacher, Main, and me. Yashima and his men had questioned Dr. Pineda about us several times, but had not yet put much pressure on the Filipinos. We were told Yashima was about forty, spoke little English, and liked American cigarettes.

I went again to Barrio Pasbul in hopes of talking to Dr. Pineda, but he was in Porac. On my return I stopped at Malleri's shack where Vacher and I had lived when the Japanese attacked the Huks. To my surprise, I found Vacher's Parker 51 fountain pen still stuck in the sawali wall. I took the pen back to Vacher.

With the continuing rain and the turbulent October winds, we saw little of the girls, a factor which only added to our depression. Forced to spend so much time together, we complained more and more about the lousy food and one another's personal habits. We accused one another of not covering personal waste. Main's singing, whistling, and muttering to himself became increasingly irritating to Vacher and me. Vacher constantly taunted Main about his fear of the Japanese with remarks like, "You're afraid of your own shadow." Sometimes I hated them both, but other times I felt each was a friend. The uncertainty of life and health irreparably eroded our ability to live together. And then came the banana incident.

A Filipino brought us a bunch of green bananas, fourteen of them. Main took them to the loft of our shack and buried them in the large rice basket where they would ripen in a few days.

The next day a check showed there were only thirteen bananas.

"Who took the banana?" Vacher asked. Main and I denied any knowledge of the missing fruit.

The following day I climbed the ladder and checked the bananas. There were twelve.

"Which one of you guys took the damn bananas?" I asked.

"I didn't take them," Main said.

"I haven't even been up there," Vacher answered.

We maliciously accused one another of having taken the bananas. The ugly disagreement continued for the next few days, and bananas kept disappearing. When only nine bananas remained, we divided them and ate them, even though they were green. Bananas were plentiful in the area, but the incident of distrust had further ruptured our relationship. I knew I had not taken the bananas and decided I could not stand the pressure of living with Main and Vacher anymore. I would leave at the first possible opportunity.

Thanksgiving was approaching, and the Cheesmans invited us for a holiday dinner. Young Roy had caught a duck in the river, and Mrs. Cheesman roasted it. She prepared fried rice with shrimp, boiled rice, kamotes, and salad. The meal was topped off with a chocolate cake. Yet even on this special occasion, the tensions between us hung heavy.

Joe Cheesman, fifty-seven years old and with no military experience, talked at length about his plan for a guerrilla force. With the written authorization he had somehow been given, he was determined to put his plan into action. He had drawn up a chain of command, and it included the three of us. Main and I listened as Vacher discussed the proposal with Cheesman. The plans struck me as rather amateurish, and neither Main nor I wanted anything to do with them. We returned to the shack, but Vacher remained behind.

"Vacher's a stupid son of a bitch for even talking with Cheesman about guerrillas," Main said. "That damn Cheesman's nothing but an old dobie citizen and doesn't know what the hell he's doing."

I knew Main was right.

When Vacher returned he taunted Main about joining the guerrillas. Then the banana incident came up again, and as they continued to argue, I took off, walked up the hill, and sat down on a log. The time had come for me to separate from them.

The next day I went to see Isabel.

"I've got to leave," I told her.

"Where will you go?"

"I don't know, but I won't go anywhere without telling you."

"Will you take me with you?"

Tears filled her eyes as she looked up at me.

"Mee-lard, you know I would go."

I wanted her with me, but for the moment I had no answer.

Chapter Twenty-eight

Rain fell all afternoon. Main and Vacher slept in opposite corners of the shack while I sat alone on the porch. The banana episode was past, but the feelings of hate and mistrust persisted.

I watched the water run off the thatched roof and splatter on the muddy ground. The unwashed rice pot sat on the porch, and I scraped the remaining kernels onto a banana leaf. As I halfheartedly munched on the dry kernels, I heard someone coming up the trail. A dark-complexioned man appeared, shirtless and barefoot, wearing only a straw hat and shorts. He carried his personal effects in a small basket, and when he saw me he stopped.

"Hi," I said. "You look like a drowned rat. You better come in out of the rain."

"Thanks. That sounds good."

"I'm Millard Hileman. Who're you?"

"Margarito Agridaño."

"Are you a Filipino?" I asked, thinking there was something different about him. The man smiled.

"You're just like everyone else around here," he said. "I'm a Mexican from Los Angeles. I was in the Thirty-first Infantry."

He joined me on the sheltered porch and talked about the past several months. I thought he was somewhat evasive about his time in the hills, but did not press him. The Mexican-American looked like a Filipino and was delighted with his success in walking past Japanese guards, bowing and moving on without a problem. His health was good, and he spoke the Tagalog dialect.

"Where you headed?" I asked.

"Zambales."

"How come?"

"There's some USAFFE guerrillas over there," Agridaño said. USAFFE was the acronym for United States Armed Forces, Far East. My visitor said that two American colonels, Peter Calyer of the 31st Infantry and Gyles Merrill of the 26th Cavalry, commanded the guerrilla group.

"I'm going over there to join them."

I suddenly recognized this as my chance to break away from Main and Vacher.

"Sounds like a good idea," I said. "I think I'll go with you."

I went into the shack and hurriedly gathered my belongings while Main and Vacher continued sleeping. I thought about leaving a note, but shrugged my shoulders, muttered, "The hell with them," and walked out.

I told Agridaño I had to stop in Barrio Pio for a few minutes. Isabel was not home, so I attempted to tell her mother I was leaving and I would come back to see Isabel soon. Mrs. Montemayor spoke little English, and even though she smiled and nodded, I was not certain she had understood me.

It was about 3 P.M. when we left the Montemayor house. We followed the trail to the Gumain River, waded across south of Pasbul, and continued on a bullcart road for two or three kilometers before heading into the hills. Occasionally we ran into Filipinos. When we explained our plan to join the guerrillas, they nodded their approval.

The trip into Zambales Province would take eight or nine hours. We had started late, and soon darkness was settling in. Agridaño and I stopped at a small farm where the owner welcomed us, fed us supper, and let us sleep near the house. In the morning he gave us breakfast and some bananas. We expressed our appreciation for his hospitality and departed.

Following a Negrito trail, we moved into the higher elevations of the Zambales Mountains where the vegetation became a dense jungle and trees obscured the sky. The jungle had seemed a hostile place when I had traveled through it with Vacher, Main, and Orlo during our escape from Bataan. Now I felt almost a part of its lush, natural beauty. The weather was good, neither hot nor humid, and as we walked along barefoot, we became aware of the abundance of wildlife. We passed several wallows made by wild pigs, and signs of deer seemed to be everywhere. We crossed the summit, found a more-used trail, and started down into Zambales Province.

When we reached a mountain stream, we sat down on a log to rest, roll cigarettes, and eat the bananas and guavas from Agridaño's basket. After all the tension back at the shack with Main and Vacher, I felt a sense of freedom and relief. I was certain, however, I would return to Pio soon to be sure Isabel understood what I was doing. Agridaño and I rested for some time, neither of us having any great sense of urgency.

It was late afternoon when we resumed our journey. White foam swirled around large boulders in the stream, the swift current and high water giving evidence of the rainy season just ending. As I jumped from one to another I slipped and struck my right knee. Pain surged through my leg.

"Oh, my God, I think I've broken my knee." I dragged my leg as Agridaño helped me to shore.

"How bad is it?" he asked.

"I don't know, but I've got to keep going or I won't be able to walk for a week."

The pain was excruciating, and I sat down on a log. Facing the stream with our backs to the jungle, I was suddenly aware of the presence of someone else.

"Margarito, there's somebody behind us," I whispered. "Turn around real quick."

At the edge of the jungle a Negrito, holding a bow and arrow, stood watching us. The arrow's tip had long barbs and a razor-sharp point, the type Negritos had designed to shoot Japanese. Agridaño slowly walked over to him, and using a combination of Tagalog and sign language, was able to make him understand we were looking for the USAFFE guerrillas. When Agridaño returned to me, he said the Negrito was with the American guerrillas, and he would lead us to their camp. Agridaño found a walking stick for me, and I hobbled painfully behind them. Fortunately, the camp was nearby.

It was not at all as we had imagined. There was little activity and little resemblance to the military base we had expected. Small Filipino-style huts surrounded the central area. To one side, rice bubbled in a steaming caldron suspended over a fire tended by a Filipino. He said someone had shot a deer earlier in the day and there would be meat for supper. We looked forward to a hearty meal.

I saw no Americans anywhere, but a Filipino assured us we would be allowed to see the American officers soon. That bothered me. I had not seen an officer since fleeing Bataan seven months earlier, and now camp officers did not even acknowledge my presence.

"Come and eat," someone called.

Agridaño and I sat on the ground with the Filipinos and enjoyed deer meat, rice, kamotes, and eggplant.

"Where are the officers?" I asked.

"We will serve them in their quarters," a Filipino answered.

"Where's that?"

"Their quarters are in another part of the camp, Joe."

We saw no Americans all evening, but were told the officers knew we were in camp, and one had arranged for a doctor to look at my leg.

At dusk a Negrito led us to a grass-and-bamboo shack with a dirt floor just off the trail. I spread my tattered blanket on the ground and lay down. The Negrito lit the small lamp, a wick floating in coconut oil. I waited for the doctor.

In about an hour an old Filipino woman came into the shack. Wrinkles were carved in her face, the marks of age and harsh living. She carried banana leaves, seashells, coconut oil, and a large candle, and she wore a necklace of garlic toes. The old woman looked at my leg and muttered while Agridaño tried to translate. She agreed the swollen, stiff leg was very sick, but she would fix it. I had expected a medical doctor, not a witch doctor.

A small boy who accompanied the old woman lit the candle. She poured coconut oil into a seashell and heated it over the flame, dipped a rag into the hot oil, bathed my knee with it, then rubbed garlic on it. As she worked she chanted in a kind of mumbo-jumbo fashion I had never heard before. She poured hot oil onto a banana leaf, added some smashed garlic, and wrapped the leaf around my knee. The old woman mumbled some words directly to my knee, turned, and left.

"What did she say?" I asked Agridaño.

"How the hell would I know? This is all new to me."

I got up with the assistance of my walking stick and went outside to urinate, carefully holding the banana leaf in place over my knee. When I returned, I blew out the lamp and went to sleep.

Late that night the old woman returned and repeated the entire ritual, again moaning and chanting as she worked on my knee. Wanting only to sleep, I became impatient with the witch-doctor routine. She completed the procedure, blew out the lamp, and left again.

Camp noise woke me in the morning. A Filipino entered the shack and said Colonel Calyer would see us after breakfast. I went outside, emptied my bladder, and splashed some cold water on my face. Then I suddenly realized I felt no pain and looked down to see the swelling in my knee had completely disappeared. I was grateful for my well-being, but had an eerie sense of wonder as I realized the old witch doctor's treatment had been effective.

A Filipino led us to Colonel Calyer's shack. Colonel Calyer, a graduate of West Point, and Colonel Merrill, from a southern military academy, were career officers, part of the old Army. Neither Agridaño nor I saluted, although we answered their questions with *sir*. They quizzed us, asking about our escape, our time in the hills, and what we wanted to do. We said simply we wanted to join the guerrillas. Calyer asked me if my rifle was in good condition, and Merrill pressed me with other military questions. I felt I was getting the runaround, and I resented the arrogant attitude of the officers. Merrill asked about my leg, and I said it was better.

"We cannot take any chances on you," he said. "We need people who can travel. You will be housed with a nearby farmer until you are needed," he said with the authority of an officer giving orders to the rank and file.

The colonel handed us signed vouchers, and we were dismissed.

CHAPTER TWENTY-NINE

A Filipino guide led Agridaño and me to a farm a short distance from the camp and twelve kilometers east of the town of San Marcelino. The colonels had made prior arrangements with the farmer, Fernando Esquibel, to house any Americans who needed refuge while they regained their health and strength. They had promised that the U.S. government would pay him after the war for boarding Americans. Agridaño and I signed the vouchers provided by the colonels and gave them to Fernando.

The Esquibel's small house sat in a clearing in the Zambales foothills. Its remoteness was marked by a jungle-covered ridge which rose behind the farm. Fernando raised sugarcane, rice, and garden vegetables, and farther back in the hills he had a small patch of pineapple. His farm was twenty hectares, about fifty acres. He had seven carabao, four Spanish ponies, six pigs, and a flock of chickens. Livestock in the Philippine provinces was a measure of wealth.

Fernando was cordial, and in a very short time we felt we knew him well. He spoke English, but his wife Eufemia did not. There were three children in the family, a daughter, Consolacion, about eight, a five-year-old son, Juliano, and a baby girl, Leonila. We had opportunity to get acquainted with the family as we joined them for their midday meal soon after our arrival. They were cordial toward us and showed no apprehension or reluctance in accepting us as guests in their home.

"You will live very well here, and you will help on the farm," Fernando told us. "There is much work to do."

He went to great lengths to explain how far behind he was and all that needed to be done. Then he rolled out straw mats and said, "You will rest now." Nothing interfered with siesta time.

I set out to gather eggs the next morning. Chickens ran loose on the farm and laid their eggs everywhere. I watched where the hens went, but Juliano and Consolacion followed me, and somehow always beat me to the eggs. It became a game.

I sat quietly watching as one hen went under the house and hopped into a pasteboard box. The children joined me, and all three of us watched the hen in eager anticipation.

As she was about to lay her egg, Juliano ran over, grabbed her, and pried the egg out with a stick. I knew then I had been outmatched, and we all laughed together.

Several days passed and there had been no word from the two American colonels who the local people called Colonel Corn and Colonel Kamote, a reflection on their demand for local produce. As a potential guerrilla wanting some action, I returned to the camp only to be told by a Filipino that I needed an appointment to see Colonel Calyer. I barged past the guard and into the colonel's shack.

"Sir, can I talk with you?" I said. "I'm still interested in joining the USAFFE guerrillas."

"Just stay with the family you're with," the colonel said. "There's no place here for you right now. We're short of food, and I cannot take on extra people."

"How in the hell do you expect me to be a guerrilla?"

"I don't expect you to be a guerrilla until I tell you. When I want you, I'll send for you."

Calyer's answer angered me.

"Is that the way it is, sir?"

"That's the way it is."

"In that case when you call on me, I may not be ready to come."

"Just remember, private, you're in the army!"

"I may be in the army, but you're not my commanding officer."

"I am the ranking officer in this area!" Calyer's voice revealed his agitation.

"So what? That doesn't mean a damn thing to me!"

I stormed out, vowing never to go back.

Two other American enlisted men, Hank Winslow and Earl Oatman, had been sent by the guerrilla colonels to a farm not far from the Esquibel's. I went to visit them and was astonished at their account of the forced march out of Bataan and their escape from it. They had worked their way through the jungle to the Fassoth Camp where they had rested and regained their strength. Many lost, sick, and tired American fugitives from Bataan had been given refuge by William and Martin Fassoth. However, the Japanese had located the camp, and it had been raided on September 26, 1942. Oatman and Winslow had crawled out a window and hidden when gunfire shattered the darkness.

They, too, had set out for Zambales Province, thinking they would join the guerrillas. Oatman was barefoot, and the razor-sharp cogan grass had cut his feet. Their experience with Colonels Calyer and Merrill had been similar to mine, and they had been sent to live with the Barone family about a quarter mile from the Esquibel farm.

"They told us they didn't need us, they didn't have enough food for us, and that we should go on about our business."

Winslow's disgust with the American officers was obvious as he spoke. They had decided, as I had, not to become involved with the guerrilla organization.

After my first two weeks in Zambales, I was confident my knee would no longer bother me and decided to go back to Pampanga to visit Isabel. Fernando did not want me to leave, fearing I would be captured by a Japanese patrol. Still, remembering my vow not to be dominated by Filipinos, I took off in mid-December, promising to return in three days. During the eight-hour journey, I thought about Isabel's statements concerning the guerrillas. Since my meetings with Colonels Merrill and Calyer, I had no intention of joining them, and I knew she would approve my decision.

Even barefoot, the walk through the mountains was easy. Warm weather and a peaceful day added to the ease and pleasantness of the trip. I entered the Plains of Pampanga, crossed the Gumain River, and arrived at Barrio Pio about supper time. I proceeded cautiously as I surveyed the area before approaching Isabel's house.

I was greatly relieved to find her at home, and we sat in the courtyard and talked all evening. She told me the Huks had been active in the area, and she was deeply concerned for her brother José. I related my experience with the guerrillas in Zambales and my decision not to join them. If something came up where I could be of real assistance, however, I would possibly change my mind.

"Will you be visiting Mr. Vacher and Mr. Main while you are in Pio?" Isabel asked.

"No. I am here only to see you. I don't want to talk to them now."

Isabel and her mother invited me to spend the night at their house. Early the next morning Mrs. Montemayor prepared breakfast, and as we ate, Isabel surprised me.

"Mee-lard," she said, "will you take me with you? I do not want you to leave again."

I looked at this gentle, pleading girl and knew I could not subject her to the dangers of a fugitive life.

"No, Isabel. I cannot take you. You will be safer here with your mother."

"Then if I cannot go with you, I will go to Manila because there is a college there."

Her words only deepened my feelings for the beautiful, young *mestiza* who was trapped in a hopeless world of war.

I returned to Zambales and was greeted with the news that Euphemia was pregnant.

"My wife, he is going to have a boy," Fernando announced proudly.

Agridaño and I joined Fernando in his rice harvest. The mountain rice grown in the Zambales foothills was a dryland crop, not grown in paddies as it was in the plains. By American standards, the harvest was a primitive operation. The stalks were cut with sickles, tied into bundles, placed on sleds, and hauled by carabao into the threshing yard. There a sturdy, wooden post was anchored in the hard-packed ground. A crossbar, fastened at the center to a circular ring, extended its arms from the center post. Spanish ponies were harnessed to the ends of the pole, and as they walked around in circles, we scattered the stalks under their hooves. The unhulled rice, called *palay*, fell from the stalks. We grabbed the trampled straw and beat it on the ground, dislodging any remaining *palay*. Husks still surrounded the kernels as we swept the rice into baskets. The baskets of *palay* were carried up a ladder to a scaffold eight or ten feet high and poured out so the wind could blow the chaff away. The *palay* was then stored.

Wealthy farmers took their rice to one of the large mills where, for a percentage of the crop, the processing was done for them. Joe Cheesman and the Fassoth brothers had both operated such mills before the war. On small farms like Esquibel's, owners milled their own rice. As the daily portion was measured out, Eufemia pounded the *palay* with a large pestle, breaking the hulls loose. She tossed and swirled the rice in large, shallow baskets, allowing the wind to blow away the hulls and other impurities. The daily task was considered women's work.

Time dragged for Agridaño and me, so when Fernando said there would be a New Year's Eve celebration in Barrio Cinemar, we looked forward to a break in the monotony. Fernando asked me on the day before the festivities to go into the barrio with him to help set up tables. Although my feet had been toughened by months of barefoot walking, I found I was not equal to my Filipino friend. Fernando moved deftly along the streambed we followed, but my feet were bruised and sore when we arrived in the barrio.

Throughout my time as a fugitive, I had tried to maintain a low profile. Even when I had visited Pio, I had confined my visits to Isabel's house, avoiding areas where people congregated. Now I was on the main street of a barrio which bustled with activity. *Sari sari* stores, little stands where impoverished Filipino owners bought and resold merchandise, offered snack foods like barbecued chicken and pork. The crudely constructed stands reminded me of children's lemonade stands in the States. I had enjoyed visiting them in the barrios near Clark Field before the war, and seeing them now made me realize how isolated my life had been for nearly a year.

Sore feet were not enough to keep me away from the next day's festivities. Long tables held fruit, vegetables, and piles of rice spread on banana leaves. Both a pig and carabao had been roasted over open pits for the occasion. For that day the war was forgotten and an attitude of laughter and celebration prevailed. The women and young girls, usually barefoot and dressed plainly, wore their best dresses and high-heeled shoes for this traditionally festive day.

The very atmosphere was exciting to me. *Basi,* a native wine made from sugarcane, was available, and in the evening there was dancing.

I was enjoying the hospitality to the fullest when a Filipino runner came with news of a Japanese patrol headed towards the barrio. The local people had developed a series of smoke signals and runners to give warning when the patrols left San Marcelino and were kept abreast of Japanese activity. Agridaño and I, along with the few other American fugitives in the barrio, left hurriedly, returning to the rural farms where we were being hidden. When Fernando came home later, he told us the patrol had not come. Our festive evening had been needlessly cut short.

There was always potential danger, yet the Japanese never patrolled near the Esquibel farm even though it was only about three kilometers from Barrio Cinemar. The patrols made the eight-kilometer journey from San Marcelino to the barrio, but never went beyond.

One Japanese patrol had been ambushed near Barrio Cinemar as it passed through a deep ravine. Filipino guerrillas and Negritos, hidden in the underbrush, opened fire on eighteen Japanese soldiers, killing seventeen. The attack had been led by a Chinese woman whose breast had been cut off by the Japanese. She was widely known as One Tit. The ambush was big news in the area, especially since the Japanese had not come back to punish the Filipinos in Barrio Cinemar. Many Japanese soldiers had been killed with the silent, steel arrows used by Negritos, and apparently the Negrito marksmanship had discouraged them.

In January I helped Fernando with sugarcane harvest. The cane was cut and then squeezed through large, steel, horse-powered rollers. Juice was collected in buckets and cooked in a large caldron. When it reached the consistency of molasses, it was stored in clay jars for future use.

With the end of the cane harvest, the season's work was finished, and again the hours dragged and the days were long and boring. Although Agridaño and I lived at the same farm and shared sleeping quarters, our relationship did not develop into one of real friendship and camaraderie. I found much pleasure, however, in visiting the Barone farm where Winslow and Oatman were living. We spent our time together talking about home, American food, the war, and our own precarious situation. We had become very fond of the Filipinos in the neighborhood and were fascinated by their simple lives and their ingenuity. Winslow, especially, was eager to experience as much of the native culture as possible. He took great pleasure in relating one experience with their inventiveness.

Rufino Barone, Antone's son, had a painful cavity in a molar, and

Winslow was reluctantly persuaded into the role of dentist. A wire with a wooden handle was heated until it glowed red. A wooden block was placed in Rufino's mouth and Winslow stuck the red hot wire into the cavity. Rufino jumped, but moments later the pain was gone. The method was effective.

In another instance Winslow had accompanied a honey-gathering party into the jungle. A Negrito climbed a tree, smoked a bees' nest with a torch, and then cut it down. The comb fell to the jungle floor where everyone ran over to gather honey in bamboo tubes. Then they ate what remained, grubs and all. The Negritos mixed the honey with water and carried it in bamboo tubes when they traveled. Drinking sparingly, the mixture gave them energy on their long mountain treks.

On one of my visits Winslow passed me a bowl containing what looked like shredded coconut mixed with brown sugar. I eagerly helped myself to a generous portion.

"What is this?" The sour taste coated my mouth.

"Fried ants," Winslow replied. He laughed at the look of revulsion he saw on my face. The Filipinos considered the ants a delicacy, and Winslow dipped his fingers into the bowl for another helping.

Antone Barone went to the cockfights in San Marcelino every Sunday. Carrying two cages that resembled suitcases, he took his prize roosters and walked into town.

"I don't wish Antone any bad luck," Winslow said, "but I sure hope one of those roosters meets an untimely death. Then there'll be chicken on the table."

Even with war threatening to impoverish the Philippine provinces, men had not forsaken their favorite pastime. The cocks were raised to fight, and the betting was heavy. Each fight was a struggle-to-death match, with the losing cock ending up in the stew pot. The gratitude Winslow and Oatman felt toward their Filipino benefactor did not extend to hoping for a winning day at the cockfights.

One evening I left the Barone farm just before dusk, and as I walked barefoot along the familiar trail, I heard something in the grass beside me. Glancing to my right I saw a twelve-foot python slithering along, keeping pace with me. I jumped to the side and quickly moved away. Fernando told me the pythons occasionally paced people, but they ate only chickens, eggs, and young pigs on the farms. The big snakes gorged themselves, and then they might not eat again for a couple of weeks.

There were several poisonous snakes in the area. Cobras always traveled in pairs, continuously crisscrossing the paths. I had observed their patterned trails in the dust several times. I saw many coral snakes along the trails with their telltale bright red, yellow, and black bands. The small snakes were slow, but dangerous. I was alert, too, to the presence of poisonous rice snakes. Even though I had always had an aversion toward snakes, I felt no particular fear as I walked the trails barefoot. Snakes were a natural part of life in the Philippines, and I was feeling more and more a part of that life.

As American fugitives we avoided towns and barrios, but on one occasion Winslow, Oatman, and I went into Barrio Cinemar. Clinton Wolfe, an American who had been with Winslow and Oatman when the Japanese raided Fassoth's camp, had arrived at the Barone farm during rice harvest and went with us into the barrio. From the 200th Coast Artillery, Wolfe was a wanderer whose flaming red hair had earned him wide reputation and the nickname Red. Although in his early thirties, Wolfe had false teeth which, combined with a highly developed sense of humor, had been the source of good-natured fun with the primitive Negritos. He had enjoyed their reaction at Barone's farm when he had taken his teeth out and clapped them together. The news about the mysterious feat spread quickly through the area. When we entered the barrio, Negritos excitedly pointed at Wolfe and expectantly began to follow him. Not one to disappoint them, he made a great show of the feat, thoroughly enjoying the attention and the amazement of the primitive people.

Wolfe's sense of humor took an unexpected twist once, however, when he approached one particular Negrito. He had enjoyed mocking them in English, knowing full well they did not understand.

"You sure are a dirty little son of a bitch," he smilingly said. "Don't you ever take a bath?"

"Sir, it is not my custom to take a bath, but I am not a son of a bitch."

His intended victim may have been the only educated, English-speaking Negrito in the area. Wolfe turned as red as his hair, while his companions broke into hysterical laughter, seeing him at the receiving end of one of his own jokes.

In March another rice crop was harvested at the Esquibel farm.

Escape

An estimated 10,000 Americans surrendered when Bataan fell on April 9, 1942.

Millard Hileman

Wally Kinder

Barrio Pasbul where Hileman found refuge.

Dr. Pineda lived in a hut like this.

Dr. Pineda

Ernie Pineda

Orlo Heinzman was buried according to Negrito custom.

Orlo Heinzman

The site on the Gumain River where Orlo Heinzman was buried.

Hileman lived with Fernando Esquibel in a hut like this in rural Zambales.

Col. Peter Calyer

Fernando Esquibel

Surrender

The Cheesman house in Barrio Salu where Hileman surrendered, and Joe Cheesman, inset.

Wendell Morgan

Colonel Yashima took his prisoners to the municipal building in San Fernando.

Bilibid

American prisoners arriving at Bilibid Prison in Manila.

Paul Vacher

Bill Main

Henry Patton

The execution chamber at Bilibid Prison.

Other prisoners who received red tags at Bilibid.

Hank Winslow

Earl Oatman

Pierce Wade

John Scott

Bill Ostrander

Alvis Loveless

Hugh McCoy

John Chernitsky

Bill Snyder

Jack Finley

Cabanatuan

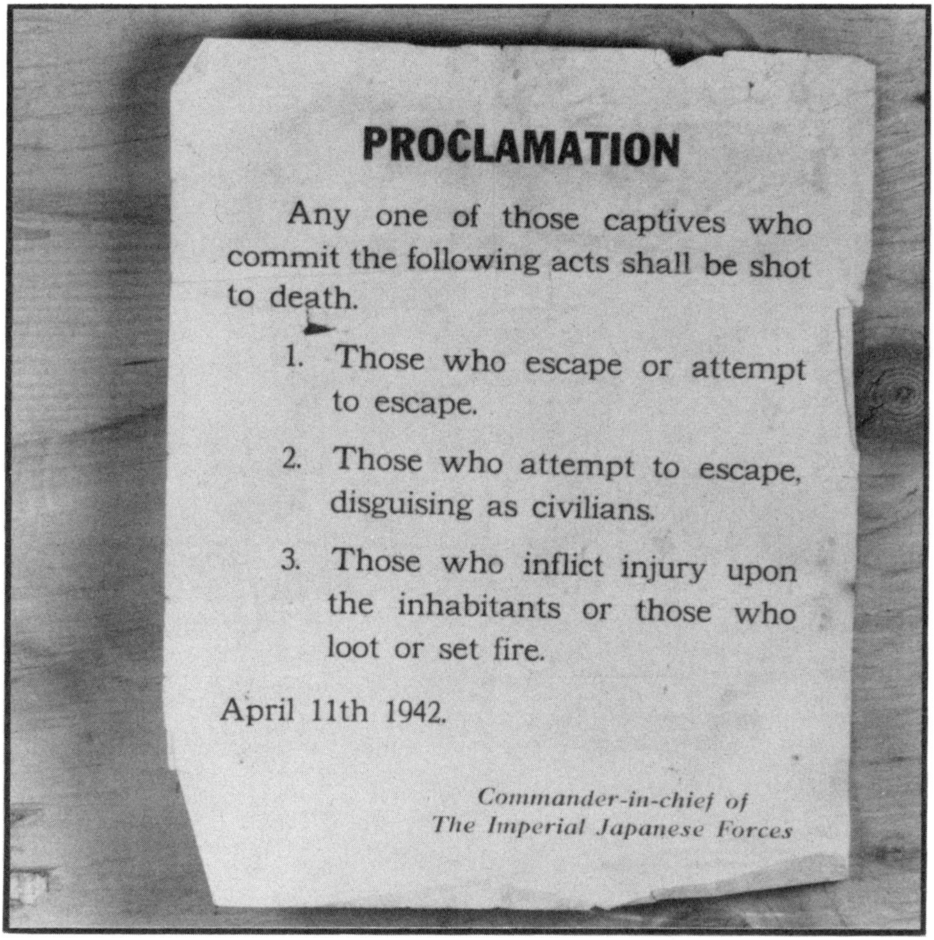

PROCLAMATION

Any one of those captives who commit the following acts shall be shot to death.

1. Those who escape or attempt to escape.
2. Those who attempt to escape, disguising as civilians.
3. Those who inflict injury upon the inhabitants or those who loot or set fire.

April 11th 1942.

*Commander-in-chief of
The Imperial Japanese Forces*

The rules were simple for prisoners of war.

PeeWee Standlee

Tom Coleman

Monty Montgomery

The Group II Kitchen where Hileman worked.

Cabanatuan was a dismal place.

Some prisoners had small garden plots.

Johnny Kratz and the Hep Cats, the band at Cabanatuan, provided a welcome break in the monotony of prison life. Pappy Harris is at the piano, right.

Hellship

Hileman was transported to Japan in the hold of the Nissyo Maru.

Mister Edward Hasse

USS Flasher

Japan

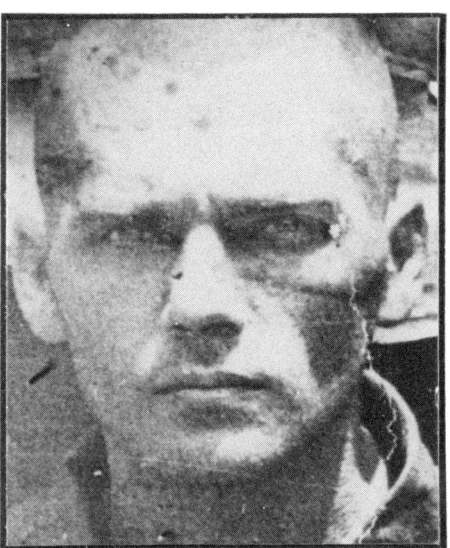
Millard Hileman

Walt Helhowski

One of the prisoner barracks at Camp 3.

The hospital at Camp 3.

Interior of the barracks.

Medical supplies for 1,500 prisoners.

A Catholic service in the barracks.

Father John Curran conducts an outdoor mass at Camp 3.

Major Rikitake surrenders his samurai sword to Major Winnefred Dorris.

This time a tribe of Negritos came out of the mountains to help. Whole families, including women, babies, and dogs, came and camped nearby. After work each day, the Negritos gorged themselves on rice. Their stomachs swelled, and they laughed and belched as they enjoyed their communal fellowship. Agridaño and I enjoyed watching them, observing their tribal life and listening to their happy chatter, though we understood none of the Negrito dialect.

Throughout her pregnancy Eufemia Esquibel had worked hard, carrying water in earthen jars, cooking, sewing, and doing household chores, but as the time for her baby approached, Fernando took her and the children into San Marcelino to be near a doctor.

"When my boy she comes, we will name it Bernardo," Fernando told us.

He said he never left his farm unattended because Negritos would come out of the hills and steal everything. With Agridaño and me there, however, he felt it was safe to leave. We fed the chickens and did other odd jobs around the farm, but there was little to keep us busy.

The family had been gone only a few days when I was wakened one morning by a loud racket. I heard the gate open and saw Fernando, his horse lathered from a difficult ride.

"Mr. Hileman. Mr. Hileman," he shouted. "My wife, he just had a boy."

After only half an hour, Esquibel mounted the small horse again and returned the twelve kilometers to San Marcelino. He had felt it was important to tell his American friends the good news.

As April progressed I found it hard to believe it had been a full year since we had escaped out of Bataan. The days were growing warmer, and the frequent night rains were a reminder the rainy season was approaching again. I had not been bothered by malaria for the past four months, but now the chills and fever returned.

About 3 A.M. on April 26, barking dogs woke me. With the Japanese garrison at San Marcelino only a few kilometers away, I was constantly alert. I grabbed my rifle, making sure there was a shell in the chamber. I pulled on my shorts and sat on the edge of my sleeping mat listening to strange noises. Suddenly, tracer bullets ripped through the roof of Fernando's house.

"Margarito, it's the Japs! They know we're here!"

I ran for the back door with Agridaño on my heels. In the

confusion of escaping, I forgot my rifle. We ran up the hill, circled back, and in the darkness we heard voices and realized Negritos were ransacking the Esquibel house. Silently we watched and waited until they left about sunrise. When we investigated, we found the rice bin was empty, Eufemia's treasured sewing machine was gone, and my rifle was missing. My fury was compounded by malarial chills as we left for the Barone farm.

Antone Barone told us there was a band of bad Negritos in the hills who stole from Filipinos whose homes were left unguarded. They probably did not know Agridaño and I were in the Esquibel house. We ate breakfast with the Barones, and when we left to go back to Fernando's farm, Rufino Barone gave me his Garrand rifle, and he gave Agridaño a forty-five-caliber pistol.

By now my malarial chills had turned into a high fever, and I found myself fighting delirium on the road between the two farms. When I spotted a Negrito peeking over a rock, I impulsively took aim and shot at him. The Garrand jammed, and I sat down in the open road, cursing as I tried to kick the charging handle open with my foot. Several Negritos fired back. Bullets hit all around me as I got the rifle working and returned their fire. Racing back to the Barone house with Agridaño, I knew the Negritos had recognized me and I would have to leave the area. Despite the shooting incident, Agridaño chose to stay.

"Tell Fernando I've gone back to Pampanga," I said to him.

The Negritos had raided the Esquibel farm in the early morning hours of April 26, 1943. Feverish and confused, I left Zambales that afternoon.

Chapter Thirty

Shooting at the Negritos had been a stupid mistake, and I knew it. Now, unarmed, sick, angry, and alone, I set out barefoot for Pampanga with my worldly possessions: a fatigue jacket, a mess kit knife, the silver spoon Isabel had given me, an old razor with dull blades, an eggplant, and my tattered shorts and shirt. I followed the hard dirt trail into the hills. The morning sun had been hot overhead, but it was soon blotted out by the inevitable appearance of heavy afternoon clouds.

My whole body seethed with anger and hate. I hated myself, my impulsive behavior, my appearance, my malaria, and my whole situation. As I sat on a rock, shivering with a malarial chill, it began to rain. Mentally, I had never been so despondent. I felt terribly alone as darkness began to swallow the day, and I wondered if I would survive the night. Soaking wet, thirsty, and with my head throbbing in pain, I began stumbling through the darkness hoping to find water. When I came to a small stream, I fell on my stomach and drank the cool water in desperate gulps.

I ran my fingers through the gravel on the stream's bottom, instinctively looking for snails. I found a couple, broke the shells with my dull knife, and sucked the insides out, sand and all. I gagged down some of the raw eggplant.

Rain kept falling as thunder and lightning shattered the silence of the isolated hillside. My fever began rising, as it always did after the malarial chills. The lightning bolts illuminated dozens of slimy black leeches clinging tenaciously to my arms and legs. They had swollen to the size of my fingers as they sucked my blood. I began flipping them off with my knife, sometimes having to dig out the heads which broke from their bodies.

My mind faded in and out of a delirium. Fever, chills, and confusion deepened my depression, and I longed to die. I had heard once that bleeding to death was painless, and decided to let the leeches suck my blood until I joined Orlo in the deep sleep of death. The will to die was overcoming my will to live, yet something inside refused to let go. I had a strange sense of observing a spiritual struggle going on within myself, a struggle between the forces of life and death. At that moment death seemed easier than life. Then I thought about my parents and about Isabel. If I died wild pigs or dogs would eat my body, and the people who cared about me would never know what happened.

"I can't let this happen. I'm only twenty-eight years old, and my life is all ahead of me."

Slowly the force of life grew stronger, and I knew I had reasons to live. I struggled weakly to my feet, and with only the light offered by flashes of lightning, flipped the remaining leeches off myself with my mess kit knife. I staggered down the trail, found a rock overhang offering protection from the rain, and lay down on the cold, wet earth to sleep.

Dawn was breaking when I awoke. The leeches were gone, and my fever had diminished. I ate the rest of the eggplant and resumed my journey. I had followed the jungle trail to a familiar point where it started into the lowlands when the chills returned, and I weakened. I sat down on a fallen log, then lay on the ground next to it as the attack became worse. Curled up and shivering in the warm sunlight, my back cramped, and intense pain surged through my whole body. Again I was aware of death creeping near.

The chills subsided, but the fever continued to ravage my body, and as my temperature rose, thirst drove me to my feet. I groped and stumbled down the trail, hoping to find anything which would ease my suffering. I came to a mud wallow, probably one used by wild pigs, and fell facedown at its edge, ravenously scooping the filthy water into my mouth. Instead of quenching my thirst, it only complicated my condition as mud coated my throat. In my semidelirious state, I knew only one thing: I had to keep going until I found help.

By late afternoon I reached the lower elevations near the Zambales-Pampanga border, a few kilometers from the Gumain River near Pasbul. I sighted a small sawali shack along the bullcart road. In this remote region farms were marginal operations, and impoverished farmers worked hard for a meager subsistence. I staggered to the shack and sat down on the porch.

I was too sick to respond to the old man who appeared in the doorway. He went back into the house and brought me a bowl of rice and some fish.

"You will eat now," he said. "I will give you some fish I got only today at the pond near Manila Bay."

My fever had subsided, but too exhausted to eat, I pushed the food away and fell asleep on the porch.

It was dark when I awoke, but as soon as I began to move about, the old Filipino came out again with food.

"How long have I been asleep?" I asked.

"A very long time, Joe."

With rest and food, I felt strong enough the next morning to go on my way. I washed, had a drink of water, and prepared to leave, never having bothered to ask the name of my compassionate host. He gave me a terry cloth towel to wipe the feverish sweat from my forehead. I thanked him, wrapped the towel around my neck, and resumed my journey.

As I continued eastward landmarks became familiar, and my spirits lifted. I was nearing Barrio Pasbul and would soon cross the Gumain River. I actually looked forward to seeing Main and Vacher, but decided to stop in Barrio Pio to see Isabel before going on to their shack.

Dirty, unshaven, and with tattered clothes, I hated the way I looked, but I had to see Isabel as soon as possible. Mrs. Montemayor answered my knock, and despite my appearance, welcomed me warmly by grasping my hand in both of hers and leading me into the house. In her faltering English she managed to let me know Isabel was living in Manila. She had returned to Pio once and had been disappointed I had not yet come back to live with Main and Vacher.

Approaching the shack where Main and Vacher had been living,

I saw Main squatted next to the fire cooking rice. He greeted me casually as if I had been gone only a day or two. It had been five months, but with time meaning so little, my leaving may well have been yesterday. Vacher was not around, and I did not ask where he was.

As we talked I realized Main was almost envious of my having been hiding in the remote Zambales Mountains. He had wanted to go deeper into the mountains ever since we came out of Bataan. He asked question after question about my working on the remote Esquibel farm and about the Americans I had met at Barone's. He was not surprised at my experiences with Colonels Merrill and Calyer and found a strange humor in my escape from the Negrito raiding party.

As he talked about recent events in the Pasbul-Pio area, I realized life there had become much more difficult. Guerrillas, often no more than renegades, had been harassing the Filipinos in the barrios, robbing them, stealing food, and threatening to kill anyone who might turn them in to the Japanese. Patrols had increased, adding greatly to the desperation of the Filipino people. Coming into the barrios, soldiers helped themselves to pigs, chickens, and eggs. With the Japanese on one side and the guerrillas on the other, people in the barrios were caught in a dangerous dilemma. They could not rely on either side for protection.

Joe Cheesman had been victimized by the guerrillas who stole from his food supply and took most of his weapons. Then those same guerrillas fled to Cheesman for refuge when the Japanese patrols entered the barrio.

Finally, Main told me about Vacher. He and Pierce Wade, an American I had never met, had been at Cheesman's when Joe had received a message from the Japanese colonel in San Fernando. The message had been a plea for Cheesman to surrender, and the three men had talked for several hours about the demands of the Japanese colonel. They knew their continued presence threatened many Filipinos who had helped them.

"Vacher and Wade walked into San Fernando and surrendered the next morning. The day after that Joe Cheesman did the same thing."

Main's voice was solemn and controlled as he spoke.

Loring and Roy had returned to their American-style home in Barrio Salu, but armed soldiers had arrested young Roy Cheesman a few days later.

Main had seen Forrest Henderson, one of the three men who had been separated from us at the Pilar-Bagac Road. He had been living about three kilometers north of Main's shack, and Main had visited him there several times. On his last visit, Henderson was dying. Sick with malaria, he had been caught in his hideout by a Japanese patrol. One of the soldiers had thrust a bayonet into him, and as the patrol moved on, left him alone to die. The compassionate Main had cleaned the blood from Henderson's wound, patched it as best he could, and cared for him during the last two hours of his life. Main did not think Henderson knew anything about Wally Kinder and George Wicks, the other two men who had started out of Bataan with us.

Soon after I had settled into Main's shack I saw Dr. Pineda. He still expressed compassion and an interest in my health, but it was apparent his nerves were frayed. I realized the Japanese had been putting tremendous pressure on him.

Henderson's death at the hands of a Japanese patrol had made the Filipino people more nervous than ever. They were all becoming more jittery and for good reason. Japanese activity had increased throughout the spring of 1943, and in Barrio Pio soldiers frequently questioned the local citizens about American fugitives reported to be hiding in the area. The Filipinos usually knew when Japanese patrols left San Fernando or Porac and would come to our shack and ask us to hide. Although near a main trail, the shack was well hidden, and we carefully camouflaged the path with branches and leaves. Japanese patrols had passed by several times, but had never seen it.

For the Filipinos, however, Main and I had become risky neighbors, especially since we seemed to be the only Americans left in the area.

Chapter Thirty-one

The warm days of April and May seemed to slip past unmarked by any particular events and unnoticed in their routine passage. We knew we should be making plans for the coming rainy season, but procrastination was the easy path to follow.

With Vacher gone, the relationship between Main and me had greatly improved. The once-fragile friendship between us was strengthened as we realized our dependence on each other.

The Filipinos continued bringing eggs, rice, and corn whenever they could, but as Japanese patrols increased they came less frequently. Main's garden was an important part of our diet, and working in it provided at least some break in the monotony. He had used bamboo to pipe water from a spring behind the shack and had successfully raised beans, kamotes, tomatoes, sweet corn, and hot chili peppers we called one-five-fives after the 155mm cannons on Bataan. In the warm tropical climate, corn grew to maturity in four weeks, and one evening, out of boredom, Main ate thirty ears, a feat I thought was revolting. Okra, too green one day, would be overripe the next. Despite the fairly adequate diet, we hated to face each day, days that dragged on and on.

In an effort to bring some relief to the boredom which was

growing daily, Main began telling Old Ned stories as he had when the weather closed in on us in the Gumain Canyon. Without Vacher and Orlo to enjoy them with me, however, the stories had lost their savor and did little to lift the heavy pallor of the days.

Occasionally Main visited Nieves Jordan who always seemed to cheer him and give him hope. His visits with her made me aware of the longing I had to see Isabel who remained in Manila. My morale deteriorated through May as my mind dwelled on her, and I wondered if I had made a mistake in not taking her with me to Zambales. As I realized more and more how deeply I felt about her, I vowed to find her after the war, if not sooner. I thought about a possible future with her, and knew if we married, I would stay in the Philippines. My family would never adjust to my marrying a Filipino girl, even one as gracious as Isabel.

The only Americans remaining in the area by this time were Main and myself, a factor which made everyone nervous: the Japanese, our Filipino friends, and us. So it was not a surprise when Carling Fejardo, the local Filipino who had shown a particular interest in our activities, visited on June 18, 1943.

Fejardo joined us for supper, and through his many questions we began to realize the purpose of his visit.

"Isn't life in the mountains hard on you? Do you not worry when you get sick? Maybe a Japanese patrol will find you. Do you not fear they might kill you?" Fejardo asked. "I think you would be better off now with the Japanese."

"What the hell are you talking about, Carling?" I asked.

Fejardo reached into his pocket and pulled out a note.

"I do not want you and Mr. Main to be unhappy with me. I am your friend," he said. "The colonel in the Japanese garrison in San Fernando has given to me a note to give you and Mr. Main." The note was addressed to Mr. Hileman and Mr. Main.

It came from Colonel Yashima, the Secret Police commander in Pampanga Province. Yashima wrote that Main and I were a threat to Japanese interests in the area, and he invited us to come into San Fernando to discuss surrender.

"Carling, you can just turn around and take that note back to Yashima and tell him to stick it in his ear," I told Fejardo. "We have no intention of going in."

"What if he sends a patrol after you?" Fejardo asked.

"He's had that opportunity before and hasn't caught us. Apparently he's unable to do that," I said. "Tell the colonel we're not going to meet with him."

"All right, I will tell him."

Fejardo's tone seemed to be a mixture of disappointment that he had failed and apprehension about our decision. He left a few minutes later.

Colonel Yashima's note deeply disturbed us. The evening was long as we stared at the fire and discussed our options, which were few. Then we fell silent, each of us lost in his own thoughts.

I was keenly aware of Isabel's absence and not being able to share this concern with her. I had learned to rely on her inner strength and wisdom, and as the coals grew dimmer, my thoughts remained with her. Near dawn the fire died, and we went to sleep.

The next day, June 19, Main and I hid on the hill behind our shack and watched a tall black finger of smoke rise above the barrio. We were sure a Japanese patrol had torched a house and wondered what else they may have done. When the Japanese finally left the barrio, several villagers came to see us.

Visibly shaken, they told us a Japanese patrol had come into Barrio Pio, burned a house, and tortured several people. After beating them, the soldiers jammed slivers of bamboo under their fingernails and ignited them. The Japanese had threatened to kill some who they thought were withholding information. This was a most trying period for the Filipinos, for they had already begun to mistrust each other. Neighbors and friends, and in some cases, even family members were suspected of collaboration with the Japanese. Yet, according to the information given us, none of the Filipinos told the Japanese soldiers where we were hiding.

That evening Fejardo came again with another note from Colonel Yashima. If we did not come in, the Colonel said, he would punish everyone in Barrios Pio and Pasbul who had helped us. The message was given added thrust by the enclosure of a list of people who had given us aid, including the Pineda family, the Jordans, Benito Malleri, and even Mrs. Valentine, the seventy-year-old widow who had occasionally given us food. In the case of the Pinedas, Colonel Yashima said special efforts would be made to punish the whole family. I was shocked to see the list included almost everyone who had helped us during the past year, but I was greatly relieved that Isabel's name was not listed. Colonel Yashima said our Filipino friends would be punished, even if we left the area. Only our surrender would save them.

Main and I were stunned by the explicitness of the message. Its implications were far-reaching, and we needed time to think. We asked Fejardo to keep the note and return the next night.

"I will not give it back to Colonel Yashima," he said. "I want to be your friend."

"I'm not so sure about that," I said.

I did not fully trust Fejardo, but the next night he returned with the same note. Realizing he could have given the Japanese our exact location, my faith in him increased somewhat.

Main and I had come to a decision on how to handle the peril posed by Colonel Yashima.

"Carling, I am going to write the colonel a letter, and you will give it to him," I said. "I do not want you to look at it." I was not sure the curious Filipino would resist the temptation, but the order would impress him with the note's importance.

I turned the colonel's note over and wrote an answer on the back.

> If you will meet us at the Joe Cheesman house in Barrio Salu, near Del Carmen, on Wednesday morning at 9 A.M., we will talk with you. Come alone and unarmed.

I put the note back in the envelope, resealed it, and handed it to Fejardo for delivery.

"We'll be there, but I'll bet he won't," I said to Main after Fejardo disappeared down the trail.

During the past month I had grown closer to Main. Now as we faced an uncertain future, Main seemed to be in full agreement with the decision to meet with the Japanese colonel.

The next day, June 21, we waited for Fejardo's return. He did not come, and we grew anxious.

Fejardo returned on Tuesday morning, June 22.

"Mr. Hileman," he said apologetically, "I was so late last night, but the colonel said he will come to see you as you asked him to on Wednesday morning at nine o'clock."

Ferjardo left for San Fernando.

That afternoon Main and I told the Filipinos about our arranged meeting with Colonel Yashima. They already knew, and I realized Fejardo had read the note and spread the news through the barrios. The Filipinos seemed relieved that we would be leaving. Several stopped by the shack to tell us we had made the right decision. We were assured it was not a matter of their disliking us, but rather a concern for their own safety.

I handed my Japanese binoculars to Ernie Pineda.

"Give these to your father. Tell him we appreciate all he's done for us."

Main left to tell Nieves Jordan, and she agreed we had made the right decision. I respected her words of reassurance. During the past year I had developed a deep appreciation for the wisdom of Filipino women. Nieves invited us to the Jordan farm where her mother was preparing a big meal in our honor.

"Beel, there will be better times ahead for you and me," Nieves told Main after our farewell supper. We said a final good-bye to the family of women who had done so much for us and walked silently back to our shack.

I put my few possessions into my musette bag, including the terry cloth towel the old farmer had given me on my last trip from Zambales to Pampanga, and the shorts and little silver spoon Isabel had given me. Main and I put on native straw hats, and Main wore ill-fitting shoes Nieves had found for him. I walked barefoot as I had for the better part of a year.

As we started towards Barrio Salu and our meeting with the Japanese colonel, our decision weighed heavily on our minds. I knew Main was torn by the thought of leaving Nieves and the rest of the Jordans behind. His love for Neives was no longer something he tried to hide.

"Goddamn it, Hileman, I sure hope this is really the right thing to do. Sometimes I think I'd just as soon go farther back into the hills and sit the war out. It won't last forever, and I know Neives would go with me."

I was not surprised at his words, knowing he still had reservations about our decision. I had been the one who wrote the note to Colonel Yashima, and even though we had apparently made the decision together, I knew his heart was not really in it. Now I was not about to let him screw things up. We could not split up; we had to either surrender or escape together.

"Main, we've gone too damned far to change our minds, so just get that bullshit out of that thick head of yours. Running out now would be the worst thing we could do. Sure, maybe the Japs would never get you and Nieves, and I know I could keep away from the bastards forever. Hell, we've proved that, but goddamn it, man, we've got to think about more than saving our own asses. What about the Filipinos? You saw what happened in the barrio on Saturday. That was only a sample of what the Japs will do to them if we run out, and I can't have that on my conscience."

"I know, but when I think of just walking in and surrendering to that son of a bitchin' colonel, it gripes the hell out of me."

"I don't give a damn about that chicken-shit colonel either. I'd just as soon shoot the son of a bitch as look at him, but we've got to think about the Filipinos. Hell, they've risked their lives for us for a year, and we can't leave them in this kind of a hole. The Japs would kill everyone in the barrios, and they've treated us like family. We just have to do what's best for them."

We continued on in silence as we passed the Spanish Church with the white dome. The church, though it was old and run-down, seemed suddenly to loom on the landscape as a symbol of the inner strength and stability of the Filipino people. As it had offered refuge and hope to them through the years, it now seemed to offer me a hope which had been dimmed. Even though Orlo was dead, Vacher had surrendered, and Main and I faced an unknown future, the white dome seemed to hold a silent promise that I would see it again.

I turned to look at Isabel's house and wondered for the first time if her mother owned or rented the old Spanish house. It had been an emotionally safe haven for me when Isabel was there, but she was gone now and once again I was leaving. I suddenly realized I had never asked Isabel's age and did not even know her birthday, although my birthday had brought us together. She had been so sensitive to my needs, yet in many ways I now felt I had been insensitive to hers.

Where the road forked, we bypassed the familiar bullcart road to Porac and followed the road which passed through the sugarcane plantation, past the Del Carmen airstrip I had inadvertently discovered earlier, and on to the Cheesman house in Barrio Salu. Neither of us had been there before. In fact, I realized the cautious Main had probably never left his shack, except to visit the Jordans, Cheesmans, and Henderson.

Although I had not visited Salu, I knew where it was, and I knew the Cheesman house was the only American-style house in the barrio. The Cheesmans had abandoned the house when the Japanese advanced into Bataan. When we had eaten Thanksgiving dinner with them, it was in the remote shack where the family was hiding.

"Goddamn, it's sure quiet around here," Main said as we approached the barrio. "Let's lie in the weeds a while and see what's up."

Suddenly the possibility of ambush seemed a stark reality, and we spent an hour watching the house. Finally satisfied it was empty, we cautiously moved toward it, found it deserted, and began looking around.

The Japanese had used the big house as an office during the fighting. Furniture had been torn and burned by smoldering cigarette butts. Shutters hung loosely on broken windows, cupboard doors had been ripped off, and broken dishes were scattered across the floor. The Japanese had cut mattresses, most likely in a search for hidden money or jewelry, and pots and pans were thrown outside. The once beautiful house was in shambles.

Nervously, Main and I explored the farm. Behind Joe Cheesman's old mill, we crossed a dry ravine and found an unharvested cane field where we could hide in the event we were ambushed.

Back in the house that evening, we talked for hours about our escape from Bataan and the events that followed. We discussed our present situation, what lay ahead, and what we were leaving behind. During my fourteen months as a fugitive, I had lost my fear of the Japanese. I had lived near them, watched their movements through my binoculars, and had never come close to being captured. I was sure I could flee and survive even now, but that alternative threatened many people. We would wait for Colonel Yashima in the morning.

Main and I spent a quiet night in the deserted house. Dawn broke, and as we looked around, everything appeared quiet.

About 8:30 A.M., we grabbed our bags and crept behind a hedge near the house. Our moment of truth had arrived.

Chapter Thirty-two

Completely hidden from view and with our escape route in mind in the event things did not go well, we lay quietly waiting.

"I don't think he'll show up," Main whispered.

"Oh, he'll show up all right. I just hope he doesn't have too much company with him."

For all we knew we were walking into a trap. Perhaps a patrol, rather than the colonel, would come.

I had hardly finished speaking when a car appeared in the distance. Acacia trees lined its way as it moved along the rutted road, passing several small shacks scattered among the sugarcane fields and rice paddies. We watched the 1941 Chevrolet sedan approach and stop a short distance away. A Filipino driver sat behind the steering wheel, and a Japanese officer sat alone in the backseat.

"We could kill the son of a bitch," Main whispered.

Main's impulsive outburst surprised me. He had always been cautious, and even cowardly appearing, but I knew he was serious now.

"We have to talk with him," I said. The threat to our Filipino friends in Barrios Pasbul and Pio had deeply impressed me, and I knew the Japanese would kill them if we assassinated the colonel.

When we were sure the colonel was traveling alone, we stood up and cautiously approached the dark blue sedan. The driver got out and stood somewhat stiffly beside the car. He opened the back door, and the Japanese colonel stepped out.

"This is Colonel Yashima," the Filipino said.

The officer was a striking figure. Taller than the average Japanese, he was a handsome man who looked sharp in his tailored uniform. His black boots had been highly polished, and his hat bore the insignia of his rank. Most remarkably, he was unarmed, and I suddenly realized Main and I were not the only ones at risk in this situation. In his vulnerability to guerrilla ambush and the fugitive Americans he was meeting, Yashima shared that risk. The colonel smiled as he reached out to shake hands.

"The colonel wants to talk," the Filipino said. He acted also as translator, and as he spoke I sensed his unnatural relationship with the Japanese. I took an immediate dislike to him, not only because I thought he was a traitor to his people, but because it seemed he tried too hard to please the Japanese officer.

The colonel motioned for Main and me to join him in the car. We hesitated, but were assured nothing would happen to us. As we took a step toward the car I whispered to Main, telling him to grab the keys if the driver tried to start the engine. I climbed in back with the colonel, and Main joined the driver in the front seat.

Colonel Yashima pulled a pack of Lucky Strikes from his pocket and offered cigarettes to us. We nervously accepted. Through the translator, we engaged in small talk as we smoked. Several times, as the Filipino translated, the colonel haltingly interjected words and phrases in English.

Yashima reached for a bottle of wine.

"You like?" he asked.

He opened the bottle, and Main and I slowly sipped the high-quality wine from it as we smoked another cigarette. We were astounded at his knowledge of our movements for the past year. He seemed to know all about us, and through the interpreter, even mentioned Orlo's death and burial. When the wine bottle was empty there was a decided change in the colonel's attitude.

"Now that we've talked, you can do one of two things," he said. His voice was steady and controlled with the crispness of military authority. We could return to San Fernando with him, in which case he promised good treatment as long as we were under his jurisdiction. Our second option was a return to the jungle. He warned the second choice would mean punishment for everyone who had helped us in Barrios Pio and Pasbul.

Main and I were tired, and we had become disillusioned with the length of time it was taking for the American army to return to the Philippines. We had not seen an American plane since the fall of Bataan. We also knew the Japanese would carry out their threat to imprison and possibly kill our Filipino friends if we fled. The list Carling Fejardo had brought, naming everyone who had helped us, was accurate. Our continued presence in the area threatened the lives of many people.

Seated in the car, I thought it was highly probable Japanese soldiers were hidden just beyond sight, ready to ambush us if we chose to return to the jungle. If not, there would certainly be greatly renewed efforts to capture us, and there would be no leniency. There could be only one practical choice. Colonel Yashima seemed like a man of his word. To protect our Filipino friends and save ourselves, Main and I agreed to go to San Fernando with him. It was June 23, 1943. After fourteen months on the run, we were now prisoners of war.

"As long as you are with me, nothing bad will happen to you," Colonel Yashima said through his interpreter.

Chapter Thirty-three

The rainy season had begun, and the road was wet as the car moved towards San Fernando. Sunlight broke through the clouds, and a steamy mist formed on the dirt road. I was apprehensive about my decision, but relieved to have it over with. Life on the run had been difficult, especially the past few months. Both Main and I were exhausted.

The colonel was obviously pleased with himself. He smiled as he pointed out landmarks and made several attempts to talk with us through the interpreter. Main and I, however, rode in silence as we gazed out the window at the sugarcane fields. I thought about Isabel, Dr. Pineda, and the other Filipinos who had risked their lives for us and hoped their peril would be abated by our surrender. I thought about George Wicks and Wally Kinder and the mix-up at the Pilar-Bagac Road and wondered if they were still alive. And what about Vacher? Would I ever see my old friend again? Then a chill ran down my spine as I wondered if I would survive even to see this day's sunset. There were many questions without answers as the car rolled on towards San Fernando.

I studied my captor for a moment, speculating the colonel might have been a successful businessman before the war. I asked no questions, but did feel certain I knew one thing about him. The colonel was a man of courage who had come to meet us unarmed and alone, except for his driver. He had proved himself, up to this point, to be a man of his word.

I watched the people on the street as the blue sedan moved through San Fernando. Only the Japanese drove cars and trucks. Filipinos were walking, riding bicycles, and leading carts drawn by carabao or small ponies, apparently going about their daily business. Yet their natural joviality was missing, hidden under the burden of living in an occupied country.

My reflective thoughts ended abruptly when the sedan stopped in front of the municipal building in San Fernando. Main and I stared at the large block building which housed government offices, wondering what it held for us. The colonel directed us to the door and left. An overhang covered a cement walkway leading to wooden double doors. It was hot, and both doors were open. We picked up our meager belongings and followed a guard into the building. When we entered the large, dim lobby with a high ceiling and dark wood-paneled walls, we could hear typewriters and phones ringing in several offices as Japanese administrators went about their jobs.

The guard left us standing in the lobby, and no one paid any attention to us. We quietly sat down on a high-backed bench next to the wall and watched Japanese officers hurrying in and out of their offices. After an hour, a thin private in a baggy uniform approached us.

"I speak English," he said. "Do you like music?"

"Yes."

"What kind?"

"Any kind, I guess." I was in no position to be particular.

"Do you like Nelson Eddie and Jeanette MacDonald?" the soldier asked.

"Yes." I had little interest in the Japanese private or his taste in music and kept my answers short.

The private left us in the lobby, but returned moments later with a hand-crank phonograph and a stack of records. He sat down with us and began to play the records, beginning with "Indian Love Call." As we listened to the American music, he tapped his foot in rhythm and talked about the famous duo's songs and movies.

After about twenty minutes, a young lieutenant emerged from an office and said, "You will eat now."

Apprehensively, Main and I followed him down a hallway and into the officers' mess. A long, highly polished wood table stood in the center of the room, neatly set with fine white china. Several Japanese officers were seated, eating their lunch. They continued talking, seemingly oblivious to our being seated in their midst. Food was being passed back and forth at the table, and even as Main and I nervously passed the bowls, there appeared to be no awareness by the officers we were even present.

When the officers began leaving, we quietly slipped out of the room and returned to the bench in the lobby where we waited for another hour. Finally we were asked our names and serial numbers, and a guard led us outside, around the building, and to the provincial jail. We entered the prison's dirt compound where single-storied concrete cell blocks lined three sides. Each cell opened with a door of steel bars. A small cement building in the center of the compound housed the latrine and bathhouse.

The sergeant of the guard met us near the prison office and took us to our assigned cells. I was surprised no one checked the small sacks of personal belongings we carried. I squinted as I gazed into the dimly lit cell. It was barren, without furnishings of any kind. There were no windows, and during the day the only light came through the barred doorway. The cell, which housed three other Americans, faced the swinging doors of the latrine. The sergeant led Main to another cell.

The barred door slammed shut, and I turned to look at my three cellmates. My immediate reaction was one of repugnance as I quickly observed their unkempt beards and their tattered, unwashed clothes. Then with a sudden flash of self-revelation, I realized I looked no better.

I introduced myself to the man nearest me, but my new cellmate only stared wordlessly back. One of the others walked over, extended his hand, and introduced himself.

"Glad to know you, Hileman. I'm Tom Rayburn. We've been waiting for a fourth. Do you play bridge?"

"No," I said tensely, "and I don't want to learn."

"Sit down!" the third man commanded, pointing to the floor.

"I don't want to play bridge. I don't even know how," I protested.

"Deal!" he ordered as he tossed me a deck of worn cards. "You can be Rayburn's partner."

I had no choice. The other three wanted to play bridge. I had played several other card games in the past and was a good player, so learning the game came readily. For the next few days I played bridge, with Rayburn as my partner, from the time we woke until 10 P.M. when the cell's dim light was turned off.

My first prison meal, about 6 P.M., was a sharp contrast to the lunch in the Municipal Building with the Japanese officers. Guards brought small buckets of unseasoned rice and watery vegetable soup to the cell blocks. Each bucket was intended to feed ten men. Breakfast the next morning was *lugao*, a rice gruel so thin we could drink it.

Guards escorted us to the latrine one at a time. I relieved myself, washed my hands and face, and dried myself with the small towel the Filipino farmer had given me a few weeks earlier. Although facilities were available, I was not allowed to bathe. Prisoners were taken to the latrine on a regular schedule, though with the prevalence of sickness and disease extra trips were often a necessity, but never without a guard. Inside the latrine, holes were cut in a board placed over a slanted metal trough. After each use, water released from a storage basin washed the waste away. The building smelled foul, and flies filled the the air and crawled over everything. Although the arrangement was poor, it did have one benefit for me. I saw Vacher being taken to the latrine. My friend who I had not seen for several months was alive and imprisoned just two cells down from me.

On my second night at San Fernando, a short, stocky Japanese sergeant entered the compound carrying a sack. A guard unlocked our cell door, allowing him to enter. He handed each of us a bottle of San Miguel beer and visited casually for some time before going on to another cell. Sergeant Nakamura, who served in the cavalry unit stationed in a field across from the jail, seemed to have an intense desire to learn English and to know as much as possible about the United States. I was told he came to the jail whenever he could to practice the language and brought beer for the prisoners who helped him. In turn, he taught us Japanese words we would need to survive captivity. The prisoners had affectionately nicknamed him Sarge. When Nakamura learned this, he was pleased.

The next evening I heard a disturbance in the jail office. Peering between the bars, I saw Nakamura and a guard of lower rank step outside. Nakamura put his sack down, and as we watched, the cavalryman slapped and kicked the guard, then reached down, picked up his beer, and proceeded towards the prison cells for another English lesson. Nakamura had told some of the prisoners he did not like war, and he resented the possibility of being transferred to the island fighting in the South Pacific. In a candid conversation, he had said he thought the Japanese warrior custom of *Hari Kari* was bullshit, a word he had learned from Vacher and Pierce Wade on one of his visits. In civilian life Nakamura had been a policeman in Kobe. He wanted only to go home, resume police work, find a girlfriend, and enjoy his beer. We all liked the friendly Japanese sergeant.

We did not see Nakamura again and wondered if he had been too outspoken about his feelings or perhaps too eager to fraternize with the enemy. We never found out.

Early in the afternoon of my fourth day at San Fernando, a sudden commotion came from the breezeway leading into the compound. We stopped our bridge game, walked over to the bars and looked out. Four guards were pulling a rope, on the other end of which an American prisoner struggled. The rope was tied to his waist and looped loosely around his neck, and his arms and legs were bound.

I learned later the prisoner was Wendell Morgan, a native of Louisiana. A Japanese patrol had caught him and another fugitive hiding in a marsh the previous day. Both were suffering from malaria and malnutrition. Bound with ropes, they had spent the night in a garrison guardhouse and had been brought to the jail at San Fernando that morning. The Japanese had accused Morgan of being a guerrilla, but he had maintained his innocence under interrogation. He had passed out during the questioning, been revived by the guards, tied up, and dragged into the compound.

It was apparent to us Morgan had been severely beaten. His face was bruised and swollen almost beyond recognition. He defiantly hollered and cursed as two Japanese soldiers and two Filipinos pulled him through the compound. The guards kicked him all the way to the latrine where he was forced through the swinging doors directly across from my cell. The swinging doors, raised about eighteen inches above the cement floor, allowed partial visibility into the latrine, and I watched as Morgan was laid out on the floor.

The beating continued, and jackets and shirts came off as the guards perspired in the heat. One guard jammed the end of a garden hose into Morgan's mouth and wrapped a length of burlap around his head. The water was turned on. I heard the gurgling sounds of the drowning man as Morgan fought for life. Morgan swallowed water, his stomach swelled, and he fell silent. Guards jumped on his stomach and fluids spewed from their victim's mouth, nose, ears, and bowels. The blow killed him.

The bloated, battered body was left on the floor of the latrine all day, a message for others. Flies hovered over the dead man when I used the latrine that evening. I stared in horror as I stepped around the body.

The sadistic execution terrified me. I had seen death in war, but nothing had prepared me for the horror I had just witnessed. I seriously questioned my decision to surrender. My own experience with Colonel Yashima, Sergeant Nakamura, and the guards had been good up to this time. Now terror, anger, and hatred gripped me as I looked at the body of the American so brutally murdered.

"He was a very bad American," guards told us. We never learned what constituted a very bad American.

On my fifth day there, a guard came to our cell and called me out, along with Tom Rayburn. We joined several other prisoners who were assembled in the compound, and then marched to a truck. Among them were Main and Vacher. I wanted to talk with Vacher, but at the moment, only an exchange of nods was possible. Both Vacher and Main appeared to be in pretty good shape, and I smiled to myself as I realized the fastidious Main had shaved that morning.

We climbed into the back of the truck. Two guards rode with us, while a third sat in front with the American prisoner who served as driver. Guards kept us silent. All of us had been classified as spies or guerrillas, and discipline was tight.

As the truck pulled away from San Fernando, I thought again about the execution I had witnessed the day before. Now I was leaving the protection promised by Colonel Yashima and wondered what lay ahead. The truck hit a bump, and I felt a knee push into my back. I turned to see the shining steel of a guard's bayonet just inches from my face.

Riding along in forced silence, I studied the landscape. The road was in a state of disrepair and bridges had been damaged from the withdrawal into Bataan, but on the streets chickens and pigs meandered about, children played, and adults went about their business. The truck stopped, and those who had money were allowed to buy fruit. I gazed at the sad, drawn faces of the Filipino people. Adults seemed afraid to show any emotion, but seeing the hungry American soldiers with no money, vendors gave us fruit. Having eaten, we resumed our journey.

In the hills I had been isolated from civilization. Now as the truck entered Manila, I noted how little the city had changed after a year of war, yet the Filipino people had changed, and so had I. I contemplated escape, but decided to wait. Perhaps there would be a chance later.

The truck stopped at a large gate, the only opening in a high stone wall facing the street. Electrified barbed wires ran along the top. I realized escape would be impossible here.

"This is Bilibid Prison," the American driver announced.

"*Kora! Kora!*" a Japanese guard yelled.

Thanks to Sergeant Nakamura we knew the order meant hurry, so we scrambled quickly out of the truck. The guard ordered us to attention.

"*Kiotsuke! Kiotsuke!*"

A new phase in my imprisonment had begun.

Chapter Thirty-four

*B*ilibid Prison was old, a remnant of Spanish colonization built a century before Admiral Dewey had come to Manila in 1898. Its outer walls formed a great square in the center of which stood a round, domed office building. It looked like the hub of a great wheel with walls extending from it like spokes to the outer perimeter.

We were led to a high-security compound within the larger confines of the prison area. The front of the compound was marked by a two-foot-high concrete wall, on top of which was stretched a six-foot woven-wire fence. The remaining three sides of the compound were fifteen-foot cement walls. Toward the rear of the high-security area was an ominous-looking building. A large cell with a heavily barred door was centrally located at the front. Over the door was a sign which read Execution Chamber. On each side, staggered in a kind of stair-step fashion, were three solitary confinement cells, each with its door facing the front.

Forced to stand formation in the hot afternoon sun, we faced the formidable structure. It seemed they hoped to intimidate us with its threatening appearance. Some prisoners fainted, a few were beaten, and one was stabbed with a bayonet.

Standing in the sweltering heat, I glanced at Vacher. I had not been able to talk with my old friend at San Fernando and wondered now if I would have that opportunity. I also wondered if the Japanese at Bilibid knew we had escaped from Bataan together fourteen months earlier.

After the formation, guards herded us into the execution chamber and closed the barred door behind us. About two dozen men were crowded into the dark cell. Its walls had been whitewashed, there were no windows, and a solitary light bulb hung from the ceiling. What it illuminated presented a chilling scene.

A concrete slab in the center of the cell held the prison's antiquated electric chair which was still connected to a switch on the wall. An iron band, made to fit over the victim's head during an execution, was bolted to the back. Unbuckled leather arm and leg straps were fastened to the chair, and there were deep gouges in its wooden arms, visible reminders of victims who had dug their fingernails deep into the hard wood during executions.

I laid my straw mat next to the cement pedestal and looked around for Vacher. We had been allowed no opportunity to even greet one another earlier, and it was good to be reunited even under such adverse circumstances. Main joined us, and the three of us talked at great length about our time in the hills and our gratitude to our Filipino friends. Vacher had voluntarily surrendered, as Main and I had, yet we did not discuss the details of our becoming prisoners. It was as though each thought surrender would be perceived by the others as weakness. Nonetheless, we were back together, sharing a closeness we had seldom experienced in the hills.

As the three of us sat together on the floor next to the electric chair, we were joined by another American, apparently well known to Vacher.

"How're you doing, Killer?" Vacher said. His question was directed at the newcomer, a skinny-looking guy with a week's growth of beard and a ready smile. An old straw hat was tilted sideways on his head. He sat down and rolled a cigarette from some native tobacco he shook from a beat-up Union Leader can.

"Pretty goddamn good for an old Georgia hillbilly. These guys friends of yours?" he asked Vacher.

"Yeah, we came out of Bataan together."

Before he had a chance to introduce himself, someone called to him from outside, and he left.

"That's Pierce Wade, the guy I met at Cheesman's just before the Japs got us. He's the biggest bullshitter you've ever heard. He served in the Canal Zone before coming to the P.I., and when you hear his stories you'll know why I call him Killer."

With two dozen prisoners crowded into the cell, we spread our mats wherever there was room. I had never lived in such close quarters with so many men, and the stench of filthy bodies filled the cell. All of them had endured numerous and varied hardships during the previous year, and their appearance gave evidence of the privations they had suffered.

Among them were my two friends from Zambales, Hank Winslow and Earl Oatman. They had become separated in Zambales, but both were captured in the spring of 1943. Winslow and another prisoner in the cell, Bill Ostrander, were captured by Huks, taken to San Marcelino, and then transported to a nearby jail. Placed in a darkened holding cell, they had not known if it was day or night. In the blackness, the threat of death had been constantly on their minds. After two weeks, a guard woke them just before sunrise and they were allowed to bathe in an artesian spring just outside the jail. As the sun rose they were marched down the barrio street, both expecting execution. Instead they had been put on a truck and transported to San Fernando, and from there to Bilibid.

Two others in the cell, Hugh McCoy and Ray Schletterer, had a similar experience. Guards had taken them from their jail cells, marched them outside, and ordered them to dig holes. They had assumed they were digging their own graves.

"Let's show them what real men are made of," Schletterer had said to McCoy, both men sure they would be shot when they finished digging. Instead, the Japanese filled the holes with garbage and marched the prisoners back to their cells.

There were others, men I had not previously known. All had fled after the American surrender of Bataan, and all had survived a year of hardships, suffering, and pain. Each was unique. Jack Finley of New Mexico had served in the 200th Coast Artillery with his father. They had been separated after the fall of Bataan, and he did not know if his father was still alive. John Scott had walked into town and surrendered to protect the Filipino family who had cared for him. Some had been turned in by Filipino collaborators when the Japanese offered rewards for their capture. A few had been active in guerrilla organizations, but most were simply fugitives hoping for the return of American forces. We all shared the common experience of escape, survivors who had been willing to take chances. We quickly fell into the prison routine.

In the close confines of the prison cell, we seldom talked about anything as personal as women or home. With nagging hunger and malnutrition common to all of us, food became the central focus of our survival and of our conversations. Emotionally, food was a topic that represented freedom and hope without touching our personal lives and was something everyone could discuss without pain.

On one occasion we sat around talking about pie. Each of us took his turn describing in detail his favorite pie. Some even described the process of planting and harvesting the fruit, of preparing the filling, and finally describing the mouth-watering taste of the finished product. After all the others finished, Sill Herring spoke.

"Oh, hell. There ain't but one kind of pie." The compact, dark-complexioned man from Louisiana spoke with a decided Southern drawl. "That's sweet potater pie!"

Our usual daily food ration, brought in twice a day, consisted of rice and seaweed soup. There was never enough of either, so we learned to eat in tiny bites to make the meager rations last longer. Hot tea was brought to us in wooden buckets.

Occasionally the Japanese brought us mongo bean soup. Hungry, emaciated prisoners scrambled into line. Boiled in a five-gallon can, the soup separated and the solids fell to the bottom. John Scott and I happened to be in the back of our line with a lieutenant colonel from one of the solitary confinement cells.

"Colonel, tell that flunky to stir the soup so those guys in front get their fair share of solids," Scott suggested.

"Oh, you're just mad because you're not getting the gravy," the officer said.

"I just don't think it's right that the first guys don't get any of the solids."

The officer ignored Scott's request.

We watched the thin prisoners in front of us get a cup of watery soup. Then we watched the colonel, a man who was healthy and strong. When he reached the can, his ration was a cup of beans scooped from the bottom. The colonel reinforced Scott's disgust, and mine, for officers who were supposed to be gentlemen.

Close quarters created friction, and there was constant arguing, but no one complained about his personal situation. We all shared an uncertain future. Most of us were convinced isolation in the execution chamber meant we had no future of any kind. We conditioned ourselves for the day when Japanese soldiers would march us to our execution. Emotionally, I learned how a condemned man felt when all hope was gone. I doubted any of us would complain, even if the Japanese told us we would be executed in the morning.

It was the rainy season, and the cell was damp and moldy. Yet we slept on the floor with only straw mats, canvas shelter halves, or worn blankets. Prisoners from the main population, outside the maximum security area, brought us buckets of warm water for shaving and, as Main called it, a whore's bath, which was wiping off with a damp towel. Clothing stayed soiled and damp all the time. Some prisoners grew beards, but having experienced an unkempt beard in Pampanga, I now preferred the pain of shaving with the dull Army-issue Gillette razor I had carried since the war started. Outside the cell was a urinal and toilet where tap water washed waste down a metal trough. Despite the adverse conditions, we adapted.

During the next few days more prisoners were brought in, bringing the total in the maximum security area to thirty-five, most of them enlisted men. Soon after the last ones arrived, the entire group was assembled in the compound. A high-ranking Japanese officer, accompanied by his orderly and several guards, stood on a wooden box and addressed us. We had been designated Special Prisoners, he said, and would be kept segregated from the regular prison population. He went on, laying out the prison rules. When any Japanese soldier walked by, even privates, we were to bow from the waist at a ninety-degree angle and hold it until the bow was acknowledged by a salute or nod of the head. In the presence of Japanese guards, we were always to stand at attention. The officer assured us that escape from Bilibid was impossible and then concluded by saying we would be held there until our guilt or innocence was proven.

Guilty or innocent of what? I wondered to myself.

I learned the answer when we were returned to the cell after the formation. Pierce Wade, the sergeant who had surrendered with Vacher, had learned the prisoners in our compound were being held for military trials. The Japanese suspected we had connections with organized guerrilla units.

Inside the Special Prisoner compound discipline was loose except during roll call, or *tenko*. After breakfast we lined up and counted off in Japanese. If we made a mistake, we were beaten or struck with a rifle butt. Fortunately Sergeant Nakamura had taught us at San Fernando how to count in Japanese.

After roll there was some freedom. Cell doors were not locked during daylight hours, and we could move around inside the compound. We were not allowed to communicate with the general prisoner population outside the compound, however.

The world, for Special Prisoners, was small, consisting only of our cell block, the small exercise yard, and what we could see of the main compound through the woven-wire fence in front. Seated on a low cement wall next to the gate, we watched the haggard internees in the main population as they walked by.

They were reluctant to talk with us, having been warned by the Japanese to stay away from the Special Prisoners' compound. Fraternization could lead to punishment. The rule was not strictly enforced, however, and some dared to ignore it.

During my first week at Bilibid, I suffered a relapse of malaria. On a day when the sun broke through the clouds I sat on the two-foot concrete wall by the gate wrapped in my blanket, yet shivering with a chill. A Navy doctor outside the compound saw me.

"It looks to me like you've got malaria," he said.

"Yeah, and it's probably going to get worse."

"I'll get you some quinine. Come back here tomorrow afternoon, same time."

The doctor instructed me to follow his prescription exactly. On the first day I was to take nine five-grain tablets. The next day eight, the third day seven, and so on for nine days. I agreed, but I had never taken forty-five grains in one day and the dosage scared me.

I was shivering with malarial chills again the next afternoon when the doctor returned and slipped me an envelope with enough quinine tablets for the nine-day treatment.

"Don't forget the dosage," he said as he walked away.

I was still skeptical about taking nine tablets, but decided I had nothing to lose. My head spun dizzily and my ears rang with a loud, roaring sound. On the fourth or fifth day, the doctor saw me and asked how I was doing.

"I don't know," I said weakly. "I'm too rummy to think." But as the days passed, I improved, and when the pills were gone, the malaria was gone too.

I returned often to the concrete wall where I could take advantage of the warm sun. It was there I reflected on my situation. I thought about the comparative freedom I had known as a fugitive during the previous fourteen months. I had been able to come and go, to choose my friends, and I had been able to control my life to some degree. I had never feared capture during that time. I remembered Dr. Pineda, Fernando, and Isabel: all had been special friends. Now my situation was uncertain, wholly out of my hands, and I hated being in prison. At the same time I realized my decision to surrender had been unavoidable. As I watched the gaunt prisoners with vacant eyes pass the maximum security compound, I resigned myself to my fate, whatever it might be.

During our first two weeks at Bilibid, the Japanese left Main and me alone and there were no interrogations, but after talking with Pierce Wade and others, we knew it was simply a matter of time.

Chapter Thirty-five

The day after our arrival at Bilibid, Main and I were sitting on the low concrete wall by the gate talking about the change in our status. We were still puzzled by our brief incarceration at San Fernando and wondered what lay ahead for us at Bilibid. As we talked Pierce Wade joined us.

"Vacher tells me you guys were in San Fernando only a few days before getting shipped down here."

"Yeah, we sure didn't know that Jap colonel was going to get rid of us so soon," I said. "Now we're wondering what the hell is next."

"Well, I can tell you one thing for goddamned sure," Wade warned us. "If they didn't question you at San Fernando, you can be sure they will grill the shit out of you down here. Those little bastards do a real job on you. They kicked Vacher and me around for about a month back in San Fernando, asking a lot of stupid questions."

"What kind of stupid questions?"

"Well, just a bunch of shit that makes no sense," he said. "They want to know where you lived back in the States. Might even ask you if the road in front of your house is paved or graveled, or if you had a girl. No matter what you say, they'll hit you with one of those big swords they all carry. I don't know a damn thing about where you birds have been or what you've been doing, but you had better be goddamned ready to tell a lot of lies. Don't mention any other Americans or they'll never let up on you, and for God's sake don't mention anything about your Filipino friends or they'll be in real trouble."

Main and I listened closely as Wade told us about his experience with interrogations, and during the next two weeks we learned more about the peril we faced. Several Americans in similar situations had been executed. Shortly before we arrived at Bilibid, Colonel Claude Thorpe, who had led an ambush on a Japanese truck convoy before his capture in late 1942, had been shot.

Another officer, Major Ralph Praeger, died an especially cruel death just after our arrival. Praeger had salvaged a radio transmitter and had been sending information to Australia after the American surrender in the Philippines. The Japanese knew Praeger used the American code, and they wanted it. Praeger was beaten with a baseball bat and then hung by his thumbs for forty-eight hours, during which time the beatings continued. The unconscious Praeger, with a guard pulling each arm, was dragged into our maximum security compound and thrown into one of the solitary confinement cells. Praeger died from the constant beatings, but never disclosed the American code. His courage touched all of us, and I wondered if I could have done the same. I doubted it, but I knew I would be tested in other ways.

"Don't be afraid to lie to the bastards, and keep your story simple," Wade advised us. Having heard the Japanese officer declare we would be tried to establish our guilt or innocence, and having talked to Wade and others who were already undergoing interrogations in Bilibid, Main and I were convinced we had to carefully plan our strategy.

"What are we going to tell them?" Main asked me.

"I don't know, but it sounds like we better forget we ever heard of people like the Pinedas and Jordans."

"How the hell do we know that damned colonel didn't send some kind of report down here with us? Hell, he even knew we buried Orlo on the river. That scares the hell out of me."

Colonel Yashima knew the details of our year in the hills, and if he had forwarded our records the Japanese interrogators would know the truth about us. Yet even with the risk that our records were already at Bilibid, we decided to gamble on a lie. Our story had to be simple and consistent. Following Wade's advice, we decided to tell the Japanese we had not known any of the men in the cell prior to arriving at Bilibid, including Vacher. We would say we had been cut off from American forces before the surrender of Bataan. We were convinced telling the Japanese about our escape after the surrender would be dangerous. We would say we had lived in the hills with a Negrito named Pedro and had no contact with any other Filipinos or Americans.

"I sure don't know about the Negrito story," Main said. "If I was a Jap, I don't think I'd believe it."

"Yeah, but we don't have much choice, do we?"

Fortunately for me, interrogations did not begin until I had recovered from my bout with malaria. The sergeant of the guard came into the compound, and we scrambled into formation.

"Hileman! Main!"

Others whispered their support as we were escorted out of the compound to the round building at the center of the prison area. We were met at the door by a scholarly looking Japanese interpreter wearing thick glasses and a short haircut. Prisoners called him Joe College. An officer sat at a table in the interrogation room, and a short, stocky guard wearing horn-rimmed glasses and a black beard stood near the table holding a golf club.

I glanced around the room as we entered. There was a telephone on a small desk, a bench against one wall, and two doors leading to other offices. A table on one side of the room had six chairs, and the interpreter ordered us to sit on one side of the table. He took a seat at one end, and the officer sat at the other.

"You! Up!" Joe College ordered Main. Main jumped to his feet. "You Hileman?"

I rose and Main sat down. Embarrassed by his mistake, Joe College decided the first position had been okay, and Main and I changed positions again.

"You!" he said to me a few minutes later. I jumped to attention. "Your name!"

"Millard Hileman," I said, then gave him my Air Corps number, 19039129.

"No! No! Only name. We do not have use for numbers. You not to use numbers anymore! You sit." He pointed to Main again.

"Your name!" he said.

Main paused, remembering what I had been told about serial numbers, and then cautiously said, "William Main, United States Army."

"Okay, your number!" Joe College demanded. Main shakily answered.

As the two officers interrogated us, the guard strutted around the room brandishing the threatening golf wood. He placed it on his shoulder as though it were a rifle, used it as a cane, and even dragged it hobby-horse fashion between his legs. When the interpreter seemed to run out of patience, the guard faked blows at us. Golf Club, as the guard was called by the prisoners, had a habit of snorting noisily like a prize fighter, sometimes doubling up his fist and sparring across his face and nose as if he were wearing boxing gloves.

Golf Club left the room during the interrogation and returned in a few minutes with a bowl of bananas. Joe College took one and made a show of peeling and eating it. The interrogating officer did the same. Main and I hungered for a banana, but watched silently. Golf Club reached for one of the bananas.

"*Joto Nai! Joto Nai!*" the officer yelled at the embarrassed guard, and an angry exchange of words followed. Finally Golf Club was permitted to eat a banana, and the questioning continued.

The interpreter asked our fathers' names, mothers' names, and our mothers' maiden names. When Main had trouble remembering his mother's maiden name, Golf Club struck him over the shoulder with the wood. Main fell, and Golf Club kicked him. When he got up, Joe College gave him a cigarette.

"You like banana?" Joe College asked Main. "Okay, okay. You eat one."

Main reached for the banana, but as his hand moved forward Golf Club cracked him across the wrist with the shaft of the club. Main winced in pain and dropped the banana.

Questioning continued for several hours, and finally we were each given a banana and marched back to the maximum security compound.

"How was it?" Wade asked when we returned to our cell.

"Just like you said it would be, a bunch of stupid questions," I said.

"You didn't tell them anything, did ya?"

"They didn't ask anything important, but Golf Club whacked

Main a couple of times. He's sure an ornery bastard."

"Yeah, but to know him is to love him," Wade said sarcastically.

During the next few weeks, the routine continued. Guards came to the maximum security compound, called out our names, and took us to the round office building where a military interrogator, an interpreter, and the menacing guard awaited us.

We faced several different interrogators and interpreters. Some were military, others were members of the *Kempitai,* the Japanese secret police. Golf Club, however, was always the guard. He was persistent and dedicated, maintaining his threatening manner at all times.

Interrogators continued asking meaningless questions while Golf Club menacingly strutted back and forth in front of Main and me. Periodically one or the other of us felt the sudden jab of the four wood, and on several occasions I suffered painful blows across the back or neck. We often fell when hit, but part of that was acting, and we went down easily. I had glared at Golf Club during an early interrogation, and that act of fearlessness seemed to have won a certain amount of respect from him. It always seemed that Main received more blows than I did.

Main's old habit of mumbling made his answers difficult to understand and resulted in one especially brutal beating. Golf Club smashed Main's nose and hit his eye so hard it turned purple and swelled shut. At one point the sergeant swung the club at Main's head, narrowly missing as the intended victim ducked. The blow, delivered with fatal force, smashed into the desk.

"You guys shit! You guys shit!" was Golf Club's much-used expression. In lighter moments, I found the aggressive guard's words humorous.

Interrogations and treatment varied. While beatings were common, occasionally we were treated well and were given pineapples or bananas. On other occasions Golf Club gave one of us a cigarette, lit it, then snatched it from our mouth and ground it out with the toe of his boot, though once in a while we were allowed to finish a smoke. The moods of Golf Club and the interrogators ran the gamut from arrogance and brutality to smiles and feigned friendliness. The Japanese were unpredictable.

Interrogators asked a wide variety of questions, most of them dealing with our time in the hills. They asked for the identities of people who had helped us and sought in various ways to determine if we had participated in any guerrilla activities against the Japanese military or the Greater East Asia Co-Prosperity Sphere. They were especially interested in the Fassoth Camp, but Main and I had not been there, so we did not have to lie about that aspect of our escape. Questions often seemed irrelevant to me. They asked about my father's profession in the U.S. and seemed pleased when I said he was a farmer. When they asked for my parents' address, I gave them their route and box number in Vancouver, Washington. Interrogators tried to understand my explanation of an address being a box, and when none of my answers satisfied them, I was beaten. Afterward they gave me a banana and took me back to my cell.

Throughout the interrogations, Main and I feared Colonel Yashima would send our records from San Fernando. We wondered if withholding them could be the Japanese colonel's way of keeping his word about protecting us. In any case, the records apparently were not forwarded.

In interrogation after interrogation, we stuck to our story about living with the Negrito named Pedro and never disclosed anyone else's name. Both of us felt our chances of survival were slim, but we were determined to protect our Filipino friends to the end.

Week after week Main and I were questioned, abused, and beaten. We woke stiff and bruised in the morning, and then endured the hours waiting for the next session. Sometimes we were called in every day. Sometimes we would spend a day or two in our compound anxiously awaiting the next session. The stress of waiting was almost as bad as the interrogations themselves.

All the Special Prisoners suffered through the interrogations. Life and death for each of us was a daily uncertainty, a factor that brought us together in spirit. We compared beatings and often sought advice from Wade who had become a dominant personality in the cell.

Even in this hell of despair, we managed to find some joy.

John Scott, one of two college graduates among the Special Prisoners, was able to maintain a high level of self-discipline and accepted his imprisonment with less stress than most of us. He had somehow obtained some crayons and spent several days drawing a detailed map of the United States on the cell wall. We all became interested in his project and the hometown of each of us was carefully marked. As Scott worked on his map one day, a guard entered the cell. Everyone snapped to attention and bowed.

"What you do? What you do?" the guard demanded.

When Scott managed to explain the project to him, the guard smiled and nodded his approval. He liked the map, and each time he came on duty he visited the cell to check its progress. Other guards became interested. They would enter the cell, select a prisoner and ask, "Where you from? Where you live?" The prisoner would obligingly point to his hometown.

Another Special Prisoner who became involved in a project which eased his situation was Bill Snyder who had been captured with Major Praeger. Though Praeger had been killed, Snyder was still in an isolation cell, the last cell on the left side of the block. A large rosebush grew next to the wall behind his cell, and through the small barred window, he broke off a thick branch. Tediously working for a period of several days, he painstakingly carved an entire chess set using a piece of glass and my mess kit knife. When it was completed, I made a chess board out of heavy cardboard, and Snyder taught me the fine points of the game. We spent many hours together playing chess, though with his experience he often checkmated me in three or four moves.

The Japanese seemed to have a particular interest in music and entertainment and allowed prisoners in the general population at Bilibid to organize variety shows. The Special Prisoners were not allowed to participate, but Vacher and I knew Main had a good tenor voice and wanted him to audition.

"I can't do that," Main declared. "I've never sung in front of a crowd in my whole life."

"Bill, this isn't a crowd, and it could be a break for you," I said. "You might even miss a turn in the office with Tojo and Golf Club."

"But I don't know any songs."

Vacher and I assured him we knew the words to several popular songs and would teach them to him. The men in the cell persuaded the Japanese to allow Main to audition.

From our compound we listened to Main's audition on the other side of the wall. We could not see him, but could hear his rich tenor voice as he sang. Main returned excited. He had been accepted.

During the next several days Vacher and I taught him the words to "Rosalie" and "Rose Marie," and he already knew "Danny Boy," the song that had so annoyed Vacher and me on the Gumain River. Guards congregated at the gate to listen when Main practiced. They grinned approvingly, and Main's treatment improved.

After the months of hate that had existed in the hills among the three of us, Vacher and I now felt good about helping our friend. Main's excitement infected the other prisoners, and all shared the experience. The Japanese did not allow us to attend the show, but from our compound we could hear Main sing and the crowd's approval.

Singing of a different sort woke us one night. Two men were being dragged into the compound singing "How Dry I Am" and "Yes, We Have No Bananas." Guards placed them in the solitary confinement cell next to the latrine, but the singing continued for hours. The next morning I learned what had happened.

Two American civilians, Jake Moran and Blackie Wills, had been on a work detail in the port area of Manila with several other prisoners. Somehow they had managed to steal some alcohol and got roaring drunk. They were caught, beaten, and brought to Bilibid. Despite the beatings, they had continued their singing. For the remainder of my time at Bilibid, the two civilians were held in a solitary confinement cell in the Special Prisoner compound.

Interrogations and beatings continued throughout the summer. Everyone in the cell had many turns at it, and for the most part, all handled the repeated interrogations well. We were all strong men who had shown courage and initiative in escaping into the hills, and after months of deprivation and hardship, most of us felt there was not much the Japanese could do to top what we had already experienced. In many ways we felt superior to our captors and reinforced each other's morale. In one instance, however, a prisoner suffered a breakdown.

Dan Cahill was a big, tough-looking man whose emotions reached the breaking point one night.

"I want to go home. I want to go home," he kept sobbing in the darkness.

"Shut up, you son of a bitch," someone shouted. "Hell, we all want to go home."

Others began ridiculing the despondent man, and he became the butt of ruthless jibes and insults.

As the taunting continued, suddenly a different tone of voice emerged from the darkness of the cell. It was Harold Todd Irving who was reciting Rudyard Kipling's poem "If."

> If you can keep your head when all
> about you
> Are losing theirs and blaming it
> on you;
> If you can trust yourself when
> all men doubt you,
> But make allowance for their
> doubting too;

Irving continued uninterrupted through the poem. His words cut through the darkness, and everyone was silent as he came to the concluding lines:

> Yours is the Earth and everything
> that's in it,
> And—which is more—you'll be a Man,
> my son!

After only a brief period of silence, Pierce Wade, in a change of tone and mood, began to recite some of Robert Service's poems of the Yukon, adding some original parodies. We were torn between laughter and tears as the rhythm of the poetry and the camaraderie it engendered provided the necessary comfort. Cahill stopped crying, and gradually we all drifted into a peaceful sleep.

Nearly everyone suffered from medical problems, but perhaps the most painful were tropical ulcers that formed open sores filled with pus. All of us had them, but none like the one on Alvis Loveless's instep that had eaten its way to the tendons in his foot. While he was still at San Fernando, a Japanese guard had smashed it with his rifle butt and then made Loveless clean the blood and pus off the rifle with his dirty shorts. Loveless had not complained, although he often said, "My time's a-comin'." At Bilibid a Navy medic treating Loveless poured silver nitrate into the open sore. Tears streamed down his taut face as he endured excruciating pain. Like the others, I respected his courage.

Many of us suffered from ringworm and tried with little success to keep from scratching the itchy infections. Medics gave us a red liquid to treat the contagious fungus. It burned when applied, but after two treatments the ringworm usually disappeared.

Pierce Wade had a severe ringworm on his buttocks, which he had scratched with the sharp edge of a tobacco can lid. Lying face down on the floor, he asked Mike Slish to apply the medicine. I watched Slish carefully dab it on, aware of the pain it caused, but his slowness and concern only prolonged Wade's agony.

"Mike, just pour it on," Wade said, wanting Slish to apply the medicine quickly.

Slish obediently poured the fiery red liquid over the infection. It ran down the crack of Wade's buttocks and covered his scrotum, burning unremittingly.

"Oh, my God!" Wade shouted as he jumped to his feet. "What in the hell did you do that for?"

"You said to pour it on."

Everyone laughed.

The diet at Bilibid caused a variety of health problems. There was no protein, and we suffered from vitamin deficiencies. The lack of niacin caused pellagra, and sores developed in our mouths, skin peeled off, and our scrotums itched, burned, and turned a scarlet red. The absence of thiamine in our diet led to beriberi, a disease that caused painful swelling in our feet and ankles. Special Prisoners received smaller rations than those in the general population at Bilibid, and the Red Cross packages occasionally distributed to other prisoners were withheld from us. Our bodily functions changed, and it became common for prisoners to urinate five or six times a night.

Prison officials stationed a guard on the bench next to the latrine at night. Occasionally one of them would beat a prisoner who failed to bow as he rushed to the latrine, and sometimes prisoners were beaten with no provocation. The guards were rotated every two hours, the sergeant of the guard marching the replacement in to relieve the first guard who returned to quarters.

During one of my many nightly visits to the latrine, I saw a young guard sleeping on duty. Private Ito, who had been more lenient than most guards and had caused no problems for us, was stretched out on the bench sleeping. His rifle was lying on the cement floor.

I went on to the latrine, and as I returned, I paused again near Ito, wondering if I should waken him.

Oh, what the hell, I thought as I returned to my cell. *Let the little shit find out for himself.*

I was still awake when the sergeant of the guard came in.

"*Kiotsuki!*" he yelled. Ito snapped to attention.

We could hear the slaps and thuds as the sergeant beat him savagely. When Ito returned to his post the next night, his nose was crooked and his eye swollen shut. We found it difficult not to laugh or enjoy the guard's embarrassment. I could have prevented Ito's beating, but had not, feeling little compassion for the young private. Instead, I felt I had made a small contribution to the war effort by adding to the frustrations of one more Japanese soldier.

After two months of interrogations and beatings, we heard that a high-ranking attorney from Tokyo planned to visit Bilibid. Interrogations ceased, and we sensed a change in the attitude of the guards. Something was happening, and it involved the expected visitor.

On Wednesday, August 11, 1943, armed guards marched into our compound.

"*Kiotsuki! Kora! Kora!*" a Japanese sergeant shouted.

We scrambled from our cells into the compound. Vacher, Main, and I followed Bill Ostrander. From his days on the streets of Brooklyn, Ostrander had developed a knack for always being first in line. Earl Oatman had been admitted to the hospital after an attack of appendicitis, but the other thirty-four of us stood in the hot morning sun wondering what was happening. The sergeant casually walked down the line handing red felt patches to the first seventeen of us. Those who received red tags were ordered to remain while the others were dismissed. Calling us to attention, we were instructed to pin the tags on the left side of our pants, belt high. Each tag came equipped with a safety pin.

"Pretty little bastard, isn't it," Vacher said as he fingered the red felt. "Wonder what it's for?"

Adorned with the tags, we were dismissed and rejoined the others in the cell.

"I don't know if I like this or not," Main said. "It looks like some kind of target to me."

"Don't worry," Ostrander said. "They're probably going to move us to another cell or something."

"Sure glad I didn't get one," a prisoner without a patch joked. Most without patches seemed relieved.

Throughout the summer Bilibid had been a perilous, brutal place. Now the red tags increased our feelings of uncertainty. We had been divided into two groups, half of us with red felt patches, half without. What did it mean?

On Friday the thirteenth, a day some people considered unlucky, I sat quietly talking with Main in the execution chamber when armed guards marched through the wire gate and entered the compound.

"Kiotsuki! Kora! Kora!" came the all too familiar cry.

We hurried into the compound, and those of us with red tags were told to gather our possessions. Leaving our seventeen companions behind in the ominous-appearing death chamber, we were marched out through the wire gate.

Many thoughts ran through my mind, but there was only one real question: would I survive?

Chapter Thirty-six

As the prison's large gate closed, the question of life and death hung over us as heavy as the rain clouds over the Manila area that morning. The Japanese had already executed many who, like us, had been categorized as Special Prisoners. Now we walked to a waiting truck, accompanied, as always, by armed guards.

We quietly climbed into the truck and sat down, none of us revealing our inner thoughts and fears to another. By Japanese standards we had been tried as criminals, and the decision about our guilt or innocence had been made when the red patches were handed out. Now judgment day had arrived, but what was the judgment? Were the Japanese transporting us to Fort Santiago for execution, or were we being taken to some unknown destination? I was apprehensive. I thought about my family back in the United States, about Isabel, and about my companions, especially Main and Vacher. Was this how our lives would end? It was a moment of great peril, but also a time of strange tranquility for me. I had managed to put fear out of my mind and experienced none of the terror I had known at San Fernando when I had witnessed the brutal execution of Wendle Morgan. Whatever my fate, I was ready.

For the past seventeen months good fortune had seemed to follow me. When the seven of us had run out of food during the escape from Bataan, we found canned salmon along the trail. When I had collapsed during a malaria attack on the trail near Pasbul, Isabel's brother saved me. When I left Zambales, again malaria had ravaged my body and soul, but a Filipino farmer provided food and shelter. Now, in my most perilous moment, I wondered if my luck would hold.

As the truck passed through the streets of Manila, Filipinos gawked at us: thin, destitute prisoners who were pathetic reminders of what we had once been. Before the war we had been healthy, well clothed, and cocky. Now I was embarrassed by the attention and sympathy of the people on the street. When the truck pulled into a railroad station in the Tondo District, a short distance from Bilibid, I was relieved to be away from the piercing brown eyes of the Filipinos.

The Tondo District was a dark, dreary, industrialized section of Manila. Dirty smokestacks, run-down shacks, and unsavory thugs characterized the area. Even in peacetime it had been a section of the city where a man's life could be bought or sold for a few pesos.

Guards moved us to a wooden platform under a sheet metal roof where we sat and waited. It had been raining, but the warm August sun broke through the morning clouds, leaving the dismal streets steamy and hot.

The Special Prisoners from Bilibid were joined by other American prisoners on the platform, and I was struck by the difference in their appearance. I had been told in Bilibid about the brutal work detail at Nichols Field where so many died and about the White Angel, the most feared of all Japanese guards in the Philippines.

Now I could see for myself the results of those work details. The prisoners who joined us had been forced to perform slave labor under barbaric conditions. They were thin, sick, and in poor physical condition. The heavy physical labor, short food rations, lack of housing and sanitation facilities, and the constant beatings had caused many deaths. Mortality rates on work details varied. On some, few survived to tell about the horrors they experienced. I wondered where these men had been, but did not ask.

At Bilibid most of us had exercised in the compound. Despite short rations and a bout with malaria, I had tried to keep fit by doing push-ups, knee bends, and even pacing back and forth like a caged tiger. I had suffered frequent beatings, but felt fortunate indeed when

I saw the condition of those we met on the loading dock.

A steam locomotive belching black smoke chugged up the rails and pulled to a stop at the platform. Japanese guards crammed us into narrow-gauge wooden boxcars, much smaller than the railway cars in the United States. I stood next to the steel door, stubbornly holding my position as more prisoners were pushed and shoved inside. In addition to the seventeen of us from Bilibid, another seventy-five or eighty men were crammed into the boxcar. We could neither sit nor lie down. A guard slammed the door shut, and I heard a steel pin fall into the lock. It was 10 A.M.

With a loud jolt, the car began to move. Listening to the clanking of the wheels on the track, I feared the trip would be slow and difficult. Outside the day was hot and humid. Inside the unventilated boxcar, it grew hotter and hotter, and as the temperature rose, tempers flared.

"Quit shoving, you son of a bitch!" someone yelled.

"Get off my foot, you bastard!" another shouted.

Each shout brought an equally vile response. There was no conversation, only cursing one another. I heard Vacher in the back of the car. Someone had shoved him, and he defended his position with an unpleasant outburst of profanity. The suffocating heat created a dog-eat-dog atmosphere, but I was sure my friend was capable of holding his own.

In both San Fernando and Bilibid, I had been segregated from most other prisoners. Now in the dark, sweltering boxcar, I recognized a striking difference between those of us from Bilibid and the others. The Special Prisoners had supported one another through weeks of interrogation in Bilibid and shared a bond I knew would continue to hold in whatever circumstances we found ourselves. In contrast, those returning from the work detail seemed to be each on his own. Few had buddies to help them, and there was no sense of loyalty to one another. The Special Prisoners were stronger, both physically and mentally.

The work detail prisoners suffered from malaria, dysentery, and other diseases, and the smell of urine, feces, and vomit filled the car. The foul air became suffocating. Men pushed and shoved to get near small cracks in the boxcar, hoping for a breath of fresh air. Some fainted. It was survival of the fittest.

The train stopped and the door was opened to reveal armed Japanese guards stationed on the platform, a crude series of wooden planks built over the muddy ground. We disembarked. Before leaving that morning each man had been given a rice ball for his lunch. With nagging hunger and fear of theft, most of us had eaten our rations immediately. Those with canteens had water; those without had suffered through the sweltering morning without a drink.

Now as we assembled on the platform, those with money were allowed to buy fruit, rice cakes, and cigarettes from Filipino vendors. Those with no money, including all of us from Bilibid, went without. Water was available, and many thirsty men got their first drink since getting on the train. After an hour's respite, we were again loaded into the boxcars.

I now knew our destination was Cabanatuan, the largest prisoner of war camp in the Philippines. The remainder of the journey would take about two hours. Knowing when the trip would end made existence more bearable in the sweltering, nauseating atmosphere of the closed boxcar.

Late in the afternoon the train pulled into Cabanatuan City, a small town ten kilometers from the camp. The ground was muddy as we disembarked, and the hot, humid climate of Cabanatuan offered little relief to the sweat-soaked prisoners. Japanese guards pushed away the Filipino vendors who tried to sell cigarettes and food or to offer any sympathetic encouragement.

I looked at the people who had gathered, but turned away when I made eye contact with them. I felt ashamed, as though I had let the Filipinos down.

Yelling and waving their arms, guards quickly herded us into waiting trucks. A few felt the painful blows of a rifle butt as we climbed inside. The American drivers, prisoners themselves, were not allowed outside the trucks, nor were they permitted to speak to the new arrivals. The seventeen of us wearing the red patches were loaded in one truck, separated again from the others. By luck of the draw, we had survived the peril of Bilibid's death chamber and thought we no longer faced the danger of execution.

I thought about my trip from San Fernando to Bilibid three months earlier. What kind of health, food, and work conditions would I find at the camp where we were being taken? How would I be treated? Throughout my confinement, I had been allowed to associate only with those whose experiences were similar to my own in the hills. I wondered what those who had surrendered at Bataan would think of me and if I would see anyone I had known from the 698th Ordnance. During the past seventeen months I had heard virtually no news of the war and was anxious to know if other prisoners would have news they could share with me.

The truck turned off the road and passed through the gate into Cabanatuan prison camp. It stopped on the main street, General Homma Boulevard, named after the Japanese commander in the Philippines. Two eight-foot-high barbed-wire fences surrounded the camp, and wooden guard towers were strategically situated between the fences. Guards armed with machine guns leered down at us.

As the truck came to a stop, I could see Filipino-style buildings just inside the gate on both sides of the road. They were the Japanese barracks and administrative offices. We quickly lined up on the wet gravel road, and guards marched the prisoners from the other trucks into the main compound. Only the seventeen of us remained, and I was gripped again by the peril of being designated as a Special Prisoner, segregated from the others.

A sergeant emerged from an administration building, and with a great show of authority, walked toward us.

"*Kiotsuki!*" he shouted.

Although exhausted, we snapped to attention and bowed. We stood in the late afternoon heat facing a wooden box, and after a few minutes a Japanese officer appeared. A small man with a thin moustache, he strutted down the office steps and walked to the box. His white shirt was spotless, his boots highly polished, and a samurai sword hung from his waist. To assure that he could look down on us, the officer stepped up on the box and began an hour of uninterrupted oratory.

"You will have none of the privileges of regular prisoners," he began in flawless English. "You will not be allowed to talk with other prisoners, and you will continue wearing the red markers. Other prisoners have been warned about you."

As Colonel Shigeji Mori continued his speech, I was aware of the officer's perfect English. His precise manner reminded me of a Japanese optometrist I had met in Manila before the war. He had examined my eyes, but the war broke out before I got my glasses. The American authorities had caught the optometrist with radio equipment and arrested him for espionage. Ironically, the optometrist's name was Dr. Saboteur.

"You are criminals," Colonel Mori concluded. "You will be isolated and punished while you are here."

Chapter Thirty-seven

Colonel Mori's words swirled around in my mind as we were marched into the barracks area of Cabanatuan.

"Jap propaganda bullshit," Vacher mumbled to me. We walked down the pathway between long rows of barracks which were all alike. Raised off the ground as a protection against flooding during the rainy season, each barracks was about fifty feet long and twenty feet wide. They were constructed of native bamboo and sawali with cogan grass roofs.

Guards moved us into an empty barracks across from the Group II kitchen. When I stepped inside, the split bamboo floor squeaked under my feet. There were no individual cots or bunks, but a raised platform covered with cogan grass was built along the length of each wall. Dividers marked off individual sleeping areas. The sawali walls were built up only four feet, and above that height they were open, offering an unobstructed view of the area.

The Special Prisoners were isolated from the others who stared curiously at us and our red tags, but avoided any communication. The Japanese had warned them to stay away from us, and they did. It was understood contact with us could result in beatings and possibly death.

As the thin, sickly prisoners lined up at the kitchen across from our barracks, the effects of their imprisonment were all too apparent. Dull stares came from their sunken eyes. Their cheeks were hollow, their beards scraggly, and ribs protruded from their sides. Most were dressed in G-strings, the only clothing prisoners wore during good weather. They stood barefoot in line with mess kits, canteen cups, empty tin cans, coconut shells, or any receptacle that could hold food. Prisoners on the kitchen detail dished out their meager rations.

I could smell the soup made from the radishlike daikon, sweet potato vines, and whistle weed, a tough fibrous swamp green that was difficult to chew or swallow. Watching the other prisoners receive their ration of soup and rice reminded me of the gnawing hunger in my own stomach, but we would not be fed until they had eaten. There was little left, and we were given very small portions.

The latrine near our barracks was a trench in the ground, partially protected by sawali siding and a cogan grass roof. Long poles extending from each end were used to move the portable shelter when the trench filled. Rough wooden planks several inches apart formed toilet seats that could accommodate twenty-five men at a time, and there was no privacy. A guard escorted us to the latrine during the day, making certain there was no fraternizing with others. At night, however, we were allowed to go alone. I found the stench overwhelming and swarms of large green flies buzzed around.

A water spigot provided drinking water where we were allowed to fill our canteens. A wooden platform nearby held a barrel with holes drilled in the bottom, the prison camp version of a shower. One prisoner poured water into the barrel while another stood beneath it, then the two switched positions, providing showers for both.

I received my first issue of clothing the morning after our arrival: two G-strings and a pair of wooden clogs. The G-strings were simply a cord with a length of muslin fabric attached. The cord was tied around the waist, and the fabric brought between the legs and tucked under the cord in front. G-strings reminded me of baby diapers. I also received a used blanket, probably one that had belonged to a prisoner who had died in the prison camp.

During our first few days at Cabanatuan, the Japanese administrators seemed totally oblivious to the presence of the Special Prisoners. We were isolated, but ignored. It was as though they did not know what to do with us. Our status meant we could not leave the camp to work on outside details, so most of my time was spent in the barracks playing cribbage or teaming up with Tom Rayburn in bridge games. I left the barracks only to use the latrine or to get one of my two daily rations from the kitchen.

Cooks at the Group II kitchen across from our barracks worked only every other day. On the alternate day they were free to move about camp, but were not assigned to outside details and never left the main compound. The cooks heard that Rayburn and I played a good game of bridge, and despite the camp rules concerning fraternization, invited us to the kitchen crew's barracks for a game.

We joked about the isolation and punishment of the Special Prisoners, being held inside the compound and not having assigned work. Finally, however, the Japanese decided we should be responsible for duties around the camp. I was assigned to the kitchen detail helping the rice cook, Jerry Emerick, who I had met at the bridge game.

The Group II kitchen, unlike the barracks, was built on ground level and surrounded by a ditch that kept water from running into the structure during the rainy season. A thatched roof and sawali walls formed part of the kitchen. The rest was open, and the hard dirt floor was uncovered. Food was cooked in large black caldrons set on stone and bricks which formed the fireboxes. Kitchen personnel tried to keep it clean, but it had become known as Fitch's Filthy Kitchen, named after Major Fitch, the American officer in charge. Despite the efforts of the crew, the Group II kitchen was far from sanitary.

Monty Montgomery, the mess sergeant, ruled the kitchen with an iron hand. He was a big man who looked well-fed himself, and the prisoners who ate at his kitchen were fed better than those who ate in the other two kitchens at Cabanatuan.

I adjusted readily to the every-other-day work routine followed by the kitchen crew. On workdays I rose at 2:30 A.M., washed rice to remove dirt, rocks, and weevils, and carried wood to keep the fire hot under the huge caldrons. By the time other prisoners awoke for breakfast, the steamed rice mixed with barley was ready. After breakfast I scraped out the browned rice which clung to the sides of the big caldron. Called *bungee* it was thought to be a deterrent to dysentery, but even without that added quality, *bungee* provided extra calories and was a fringe benefit for the kitchen crew. After washing the large caldrons there was time to rest or play bridge before we began cooking rice for supper. Soup made from vegetable greens, with occasional small amounts of meat or fish, was usually a part of the evening meal. The small bits of food I was able to steal from the kitchen as I worked added to my meager diet.

Bags of dried corn began arriving at Cabanatuan, and Montgomery decided to make hominy from it. Though I knew nothing about hominy, and in fact had never eaten it, I nonetheless became the chief hominy cook for my shift in the Group II kitchen.

Under Montgomery's guidance I soon mastered the task. I scooped generous portions of ashes from the cooking fire into the water boiling in two large caldrons, creating a lye solution in which the corn was cooked. After an hour, the mixture was rinsed in cold water and then boiled another hour in fresh water to remove the hulls. When the hulls were separated, a third hour of cooking was needed to make the hominy palatable. The kitchen crew constantly tasted the hominy after it passed the lye solution, and by breakfast our hunger was already satisfied. While hominy provided an addition to the meal, rice remained the mainstay of the prison diet.

Bridge helped pass the hours on my days off, but there was lots of time for thought and introspection. Having passed my twenty-ninth birthday at Bilibid, it seemed life was passing me by, and there was no indication when my imprisonment would end. I remembered the relative freedom of my birthday in Pampanga when Isabel had baked me a cake. She had been the one good thing in my life since the outbreak of war, but I had not seen her for nine months, and there had been no word of her since my surrender to Colonel Yashima. I wondered if she had been arrested, a nagging thought which haunted me in my quiet moments. I sometimes wished I had taken Isabel to Zambales with me when she had wanted to go. Then at least I would know what had become of her. Now all I had was the overwhelming awareness of separation and imprisonment.

With imprisonment I seemed to have no future, only a sense of doom. When I had an opportunity to write a twenty-five-word note to my parents to let them know I was alive, I did not do so, thinking I would not live to see the war end anyway. My self-esteem had been low before I surrendered, and it continued to sink. Although I was in relatively fair physical condition I fell into a state of depression, a depression which seemed to appear and disappear like the rainy season's black clouds.

Chapter Thirty-eight

I dropped a pinch of tobacco into a scrap of toilet paper and rolled a cigarette. The poor-quality paper did not hold well, but I lit the cigarette, inhaled deeply, and gazed out at the dirt paths between the barracks we laughingly called streets. Many had been given American names, the one next to my barracks being Broadway.

Sitting at a small wood table near the barracks, I watched the prisoners from the main population. Scrawny men enduring the harsh realities of prison camp, they all seemed to look the same as they passed by indifferently. On the days I did not work in the kitchen, I spent much of my time watching them, wondering what horrors they had known. As I thoughtfully took a long drag from my cigarette, a familiar figure passed by.

"Hey, PeeWee!" I called.

Looking up in disbelief, it was several moments before PeeWee Standlee, my friend from Clark Field, recognized me. Ignoring the order to avoid prisoners with red tags, he walked directly toward me.

"My God, Hileman, I thought you were dead," he said. "How did you get here?"

"Came from Bilibid. How about you?"

Before he could answer, a guard noticed him talking to me, so with a quick promise he would be back, Standlee walked on to his barracks. He was well aware punishment in prison camp could be swift and brutal.

It was several days before I saw Standlee again. I was sitting with Vacher and Main after supper one evening when he came to our barracks.

"Is that all you guys do, just sit around? How come you aren't out working like the rest of us?"

"Haven't you heard?" Vacher said. "We're criminals! The Japs are afraid we might escape."

"Hell, we need all the help we can get out on the farm."

"What farm?"

"The Japs have a farm outside the camp. I've been working there about three months."

"What happens to the stuff they raise?" Main asked. "We sure as hell haven't seen any of it since we've been here."

"No, and you probably won't."

Standlee went on to tell us the produce was delivered to Filipino markets or to Japanese garrisons. Corrupt Japanese officers sold some of the vegetables on the black market. Only the culls were sent to the prison kitchens. For prisoners working on the farm, the penalty for stealing vegetables was, at the minimum, a severe beating, and it could lead to death.

Standlee had seen one man lose his life for stealing peppers and onions. When caught trying to sneak the vegetables into camp, guards had hit him with a two-by-four, breaking his ribs. Then they tied him to a post inside the front gate and left him in the hot sun all day. That night guards ended his life with a bayonet and posted a sign beside the dead prisoner that said Do Not Pick The Vegetables.

Although the prohibitions against fraternization continued to be the rule, guards relaxed somewhat and began to regard us as regular prisoners. It seemed our red tags were gradually losing some of their significance. That made it easier for Standlee to visit more often, and through him we learned about some of our friends from the 698th.

Six or seven of them had managed to stay together during the forced march out of Bataan. I was relieved to learn Alva Carpenter had been included in that group after Vacher forced him to leave our escape party. Because of the mutual support they offered one another they survived the march while hundreds of others died along the way.

From the first day of marching, Standlee had witnessed the horrors of the deadly trek. Stragglers who were too weak or sick to keep up with the others fell to the side of the road. Their weakness prompted guards to drop out of line, and a rifle shot echoed the death of the prostrate man. Guards rejoined the group, often laughing and joking as they drove their beleaguered captives onward.

In a surprising contrast to such sadistic behavior, Standlee had witnessed the compassionate nature of one Japanese guard. Homer Boren had suffered severe leg cramps and was unable to walk any farther.

"We could see guards looking for stragglers down the road," Standlee said, "and Homer kept telling us to go on without him. Hell, I wasn't about to leave him there."

As they considered their quandary a Japanese soldier approached them. Recognizing the problem, he reached into a leather pouch and handed Boren two small brown pills. He lay on his back and kicked his legs, demonstrating the pills would make Boren's legs move.

In just moments Boren was able to walk with help and very shortly was able to walk on his own. They soon realized the pills were opium, and in a world where chaos and murder characterized the Japanese soldier, this one had saved Boren's life.

Standlee did not know whether anyone from the 698th had died on the march, but some had died at Camp O'Donnell, the first prisoner of war camp where they were taken.

"I guess we thought we'd be better off when the march ended, but we were wrong. O'Donnell was a hellhole."

The starvation diet, severe water shortages, and lack of sanitation had further weakened prisoners, and many died. Standlee said Sergeant John O'Conner had died there.

I remembered O'Conner's colorful greeting when we had arrived at Clark Field in 1941, but I had come to respect him as a soldier. The last time I had seen him was in Bataan where he was sitting on the ground with his rifle, giving vent to his frustration as he fired shot after shot at passing Japanese aircraft. I was sorry to hear about his death.

Standlee had been on the burial detail at O'Donnell, and I listened in morbid fascination as he described burying the endless number of dead prisoners. Corpses were tossed out the windows of Zero Ward, the section of the hospital where prisoners were taken to die. They were picked up each morning by the burial detail and carried a couple kilometers to the cemetery.

In the beginning he had tried to handle the dead with some dignity and was appalled by those on the burial detail who had examined bodies, trying to find those lightest to carry. After a few trips, however, Standlee found himself doing the same thing. The dead were laid on sawali shutters, and each of four men grasped a corner as they began the long barefoot march to the cemetery. Often the gaunt prisoners carrying the dead slipped, and the corpses fell to the ground. The living cursed the dead as they lifted them back on the shutters. At the grave pit, bodies were dumped one on top of the other. Efforts toward orderly burials and accurate records of the dead had collapsed early. Standlee estimated the dead, both Americans and Filipinos, numbered in the thousands.

"I'll bet you were glad to get out of there," I said to Standlee.

"Yeah, but it wasn't much better when I first got here. They were dying just as fast as they did at O'Donnell."

"What ever happened to Bump?"

Grover Bump, the only member of the 698th injured when the Japanese had attacked Clark Field, had been severely burned and hospitalized. He had returned to our unit shortly before the surrender of Bataan.

"Bump is about the luckiest son of a bitch you can imagine. He not only survived those burns, but he was one of the few guys ever to live through diphtheria in the Zero Ward here. He's probably somewhere in Japan now. He and Homer got shipped out together just before you came."

Standlee's stories made me appreciate how fortunate I had been. I did not fully comprehend all the horrors my friends had experienced, but I began to realize their imprisonment had been worse than anything I had gone through during my months on the outside. Even now, the Special Prisoners' isolation in Cabanatuan was ironically working to our advantage.

CHAPTER THIRTY-NINE

*I*t has been said no man is an island, and men, no matter what their situation, need others. This was never more true than in the confines of prison camp.

Prisoners formed small groups, usually two to four men who honored an unwritten pact of mutual survival. Such support centered around obtaining and sharing extra food, and the activity became known as *quanning*. The word was coined from the Filipino word *quan* which refers to a small kitchen.

Despite the friction we had experienced in the hills, Vacher, Main, and I trusted one another and instinctively became *quan* partners. A fourth man, Henry Patton who we had met in Bilibid, joined us. Patton's strong personality had clashed with Vacher's at various times, but I was friends with both of them, so we were brought quite naturally together.

When any one of us, through any means, succeeded in finagling extra vegetables or meat, we shared it with the others. Protein was scarce in the prison diet, so whatever we could catch, buy, or steal, including rats, iguanas, or dogs, was divided with the *quan* group. Vegetables were somewhat easier to find, but that, too, required some ingenuity. Some were smuggled into camp from the prison farm, some were purchased inside the camp on the black market, and some raised in small prisoner-owned gardens. Two other Special Prisoners, John Chernitsky and Bill Snyder, had staked a claim to a small cooking area behind the kitchen and for a share of the meal would cook whatever extra food we scrounged.

Each of us hustled for the group. I stole rice in the kitchen, especially the browned *bungee* left on the sides of cooking pots. Vacher, who worked in the laundry, stole soap, a precious commodity we could use ourselves or trade for food. Patton worked in the latrine, a nonproductive area for hustling anything valuable, but he ran a poker game that helped supply our group. Only Main seemed to have a problem contributing.

At one point Patton suggested to Vacher we should get rid of Main, but Vacher's loyalty to our friend would not allow that. Despite the disagreements and jealousies which were often evident, our *quan* group remained together.

"Hey, Hileman, I just ran into Tom Coleman," Vacher said when he came from the laundry one evening. "Can you beat that? I thought he was dead."

I could hardly believe what Vacher was saying. I had not seen Coleman since we had spent a weekend together in Manila two and a half years earlier. Even as we talked, I recognized him walking up the street.

"Goddamn, Hileman, I figured you to be long dead! Vacher tells me you guys spent more than a year out in the boonies."

"Yeah, that's right, but how about you? I didn't even know if you made it to Bataan. Where the hell you been, anyway?"

"I was a machine gunner on the front lines with the infantry Air Corps. Got any idea what the average life span of a machine gunner is?"

Coleman did not wait for an answer.

"You measure it in minutes, I can tell you that. The goddamn Japs tried hard enough to kill me, but when they finally broke the lines we made them pay. That old thirty-caliber machine gun was really smoking! We piled Japs up like cordwood that last day. They were stretched all over the barbed wire. It was the most gruesome thing you've ever seen."

"How did you make it out of there?" I asked.

"Guess I'm just a lucky bastard. Got no business being here, but

I always knew I'd make it through."

I sensed Coleman had not changed much, and the old bond between us remained. The rules against fraternizing with us had eased, and Coleman became a regular evening visitor, often sharing a *quan* meal with us. One of his visits may have prevented a possible split in our group.

Vacher was always looking for coffee. When his supply was adequate, he was generous, but when it was low, he carefully guarded it. His selfish attitude angered Main, and a heated argument was in progress when Coleman appeared.

"If you want to fight, why don't you take me on?" he challenged Vacher.

The two former strong men glared at each other. From their days together in California, each knew the other's strength. Vacher was stronger, but Coleman was more skilled and had fought professionally. As they eyed each other angrily, Main spoke up.

"Come on, you guys. A cup of coffee isn't worth fighting over. Save your damned strength. You'll need it before you get out of here."

Vacher kept the coffee, and the incident was dropped. The uneasy relationship between Main and Vacher resumed as though the argument had not taken place, and our *quan* group remained intact.

During one of Coleman's visits, he and I decided to try our luck at raising a garden. We found an unused plot just down the street from my barracks, checked out a shovel and hoe at the supply shed, spaded the ground, and planted tomatoes, okra, beans, and eggplant. We carried water in the five-gallon can we used for cooking. Vacher complained, fearing we might ruin his coffee pot, but finally gave in and even helped carry water. The tomatoes and okra did not grow, but our disappointment did not stop us from replanting.

The produce that came from the garden added some much-needed vegetable to the diet of my *quan* group. With Patton's poker game, my stealing from the kitchen, and the constant trading, we maintained a relatively adequate diet. By prisoner of war standards, our group ate better than most, and I gained about thirty pounds.

The quantity of food had improved, but the needed nutritional value was still low. There were not enough vitamins, and protein was sadly lacking. This brought us into a conflict between our peacetime values and prison camp survival.

Shortly after we had arrived at Cabanatuan, a stray yellow cat wandered into camp and settled in at the Group II kitchen. He had become a real pet to the cooks, especially Jerry Emerick. Vacher, with his bent for nicknames, named the cat Tojo after the Japanese prime minister. Even Montgomery, the hardheaded mess sergeant, made sure Tojo ate well. Over the next few months, Tojo endeared himself to everyone around the kitchen, bringing us much pleasure and reminding us of family pets at home.

Hungry prisoners often teased Emerick about eating the cat.

"Emerick, if you ever get that yellow son of a bitch fattened up, I'm going to pop him in Chernitsky's *quan* bucket," Montgomery had joked.

One morning Emerick, Tom Rayburn, Bill Ostrander, and I were playing bridge outside the cooks' barracks. Although sparing in his affections, Tojo rubbed against Emerick's leg before following Montgomery into the barracks.

Moments later, a screaming yowl followed a loud crash. We dropped our cards and ran inside to see what had happened.

The yellow cat lay on the floor, his back broken. His favorite place to sleep was on a two-by-four which lay across two stringers in the rafters above Emerick's bunk. The board was not quite long enough to reach the third stringer, and apparently Tojo had jumped on the overhang, causing the board to come crashing down. It hit the cat, snapping his back.

Emerick rushed over to pick the cat up, and its hind quarters hung limp. He stroked Tojo's head, but avoided petting his broken back as the rest of us watched in stunned silence.

"Emerick, you can believe this or not, but I'm as sorry as the rest of you about this," Montgomery said. "Hell, I like that damn cat."

We all liked Tojo.

As we stood there looking at the cat, John Chernitsky came in.

"Well, I suppose the humane thing to do is put him out of his misery," Emerick said.

"Give him to me, Jerry. I'll go finish him off," Chernitsky said.

Chernitsky grasped the cat by the tail, and as he carried it outside, Tojo's head made a steady, hollow sound as it thumped across the bamboo floor.

Chernitsky returned moments later, still holding the cat's tail.

Tojo's throat had been slit, and blood matted his yellow hair.

"I'll skin him and get the stew pot started," Chernitsky said.

"What the hell you talking about, Chernitsky?" Emerick snapped. "Ain't nobody going to eat that cat. Hell, that's just like eating one of your friends."

We all sensed Emerick's dilemma, but protein was rare in our diets, and the cat would make a healthy stew.

I looked down at the floor as I thought about Tojo. It had seemed almost like a touch of home to find him silently sleeping next to the fireboxes when I came into the kitchen to work before sunrise. Even the guard we called Big Speedo petted Tojo when he made his morning rounds. The cooks had taught Big Speedo how to say "Nice Kitty," and he always talked to the cat as he petted him. None of us had dared to tell him, however, the cat was named after the Japanese prime minister.

"Well, I guess the smart thing to do is let you cook him," Emerick said. "Ostrander, do you have any vegetables stashed away?"

Ostrander smiled as he got up and headed for his bunk. He was the vegetable man in the kitchen and always had some extra hidden away. We began anticipating stew for supper.

"Hey, wait!" Emerick called out. "I know you guys all think I'm nuts, but there's no way I'm going to let you cook that cat. Somebody go bury him."

Rayburn went to the kitchen and got the shovel used to scoop ashes from the fireboxes. He beckoned to me and we took the cat outside.

"What the hell's the matter with that guy?" I said. I wanted to eat the cat.

Finding a soft place in the dirt underneath the barracks, we dug a hole. Rayburn tossed the cat in, and I covered him with dirt.

Emerick was alone when I went back into the barracks. We sat quietly talking as Vacher walked in carrying a can of freshly brewed coffee. He poured a cup for both of us, and we told him about Tojo.

"Emerick, you're dumber than I thought. You mean to tell me you buried that cat?" Vacher was dumbfounded. "Bury a cat in a concentration camp? What the hell's going on here?"

Emerick's distress was apparent as the impact of Vacher's words hit home.

"Tom, go dig up the cat," Emerick said. "We'll eat him."

Rayburn came in moments later carrying the cat. With glazed eyes, Emerick studied his dead pet.

"I'm sorry, you guys," he said. "I just can't do it."

I understood Emerick's feelings, but was somewhat disgusted by his indecision as I watched him turn to Rayburn and tell him to bury the cat again. Vacher began laughing.

"Shit, you guys make me sick," Vacher said as Rayburn took the cat out again. "You're a bunch of damn perverts, that's what you are."

Vacher looked at Emerick and began recalling historical events related to similar situations.

"How about the Donner Party in the Sierras back in the early days?" Vacher said, referring to a wagon train stranded in the mountains.

"They ate each other. Hell, they'd have been glad to have cats to eat," he continued. "Wait until I tell Main about you jerks. Did you ever hear him tell the story of how he and Old Ned got so hard up when they were up at the mine in Seneca they had to eat wildcat and cougar all winter?"

I had been around Main for a long time, and I had never heard that story. I was sure Vacher had dreamed it up to fit the occasion. The tactic worked.

When Rayburn returned, Vacher and Emerick broke into laughter.

"Tom, go dig up that damn cat. We're going to have some stew," Emerick said.

So once again Tojo's body was dug up. Ostrander got some vegetables, and Chernitsky cooked Tojo. The kitchen crew at Fitch's Filthy Kitchen enjoyed cat stew that evening.

In the conflict between values and survival, the instinct to survive had proven stronger. We had been torn between the desire to bury a pet and our need for protein, and Tojo had become the main course in a prison meal.

A few mornings later Big Speedo came into the kitchen as we were starting breakfast. He glanced around with a puzzled look on his face.

"Where Tojo? He sleep?"

We thought the cat's name had been a well-kept secret. No one answered, and Big Speedo did not press the issue. Apparently, he never learned what happened to the yellow cat who had been a kitchen pet.

Life in a Japanese prison camp presented many contradictions. One centered around the prison band, perhaps the most surprising diversion I experienced as a prisoner of war.

Johnny Kratz, an accomplished musician who had attended college with Meredith Wilson and whose talent was on a par with Wilson's, was a prisoner at Cabanatuan. The Japanese obtained instruments in Manila, and Kratz organized a band, alternately called Johnny Kratz and His Hep Cats or J.K. and the Ten Rice Balls. There was no printed music available, but Kratz, drawing on his memory and his expertise, wrote band arrangements for many popular songs. Among the prisoners there were a few musicians who had performed professionally before the war. Others were talented nonprofessionals. They joined Kratz, and we became convinced the band's quality rivaled that of the big bands we had heard in the United States.

Lieutenant Kunel, the trombone player, had sung professionally and sang with the band. His two front teeth were missing, and as he lisped through the C's in "Cecilia," we rollicked with laughter and enjoyment.

One evening a week the band set up a portable stage and performed near the Group II kitchen.

Sitting at the small table next to my barracks, I listened to popular songs like "Deep Purple," "Stardust," and my favorite, "Cocktails For Two." The setting sun turned the sky a brilliant red as the music floated through the air. Closing my eyes, I could imagine myself with a beautiful woman at the Edgewater Hotel in Chicago, sitting at a fine table eating the best steak in the house. My imagination was in sharp contrast to the watery rice and whistle weed soup which made up my diet. Only the music was comparable.

As the band played I thought about Isabel and felt sorry for myself. The sweetness of the music made me bitter. At such times I regretted my surrender and cursed myself for leaving her.

Vacher and the rest of us encouraged Main to sing with the Kratz band, but he rebuffed our suggestions. However, the music often inspired a kind of sing-along when all of us joined together in the familiar songs. When Main joined in, the rest of us dropped out, and the shy tenor would find himself singing a solo. Try as we might, though, we could not get him to sing before an audience like he had at Bilibid.

"I don't know the words," he protested.

"That's a piss-poor excuse," I chided him. "You haven't got the guts to get up there and sing where we can all hear you."

Main agreed. He never sang a solo in Cabanatuan.

Every prisoner needed help at one time or another. My hour of need came just before Christmas 1943. I had tried to ignore the onset of a severe sore throat, although friends encouraged me to go to the infirmary to see if I could get some medicine. My throat became so swollen I had to hold my head back like a chicken to swallow. I often threw up whatever I tried to eat. Vomit came out my nose, and afterwards I blew out chunks of rice.

Emerick covered for me in the kitchen so I could rest. Still I refused to go on sick call, choosing instead to remain in the barracks. My refusal was based on the reputation of the American doctor in charge of the infirmary. A large gap existed between enlisted men and officers, and prisoners maintained that enlisted men going to him were denied being excused from work unless they were so ill rigor mortis had set in. The doctor became known as Rigor Mortis. We hated him, and I wanted nothing to do with the notorious doctor.

After a few days rest, I felt somewhat better and returned to the kitchen. A week or two later I was describing my symptoms to a young doctor who stopped by the Special Prisoners' barracks. The doctor told me I had been suffering with diphtheria and said most patients admitted to the diphtheria ward died. I had survived in part because Emerick and others had taken care of me. Having friends was important.

Despite periodic frictions, I needed my friends and they needed me. It was a matter of survival, both physical and mental. I remained loyal to the Special Prisoners and to the cooks at the kitchen. I had regular contact with Tom Coleman and occasionally saw PeeWee Standlee. Beyond that small circle, I did not associate with others. They did not matter to me.

Chapter Forty

"One canteen cup of rice, twenty pesos," someone called as he walked up the street by my barracks.

"I've got two cans of Borden Instant Coffee, five pesos each," another called.

Buying and trading food was a regular part of camp life, but the bartering was especially active after the two or three times Red Cross packages were issued. The packages contained American cigarettes, instant coffee, tooth powder, canned cheese and butter, dried prunes, and other treasured items such as chocolate. Two men had to share one package, so each item in it was carefully divided. An unspoken law in prison camp required the man who split anything in two would give his partner first choice. The packages were an important link with home, and the commodities they contained were highly prized.

After splitting the packages, trading began.

"Who wants five Chesterfields for five Camels?" someone would ask.

"One can of cheese for one can of butter," another offered.

The first Red Cross package I shared was issued at Christmastime 1943. The Japanese commander lined us up for a speech saying because we were criminals our rough treatment was justified, but because of his compassion and the kindness of the Japanese people the packages were being issued. His words angered me, but nevertheless, I was pleased to get the American goods.

Red Cross packages were issued only two or three times during my imprisonment at Cabanatuan, yet Red Cross goods were always available for a price. Japanese officers had access to the boxes, and some of them collaborated with a mafia-type organization within the prison. They regularly bribed certain guards and gained access to the packages and their contents. Even though the system exploited some prisoners, it was beneficial to the general population as it circulated items which would otherwise have been distributed only among the Japanese. Even those of us not directly involved in the organization benefited from the money and goods circulated through the prison economy.

Bartering of all kinds was a necessary part of our survival. Barbers, for instance, traded haircuts for cigarettes, food, or money. Some prisoners who were artistic etched names, pictures, or insignia on canteens and mess kits in exchange for commodities. Trading was commonplace, but one form of trade had drastic, even fatal, results.

Some prisoners for whom cigarettes had become a consuming priority were willing to trade their next day's ration of rice for a cigarette. A few became so indebted they literally starved to death. Standlee had told me such trading had contributed to Alva Carpenter's death.

Prisoners needed discipline to survive. The Special Prisoners supported one another in following one fast rule: Never trade food for cigarettes.

Most prisoners developed some kind of scheme to get money, food, or other commodities. Henry Patton ran a hard-nosed poker game in my barracks. It became known throughout the camp as Pat's Poker Game.

Patton was strong and cantankerous and always seemed to be in a foul mood during the games. Consequently Vacher nicknamed him The Mean Old Man.

Playing poker seemed to be a natural way for American prisoners to pass time, but since most did not have money, commodities like coffee, rice, salt, and sugar were used for their betting. With the high premium placed on tobacco, Patton offered free cigarettes when they played. In return, he took five percent of each pot.

Perched on the sleeping platform, Patton sat chain-smoking and watching the game like a hawk. He suffered from a chronic lung problem that caused him to cough and gag until tears streamed down his reddened face. Then he would take another drag from his cigarette. The game went on day and night, and Patton never got enough rest, which only added to his irritability.

He ruled the game with an iron hand. When one man went broke, another was ready to take his place. Cheating was not tolerated, as one officer found out.

Two American lieutenants wanted to play, and Patton let them in the game, but spotted one of them cheating. He jumped from the platform, accusing the officer of the violation.

"Private, don't forget you're talking to an officer," the cheater said.

"The day has long passed when I'm going to practice military courtesy and call any son of a bitchin' officer sir!" Patton screamed.

He grabbed the officer, dragged him to the door, and kicked him in the seat of his pants as he warned him not to come back. Vacher was grinning from ear-to-ear during the altercation.

Japanese guards did not tolerate gambling and were suspicious of any card game. Tom Rayburn and I were playing cribbage on a homemade board one day when a guard walked up. A blanket covering the table made it easier to pick up the cards.

"No gamble!" the guard ordered.

"No gamble," I replied.

The guard did not believe me, grabbed the blanket and jerked it off the table. Cards, cribbage board and pegs went flying, but there was no money. The guard could not believe Americans would play cards without betting. He forced Rayburn and me to stand at attention as he slugged us. Then he made us slap each other. We tried to slap hard enough to satisfy the guard, but not sufficiently to hurt one another. A crowd gathered, and the guard became embarrassed and walked away. Rayburn and I picked up our cards and resumed playing.

Guards constantly threatened Patton's game, and precautions were necessary. He gave cigarettes to prisoners who stood watch at the front of the barracks.

"Keep it low. Here comes old baggy pants," was a common warning.

Sometimes the lookout started singing a song to warn the players, usually identifying the approaching guard. Among them were Hammer Head, The Jerk, Four Eyes, Shit Face, Big Speedo, Ak Ak, and Air Raid.

One guard caught Patton and the players by surprise. He watched awhile, took a can of Borden Instant Coffee, and left. Patton put a watch at the door, knowing the Japanese guard would return for another cut. He did, but there was no game in progress when the guard entered.

Patton prospered through the poker game, and as he did so, he shared commodities with his *quan* partners, Main, Vacher, and me. In the brutal prison economy, the game enriched our diet and kept us smoking. Patton kept the cash, and when he left Cabanatuan his musette bag was stuffed with paper money.

Chapter Forty-one

I took a deep drag from my cigarette and gazed across the street at the bulletin board which served as the message center. There were many gardens listed for sale, but few customers. Posted next to the For Sale notices were neatly typed lists of prisoners scheduled for transfer to other camps. Their destination had not been announced, but we generally assumed they were being sent to Japan. At the rate prisoners were leaving, the camp would soon be empty.

The garden Coleman and I shared was finally producing fairly well, but we had to sell because Coleman's name was on the shipping list. The garden would have been worth a good price a few weeks earlier, but the real estate market was saturated now with garden plots, and we sold ours for two packages of Picadura, a rather high-grade Philippine tobacco.

I took another drag on my cigarette and considered the list of names, including those of my two close friends, Coleman and Standlee. Both had stopped by earlier in the day to say their farewells. Coleman was a friend from home, and being reunited with him for the past few months had given me a sense of connectedness and hope. Standlee was from the 698th, one of that special group of friends I had made at Clark Field before the war. I was sad to see them leaving.

For a few moments I allowed myself to remember better times, and thoughts of the happy prewar days at Clark Field filled my mind. I missed the social gatherings under the barracks drinking gin and grapefruit juice with Standlee and the others, but then reality hit me like a clenched fist. So many from those days had disappeared or were dead, including Orlo Heinzman.

The memory of his death still haunted me. During our escape, I had wondered often who of us would be the first to die and who would be the last to survive. How ironic that the youngest had died first and had predicted his own death a year before it occurred.

My thoughts snapped back to my present situation when one of the Special Prisoners rushed into the barracks.

"Hey, you guys. They've added our names to the list. We're getting out of this mud hole too."

At dawn the next morning, July 13, 1944, we scrambled from our barracks and lined up for the last time at Cabanatuan. Although our Special Prisoner status no longer held its former significance to the Japanese, we were the last of the contingent being shipped out to board the waiting trucks.

Rain had fallen the night before, and the day promised to be hot and humid. The road was a muddy mess as the trucks carried us to the rail station at Cabanatuan City.

While we sat waiting on the platform, my thoughts turned to the change that was taking place. I was apprehensive about it, certain that any change would be for the worse. Internment at Cabanatuan had been a relatively decent experience, all things considered. I had gained weight, and my health was greatly improved. I glanced around to see how others were reacting to our changing situation. Vacher was talking with Patton, and Main was rolling a cigarette with some scrap newspaper. I thought about how lucky we had been, missing both the march out of Bataan and O'Donnell. By the time we had arrived at Cabanatuan, conditions there had improved, and as Special Prisoners we had not worked on the brutal details outside the camp.

I was startled from my reverie as guards began swinging bamboo sticks and yelling, pushing, and shoving us into the boxcars. There was a general state of confusion on the platform, but the Special Prisoners managed to stay together. We were among ninety who were stuffed into a small boxcar. I had learned some important survival tactics on my trip from Bilibid, and this time I had a full canteen of water.

When my eyes adjusted to the darkness of the boxcar, I realized it had been used to haul other prisoners. Chunks of wood had been gouged out in a futile attempt to make breathing holes, and consequently the inside walls were splintered and rough. The area next to the door provided the only movement of air and was premium space. Everyone wanted to station himself close to it. One prisoner smuggled an iron pipe into the car, and when the steel door closed, he tried, without success, to pry it open.

The overall din subsided somewhat, but vile comments could be heard throughout the car. Yet I found this trip different than my first experience in a boxcar, perhaps because of the mutual support among the Special Prisoners. Instead of the dog-eat-dog attitude that had marked the trip to Cabanatuan a year earlier, there was compassion for the sick and weak. The Special Prisoners made room for the sick near the door and made space for those too weak to stand. I shared my water with a stranger, a small act of compassion, but one that made me feel good about myself.

The train stopped several times, and we were allowed to disembark for brief periods. Filipino vendors met us at every stop, eager to sell fruit. Unlike the trip a year earlier, most of the Special Prisoners now had small amounts of cash. The compassionate vendors, when they had sold what they could, gave fruit to the prisoners who had no money.

The air in the moving boxcar hung heavy with heat and the smell of urine, feces, and vomit. For the most part, the ride was quiet, and some of the occupants even joked about getting a free trip to Japan. As they talked, I realized many did not know where Japan was located, and because I had always enjoyed studying world geography, their ignorance astonished me.

We got off the train at Tondo Station in Manila, and with only two guards accompanying us, walked about a mile to Bilibid Prison which also served as a distribution center. Sad Filipinos watched silently as we were marched through the city in tattered rags and G-strings.

I noticed a young boy form a "V" for victory sign with his fingers. He carefully made the sign at his side when the guards were not looking.

When an old woman handed a bunch of small bananas to one of the prisoners, I was reminded of Fernando and the time I had spent with him in Zambales.

"You will cut down the old banana tree, and a new one will grow at his feet," Fernando had said.

I was still thinking about Fernando and his simple life when I realized we had arrived at Bilibid.

We walked by the maximum security compound and the death chamber where I had been imprisoned a year earlier. There were no signs of prisoners there now, and weeds grew in the compound. Apparently no one had occupied the cell with the electric chair for some time. I wondered about those who were still being held there when I was transferred to Cabanatuan.

We were marched to a large warehouse I had not seen before, but then I remembered I had not been allowed to leave the small compound except for the gruelling interrogation sessions. We were led up a rickety wooden stairway to the upper floor and into a large storeroom with no furnishings. At the far end was a bathroom. I sat down on the wooden floor next to the wall.

"Kiotsuke!" a fat Japanese sergeant yelled.

We scrambled into formation, and I knew a speech would follow.

A Japanese officer strutted into the room, and with the fat sergeant standing at attention, he stepped up on a small box. I thought he looked like an effeminate reject with limited usefulness to the army, the sort of officer I hated. Lieutenant Kohari wore horn-rimmed glasses, and gold fillings emphasized his buck teeth. In halting English he informed us he was the transportation officer. He began by telling us how fortunate we were to be selected for the trip, and how well we would be treated on the Japanese mainland. We would board ship in the morning, he said.

"What a bullshitter this prick is," Vacher mumbled to me. "Bucktoothed son of a bitch looks as queer as a three-dollar bill.

"Those slant-eyed bastards have only one thing in mind," he continued. "They want to get us up there and work our asses off. Then they'll probably shoot us when Uncle Sam invades their shitty country."

That thought shook me.

The Japanese lieutenant noticed Vacher talking and fell silent as the sergeant strutted over and struck him across the face. Vacher's neck and face grew red with anger, and the sergeant hit him again. I feared Vacher would swing back, but he submissively took the blows. When the sergeant had accomplished his disciplinary task, Lieutenant Kohari concluded his speech.

"I may not get even with that son of a bitch, but I'll get even," Vacher said afterwards. "I'll make it my business to kick the shit out of every Jap I see for the next ten years."

After the speech, American prisoners who were currently held at Bilibid brought buckets of rice and daikon soup. They revealed no apparent interest in those of us being held in the warehouse, and they left quickly.

The Special Prisoners were no longer isolated from the others, but were included now in the general prison population. As I roved aimlessly among the fifteen hundred men crowded into the warehouse, I found Standlee and Coleman who had said good-bye to me the day before. I talked with others, mainly seeking information about friends from the 698th, but learned nothing.

As darkness fell I settled down on the floor next to Vacher. Somehow, in an uncertain situation, I was always drawn to my friend from California. Between the coming and going of the Japanese guards, we quietly discussed our trip. How long would it take? Was there a danger the U.S. Navy might sink our ship? What kinds of jobs would we be given in Japan? We had both worked primarily under American supervision at Cabanatuan and did not look forward to taking orders directly from the Japanese.

Vacher's knowledge had always amazed me, and on this night he talked about Japanese shipbuilding and industry. He talked about the number of Japanese industrial technicians and military officers who had been educated in the United States. I remembered that in my ROTC days in high school Japanese were even then training in the U.S. Vacher talked about Emperor Hirohito, calling him Pip Squeak. He said the Japanese monarch was an effeminate little son of a bitch who had little control over the government.

"The real bastard in their government is that sawed-off prime minister, Tojo," he said.

I remembered loading bombs with Vacher at Clark Field where he had inscribed one with the words For Old Hard-ass Tojo.

I lay awake most of the night, mulling over the events of the past three years and wondering what lay ahead. I knew the future would be difficult, but even in my wildest imagination there was little to prepare me for the hell of the next three weeks.

Chapter Forty-Two

The sound of footsteps on the squeaky stairway woke Vacher, and he leaned over and shook me. Prisoners around me began to stir from their restless sleep as a guard entered the storeroom.

"You now prepare for leaving," he ordered in broken English.

I could see the pinkish tint of the predawn sky through the window as I went to the bathroom and washed my face. I sparingly used the little bar of soap I had smuggled from Cabanatuan, and dried with the small towel the Filipino farmer had given me seventeen months earlier. It had become faded and worn, but remained a treasured possession.

After roll call we were given rice and soup for breakfast. The ample portion of rice was hot, well cooked, and had shrimp in it. The okra and whistle weed soup had the added luxury of bean curd. We ate heartily of the most ample meal we had been served by the Japanese.

It was still early when a guard led us down the stairs and across the compound to a supply house where we received an issue of new clothing, including heavy British overcoats. Prisoners joked about the overcoats, but I thought they might prove useful and determined not to let mine out of my sight. We were instructed to put on the new clothes and to carry what we had been wearing.

It began to rain, and by the time we started our march to Pier 7, we were soaked. When we crossed Dewey Boulevard and entered the port area of Manila, I recalled my arrival on the USS *President Pierce* at the same pier in June, 1941. The three years since seemed like an eternity.

The morning sun had begun to burn off the clouds as I got my first look at the *Nissyo Maru*, an old transport ship tied to the pier. Its crewmen pointed and laughed at us.

Again we experienced the unpredictability of our captors when, at the pier, they made us return all the new clothing except the overcoats. We were left with only the tattered clothes we had worn at Cabanatuan. Apparently the Japanese had wanted to impress the Filipino people who watched us being marched to the dock.

I folded my newly acquired coat and used it for a cushion as I sat down on the dock and leaned against a building. An open truck with a large-caliber machine gun mounted in back was parked at the far end of the pier, the machine gun pointed at us. A few guards milled around on the dock, but discipline was light and we were allowed to move about and talk with one another. The Catholic chaplain, a prisoner himself, walked among the worried and frightened men, offering counsel and encouragement. His presence lent a ray of hope to the disheartened prisoners.

I went to a latrine in one of the buildings and filled my canteen for the third time that morning. I had already drunk two canteens of water while we sat through the worrisome hours on the dock. Malaria had not bothered me at Cabanatuan, but my extreme thirst indicated an attack was coming on as I prepared to leave the Philippines.

We had waited for hours when finally we saw the flexible hatch cover being rolled back by a stationary wench on the ship's deck. The hatch cover was made from large wooden planks cabled side by side to form a fifteen-foot square.

A guard instructed us to throw our belongings into a net, but I kept my mess kit, canteen cup, and overcoat. I tore up some paper, hurriedly rolled some cigarettes, and stuffed them into my pocket. The rest of my meager belongings, including a pouch of Picadura tobacco, my dull razor, and a toothbrush were left in my musette bag. I tossed the bag in the growing pile and watched as the crane hoisted the net and lowered it into the hold.

We were lined up for roll call, then moved into a warehouse on the dock. The building was stifling and steamy from the intermittent rain and hot morning sun. The guards left the building, but would not allow us out.

After an hour in the hot, humid warehouse we were lined up for boarding. I was one of the first to walk up the wooden plank, cross the deck, and approach the temporary wooden stairway which had been lowered into the hold by a crane. I glanced back at the dock and saw Vacher and John Scott emerging from the warehouse. I waved, and Vacher yelled something, but his words were drowned out by the confusion and the shouting of the guards. I started down the stairway into the dark hold.

It took several moments for my eyes to adjust to the strange, dark world that was enveloping me. The hold had been used to haul horses, and although it had been partially cleaned the smell caused my stomach to go into spasms. With each step downward, hatred for the Japanese throbbed within me, and by the time I reached the floor, I was obsessed with anger and contempt for everything around me.

When my eyes adjusted to the darkness, I was surprised by the small size of the hold. There was not nearly enough room for the fifteen hundred men being loaded. Prisoners were already swearing at one another and vomiting. I saw one man suffering from dysentery pull his pants down and spray feces in all directions. Someone kicked him into his own waste.

Along the outer walls were small pigeonhole niches that had been used as sleeping quarters by Japanese troops at one time. I claimed one by putting my meager possessions in it. Two men nearby were fighting for another. Japanese guards yelled down at the prisoners from the deck, and below, prisoners yelled at each other. The noise was deafening. Pandemonium reigned as frightened, angry Americans began to sense the inhumanity of the situation. They reacted like crazed animals in a cage. Rifle butts and swords struck reluctant prisoners as more descended the stairs. I was experiencing for the first time the kind of terror those on the forced march out of Bataan must have known. The yelling and screaming were uncontrollable.

Even the Japanese were out of control. I watched one guard wending his way through the bedlam of confusion. He reminded me of a snake ready to strike its next victim. When our eyes met, I stared unblinkingly at him and he moved on.

One prisoner passed out and fell against another who pushed him down and kicked him in the back.

"Hey, you dumb son of a bitch. Can't you see he's unconscious?" I yelled. "Leave the poor guy alone, you shittin' animal."

I picked the victim up. His eyes were open, but he was incoherent as he was passed over the heads of the others to the stairway. He was carried to the deck, despite threats from guards who wanted him left below.

Prisoners kept filing in. One, a big man, threw a body block on a guard who fell from the stairway and landed in the hold. Each time he tried to get up, he was knocked down by several Americans who beat his face to a pulp. His clothes were torn nearly off, blood covered his chest, and terror was written in his swollen eyes.

"Let's kill the little son of a bitch and see if they want to start something down here, the bastards," someone yelled.

I feared for the guard's life, not because I cared about him, but rather because I worried about retribution if he was killed. I shoved my way through the mass of humanity for a closer look. The guard was on his feet, staggering around. Men continued hitting him as he worked his way up the stairs. Two other guards who had been watching from above as the prisoners beat their colleague left. I feared they had gone for help, but they did not return. I wondered if there were enough Japanese to stop us if all fifteen hundred prisoners rebelled.

The heat, stench, and smell became heavier with each passing minute. More men fainted, fights broke out at the slightest provocation, and the cursing became louder. Finally the flow of prisoners stopped. We were packed in like sardines, standing shoulder to shoulder.

Apparently the size and behavior of the unruly mob influenced the Japanese to move five hundred men into the front hold, and I saw Vacher and John Scott among those who climbed the stairs. As I watched them go, I realized the supportive strength of the Special Prisoners was being weakened.

I returned to the cubbyhole where I had stashed my coat just as someone was rolling it up and stuffing it into his shirt.

"What the hell are you doing with that coat?" I demanded angrily.

"It's not mine," the man said. "I'm just using it."

"That's my coat!"

Having no desire to fight, I was relieved when the coat was handed back to me.

Men were struggling for survival in the overcrowded hold, and I looked around for needed support. I had little trust in anyone other than the Special Prisoners from Bilibid and Cabanatuan and was able to find two of them, Ray Schletterer and Mike Slish, who came back to my cubbyhole with me. They put their belongings in it, and together we stood our ground. There was not enough room for all three of us to lie down, so we took turns. Schletterer and Slish were big men, and I was relieved to know there were two friends nearby I could count on.

When the five hundred prisoners had been moved to the forward hold, the wooden stairway was removed. Now the only way out of the hold was the metal-rung ladder bolted to the starboard wall. Through the opening above, the sky was visible, and I could see it was dusk. The loading process had taken all afternoon.

"Chow's coming down!" someone shouted.

Rice and soup buckets were being lowered into the hold with ropes. A thousand hungry men pushed their way toward the buckets in a scramble for food. The soup bucket was spilled, but was raised for refilling as the rice bucket was lowered into the hold.

I worked desperately to push my way toward it, but it was emptied before I reached it. As the refilled bucket was being lowered two men dove for it. Schletterer kicked one in the shins, and he let go of the bucket. Slish grabbed the bucket, held on, and lowered it to the floor. The man Schletterer had kicked struck out at a bystander, and the fight spread until everyone in the area was involved. Those behind us swore and shoved, and I continued to work my way to the bucket. As I filled my canteen cup, someone knocked me to the floor, but I managed to keep from spilling the precious rice. While men fought and wrestled on the floor, the soup bucket was lowered again, and more men fought. In this desperate drama, I became aware of an overwhelming hatred of my fellow prisoners.

Over the roar I heard someone yell and looked up to the opening to the hold. The melee had enraged the Japanese, and several of them stood at the opening with automatic rifles aimed at the mob. One began shooting and hit the soup bucket. Fortunately no prisoners were wounded, but the soup poured out of the riddled bucket. One prisoner tried to stuff a dirty cloth into the bullet holes. The futility of his efforts amused me as I wondered if the same cloth might have been used to wipe his ass. The bullets ended the riot.

When we had eaten our meager rations, a barrel of hot water was lowered into the hold so we could wash our dishes. The thought of washing dishes in a place where the floor was already slick from men defecating and vomiting seemed ironically absurd. The odor permeated every part of the hold.

Shouting, cursing, and fighting filled the hold with a constant roar. As never before in my life, I witnessed mob violence, greed, and man's inhumanity to man. That day I learned the deeper meaning of hate. I hated the Japanese, I hated my fellow prisoners, I hated my situation, and I hated myself. The hold smelled like a full toilet, and I felt like shit.

The shrill blast of a whistle suddenly cut through the roar of the mob. I looked up to see the Catholic chaplain, Father John Curran, standing on a shipping crate in the center of the hold. Everyone fell quiet for the first time since descending into the bowels of the *Nissyo Maru*. A clean-cut, well-built officer, Curran's physical appearance commanded respect.

"I'm the ranking officer here, and the rules I set forth will be obeyed!"

Father Curran put a special emphasis on the word *will*.

"My rules will be obeyed when food is lowered," he said. "There will not be any more riots such as we witnessed this afternoon."

In a firm, clear voice Curran was taking charge and establishing some order. The lower hold where our personal belongings had been stored would be off limits, he said. Guards would be posted at the two corner hatches leading to it. Personal property needed protection, and trespassers would be punished. The Japanese had ordered there would be no smoking in the hold, and Curran emphasized the rule would be enforced.

"No one wants a cigarette more than I do, but anyone caught smoking will answer to me," he said.

Men had been smoking earlier in the day, and I had welcomed the smell of cigarette smoke in the foul-smelling hold. I knew, however, Curran was right, and decided I would chew the tobacco stored in my pocket.

"We're not going to live down here in our own shit," Curran said. "Hear me, and hear me good. If you make a mess, you're going to clean it up."

Toilet facilities constructed topside consisted of a framework suspended over the starboard side of the ship. Built with railings, it was safe. A board with round holes served as a makeshift toilet. For emergencies a slop bucket had been placed next to the steel ladder leading out of the hold. The sick, Curran said, should sleep near the bucket.

As the ranking officer, the chaplain would have daily audience with the Japanese. There were no medical personnel in the hold, but he would try to get quinine and other needed medical supplies. He said he did not know how long the journey to Japan would take, but if anyone wanted to talk during the journey, he would be available to listen. In the midst of a man-made hell, this man of God had risen to take control. I felt a sense of relief. Instead of chaos, there would be order. Father Curran was a man to be respected.

Trapped in a strange, forbidding world where men's actions were as vile as the odor they created, I pulled one of the Picadura tobacco cigarettes from my pocket, broke it open, and stuffed some tobacco in my cheek. I wondered where to spit, but decided it did not matter because the floor was already slick with vomit and feces. I felt queasy and worried about malaria when I felt a familiar chill.

I could hear the crane loading supplies while men continued arguing and cursing in the hold. From the deck above, armed guards stood watching the scene below.

Chapter Forty-three

From the dark hold of the *Nissyo Maru,* I gazed out the open hatch as others slept, talked in muffled tones, or coughed and gagged in the stifling air. I could see the stars, peaceful white beacons in a sea of black. It seemed strange those same stars lit the night sky at home. Navigators had used them for hundreds of years to guide ships across open water, and soon they would guide the *Nissyo Maru* to Japan, the land of our enemies.

Japanese officers on deck shouted orders, and the crew scrambled to obey. Powerful engines vibrated through the ship, and I watched the stars move across the hatch as the ship backed away from Pier 7.

Almost immediately a loud scraping sounded against the steel hull. Quiet followed. The engines began pounding again, only to be interrupted by a loud metallic clank which echoed through the hold. Once again the ship fell silent. I listened to the agitated voices of Japanese sailors as they scurried around the deck above. Then I heard a small tugboat as it nudged the *Nissyo Maru* back to Pier 7, and I felt the ship bump into the dock.

Below deck, rumors ran wild. Someone suggested a prisoner had jumped overboard, but that did not explain the loud noise. Mike Slish, coming from the latrine topside, said a guard told him the ship had hit something and broken the propeller. The start of the trip would be delayed, but he did not know for how long.

A malarial chill ran through my body, and as I began shaking uncontrollably, I clutched my British overcoat. I knew fever would follow the chill. Instinctively I checked my canteen and was relieved it was half-full, but it had to be conserved. Malaria victims would get no special treatment on the *Nissyo Maru*, and that meant no extra water. My back began to cramp as I folded the overcoat, lay my head on it, and fell into a restless sleep.

With the ship tied to Pier 7, the Japanese halted the steady line of prisoners using the latrine on deck. Despite the stench, the slop bucket was the only place we could relieve ourselves. We knew the Japanese would close the hatch if the disorder and mayhem resumed, and we feared suffocation in the stagnant, rancid air. That threat, and Father Curran's commanding presence, were effective in maintaining control.

Before the morning meal was lowered, the chaplain organized a system of food and water distribution. In whatever quarter of the hold a man found himself when water or food was lowered, he was to take his turn with that group of approximately two hundred fifty men.

After forcing my way to the bucket and receiving a small portion of rice for breakfast, I struggled back to my cubbyhole to eat with Slish and Schletterer. With malaria weakening my physical condition, I would need friends.

I took a good-sized pinch of tobacco from my pocket and stuffed it into my cheek. For the most part, Curran's No Smoking rule was being observed. Schletterer quit tobacco altogether, but Slish and I chewed.

My thoughts turned to the other Special Prisoners from Bilibid. I knew Vacher and Scott had been moved out, but I assumed the others must be scattered throughout my hold. However, with Slish and Schletterer with me for support, I made no effort to find them.

Slop from the slick floor soiled my shoes and clothing, and I could not remember the last time I had bathed. The heat and stench rose as the morning sun climbed in the eastern sky. The only consolation was the absence of flies and mosquitoes.

I was eager to set sail, certain the movement of the ship would create a circulation of air through the hatch. The ship would not move that day, however. Word came that both the rudder and propeller had been damaged, and the parts had been transported to Subic Bay for repairs.

Waiting in the hot, humid, vile-smelling hold became a nerve-racking ordeal. The minutes dragged into hours, and the hours into three agonizing days. There was not enough water, and I carefully guarded my canteen as the intermittent chills of malaria became more pronounced. The chills would subside and fever would sweep through my body, demanding the relief of water. All I could do was wait.

Finally, late in the afternoon of July 19, word came down the propeller had been repaired. The prisoners cheered when it was announced we would leave the next day. No one wanted to spend more time in the hold of a ship tied up at the pier. We listened as a crane lifted the propeller into place on July 20 and soon felt the vibration of engines. Someone came down the ladder and confirmed we were under way.

As the ship moved into Manila Bay we were allowed on deck to use the latrine. A few at a time, prisoners rushed topside, most of them wanting a last look at Manila. Long lines formed before the four-hole board suspended over the water. I struggled up the steel ladder and joined the others.

The ship sailed past the Bataan Peninsula, and I stood gazing at the cloud-covered peak of Mount Bataan. My mind went back twenty-eight months to the day the seven of us had found the telephone wire leading to the summit. I remembered our surprise and disgust when I had kicked dirt off the elevation marker and realized where we were. What an unnecessary expenditure of strength the mountainous climb had been. It was there we had seen the bullet birds which dived at us repeatedly, reminding us we were fugitives in a foreign land.

"What the hell," Orlo had said. "It's all downhill from here. We got it made."

I felt a surge of pain when a Japanese guard kicked me, bringing a quick end to my reverie. Soldiers were shoving everyone back into the hold, seemingly not wanting us to look back at Bataan and Corregidor.

"I'm glad," someone mumbled. "No one but a damn pervert would want to see that shithole again."

Having formed a deep, personal attachment to the country and its people during my months in the hills, I did not agree with the man's sentiment. Sadly I climbed down the metal ladder and worked my way back to the cubbyhole and to Slish and Schletterer.

With malaria relentlessly sapping my strength, I did not get in the chow line that evening, but remained curled up in my small compartment, drifting in and out of restless dreams. When I woke it was dark, and I had to weave my way through the sleeping mass of men as I struggled up the ladder to the latrine. It had rained while I slept, and the deck was still wet, but the clouds had disappeared. I stared at the brilliant stars and listened to the rhythm of the ship's engines as we moved northward. I soaked up the cool evening air for a long time before a guard walked toward me, brandishing his bayonet. Submissively, but with reluctance, I returned to the dark hold.

An occasional forbidden cigarette glowed in the darkness, and I secretly hoped one would blow up the ship. My misery was filling me with bitterness and hate, and I was fast losing my compassion.

The next day Father Curran stood on the shipping crate he used as a platform and introduced Mr. Haase. A Navy man who had been imprisoned at Bilibid, Mr. Haase had been appointed interpreter for the prison ship. His clean uniform was out of place in the slimy hold, and I jealously wondered where he was quartered. Mr. Haase spoke Japanese, and I found myself distrusting him, convinced he was being given privileges denied to the rest of us.

A sudden change in engine speed woke me on our second night out of Manila. The ship was turning, and as I watched the stars through the hatch opening, I realized the *Nissyo Maru* was in a zigzag pattern. American submarines were apparently in the area, and the prison ship was an unmarked, easy target. Listening to the explosion of depth charges being dropped by the ship's destroyer escorts, I wondered when a torpedo would hit our ship. Officers on deck were barking orders as the ship zigzagged three times before straightening its course. When the danger had passed, we were angered to hear the celebration and laughter of the crew above.

Diarrhea kept me climbing up and down the ladder, and each trip was a struggle. Many others were experiencing the same problem, but some of them lost all self-respect and sprayed watery feces where they lay, adding to the stench and filth in the hold.

Each time I went up to the deck I hated more the thought of going down again, but under the threat of bayonets, I continued climbing back into the dark hold. By day the only light came through the hatch, and at night, two dim light bulbs cast an eerie glow over the misery below deck.

My morale continued to decline, and both Slish and Schletterer fell into the same depression, though they did not share the added burden of malaria. Thirst became a compelling force, in a sense a slow form of strangulation. Each time the water bucket was lowered, I forced my way with others toward it. The crowding and shoving caused many fights, often for only a few drops of the life-sustaining liquid. Men angrily lashed out at one another, using whatever means they could to gain access to the precious water. I was witness to one incident where a full canteen, swung by its attached chain, became a lethal weapon. Whenever a prisoner succeeded in filling his canteen or canteen cup he drank it, not daring to risk spillage or theft. Some who did not make it to the water bucket drank their own urine. Others died of thirst.

The same desperation surrounded food. As prisoners fought, others watched for an opportunity to steal unguarded rations. Thirst and hunger drove us to behave like threatened animals. At times Father Curran was able to gain some semblance of order. Other times, chaos reigned.

In this living hell, hate consumed me. I hated everything and everyone.

An explosion woke me from a fitful sleep. Prisoners who were on deck were quickly pushed into the hold by panic-stricken guards. They fell to the floor or landed on other prisoners as the wenches were started and the hatch rolled shut. There was absolutely no way of escape from the hold of the *Nissyo Maru*.

The ship began its zigzag pattern again, and in the darkness we heard the *ka-whump, ka-whump, ka-whump* of Japanese depth charges. In stunned silence, we listened to the churning motors of two torpedos as they passed under the ship. Because of its light load, the ship sat high in the water, and the lethal projectiles passed harmlessly beneath. Moments later a second explosion rocked the quiet, and through cracks in the hatch I could see the glow of fire against the night sky. One of the ships in the convoy apparently had been hit.

The heightening fever of malaria was causing me to fade in and out of delirium, and under the dim lights of the hold the fear etched on gaunt faces seemed to assume a personality of its own. Fearful men deserved to die, I thought, and the thought itself gave me a morbid sense of satisfaction. I pounded my head against the steel hull, knowing it was all that separated me from the water. I hoped if I could not pierce the bulkhead, a torpedo would. Then the hold would flood and end my misery. I had heard drowning was relatively painless, so death would be easy. In my delirium I imagined screaming prisoners clawing at each other as the hold filled with water. I continued pounding my head against the steel hull, and blood began streaming down my face.

"What the hell are you trying to do, kill yourself?" Slish shouted.

I cursed incoherently as Slish and Schletterer talked to me in quiet, reassuring tones. I eventually calmed down, and when I regained my sanity, I could not explain my actions. We talked a while, and I drifted off to sleep.

"You sure did raise hell last night," Slish said when I woke the next morning. "I've never seen anyone so totally out of it."

I felt my battered head and realized Slish had somehow found a bandage and covered my cuts. I remembered only that I had wished the ship would sink and kill all of us.

Now as I gazed around I was aware the level of cursing and fighting was increasing again, undoubtedly in reaction to the realization we had been the targets of American torpedos the night before. The yelling and screaming grew to a deafening roar as the hold became a den of uncontrolled mayhem. As the tempest swelled, guards lined the hatch and aimed guns down at us. We immediately quieted down.

In my irrational mental state, I was sure one moment we could band together, overpower the guards, and take control of the ship. Moments later I sensed an overwhelming distrust for my fellow prisoners and was convinced they were incapable of cooperating in any action, even if it meant our mutual survival. I hated everyone.

A small hatch at either end of the hold led to the lower deck where our personal property had been stored. When men in the hold began to appear with canned milk, fish, and other food products, it was obvious some were looting the personal belongings of others. Even in my condition of intermittent delirium, the thought of Americans stealing from Americans offended me. I had heard about the dog-eat-dog attitude in the early days at O'Donnell and Cababanatuan when corrupt officers and guards had hoarded medical supplies and food while others had gone without. Now I was witnessing that same self-seeking disregard, and my hate turned to rage.

Father Curran, in his attempt to establish order and fairness, had posted guards at each hatch, but it seemed some of them were receiving a cut from looters who sneaked below. I determined to do whatever I could to avenge the wrong against my fellow prisoners, and my opportunity came. In an unannounced scheme to stop the looting, Curran changed guards in midshift. I was called to guard one hatch.

I had been there only a short time when I heard a tapping from below.

"Hey, Turk, open up. I'm loaded," someone called.

I lifted the hatch, and a hollow-eyed stranger with his arms loaded looked up at me. His surprise was apparent.

"I'm not Turk, you bastard. Who are you?" I said.

"Where's Turk?"

"He's gone. What do you have?"

"Cigarettes and some cans. Don't know what's in them," the looter replied. "Got them out of a musette bag down below. Here, take it, and we'll split it when I get up."

"You son of a bitch," I shouted. "You're not coming up!"

I grabbed the looter's ears, rammed my foot against his Adam's apple, and pushed him off the ladder. He grunted when he hit the floor twenty feet below, and I slammed the hatch shut. Silence followed. I wondered if he was dead, but did not bother to investigate. Consumed with hatred, I had lost all compassion and feeling for others. I wondered if I would ever again be capable of normal human emotions. I felt totally alone.

With my raging fever and the horror of life below deck, the days and nights blended together. I lost all track of time, aware only of an insatiable thirst for cold water. My mind ran rampant as dead men were passed through the hold and thrown overboard. A living hell raged all around me.

Then Slish came scurrying down the ladder one day and said he had sighted land.

"How long has it been since we left Manila?" I asked.

"How the hell should I know?" Slish said. "I've been so busy trying to keep you clean I haven't had time to look at the calendar."

Smart ass, I thought to myself. We wondered if what he had seen could be Japan, but decided we had not been at sea long enough to have gone that far. The *Nissyo Maru* docked at Takao that night, in Formosa.

The next morning we were allowed on deck in groups of fifty. The first group returned excited. They had stripped, and guards had showered them with fire hoses. I eagerly awaited my turn.

I struggled up the ladder and took off the G-string and GI undershirt I was wearing. Both articles were crusted with filth, and I held them in my hands, hoping they would be cleaned too, as the hose sprayed a cool stream of saltwater on me. My malarial fever raged, and my head throbbed as I looked around. The August sun cast a hot, dry heat down on the deck unlike the humid climate of the Philippines.

A crane lifted bags of rice from the dock into the supply hold. Some leaked, and men rushed to gather the few raw kernels that fell to the deck. With my mouth parched and dry, I had little desire for the harsh, dry kernels, but something else caught my eye.

The crane had begun lifting blocks of ice. My mind flashed back to my malaria attacks on the Gumain River and my craving then for an ice-cold Coca Cola. I watched the ice blocks with steady eyes as the cargo net swung them toward the supply hold. The crane operator tried several times to place the ice next to the hold. When he finally had it in place, he dropped his load. Ice shattered, and pieces slid helter-skelter across the steel deck. A chunk about the size of a small drinking glass slid toward me. I ran for it, but just as I reached for it, someone else's hand grabbed it.

"Break it in two!" I shouted.

The other prisoner ignored me.

I grabbed his hair, and naked, we began struggling for the piece of ice.

"Leave me alone, you son of a bitch," he said.

I grabbed his throat and felt my fingernails penetrate the skin as I tightened my grip. Still he held on to the ice.

"Let go. Let go!" he gurgled.

I continued choking him, aware only of my driving desire for that piece of ice. I was ready to kill for it, and as my grip tightened, my opponent was unable to speak. Even with malaria, my strength was superior to his. The muscles were bulging in my arms and neck, and my teeth were clenched. My thoughts drifted in and out of reality, and the small world around me became a blur as blood oozed between my fingers. Finally, the ice slipped from the choking man's hand, but as I eased up, he grabbed it again. I tightened my grip, and only a gurgling sound came from his lips when he tried to speak. A crowd gathered as I grabbed his head in both hands.

"Let go or I'll kill you and throw you overboard," I screamed.

The man lay quiet, water dripping from the ice clenched in his fist. There were other pieces of ice, but my opponent had the piece I wanted.

"Let him go," a bystander finally said. "You're killing him. Here's a piece of ice for you."

He put it down next to me, and I kicked at his groin, wanting to kill him too. He dodged, and I began beating the first man's head against the steel deck. The beaten, pulverized prisoner released the ice and lay motionless. I victoriously picked up the ice and sat down on a steel railing, holding the prize possessively in both hands. Much of it had melted, but I savored the coolness of the remaining fraction. Someone stepped out of the crowd to pick up my limp opponent.

"Don't bother," a spectator said. "Looks like he's dead."

"I'll throw him overboard as soon as I finish my ice," I said.

Mike Slish walked over to the still, unmoving body of my victim, knelt down, and lifted his head. Blood covered Slish's hands as the man slowly regained consciousness, and Slish helped him to the hold.

He returned for me, picking me up and carrying me to the hold where someone else helped me down the ladder. Returning to my niche, I fell asleep.

I woke sometime later wearing my dried G-string. Slish had dressed me. I could remember the ice sliding across the deck and my crazed desire to have it, but the rest of the events were a blur. When Slish and Schletterer told me the details of the incident, I felt only a kind of numbed sense of satisfaction. The fight had brought about one change in me, however. I had regained my will to live.

CHAPTER FORTY-FOUR

In the span of two weeks, I had changed. When I had ridden the train from Cabanatuan, I had shared my water with a stranger. At Bilibid prior to boarding the *Nissyo Maru*, I had sought information about old friends. After spending time in the hold of the prison ship, however, I had tried to kill a man for a piece of ice. I had emerged from that fight strong-willed, determined to survive. I acquired an almost sinister attitude towards my survival, and an all-consuming hatred drove me. Those around me no longer mattered. My survival was in my own hands now, and I would not depend on others. Even Slish and Schletterer who had taken care of me were valued only as they served my needs.

We stayed only one day to replenish supplies in Formosa, and the *Nissyo Maru* continued toward Japan. Conditions in the hold became more tolerable with larger rations of food and water, and fewer men died.

It was a week later when I sighted land during a visit to the latrine. Green trees blanketed rolling hills, and waves pounded the rocky shoreline of the Japanese coast. I returned to the hold and fell asleep as the engines continued their rhythmic rumbling. Late that night the silence woke me, and I lay awake wondering what the next day would bring. As the sun rose I knew the day would be hot.

Guards lowered extra buckets of food into the hold. We wolfed down the rice and bean curd which had little taste but was rich in food value. For the first time, second helpings were allowed. Apparently the Japanese wanted us to be in a good mood when we disembarked.

Rumors circulated through the dark hold. Some said we were in Tokyo Harbor, but I correctly guessed we were more likely on one of Japan's southern islands. I had heard we would be sent to mine coal, and the thought of going underground filled me with dread.

Word came that the *Nissyo Maru* was docked in Moji, a Japanese port on Kyushu, the southernmost of Japan's major islands. We anxiously waited several hours in the dark, stifling hold while those in the front hold disembarked.

When we were finally brought up on the deck, the sun's blinding glare hurt my eyes as it had during daylight visits to the latrine. Below, on the pier, lines of men from the front hold were already being marched away. I looked for Paul Vacher and John Scott, but could not see them in the mass of bedraggled men.

Japanese doctors walked up the plank and began giving us cholera shots, and I noticed they did not disinfect the needle as they moved from prisoner to prisoner. Having received our shots, we formed a line near the ramp and passed by the doctors. Each of us dropped his pants and bent over as a glass rod was inserted into rectums for a feces sample. An epidemic of amebic dysentery had caused many deaths in Japan before the war, and the Japanese were not taking any chances with infected prisoners. Once this was completed, we walked down the plank and sat on the hot pavement. I needed to urinate, but there was no available facility. I sat with the others for two hours in the hot sun.

Japanese civilians gave each of us a rice ball, and not wanting to lose my lunch to theft, I ate it immediately. Finally guards lined us up and marched us a few blocks to waiting electric streetcars.

As I looked at the line of cars my mind flashed back to a day in Los Angeles when I was sixteen years old. I had bought a day pass and ridden the Pacific Electric Big Red Cars, as they were called in Southern California, all day long.

When I boarded the Japanese streetcar, I sat down and urinated into my canteen. The car started moving, and I threw the canteen out the window.

We were seated three to a seat. I knew neither of the men beside me, and when one of them asked me a question, I ignored it. I was on my own and in no mood for casual conversation, neither wanting nor needing company. I was relieved to be off the ship and on solid land and renewed my vow to survive.

I watched through the window as the streetcar slowly wound its way to an unknown destination. Green countryside and rice paddies separated small towns, and there were orange trees similar to those in California. I watched the people on the streets. Most walked, but some rode bicycles or drove small trucks powered by charcoal generators mounted in back. We passed a bay dotted with fishing boats, and I noticed most of the fishermen appeared to be women, children, and old men. The military and wartime industries had drained the pool of young adult men.

The serenity and beauty of the country was a sharp contrast to the brutality and ugliness I had experienced on the *Nissyo Maru.* For a brief time I seemed far removed from the circumstances of war, and I was at peace with myself. Looking ahead I saw a large industrial building with six tall smokestacks. Black smoke curled up from them in ominous contrast to the brilliant blue sky. Then the brakes squealed as the line of streetcars came to a stop.

Before me lay the prison camp in Tobata, a suburb of Kokura. The wooden buildings gave the camp a different appearance than the sawali and bamboo structures of Cabanatuan. Barbed wire and guard towers surrounded the compound.

Since we had disembarked the *Nissyo Maru,* guards had treated us politely, speaking to us with a reserved compassion and kindness. With our arrival at the camp, however, guards once again began cursing, yelling, and kicking us. Many prisoners felt the painful blows of bamboo poles.

I had never seen bamboo poles like the ones the guards were swinging. About four feet long, the ends had been split into half-inch sections, similar to a broom. The sharp, slapping sound they made as they struck an object was both threatening and irritating.

We were marched through the large, wooden, double gates which swung open and exposed the compound. Surrounded by an eight-foot wooden fence, Camp 3 reminded me of an American frontier fort. To the right of the gate was the *eso,* a small jail with no windows and bars for a door. On the left was the Japanese headquarters building. Straight ahead, at the far end of the street, was the kitchen. Ten large barracks lined the compound, six on one side and four on the other. The foul odor of sewage hung heavy in the air.

Thin, hollow-eyed prisoners, many of them dark skinned, stared at us. Officially known as Camp No. 3 of Fukuoka District, prisoners of many nationalities were incarcerated here. They included Dutch-Javanese, Malaysians, Portugese, Arabs, Indonesians, Indians, and Chinese. There were a few Americans, some had been captured on Wake Island early in the war and some were sailors from the USS *Houston,* an American cruiser sunk during the Battle of the Java Sea in February 1942.

In the same manner as the camp commanders at Bilibid and Cabanatuan had addressed incoming prisoners, a Japanese officer appeared before us when I entered Camp 3. While we stood in formation, a small, bandy-legged officer stepped on a wooden box, lifting himself head and shoulders above his taller American prisoners. Major Yaichi Rikitake appeared too old for combat, and I surmised his assignment as commander of a prisoner of war camp would free a younger man for more active duty. His uniform did not fit, and his scuffed boots were unpolished. A close-cropped mustache highlighted his round face. He spoke no English, but at his side were two Japanese interpreters.

"You are criminals. A Japanese soldier would have taken his own life rather than surrender," Rikitake said, ignoring the difference in cultures.

"You Americans have slipped into a lazy way of life, unlike the frugal life of the Japanese soldier. You do not deserve to win the war."

Rikitake told us we were to work hard in the Yawata steel mills and be paid according to the standards of the Japanese army. During our imprisonment, he said, we would be fed the same rations Japanese workers received. Meals would include rice, greens, soup, and fish or meat. The camp commander also said we would be allowed two weeks rest before beginning work.

We retrieved our personal belongings that had been stored in the lower hold of the *Nissyo Maru.* Knapsacks and musette bags had been ransacked by looters on the ship, but only canned food and tobacco had been taken from mine. It still contained my Army-issue Gillette razor with one blade, the spoon Isabel had given me, and a few other items.

At the camp supply, Corporal Nagadura issued each of us a pair of green pants and a jacket, both made of a burlap-type, loosely woven fabric. I wondered when I was handed split-toe rubber shoes and wooden clogs for our *yasumi,* or rest days, how I would adjust to the strange footwear. The clothing was intended for both summer and winter wear. Each man was given a small wooden box to carry his noon rations, and each of us carefully wrote his name and number on his *bento* box.

The barracks were plain wooden buildings placed at ninety degree angles to the street. Each was about twenty-five feet wide, one hundred fifty feet long, and twenty feet high. The entryways were doorless openings at the end of the building. Two rows of small, dirty glass windows ran along each side. One row served the upper sleeping bays, the other the lower ones, and both had vertical two-by-two wooden bars over the windows. Each light-framed building housed one hundred fifty prisoners.

I was assigned to *di hachi kutai,* number eight barracks. Two tiers along each wall formed the sleeping area. The lower tier was raised six inches off the cement floor, the upper tier was up about six feet and reached with wooden ladders. Each sleeping bay had a small shelf for personal articles.

Two long wooden tables were placed lengthwise down the center of the barracks. In the central area between the tables was a small, coal-burning stove. Low-watt light bulbs hanging from the ceiling provided the only light at night. Dim blue lights were used during air raid blackouts. All lights were turned off at 10 p.m.

The latrine at the far end of the barracks was the width of the building. A cement trough in the floor served as a urinal, and there were six holes for squatting above tanks under the floor.

Each prisoner was given a number used for identification during the first few days, and it designated our assigned sleeping space in the barracks. When I had matched my number, 1051, with the proper bunk, I found myself staring into the deep blue eyes of the slender man next to me, number 1050.

"Walt Helhowski here," he said as he reached out to shake hands. "Sixtieth Coast Artillery from Corregidor. Polack from Pennsylvania."

"Millard Hileman, Six-ninety-eighth Ordnance, Clark Field."

Helhowski greeted me with a firm, warm handshake. Although I had declared my independence from others, I was immediately drawn to this man whose name came alphabetically next to mine.

Several things about Helhowski drew my attention. He seemed to be a man who had his act together. His musette bag was complete with a needle and thread, a mess kit with cup, a good toothbrush, and more than one razor blade. He also had a good supply of tobacco. Compared to the Pennsylvania Polack I was impoverished.

Helhowski had spent time at O'Donnell and Cabanatuan after the surrender of Corregidor. In both camps he had volunteered for the kinds of work rewarded with a slight increase in rations, even though the work might be unpleasant. This included the burial, wood, and farm details. In addition, he dog robbed in prison camp. Dog robbers were enlisted men who washed clothes and did housekeeping chores for captured U.S. officers.

They were often derided by other prisoners, but with Helhowski, survival was the top priority. Throughout his prisoner of war experience, he had deliberately chosen to associate only with people who shared his principles of survival and avoided those who gave up easily. Helhowski was an organized, easygoing man whose Polish ancestry had provided him with a disciplined character and a strong Catholic faith.

I turned as a third prisoner approached and reached out to shake hands. He was Curley Hoyle, number 1052. The three of us exchanged greetings.

"Well, I wonder how long we'll call this place home?" Helhowski said.

As we talked, a Japanese sergeant and an American major came into the barracks together. I studied the two men as we lined up and began counting off in Japanese.

Takada, the Japanese sergeant, was in charge of the camp guards, and I knew that meant he carried a high degree of power. As we counted off in Japanese, several men made mistakes. Takada rolled his eyes upward each time and in a disgusted voice muttered, "Oh, boy," a phrase he had learned from Americans already in camp. The sergeant tolerated the mistakes now, but that would change.

The American officer, Major Winnefred Dorris, was the senior officer in the barracks. He had been assigned to a small room near the entry which he would share with Mr. Haase, the interpreter. Although Dorris displayed no particular spunk toward the Japanese, he appeared to be pleasant and trustworthy.

Lying on my straw mat that night, I wondered what my job would be and whether I would work with Helhowski.

Chapter Forty-five

Guards charged into the barracks before sunrise, yelling and swinging their threatening bamboo poles. They slapped them noisily against tables, bunks, or sleeping prisoners. We snapped awake immediately or suffered a painful blow from one of the ominous weapons. Scrambling to attention at the foot of the sleeping area, we bowed before counting off in Japanese.

Sergeant Takada rolled his eyes at every mistake, muttering "Oh boy! Oh boy!" His clean-shaven face, stocky build, and neat uniform accented his look of authority. Stars on his cap and sleeve denoted his rank. I studied him, certain it would be only a matter of time before he would tire of our errors and begin beating us.

After a meager breakfast of rice and a hard roll, we assembled in the compound for another count. Sergeant Takada announced there would be a barracks inspection in a few minutes. We lined up at the foot of our bunks and waited. More than two hours later Major Rikitake arrived, walked hurriedly through the barracks, and left.

The Japanese major was accompanied by Mr. Haase, the immaculately dressed interpreter I had first seen in the hold of the *Nissyo Maru*. I had not trusted him then, and seeing him with the Japanese major served only to deepen that feeling.

A lecture on military courtesy followed the inspection. As at Bilibid and Cabanatuan, we were to bow from the waist whenever we met a Japanese officer or enlisted man, or salute if we were wearing a cap. In the barracks, the first man to see a Japanese soldier was to snap to attention and yell, *"Kiotsuke! Kei Rei!"* calling the others to attention and to bow or salute.

Any Japanese soldier, from Major Rikitake down to the lowliest private, would slap, kick, or strike anyone who failed to acknowledge them.

Later that morning we were taken into the compound where our heads were shaved. As we lined up for a group photograph I was suddenly aware the uniformly shaved heads had somehow reduced the individuality of each man. Each of us was given a white card bearing the ID number we had been given the day before. I pinned the card to my chest and sensed deeply the humiliation and anonymity of being known as *ju go ju ichi*, or 1051. It was August 6, 1944, my thirtieth birthday, a day marked by losing my personal identity and being reduced to the nonentity of a mere number.

With the details of first-day orientation behind us, I spent the rest of the morning visiting with Walt Helhowski. The more we talked, the more I liked the Polack from Pennsylvania. He told me his parents had immigrated from Poland, but his mother, proud of her Polish heritage, had not become an American citizen. Helhowski had joined the army to escape the drudgery his father had known for years in the Pennsylvania steel mills. Now, in Japan, he would be working at the Yawata Steel Mills. I joked with my new friend about the irony of his circumstances. Helhowski's parents were conservative people who, like many immigrants, placed great value on the privilege of owning their own home and taking care of their possessions. I began to understand why Helhowski was so adept at maintaining order in his life. His discipline and his principles of survival were influential on my decisions as I accustomed myself to the daily routine of Camp 3.

With the constant threat of beatings, I learned quickly to count in the language of our enemies, making few mistakes. We did not always line up in the same order, so my number was not always the same. It was necessary to be constantly alert to the correct sequence. One slip in counting gave guards cause to punish the offender with a knee to the groin, a rifle butt to the Adam's apple, a resounding thump of a snapping finger under the nose, or any one of many malicious pranks designed by physically small men to humiliate their larger American prisoners.

I was willing to learn whatever Japanese words I needed to survive, but stubbornly resisted learning the language. My refusal was one means I chose of protesting my imprisonment.

Many prisoners traded food rations for cigarettes as they had at Cabanatuan, but I soon realized those men were weaker than others and more prone to sickness. Helhowski rigidly maintained food must always hold priority over smoking, and I followed his example. Although I constantly craved tobacco, I did not trade my food for cigarettes.

The Japanese had an extreme dread of fire and had forbidden any smoking after lights out. Despite the rule, we always found a way to smoke. We hid smoldering cigarettes under our shirts or blankets, and often sneaked from barracks to barracks after hours looking for a light. Nothing, it seemed, could keep us from smoking. Occasionally guards, yelling and swinging bamboo poles, woke us in the middle of the night and made us scramble outside. It was their version of a fire inspection and drill.

A roster was posted on the wall next to Major Dorris's room, assigning each prisoner a turn as fire guard at night. In two-hour shifts, the guard paced the barracks or sat at one of the long tables, and when the big wall clock indicated a shift was completed, he woke the next man on the list. Fire guards usually knew who was smoking and where a light could be hustled during the night.

Every morning I carefully planned the consumption of each cigarette, deciding when I would smoke, how much, how to save the butts, and when I would finish the half-smoked cigarette. I used a bamboo holder made by the Indian prisoners in my quest to get the last puff from a smoldering butt.

Each of us was issued a ration of ten poor-quality Japanese cigarettes. Packed loosely, the tobacco fell out the end, causing no end of frustration to the smoker. I marvelled at how patiently Helhowski smoked, sitting down and carefully handling the cigarette so no tobacco was lost.

When I finished my morning smoke I went to the latrine and shaved with my old Gillette safety razor. I painstakingly sharpened my one remaining blade against the dirty glass windowpane when I finished. The tap water was cold, so I used the hot tea that came with breakfast for my morning shave.

On my arrival at Camp 3 I had listed myself as an auto mechanic. The Japanese had said we would be classified, and I hoped for a good job. Like the two weeks of rest promised by Major Rikitake, that would not happen. I was assigned instead to the walking detail, a work crew who walked to its work site, unlike the majority of prisoners who rode the train to the main plants of the Yawata Steel Works. Twenty-five or so of us were led outside the compound to a site near the big power house I had seen from the streetcar. Our assignment was to dig excavations for air raid shelters.

A Japanese civilian met our detail and addressed his new labor force.

"You are going to work hard," he said. "If you do, you will not have problems, okay?"

Mr. Omuri was middle aged, had an average build, and wore black pants, a white shirt, and traditional split-toed shoes.

It was soon apparent our supervisor was an extremely eager employee, not unlike some company men we had known back in the States. However, Omuri's exactness for detail and his zeal became sources of humor for us.

"Okay, you see? *Shaberu. Yon shaberu!*" Omuri said as he held up a shovel.

Harold Irving, one of the Special Prisoners who had learned Japanese, mimicked the supervisor with his own translation.

"Okay, you see this? This is a shovel!" Irving whispered with a snicker.

Omuri continued his detailed instructions to his crew of Americans. He bent over at an extreme angle and as if in a movie which had been speeded up, shoveled dirt in tiny bites, throwing it in every direction.

"Now you see. Now you do! Okay?" Omuri was already gasping to catch his breath.

Watching attentively, it was difficult to keep from laughing. We were still clean, fresh, and rested while sweat stained our supervisor's white shirt, and perspiration dripped off the end of his nose. He continued his demonstration, showing us how to use picks and crowbars.

He was very thorough and went into great detail as we watched him. He reminded me of an educated supervisor from the city who had read a book on tools and assumed his crew knew nothing about their use. Omuri grew tired from the work of his demonstrations.

"Okay, *yasumi* now," he said.

It was break time, and we still had done no work. "Okay, *takusan shigoto! Takusan junyo shigoto!*"

It was time to work on the big job, the big important job.

We all picked up shovels and began digging.

For the next ten days or so we laughed among ourselves as we watched Omuri. He regularly grabbed a tool from one or another, correcting us in its proper use. Occasionally we pretended not to understand how to use a crowbar or some other piece of equipment, just so Omuri would step in and demonstrate its use once more.

"You see! Okay? You do!"

It was only a couple of days before he was dubbed Okay Omuri.

The walking detail moved from site to site digging the excavations. Japanese crews followed us to do the finishing work, building wooden frames, installing steel beams, pouring cement, and covering the structures with heavy timbers. There had been no war news, but I wondered if the construction of the shelters indicated the Japanese knew time was getting short. I enjoyed the thought.

Harold Irving was working next to me on Friday, August 18. Taking the opportunity to practice his Japanese, he was talking with Okay Omuri. Omuri joked about how lucky we were to be next to an air raid shelter. Ironically, it was only moments later when the air raid siren sounded its alarm.

The siren at Camp No. 3 was located on the powerhouse, and though I had seen it, I had not heard it before. It began with an ominous, low sound which rose gradually to a high, screeching discord, sending chills down my back. Its volume and pitch created a deafening, shattering sound unlike anything I had ever heard.

"You come with me, okay?" Omuri said.

We followed him among the buildings to an unfinished shelter, one which had no roof.

When the siren ceased its moaning, we heard the steadily increasing drone of B-17s. We rushed to watch through the open roof as guards huddled on the floor. They yelled at us to get down, but we were eager to see the American bombers.

Like giant birds, seven B-17s came into view. They came in low with their bomb bays open. Japanese antiaircraft guns fired at the formation, and black puffs of smoke could be seen as shells burst high above the oncoming B-17s. American bombs began raining down in the adjacent area.

We cheered, laughed, and jumped for joy at the sight of American planes and took great pleasure in watching the guards who hovered together in the shelter. For my part, I gave no thought to the danger. I had learned on Bataan about the force of bomb explosions and how shrapnel rose at a forty-five degree angle from the point of impact. Only a direct hit could injure a person on the ground. Apparently the Japanese guards were unaware of this, and I found real satisfaction in watching them scramble as I had been forced to do during the attack on Clark Field three years earlier.

The B-17s dropped their loads and banked to the left as two Japanese Zeros gave pursuit. One American plane was hit and trailed black smoke. I watched as it caught fire and lost altitude. Soon parachutes were visible in the blue sky.

Omuri and the other Japanese were quiet when the detail returned to work, as though embarrassed their country could be bombed.

I looked forward to telling other prisoners that night about the raid. The hill which separated the Yawata steel works from the prison camp would have prevented prisoners in the mills from seeing the attack. We learned a large armory at Kokura had been the target, and I felt I had witnessed history. My spirits lifted as I related to the others what I had seen. We talked excitedly about the next raid, anticipating when it might occur and how many planes would come. We all longed for news of the war.

The crew of the burning B-17 was captured, brought to Camp 3, and executed a few days later, accused by the Japanese of invading a holy land. The crew's personal belongings were displayed in the camp office, and the Japanese invited us to view them. Most of us went to look at the papers, money, wallets, and other personal effects, but nothing displayed identified the crewmen.

There was time to visit in the barracks before lights were turned off each evening. It was then I learned about the work details of other prisoners. Helhowski's job at the mill was carrying heavy bags of cement from a conveyor belt to a machine which closed them with a wire twist. In an area nearby others were pouring a cement floor in a machine shop which housed lathes and other machinery. Some men worked in the electric shop or in the machine shops. It was all backbreaking labor, carried on under vile and hazardous conditions.

The men who worked at the mills talked about the daily train ride. When the gondola cars passed under a bridge, young boys threw rocks at the prisoners. The malicious prank angered both prisoners and guards because the rocks did not distinguish between them.

Following the bombing run of August 18, my detail came to an end. The work had been hard, and we had been hassled and slapped, but judging from the descriptions I heard about details at the mills, it had been halfway decent.

I was sent to the mills the next day.

CHAPTER FORTY-SIX

Guards marched us to the loading dock, and I boarded the waiting gondolas for the first time. I noticed old-timers hurried aboard first and sat at either end of the car where they could rest their backs against the steel walls, a prized position. The rest of us had no back support as we sat on the floor or on our *bento* boxes. Two guards were positioned at each end.

The cars lurched as the small electric engine began its trek from the loading area, and the wheels clanked as they slowly passed over the rails. Two kilometers down the track the train entered a long tunnel built through the hill which separated the cities of Kokura and Yawata. When it emerged I got my first look at the vast Yawata industrial complex. The sprawling mills and factories were a vital part of Japan's war effort, a striking contrast to the traditional culture and beauty of Kokura.

Yawata was the heart of Japanese heavy industry on Kyushu and the site of the tremendous government-owned Yawata Steel Works. Sugar and oil refineries, chemical works, paper and flour mills, glass factories, and various metal industries made up the massive industrial complex.

If not for the low range of coastal hills, the two cities might have been one. They were separated geographically by only a few kilometers, but by the standards of culture, atmosphere, and the daily humdrum tensions of industry, they were separated by centuries.

A large Japanese flag was waving in the breeze as the train pulled up to the platform in front of the main office. As we scrambled from the flatcars and lined up, I followed the example of others who removed their caps and bowed toward Tokyo, a forced tribute to the emperor. Having acknowledged the Son of Heaven, we exercised for about ten minutes, mostly stretching our necks, legs, wrists, fingers, and ankles. I soon realized the Japanese instructors were experts. I had always disliked the discipline of calisthenics designed to build and strengthen muscles, but the Japanese stretching exercises had been designed to relax muscles. Both physically and mentally, they prepared me for the day.

Guards took us to our work stations. The group to which I was assigned was mostly Javanese from the Dutch East Indies. We were led to a large enclosed area, an extension of the foundry where the castings were molded. A forty-foot-high tin roof covered the 150-by-60-foot frame building where the hot castings were delivered to be cooled, cleaned, and finished.

My attention was drawn to a huge overhead suspension crane that moved along high rails installed along the lateral walls. The track extended through the foundry and the adjoining area where I would be working. The operator sat in a glassed-in cab with a complicated electronic keyboard. Depending on the type of casting it carried, the crane used either a large electromagnet or chains and chokers with big hooks. The chains were used to carry large castings such as naval gun barrels. The electromagnet was used to carry small items, like grenades or railroad journal boxes which housed bearings. The crane picked up hot castings in the foundry area and brought them to the sand pit area for finishing work. Giant sliding doors opened to allow the crane to travel from one section to the other. The castings were dropped into a large sand pit three feet below the floor surface.

The pit itself was walled with twelve-by-twelve-inch timbers stacked three high. The heat in the entire area was overpowering, and smoke and dust created a thick haze.

As I took in the enormity of the area and slowly realized the kind of work I would be doing, I remembered something my father had once related to me. Working for a time as a logger where power machinery and cables were used, he had witnessed several accidents, one of which had disemboweled a friend when a cable snapped. I hoped the Japanese crane operators were capable.

Two large air compressors were located at one end of the building. On the spokes of its ten-foot wheel, each compressor was stamped with its maker's insignia, Murphey's Tool Works, Brooklyn, N.Y. The compressors powered air hammers which were used to clean the castings. After castings were poured, sand and coal dust had to be chiseled out. That would be my job. I had been assigned to the jackhammer crew.

On my first day we were cleaning naval gun barrels. I picked up a big air-powered drill with a ten-foot bit. I was clumsy with the strange tool and had trouble holding it as I tried to drill the hard-packed sand and coal dust from inside the barrel. A dark, muscular Dutch-Javanese man approached me.

A.B. "Abe" Nieman took the hammer and showed me how to rest it against my thigh as I worked. Following his instruction the drill ran steady when it started. At first the intense vibration hurt my leg, and with watery eyes, already in bad condition from malnutrition, I had difficulty trying to judge where to start drilling. Nieman's patience and concern helped me as I adjusted to operating the powerful air hammer.

Nieman and I became friends but, still encased in a shell of hate, I seldom spoke to the three other Americans working in the pit.

The initial phase of the chiseling work was done with the jackhammer and drill bits, working first at one end of the long gun barrels and then the other. A long-handled scraping tool was used to pull out the rough residue, and finally an air hose was inserted to remove the fine dust remaining in the barrels. The work produced a heavy, black cloud of coal dust and sand around me.

During my time in the sand pit, I cleaned castings for railroad journal boxes, grenades, and barrels for large naval guns. Working on the journal boxes did not bother me because they were only indirectly related to the Japanese war effort. The gun barrels and hand grenades, however, were directly intended for the purpose of killing Americans. Giving such aid to the enemy angered and embittered me. Prisoners working on military weapons was against the Geneva Convention, but Japan had never signed the agreement, and I had no choice.

At 10:15 A.M. we went on break, walking up a wooden stairway to the lunchroom where hot tea was waiting. The morning and afternoon tea breaks and the thirty-minute break for lunch became a part of my carefully planned daily routine.

Before breakfast I started a new cigarette, butted it, and carefully put it into my pocket. At morning tea I finished the butt using my bamboo holder to get the last puff. After eating my rice ball for lunch, I started a new cigarette, butted it, and saved the rest for afternoon tea. Others had similar routines. Some smoked a whole cigarette at the end of the shift when we gathered for the trip back to Kokura. I preferred having a short smoke during the breaks in my workday.

Many of the civilian workers at the mill were women. I had left the U.S. before women went to work in war industries, but soon grew accustomed to seeing the female workers. Most were unattractive, poorly groomed, and plain-looking women. There was one exception, a girl we called Suzy Q.

"She's our friend," Nieman told me.

He went to great lengths to explain how careful she was when prisoners were working below the big Hercules crane she operated every third day.

In her early twenties, Suzy Q was petite and attractive. Black knee-length pants and a white blouse covered her slender five-foot frame. She always wore her cap pushed back, and a long braided ponytail hung from it to her waist.

I watched nervously the first time I saw Suzy Q climb the ladder and take the controls, but after her first pass I knew she was capable of handling the big crane. When she moved the large, hot castings, she always blew the horn to warn us. If we were doing something in the pit and could not move quickly, she smiled and waited. Only when we were clear of danger would she move the large castings into place and drop them. The other crane operators showed little concern for the prisoners below, which only deepened our appreciation for Suzy Q's awareness of the potential danger.

One operator, a surly Japanese with an obvious contempt for us, was especially tough to work around. Impatient, he vented his feelings through the constant *beep, beep, beep* of the crane's horn. If the chain and hook were not removed quickly from the castings he blasted his horn and jerked the chain through our hands. We began calling him the Gunsel.

I had first heard the term *gunsel* when I was at Clark Field. Rudolph Harper, a Los Angeles cab driver serving with me in the 698th Ordnance, had told me a gunsel was anyone out of step with humanity. Alva Carpenter, the big man who threw the disarmed hand grenade into the poker tent on Bataan, was a gunsel according to Harper. I was convinced the Gunsel at Yawata was decidedly out of step with humanity. With his vicious behavior, his buckteeth, and hair hanging in his eyes, he certainly looked and acted the part. We yelled insults at the hated crane operator as we worked, knowing the roar of the compressors drowned out our words.

We also hated the building supervisor, a short man with baggy pants, a white shirt that never fit, and glasses which constantly slipped down to the end of his nose. An employee of Yawata for many years, he neither liked nor understood Americans. We called him the Runt. He expected us to understand everything he said in Japanese, and if we did not, punishment often followed.

When my air hammer broke down one day, I vainly tried to explain the problem to the Runt. Nieman stepped in.

"No good! *Joto nai. Joto nai,*" he said. The Runt became angry with Nieman's efforts and hit him over the head with the wooden club he always carried.

"Bad! *Dami, dami,*" Nieman persisted.

The Runt struck Nieman again and then, apparently understanding more than he let on, sent me to the toolshed for another hammer.

"You say in Japanese!" the clerk there ordered.

When I did not know the Japanese word for air hammer the clerk, too, became furious. Exasperated, he grabbed a shovel handle and struck me. With each blow, he shouted *"pneumatico!"* Then he gave me another air hammer.

Supervisors, guards, and Japanese workers wore masks to filter out the smoke and dust. When heavy drilling was being done, they left the area or went into closed offices. Prolonged exposure to the coal, sand, and smoke was a health threat. I asked the Runt for a filter.

"Only for Japanese!" the Runt said.

"Son of a bitch," I said to myself as I returned to my drilling, engulfed in coal dust and soot.

Guards at the mill fell into three categories: military, civilian, and *Kempeitai* who were the Japanese secret police. They alternated shifts, two days on and four days off. The sinister *Kempeitai* guards were brutal and often beat prisoners, while both the civilian and military guards were more lenient. Japanese combat veterans, as a rule, were considered the most restrained. When dealing for food, however, the civilians were more open to trading and less afraid of military authority. As long as we paid attention to military courtesy, the military and civilian guards did not hassle us.

Some days passed more smoothly than others. When Suzy Q worked, or when we had military guards, conditions were somewhat better. The ten-hour workdays, plus the two hours for the train ride to and from the plant, exhausted us. We were given one day off a month, usually a Sunday.

Chapter Forty-seven

The monotonous routine of days in the Yawata mills allowed little change, and all we had to look forward to were more days in the same vein.

Even on our one day off there was little time for rest. Guards constantly harassed us in the barracks. They lined us up for inspection, then made us wait an hour or more for Major Rikitake. The camp commander usually walked through quickly, and we would be dismissed, only to be ordered back into formation a half hour later. The severe physical punishment was not as harsh as in the early months of our internment, but the Japanese found innumerable ways to vex us.

Only occasionally was there opportunity for a break in the monotony. Bridge and poker had been important diversions at Cabanatuan, but card games were against regulations at Camp 3. However, Cat Osmanski from the 803rd engineers started a poker game on his upper bunk directly under the dim blue blackout light. Prisoners gambled for cigarettes, Red Cross canned goods, tooth powder, and toothbrushes, both used and unused. Osmanski did not manage his game as strictly as Patton had in Cabanatuan, and players often questioned his methods. He took his cut from the pot, as Patton had, but the percentage of the take was inconsistent.

I had been avoiding the game, but with an extra supply of cigarettes, Helhowski and I decided to try our luck. Helhowski did not play poker, but he enjoyed watching, and I played for both of us.

All six players anted a cigarette and the cards were dealt. With a pair of jacks I opened for two cigarettes, and the others called.

I drew three cards, and inwardly trembled as I saw another jack and two threes. I had a full house and threw a can of butter into the pot. Two players dropped out.

Someone called and raised me five yen. Toothpaste and a new toothbrush went into the pot. Four players remained as I called and raised by a can of instant coffee. Two more dropped out, and the remaining player called my raise. Osmanski took the coffee as his cut.

In anticipation of winning the rich pot, I casually leaned against the ladder in an attempt to hide my excitement. As I did so I was aware of someone on the ladder behind me. Glancing around, I saw the familiar red stars emblazoned on the cuffs of guard uniforms. We had been caught playing poker, right at the climactic moment when I was about to win a large pot.

I turned quickly and found myself face to face with the military guard we called Bucktooth. Under camp discipline, poker players could be severely beaten. Bucktooth grabbed my wrist and said, "No good." He was referring to playing poker, not my cards.

The argument which ensued between Osmanski and Bucktooth was seemingly settled when Bucktooth picked up a can of tooth powder and left.

I won the pot, but without the coffee and tooth powder its value had decidedly diminished.

On rare occasions the British prisoners were allowed to entertain us with camp shows. Helhowski and I especially enjoyed one burlesque-type comedy team. One prisoner played a sexy streetwalker, another a bum, and a third played a bobbie. Just as the bum talked the streetwalker into a free piece, the bobbie showed up. The argument that followed, carried on with decided cockney accents, brought roaring laughter to the audience. The routine was repeated whenever they were allowed to have a show, but none of us tired of the favorite skit.

A cockney song-and-dance routine featuring Mr. Ding, Mr. Dong, and Miss Prissy added to the humor and reminded me of the first time I had gone to the Follies Theater in Los Angeles. I had been so embarrassed as I left the theater I hoped no one would recognize me. Though rarely allowed, the variety shows at Camp 3 provided a welcome break in the dismal prison life.

The Japanese provided their own form of entertainment. Military guards, dressed in their best uniforms, conducted bayonet drills on the street outside the barracks. We lined the street to watch.

When they crowned their bayonet champion, a guard we had dubbed Hog Jaw, one of the prisoners loudly proclaimed the camp tailor, an American named Huskie, could beat Hog Jaw any time. Huskie, a veteran infantryman, had served with the 31st Infantry in the Philippines and in China before that.

As prisoners began badgering the Japanese, Sergeant Takada, Major Rikitake, and Mr. Haase, the interpreter, appeared. We grew apprehensive, but a challenge to Japanese pride had been issued and a contest was arranged.

Using wooden guns, Huskie and the Japanese champion faced off.

"*Banzai!*" Hog Jaw challenged his American opponent.

He grunted and shouted other military yells, and gradually getting into the spirit of the contest, Huskie began shouting too. Mockingly, he made faces, grunted, and hollered. Japanese guards stood on one side of the street, prisoners on the other, each group rooting for its own man. Most of the American cheering section expected Huskie to adequately demonstrate his skills, then let his opponent win. He would have risen to the challenge, and the Japanese would save face.

When Hog Jaw missed with his first thrust, Huskie smacked his face with the rifle butt. The guard fell to the ground, and a tremendous cheer went up from our section. For us, the blow was like a grand slam home run in the seventh game of the World Series. Huskie waited for Hog Jaw to get up, and they went at each other again.

Huskie missed with a thrust, Hog Jaw's counter went wide, and then Huskie caught him with the rifle butt again. He would have fallen no harder had he been hit with a sledgehammer. Fear gripped me as Huskie stood over the motionless Hog Jaw. Finally, the Japanese guard struggled to his feet, bowed to Huskie, and walked away.

Stunned, not knowing what to do or say, we turned and walked quietly back to our barracks. There were no more bayonet drills on the street, and the incident was never mentioned. There was no retribution, however, and we admired the good sportsmanship of the contest.

Chapter Forty-eight

I was keenly aware of the fragile quality and the fluctuation of my personal pride and self-respect, yet I seemed incapable of maintaining a constancy in my mood or outlook. At Bilibid, facing possible death, I had kept a positive attitude and had even been able to support my cell mates. At Cabanatuan I had resigned myself to accept whatever came my way. Under the vile, inhuman conditions on the *Nissyo Maru,* I had become almost subhuman in my determination to survive.

Now, in Japan, my survival instincts remained intact, but constant hunger, filth, and physical exhaustion dragged my self-esteem to a degrading low. When I shaved with the dull Gillette razor in the morning, the face in the dim mirror was frightening. I hated that man.

It seemed even the creatures of nature conspired to lower my self-respect as lice and bedbugs feasted on my thin frame. In the latrine I picked lice from my worn GI undershirt. Squeezing them between my thumbnails, I often killed twenty to thirty in one sitting and began to enjoy the popping sound they made.

"That makes twenty-four, I think," I said to Curly Hoyle, who squatted next to me.

"Hell, I've lost track, but I know I've got that beat."

I tried to rid myself of the persistent pests by boiling my clothing, but the effort was ineffective.

The barracks was infested with bedbugs: wingless, bloodsucking insects with flat, reddish bodies. Unlike the satisfaction I found popping lice, smashing bedbugs created a nauseating odor, and their painful bites repeatedly interrupted my sleep.

Walt Helhowski slowed them down somewhat when he discovered they would not cross a wet surface. By soaking the edges of his sleeping mat, Helhowski kept the pests away, at least until the mat dried. Following his example, I filled my canteen every night, and carefully patted the cold water along the edges of my mat. By the time the mats dried out and the bedbugs returned, guards were running through the barracks swinging their bamboo sticks.

"*Kora. Kora!*" Another work day had begun.

Even the most basic attempts at hygiene were difficult. Soap was scarce, and there was not enough of the Red Cross tooth powder to meet minimum brushing needs. Because tooth powder had a high value in the prison economy, Japanese guards stole much of it and many smokers traded it for cigarettes. The prisoners who kept their tooth powder had fewer dental problems, and I determined, as I had with food rations, never to trade tooth powder for cigarettes.

The sudden onset of war in 1941 had prevented me from keeping a scheduled dental appointment, and since that time I had developed several cavities. One of my teeth began to throb in pain, and I was sure it was abscessed. The lack of dental equipment made me reluctant to visit the American dentist in the prison camp, but the pain finally drove me to his makeshift chair, a converted packing crate in a tiny room at the hospital.

The dentist took a hypodermic needle from his bag, apparently filling its vial from one of the small bottles he sorted through. He gave me shots on both sides of the affected tooth, and waited for the Novocain to take effect.

"Can you feel a tingling in your tongue?"

"No," I said. "Not yet."

He looked into my mouth, inserted a forceps, and quickly extracted the tooth. I nearly ripped the sides off the packing crate.

"That damned Novocain is no good," I said.

"No good? Hell, man, we don't have any Novocain. But if I'd told you that, you'd have given me an argument."

I was glad to be rid of the aching tooth.

The quality of the food did little to heighten my self-esteem. Cooks ladled out small portions of rice and daikon soup. Sometimes the soup had small bits of fish or fish heads in it. The diet lacked protein, and we eagerly sought the pieces of fish. I discovered when I chomped down on a fish head, the eyes popped out and rolled around in my mouth like marbles. They could not be chewed, so I swallowed them whole. Occasionally seaweed or squid was added to the rice. The seaweed was tough and hard to chew, but it was vegetable, and I ate it. The squid was a valuable source of protein, and I considered the rubbery thin pieces a treat, although my teeth had deteriorated to a point where it was painful to chew. Occasionally soybean curd was added to the soup. It had little flavor, but its nutritional value supplemented the meager rations.

Only once, in the spring of 1945, was meat added to the bland diet. As we returned one evening from the mills, a strong stench filled the air. A whale had beached itself near the powerhouse, and the carcass had been brought into camp. It smelled rotten.

Spike Moran, a prisoner from New England, recognized the potent odor.

"It's not rotten," he said. "That's whale meat."

Moran, who slept in the upper bunk across from me, talked about New England cooking, especially clam chowder, swordfish steak, and Boston baked beans. He assured us whale meat always had a terrible odor, but tasted good when cooked. I looked forward to supper.

When the whale soup was ladled into my canteen cup, I walked to the table in the middle of the barracks and sat down next to Helhowski. I felt fortunate my ration included several small chunks of meat. The soup was foul-smelling, but I was encouraged when I glanced at Moran who was eating heartily.

With my first bite I imagined a surge of strength from the protein. It seemed to warm my entire body, filling it with needed nourishment. Foul smelling or not, the whale meat added an almost-forgotten quality of richness to the soup.

"I can't eat this stuff!" The man next to Helhowski pushed his ration aside in disgust.

"Don't throw it away. If you can't eat it, we'll make some kind of deal for it."

"I don't want to make a deal for rotten meat. You can have it."

Helhowski and I carefully divided the extra ration.

For the next few evenings the smelly soup was added to our meal, but then it was gone and the diet returned to watery soup and rice.

On the whole I kept to myself in the barracks, caring little for anyone but Helhowski, not bothering even to visit Tom Coleman, although I enjoyed his coming occasionally to visit me.

Coleman had seen Vacher before the prisoners from the front hold of the *Nissyo Maru* were marched from the dock at Moji, and he told me Vacher had withstood the trip well. I was glad to hear about my old friend, but was concerned now solely about myself and my own circumstances.

Coleman seemed to have a knack for scrounging extra food, and because he did not smoke, he sometimes gave me his cigarettes, though I never asked for them. Even with his generosity I resented his being a nonsmoker because it meant he had a trade commodity and I did not. I envied Coleman's survival skills and knew I could count on him. That assurance, however, only seemed to increase my own feelings of inadequacy. I hated myself, and my only satisfaction came at the expense of Japanese guards.

I had disciplined myself to stare, unblinking, at them. When they looked down or dropped their gaze, I felt superior to them. I vowed to myself to never let a guard stare me down, and each time I won a battle of the eyes I felt a sense of victory. I was determined to survive despite the bastards and found strength in my intentional defiance and deliberate hate.

As Christmas of 1944 approached we were assembled to hear Major Rikitake speak. Rumors had been circulated about a new shipment of Red Cross packages, and the Japanese commander said he was doing us a big favor in giving a box to each man. Some of the Americans resented the general distribution which included the Javanese, Indians, and other nationalities imprisoned at Camp 3, complaining the packages should be given only to us. Father Curran reminded them the Red Cross was an international organization, and of the twelve hundred prisoners at Camp 3, only five hundred were Americans.

Each box contained a package of dried prunes, so a Javanese cook who had some powdered milk suggested we pool them and he would make a prune whip for Christmas dinner. We all anticipated our first dessert since becoming prisoners.

Before going to the mill on Sunday, December 24, we were told we would have Christmas Day off. Father Curran asked Major Rikitake, who professed to be a Catholic himself, for permission to conduct a midnight mass. Rikitake approved and, in fact, thought it was such a good idea he ordered the guards to attend.

Just before midnight on Christmas Eve we were wakened as guards charged into the barracks swinging the bamboo poles and yelling, *"Kora. Kora!"*

I climbed out of my bunk, wrapped my thin blanket around my shoulders, and followed the others outside. An inch of snow had fallen that evening, covering the ground with a white blanket. Immediately sensing the cold on the bottoms of my feet, I turned to Helhowski.

"How long will this take? I forgot my damn shoes."

Father Curran, wearing his clerical robe, stood on a platform in front of us. Major Rikitake was at his left with the three interpreters, including Mr. Haase, beside him. The camp guards were assembled in formation around them. The protocol indicated this would be a serious ceremony, and serious it may have been, but I was aware of only one thing: my feet were cold. I stood numbly through the hour-long mass, thinking about having to get back on my cold mat with little to cover myself and knowing my feet would remain cold all night. We were not allowed to put any coal in the small fireboxes after 10 P.M., and the fire had gone out before the mass started.

How the hell do they expect a little firebox like that to keep a hundred and fifty men warm? I thought to myself as I shivered in the cold.

The small daily ration of coal was inadequate at best, and we consistently smuggled extra pieces into the barracks from the mills in an effort to keep a fire a little longer in the evening. Those who brought coal earned the right to stand next to the heat. There was no place there for those who did not contribute, an unwritten rule even though some had no access to it. I smuggled coal back into camp at every possible opportunity. Tying a lump or two with a string, I hung it inside my pants. I put small pieces in my pockets, or occasionally put a lump under my cap, depending on which guards were on duty. I did not like being cold.

The mass finally ended, and I returned to the unheated barracks for a cold, sleepless night. On Christmas morning, following a breakfast of rice, a hard roll, and tea, I examined the precious contents of my Red Cross box. After eating, trading, and bartering I still had a four-ounce can of Borden instant coffee, a tin of processed cheese, a can of butter, and an unopened package of ten cigarettes.

My thoughts turned to home and the traditional Christmases I had known. I remembered especially my mother's fruitcakes which were always stored in brandy-soaked cheesecloth. I had deliberately suppressed thoughts of my family, but it was Christmas, and on this day I regretted not having sent word to my parents when I had the opportunity. I wondered if they were thinking of me on this Christmas Day and if they even knew I was alive.

After the Christmas mass and a day off, we returned to the monotonous drudgery of the mills. On New Year's Day, men in the barracks sang "Auld Lang Syne," but other than that, it was just another workday.

In the spring I received a surprise. Tom Coleman came to my barracks with a box my mother and sister-in-law had sent to him. With no family of his own, Coleman had listed my parents as beneficiaries on his GI life insurance. Unknown to me he had sent them one of the form postcards from Cabanatuan, and in his message had let my parents know I was alive.

In the letter that accompanied the package, my mother asked him to share it with me if I was around. The fruitcake and cookies, mailed before Christmas, were stale, but the rest was a treasure. The box contained playing cards, dice, underwear, two pairs of socks, needles, thread, two cans of Union Leader tobacco, and brown cigarette papers. Staring at the contents, I felt I suddenly possessed all the riches a man could want. Coleman gave all the tobacco to me, and I split it with Helhowski. It was an exciting day.

While the package delighted me, it also disturbed me deeply. I thought about having ignored opportunities to write, and now a piece of home had touched me for the first time in three years. Feelings of guilt hung heavy as I rolled a cigarette, savoring the American tobacco.

Chapter Forty-nine

Shortly after New Year's, an apparent cold caused me to cough up globs of black coal dust day and night. At times blood colored the dark mucus. In talking with others on the jackhammer crew, I found some of them were suffering the same symptoms. Dr. Anderson, an American doctor in camp, had told them conditions in the pit, with its heavy cloud of smoke and coal dust, were the worst at Yawata. My cough persisted, and I went on sick call.

A Japanese doctor diagnosed my illness as pneumonia and sent me to the hospital, a fate I dreaded.

My small bunk resembled a crudely built wooden box with a thin mattress of rice straw. Although primitive, it was the first time I had slept on any kind of a bed since my surrender. The steam heat in the hospital was turned off at night, but I was given enough blankets to keep warm.

For the first two days medics paid little attention to me, but on the third day my temperature rose to 106-degrees and I became delirious, passing in and out of consciousness. I lost all track of time until my fever broke several days later. During my recovery, I learned in their struggle to bring my fever down, medics had given me the last dosage of sulfadiazine at Camp 3.

Yet even as I slowly recovered, more pneumonia victims were being admitted to the hospital. Many of them were survivors of the *Oryoku Maru,* a transport ship sunk by American planes off Luzon. Of the sixteen hundred prisoners on board, five hundred had survived, and of that group ninety, most of them officers, were sent to Camp 3. Suffering from malnutrition, starvation, disease, and exhaustion, they truly looked like the walking dead, and pneumonia quietly claimed many of them. Without medicine there was little medics could do for them. I had been fortunate. Had I not received sulfadiazine, I undoubtedly would have died with the others.

I had not fully recovered by mid-January, but the hospital was overflowing with patients, and I was returned to my barracks. One of the *Oryoku Maru* survivors, Major John Trapnell, would take my bed. I had an opportunity to visit with him and realized that contrary to my general feeling toward officers, I liked this man. An All-American football player at West Point in 1927, he was from the 26th Cavalry. Except for the few days when I was violently ill, the time away from the mills had been a welcome respite for me, and I hated to leave the hospital. Yet, as I prepared to leave, I was glad it was Trapnell who would take my bunk.

When I was discharged I was given a reddish orange tag bearing the Japanese inscription Camp Work Only. I was still too weak to work in the mill and was still coughing up globs of blackened phlegm. I spent the next two days resting in the barracks and reading *Ivanhoe,* a book I had hated in high school. Malnutrition had caused severe eye problems, and though I finished the book, I found it increasingly difficult to see the words.

My vision was deteriorating rapidly. At the end of the barracks was a large clock with a white face and black numerals. I found myself squinting and studying the clock to figure out the time, and by spring I was unable to read at all. Others, too, were experiencing vision loss, a result of the vitamin-deficient diet.

During the time I spent in the hospital and recuperating in the barracks, I gained about ten pounds. With my strength returning, Major Dorris asked me if I could handle burial detail. The work required pushing a two-wheel cart three kilometers to the crematorium. I welcomed the thought of leaving the camp and possibly seeing part of the town.

Burial detail meant picking up a dead prisoner at the hospital and taking the corpse to the crematorium on the burial cart, a simple board platform between two bicycle wheels. The cart had a handle across the back for pushing. The single closed casket was used over and over, and on the return from the crematorium it held a small cardboard box with the dead man's ashes.

It took two of us to push and pull the cart through the streets and hills of Kokura. My work partner was Pappy Harris, one of the musicians who had played piano and organ in the Cabanatuan band. Working with him, I recalled listening to the band as the sun set over the prison camp in the Philippines. Harris spoke fondly of the band members and wondered if they were still performing. He knew they were all in Cabanatuan when he was shipped out.

An older man, Harris had been in the army for a long time and talked about soldiering in China during the 1930s. I enjoyed the good-natured musician, a man who adapted well to prison life.

On our first trip to the crematorium we carried an officer from the *Oryoku Maru,* one of many pneumonia victims that winter. As we pushed the cart down cobblestone streets, we were aware that civilians stared at us. Nearly all were old men and women, or young boys and girls. Able-bodied men and women were in the military or working in wartime industries. I tired quickly from the exertion of pushing the cart up the hills, and my hip severely cramped under the strain.

As the pain in my hip throbbed, I remembered the agony of the trip I had made when I left the Jordan farm to strike out for a couple days on my own. My hips and knees had throbbed with pain then too, and a malarial fever had run rampant through my body. Isabel's brother had found me lying unconscious on the ground, picked me up, and carried me to safety. As I remembered, I thought again about Isabel, as I did every day. I hated myself for leaving her.

Limping slowly along, pushing the burial cart, I felt a sudden pain in my back. I turned to see our impatient guard ready to jab me again with his rifle butt. I pushed harder. I wanted to stare into the guard's eyes, but he walked menacingly behind us.

I could see the crematorium ahead, a windowless stone building with a slate roof. Black smoke floated lazily from the gray brick chimney towering above the building. Harris and I pushed the cart to the door, and the guard summoned the caretakers. While they carried the casket inside, we were left unguarded. We gratefully sank to the manicured green lawn to rest.

We had been warned to stay away from Japanese civilians, but as we rested, an elderly Japanese woman came out of the small house next to the crematorium and walked over to us. Harris, who had been on the burial detail before, said the prisoners called her Mama San.

Mama San offered us a tomato and a large white daikon.

"I so solly fol you," she said with a smile.

I tried to tell Mama San the guard would punish us, but when I mentioned the guard, she made a sour face and pretended to spit on the ground.

"Joto nai, joto nai," she said.

We smiled and hesitantly accepted the forbidden gift. Mama San urged us to eat the tomato and daikon immediately. Then she brought us each a piece of sweet cake. It was plain, but a rare treat for us.

We were finishing the cake when the guard, who other prisoners had nicknamed Rat Face, appeared. Seeing us with the cake, he rushed over, yelling and threatening us with his rifle butt. Mama San charged Rat Face like a bantam hen defending her nest. Her ferocious verbal attack humiliated the guard, but he submissively knuckled under to the petite, elderly woman. Mama San's husband ran the crematorium, and she left no doubt in the guard's mind who was in command on the premises of that operation. Rat Face would regain his authority when we left, and I feared a severe beating would result when we were away from the watchful eye of Mama San. However, the guard had lost face in front of his prisoners and walked behind us, grumbling to himself all the way back to camp.

Getting ready for my second trip to the crematorium, I went to the hospital to pick up the casket. Seeking the right room, I opened a door along the hallway and was struck with a horror I had never before experienced. Blood covered the floor. In the center of the room a corpse lay on a marble slab, and beside it was a chopping block with a metal cleaver. Bloody knives and other cutting instruments rested on the block, along with a human head. The head had been split in two, half of it turned away and the other half facing me. The eye facing me was closed, and blood covered the man's brown hair. I stared in disbelief, wanting to vomit.

"Boy, you look bad, and I know why," Pappy Harris said when he met me in the hall. "I saw you leaving the autopsy room. Pretty grisly in there, right?"

I nodded numbly, my pallid face giving evidence of the nausea I was experiencing.

"That's where they chop some of us up when we die," Harris said.

I had seen dead Japanese soldiers during the fighting on Bataan. Some had been dead a week or two, and maggots feasted on their swollen, rotting corpses. Nothing, however, had conditioned me for what I had seen in the autopsy room. My knees were weak as Harris and I pushed the cart to the crematorium. I never knew if the dissection was done by an American or Japanese doctor.

My duty on the burial detail continued, but I never saw the bodies we carried to the crematorium. I learned when I was on burial detail that Ray Schletterer, who with Mike Slish had taken care of me on the *Nissyo Maru,* died at the hospital after a bout with pneumonia. I wondered if his body was one we carried to the crematorium. There were two other teams on the burial detail, however, and I had no way of knowing.

Pappy Harris was taken off the burial detail and sent back to the mill. He was replaced by Bill Ostrander, one of the Special Prisoners. Rat Face was still the guard, but since the first day when he had been intimidated by Mama San he had not given me any trouble.

Pushing the cart through the streets of Kokura gave Ostrander and me opportunity to recall the similarity of our experiences for the past three years. We had both escaped the Japanese and spent time in the hills. We had been together in Bilibid and Cabanatuan and on the *Nissyo Maru.* It was good for me to be exposed to Ostrander's optimism and his Brooklynese will to survive. We regretted the regulation against bridge games in Camp 3, but somehow sensed the lack of socializing would be overcome.

Ostrander told me about a hoax he was pulling on the guards. Tooth powder was scarce, and guards as well as prisoners valued it. Ostrander traded the powder to the guards, but filled the bottom of the containers with sand. Only the surface layer was tooth powder. In surprise, I asked him if he did not fear retaliation.

"Hell, no. If they admitted they were being fleeced, they'd lose face."

The burial detail was exhausting work, but it became easier each day. The fresh air and walking improved my strength, and all too soon the Japanese doctor said I was ready to go back to work at the mill.

Chapter Fifty

Standing for roll call before the ride to the mill the next morning, I became aware of a dark depression closing in on me. Working in the fresh air had renewed my vigor in both body and spirit, but now I was returning to the stifling, dust-filled air of the steel mill, and I already sensed a revulsion for the days ahead.

The outdoor work of the burial detail had enabled me to survive the heavy pall of gloom that descended on the camp each evening when the mill workers returned. After only a few days back at the mill my mental strength diminished, and I began to succumb to the gloomy atmosphere around me. The whole camp seemed to retain a black mood day and night with nothing to break the agony and depression of the twelve-hour workdays. No one told jokes, no one laughed.

My fellow prisoners irritated me, and as a rule, I liked only those who left me alone. I tried to avoid those who wanted to visit or to start a conversation during meals. I considered the talkative man in the next bunk a loudmouth, and his habit of farting during meals became more and more aggravating to me.

Sitting next to me, he would jab his elbow sharply into my ribs and say, "Hey, how did you like that one?"

Or he would say, "Wow, Hileman, there's one right out of shit town."

As he slept, he often mumbled "Oh, shit," with each breath he exhaled. I felt like knocking the hell out of him, but contented myself with an occasional poke that forced him to roll over.

The heavy breathing and muttering of the man who slept above Helhowski were constant annoyances. He often wet his bed, and dripping urine woke Helhowski who soon learned the only solution was to waken him and take him to the latrine.

I became totally consumed with a determination to live through the hell around me, and I wanted to do it without the help of others. I sensed a need for only A.B. Nieman in the mill and Walt Helhowski in the barracks. Occasionally, however, someone else pierced my psychological shell.

I left the work area at the mill for a few minutes one day to go to the latrine. Unguarded, I left by a side door at the rear of the building and walked down the tracks next to the foundry. Passing an open office door, my eyes momentarily met those of a rather plain-looking Japanese girl behind the front desk. After a quick glance around the office, she tossed an orange out the door and went on with her work. The action startled me, and I looked furtively around before picking up the fruit. I stashed it in my pocket and continued on to the latrine. Because supervisors often used the same latrine, I did not dare eat the orange there, but found a secluded spot around the corner.

I looked at the orange for a moment, anticipating the taste before biting into the skin so I could begin to peel it. I started to toss the peeling on the ground, then thought of all the times we had picked up the peel discarded by guards. I retrieved it and stuffed it into my pocket.

Juice ran down my wrists as I hurriedly ate the proffered fruit, and I wiped it off with the ends of my burlap jacket. A feeling of guilt came over me when I realized I should have smuggled the orange into camp and shared it with Helhowski. I would save the peel for him, however. If guards found it, I would say an inspector had given me an orange, protecting the secretary behind the desk. I hurriedly finished the orange and returned to work, wondering who she was.

Guards did not check our pockets that evening. It must have been one of the days they had been bribed.

Indian prisoners who had been in camp long before the Americans came controlled the prison economy. They had mastered the language and built a trading network with Japanese civilians in the factory. It did not have the dimensions of the prison economy at Cabanatuan, but compared to others in camp, the Indians were prosperous. I had visited their barracks once and had gazed in astonishment at all the extra clothes, cans of food, cups of soybeans, and other precious commodities they had accumulated. White and broke, I felt discriminated against as I pondered the wealth of the Indians.

Through bribery they controlled the guards, often paying them not to inspect prisoners returning from the mill.

Usually the word got out so we knew when it was safe to smuggle any kind of contraband into camp. Unless they were bribed, guards severely beat smugglers. If caught with plain food such as dried fish or fruit, guards let us keep it after the beatings. If caught with something more valuable, like sugar, the guards beat us and took a cut before letting us into camp.

Over the next few weeks, the secretary threw an orange to me whenever she had the opportunity. Occasionally I got two in one day. I ate them quickly, squeezed the peeling into a tight ball and put it into my pocket. I always felt guilty for not sharing the oranges with Helhowski, but smuggling them regularly past the guards would have been difficult.

The Japanese secretary and I had developed a strange relationship. Then one day in May, as I began to eat the orange she had tossed me, I looked up and saw her near the drinking fountain. She smiled, and by natural reflex, I smiled back. She beckoned to me, but I ignored the invitation and went into the latrine. She followed me into the bisexual facility and began talking. I could not understand her and became frustrated, not only with my inability to understand Japanese, but in fear someone would see us together. She sensed my mood.

"You afraid?" she asked in English.

I nodded and she smiled. I felt I had to get back to the sand pit before anyone caught us. I was reluctant to talk with her, yet wanted to remain. The girl kept smiling.

"You name?" she asked. "Me Maji. Maji Minishi."

I feared giving her my name.

"My name's Sam," I said.

"Sam. I like Sam."

Almost in a state of panic, I edged closer to the door. Maji sensed my fear and said no more as she squatted over the concrete ditch both men and women used for urination. I hurried back to the sand pit, picked up the air hammer, and pounded furiously at a casting.

Obviously pleased with my added enthusiasm for work, the Runt smiled.

"You work fast. J*oto!* Okay," he said.

That night I told Helhowski about meeting Maji in the latrine.

"Boy, you're playing with fire. Keep doing that and you'll end up with your tit in the ringer for messing around with a Japanese girl right in the plant."

"Hell, I'm not messing around with her. I'll take all the oranges she wants to throw my way, but I don't want her any closer."

Maji often followed me into the latrine, and as the days passed she expressed her sorrow for my plight as a prisoner. I learned she had been sold into employment at Yawata by her father, just as his father had sold him into employment in the Yawata Mills. It was a common Japanese custom.

The strange friendship with Maji, confined to brief conversations in the latrine, continued. She brought oranges to me regularly and occasionally brought small rice cakes I smuggled into camp and shared with Helhowski. I knew it was a perilous situation, but as long as she gave me oranges she would remain an important factor in my determination to survive.

Maji's kindness gave evidence of goodness in the otherwise evil world of prison camp, but another worker in the mill manifested the sadistic attitude most Japanese felt towards the prisoners. He was the crane operator called the Gunsel.

Processing the ore left huge piles of slag that had to be loaded into gondolas for transport to a dumping site. Once or twice a week I was pulled from the jackhammer crew to help load the slag.

Using the electromagnet on a big crane, operators lifted fifteen hundred pounds of slag, swung it over the gondolas, cut the switch, and let it fall into the cars. The cars were on a high rail bed, and the crane operators, working from ground level, could not see where they were dropping their loads. It was my job to stand on the edge of the gondolas about fifteen feet above the ground and direct them.

The crane operator on that job was the Gunsel who began to play a dangerous game with me. Each time he swung a load over the gondola, he would see how close he could come to my precarious position on its rim. At first I accepted it as sport, but it soon became evident the Gunsel was serious in his life-or-death challenge. Again and again I dodged the heavy slag loads, shouting profanity which was drowned out by the noise of the machinery.

With only one more load before quitting time one evening, I stood on the rim of the gondola directing the crane operator. In a deliberate move, the Gunsel swung the heavy load directly at me. Realizing it was going to hit me, I jumped backward off the gondola and tumbled down the steep embankment. I fell in a crumpled heap at the bottom as pain shot up my leg.

The Gunsel dumped his load, shut down the engine, and left without looking back. Dazed by the fall, and with my foot and ankle throbbing in pain, I heard a scream. From her office window, Maji had seen what happened. She ran from the office and raced past me to the sand pit, screaming for help. Workers from the pit came running.

The Runt went into a tirade about my carelessness, but it was A.B. Nieman, a few steps behind him, who knelt down, grabbed me under the arms, and helped me up. With Nieman holding me, I was able to walk, but only with extreme pain.

I looked around for Maji as we started toward the train, but she had disappeared. She had, however, affirmed again the kindness and compassion I had seen in Asian women.

I pulled away from Nieman and hobbled to the lunchroom, got my *bento* box, and boarded the train for the ride back to camp. My foot throbbed unmercifully, and after the cramped ride through the long tunnel and to the station, I could not walk the final kilometer to camp. Reluctantly I climbed on Nieman's back, and the big Javanese ran to catch the others. He was undoubtedly the only prisoner on the crew strong enough to run with me on his back.

Camp rules stated that disabled or ill prisoners were to report to sick call in the evening after work, and carrying me to my barracks, Nieman urged me to report at once. Stubborn in my hatred, I was sure my ankle would be better in the morning.

I sat at the table in the middle of the barracks, and Helhowski brought my rice to me.

"You dumb bastard! You should have gone on sick call."

"I'll be all right by morning," I insisted.

When I tried to put on my shoe in the morning, it did not begin to fit over the horrendous swelling in my black-and-blue ankle. The pain was worse, and I could not walk. In addition to the physical pain, I was vividly aware of the possible consequences of having violated camp rules. When the call came to board the train, Helhowski and Pappy Harris carried me to the hospital and left, promising to cover for me at roll call. I hoped my friends would not be punished for helping me.

I sat on a box in the hospital hallway, waiting nervously to see the doctor. I knew there would be trouble; there always was when a rule was broken.

One of the two Japanese doctors in Camp 3, Lieutenant Ogani, came out of his office. A small man, Ogani dressed sharply. His pencil-thin mustache and hawklike nose gave him a sinister appearance, and I could see he was enraged. A Samurai sword carried on his left side jutted out in front of him.

"You sick!" the doctor shouted. "Why you not come to hospital last night?"

I tried to explain I thought I would be able to return to work, but the explanation was futile. I had broken an immutable Japanese rule.

"*Kiotsuke!*" Ogani ordered.

I wobbled as I tried to stand at attention.

Lieutenant Ogani pulled his Samurai sword from its scabbard, grasped the handle with both hands, and raised it over his shoulder. For a split second, I had a vision of the bloody head I had seen in the autopsy room. Ogani positioned himself to swing the sword, and the vision changed to one of my own bloody head rolling across the floor. I knew the end had come.

As I watched the blade swing towards my neck, it seemed to be moving in slow motion. A split second before it hit, Ogani deftly twisted the handle and struck my right ear with the flat side. I fell to the floor in a semiconscious state.

I heard Lieutenant Ogani yell at an orderly and then felt a splash of cold water on my head. I staggered to my feet.

Again as I stood at attention, Ogani swung the sword at my head, turning the blade at the last possible moment so it struck me with the flat side. I went sprawling across the floor again. This time I lay motionless, faking unconsciousness until I heard the doctor stomp off to his office and slam the door.

I struggled painfully to my feet and was told I did not have to work. Private Fukada, a medical orderly with a reputation for cruelty, placed the same kind of tag around my neck I had worn after my bout with pneumonia. Once again I was confined to quarters.

Fukada left, and I hobbled back to the barracks alone. I reached the first of the two tables that ran down the center of the barracks and sat down. Hatred welled up in me as burning pain surged through my foot, and my head throbbed from the blows from Lieutenant Ogani's sword. As I sat with my head in my cupped hands, someone spoke.

"Here, let me get you some tea."

Major Winnefred Dorris came from his room and set a canteen cup of hot tea in front of me.

The senior American officer in Camp 3, Major Dorris shared a small room at the front end of the barracks with Mr. Haase, the American interpreter. Like other officers, he did not work in the mills, received better pay, and had his own room. I had always thought it unfair that American officers were exempted from work, and their favored status had served to widen the gap between them and the enlisted men. Officers occasionally threatened insolent enlisted men with court-martial after the war, but the men only laughed, safe in the knowledge the officers had no meaningful authority in the prison camp.

Dorris was not a particularly dynamic personality, and the years of imprisonment had weakened him physically and mentally. Approaching retirement age, he displayed more compassion for enlisted personnel than most officers. It seemed to us he did not stand up to the Japanese as we thought an American officer should, but he never betrayed his men either. Despite my general dislike for officers, I trusted the major.

Dorris seemed to show a genuine interest in my physical condition and expressed concern about my ankle. He assured me I would be confined to the barracks until I could walk without pain. As we talked I became more at ease around him and was pleased when he asked about my participation in high school ROTC.

The ROTC faculty advisor, Major Ashbrook, had been an inspiration to me. On rainy days he had taken the cadets into the gymnasium and entertained us with stories of his experiences during the Philippine Insurrection when Filipinos fought Americans for independence. Ashbrook's detailed stories had made me want to visit the Philippines and may have played a role in my decision when I enlisted. I wondered about that as I talked with Major Dorris.

I confided to Dorris I had received the highest score on the ROTC battalion's competitive examination, and he sympathized when I told him I had not been able to accept the commission because I did not have money for an officer's uniform and saber.

Smoking as we talked, Dorris offered me a cigarette. I had a constant craving for tobacco, but at the same time did not want to become obligated to an officer. I asked what I could do to earn the cigarette.

"You could wash my socks."

I found the suggestion offensive, and my hatred for officers flared. I felt like hitting the old man.

"I don't need your damn cigarettes," I said.

I got up, limped to my bunk, and lay down.

"Private, you are not to lie in your bunk when you are on quarters."

"Who the hell says so?"

"Japanese orders."

I knew Dorris was right. The tag around my neck confined me to light duties around the barracks, but did not allow me to rest. I got up, hating both the American officer and the Japanese.

I had been offended by the major's offer, but the next day I reconsidered. After all, pride did not mean much and tobacco did. Dorris offered me a Red Cross pack of five cigarettes for washing his socks, and this time I grudgingly accepted.

As I scrubbed the major's socks in the latrine's small sink, I wondered about his supply of cigarettes. I wondered too about the socks I was washing. The GI issue socks were in good condition, but enlisted men had no socks. Officers did not work, but we slaved for twelve hours a day in the mills. Officers received fifty yen a month, but enlisted men did not receive even the ten yen promised them. The more I thought about the differences, the more my hatred for officers grew.

That night when I divided the cigarettes with Helhowski, I did not tell him how I got them.

Following the laundry job, the relationship between Dorris and me was strained. Both of us suffered from malnutrition, fatigue, and a deterioration of mental health. The stress of imprisonment was taking its toll, and the conflict between us came to a head a few days later.

It was spring, and the warm barracks attracted flies. They seemed to be everywhere and on everything and were especially annoying at mealtime as they hovered over our bowls of rice, landed on our spoons, and crawled on the table.

One morning Sergeant Takada came into the barracks accompanied by the ever-present interpreter, Yasu Homino. Homino, small and effeminate appearing, was reputed to be homosexual, and prisoners called him Evelyn. Dorris and I sat far apart at the long wooden table. We were not talking.

Flashing his toothy grin, Takada announced a new program to rid the barracks of flies. Each prisoner confined to the barracks would be issued a flyswatter, and for every one hundred flies killed, he would receive a very good Japanese cigarette. The dead flies would be counted in Takada's office at the end of the day.

Stupid goddamn Japs! I thought to myself. *There's no way they're going to rid this garbage dump of flies.*

I craved cigarettes, though, and swatting flies was preferable to washing the major's socks.

"You sick in barracks, you never worry more about tobacco." Takada smiled triumphantly as Evelyn translated his declaration.

Dorris and I walked to the supply office where we had to sign for flyswatters and the small glass jars in which to store our quarry. Back in the barracks, I started at one end and the major at the other. Flies covered the tables and the hunting was good, but as we swatted, the flies became skittish and flew around. Engrossed in my hunting, I worked my way down one of the long tables and moved to the other.

"Private, you are invading my territory," Dorris yelled. "I forbid you to swat flies on this table. You will, I repeat, you will move to your own end of the barracks."

I looked up at the major, thinking he was joking, and began to laugh. He swelled with anger, telling me not to refuse a direct order from an officer. I lost my temper.

"Get out of my way!" I shouted. "I'll swat flies wherever I damn well please, even if it's on top of your old bald head. Now get off my ass!"

Dorris threatened to put the incident into my permanent service record and declared he would have me court-martialed for insubordination.

"Go to hell," I said and resumed swatting flies.

A few minutes later I thought of a way to swat more flies and aggravate the major at the same time. I went to my bunk to get a small jar of molasses I had stolen at the mill. I spread a little molasses on the table and sat down. For the rest of the day I sat quietly swatting flies as they landed on the sweet brown liquid.

At the end of the day Dorris and I reported to Sergeant Takada. I counted out 980 flies, and Dorris had about half that number. We received our cigarettes and returned to the barracks where I divided mine with Helhowski.

I regretted my behavior toward the major and considered apologizing to him, but the flyswatting program was dropped the next day and the incident was never mentioned again. Our guarded friendship resumed.

Takada came in a couple days later with another program. Scattered throughout the camp, the Japanese had planted castor beans. I had noticed the tall plants with the large, fanlike leaves, and wondered what they were. The plants produced beans covered with soft, orange-brown spines. I wondered if the castor oil I had taken as a youngster had come from plants like these. The Japanese, however, had another use for the beans.

With Evelyn at his side to translate, Takada went to great lengths to assure Dorris and me that our work would contribute in bringing the war to a quick end. We would pick beans which would be used by the Imperial Air Force to lubricate planes. He handed each of us a small bucket and explained our task. Evelyn smiled, somehow making the job seem even more ridiculous.

Dorris and I laughed when we got outside. The fly incident had been forgotten, and we found satisfaction in ridiculing Sergeant Takada. We had all found Takada to be a man of multiple moods. He could be angry and depressed or jovial and friendly. Aware of his changing moods, we joked among ourselves about how his wife must have treated him the night before. My mind went back to Bilibid where guards had often provided the substance for American humor. I remembered the beating of Private Ito for sleeping on duty and even the beating I had taken myself when interrogators had not understood my parents' post office box. Despite the pain I had found the incident amusing, but at Camp 3 there had been little cause for humor. This was the first time I remembered laughing at the guards, and I sensed a certain irony in sharing my amusement with an officer.

After a few days of slowly picking castor beans, I returned to the drudgery of the mills. My foot had improved, and I was able, in a limited sense, to stand and walk.

Chapter Fifty-one

The weather grew warmer, the days longer. I sensed a change was in the air, although on some days the cold wind blowing off the bay reminded us winter had not completely released its grip. Its chill easily penetrated my emaciated body, and I looked forward to the hot bath that followed the day's work.

The bathhouse in camp had two tubs, each approximately ten feet square and three feet deep. We stripped, jumped into the hot water, and let the heat permeate our cold, tired bodies. For those fortunate enough to be first in line, the water was hot and clean. Groups that followed still enjoyed the warmth, though the water had become black with mill dust and dirt. Helhowski and I scrubbed each other's backs as the warmth of the water relaxed us. Finishing our baths, we ran back to the barracks and jumped under our blankets to conserve the heat. All things considered, the bath was the best thing about Camp 3.

The March and April weather reminded me of Southern California. I was glad winter was over and wondered if I, or any of the prisoners, could survive another winter. Pneumonia had claimed many lives, particularly from among those who had been on the *Oryoku Maru*.

As I pondered the future, important and surprising news was brought into Camp 3. It was April 13, 1945 when one of the office clerks ran up and down the street, yelling in an excited, high-pitched voice. We listened in shocked amazement.

"Roosevelto *shinde!* Roosevelto *shinde!*" the clerk yelled.

President Roosevelt was dead. I felt the urge to kill the messenger.

Through Mr. Haase, the interpreter, we learned that Roosevelt had been succeeded by Harry Truman. We looked at each other in bewilderment. None of us had heard of Truman, and now he was our president.

For the next few days, the Japanese flaunted their enthusiasm. In their eyes, Roosevelt was an evil man who had brought the war to Japan. Perhaps the Japanese reaction to Roosevelt's death was best summed up by a guard on the work train. A UCLA graduate, he had been visiting Japan when the war broke out. He had wanted to return to the United States where he probably would have served in the U.S. military, but had been drafted instead into the Japanese Army.

"Tojo and Roosevelt are both sons of bitches and responsible for the war," he said.

The guard hated war, and he hated the leaders of both belligerent nations.

"I am so sorry for you," Maji said as she handed me an orange.

Soon after the news of President Roosevelt's death reached us, Maji was replaced. I did not know where she went, but I missed her compassion and her warm smile. Even more, I missed the oranges she had graciously provided.

News of President Roosevelt's death remained uppermost in our minds well into the summer, even overshadowing news of the German surrender on May 7. During our imprisonment, we had given little thought to our president. He had been elected in 1932 and was still a strong, vigorous leader when we were captured a decade later. It was difficult to envision life beyond the prison compound, and the thought that Roosevelt had become an old, sick man had never entered our minds. When Harry Truman became president, none of us knew anything about the feisty Democrat from Missouri. Time was passing us by.

Chapter Fifty-two

A white vapor trail cut across the blue sky as we rode the work train to the Yawata Mills, ready to start our day's work. Ahead of the trail, I could see a tiny silver speck reflecting the morning sun. The sight of a vapor trail was new to us, and we wondered what kind of plane created something like that.

Antiaircraft guns located around the factory opened up, and the explosions thundered and echoed around the mill. The guns sent shells high into the air, but it was a futile effort. They exploded far below the high-flying aircraft. The impotence of the Japanese defenses thrilled us. An English-speaking guard told us about the plane the Japanese called *B-ni-ju-cu,* which we readily translated to mean B-29. When we realized the plane was American, we applauded, yelled, whistled, and cheered.

Japanese fighters from a nearby airstrip took off in pursuit, but the attempt, like that of the antiaircraft guns, was an exercise in frustration for the Japanese. The fighters climbed into the air, but were unable to reach an altitude where they could engage the B-29.

After that first sighting, we saw the plane pass over every other day and assumed it was flying reconnaissance or photographic missions.

"Those lucky bastards up there with their Thermos jugs of coffee and ham sandwiches," Spike Moran said to me.

After the futility of the first attempt against the big bomber, the antiaircraft guns around Yawata remained silent, and Japanese planes remained on the runways. In a sense, the Japanese had given up.

In August 1944, soon after my arrival at Camp 3, I had witnessed an isolated B-17 raid in the Kokura area, but we had seen no American planes since then. That raid had done little damage, but it had given us hope more bombing would follow. We wondered now, nearly a year later, if those raids were finally coming.

While the Japanese rotely went about their work during the day, at night things were different. As if in retaliation for raids elsewhere in their country, the Japanese began harassing us. The harassment began with the first night attack against Japanese targets somewhere to the north.

Moaning Minnie's ear-splitting whine woke us and was followed immediately by guards blowing whistles and lashing out at us with their split-bamboo poles. We were herded into a flimsy shelter dug into a sandy hill. Bamboo poles pounded into the ground supported the sides, and a plywood roof covered the shelter. It offered little protection.

As the frequency of the air raids increased, the high-pitched scream of Moaning Minnie tore through the night with regularity. Sleep became more and more difficult, and we spent hours waiting in the bamboo shelter as the siren continued to sound its ear-shattering warning. Inside the shelter, I found sleep was impossible. To lie down meant an immediate infestation of fleas. Sometimes we were allowed to return to our barracks for a few hours sleep, but other times we were held in the shelter until breakfast and head count before reporting to work. Though we were crowded into the shelter two, three, or even four nights a week, we never heard a bomb explode. The Japanese were deliberately keeping us awake as a means of torture and retaliation, and their tactic was highly effective.

Poor diet, exhausting physical labor, and lack of sleep caused tempers to flare, and frayed nerves led to fights, cursing, and yelling. Such reactions gave the guards cause to beat us more frequently. Flogging us with bamboo poles caused us to curse the guards, bringing more punishment. It had truly become a vicious cycle.

As Moaning Minnie sounded her nerve-shattering warning night after night, a few prisoners began hiding in the barracks. After the others left for the shelter, they went back to sleep. Guards soon discovered their ploy and began patrolling the barracks, catching and beating those who had remained behind.

I tried several times to beat the system and occasionally won what I considered a cat-and-mouse game with the guards.

The first time I remained hidden until after the guards came through looking for stragglers. Once they had passed, I returned to my bunk with a real sense of satisfaction, a sense of outwitting the Japanese. Ordinarily there were many distractions to peaceful sleep in the barracks. There seemed to be a constant undertone of whispering, and many prisoners talked in their sleep. Loud outbursts of cursing the bedbugs or the sudden screams that accompanied nightmares woke others from their already restless attempt at sleep. The silence in the barracks when I evaded the bomb shelter was an almost-forgotten luxury, but one which came to an abrupt end. I saw the wave of a flashlight as guards came through the barracks door. Cursing and hollering, they came up the center aisle of the barracks. When one of them spotted me, he struck me over the head with his flashlight, then beat me with his split-bamboo club.

Despite the beating, I continued my game of trying to outwit the guards and occasionally escaped detection, making me feel I had won a personal battle with the enemy. Winning counterbalanced the beatings and gave me a sense of having the upper hand.

When Moaning Minnie's ear-splitting siren shattered the darkness one night, I ran out the back door toward the fence and crawled under a growth of castor bean vines. There was a unique kind of satisfaction in listening to the commotion in the barracks. The whistles, bamboo sticks, and hollering seemed remote, somehow removed from my everyday life. Prisoners scrambled to the shelter, and the clean-up crew went through the barracks looking for stragglers. When they were gone, I eased back into the barracks and crawled into my bunk. One or two others had done the same thing, but I could not see them in the darkened barracks.

I was quietly savoring the victorious moment when I heard the drone of planes. I went to the window and saw searchlights cutting through the blackness. I had never seen the lights before, but they seemed to come from everywhere. In their beams I could see the large four-motor planes I assumed were B-29s. Antiaircraft guns opened fire, exploding high above the aircraft which were cruising at an extremely low level. I went outside to watch, knowing the guards would all be in the shelters.

Flak from the antiaircraft guns began raining down while I watched the planes fly a crisscross pattern, a maneuver I did not understand. They remained over Kokura for several minutes, then disappeared without dropping a bomb. Wondering what the planes had been doing, I returned to my bunk, watered down my mattress to keep bedbugs away, and drifted off to sleep.

Rumors were rampant in the morning. One said they had mined the harbor, but it was pointed out the harbor was shallow and could not handle large ships anyway. I wondered if they might have been trying to locate antiaircraft batteries, but I had no way of knowing, and there was no satisfactory explanation of the mission.

The weeks dragged with Moaning Minnie sounding almost every night, taking an ever-increasing toll on shattered nerves and irritable dispositions. Occasionally we could hear the far-off drone of aircraft overhead in the darkness, yet Kokura and Yawata remained untouched. It seemed I had gone nights on end without sleep, and I was losing more weight as well. During the day the Japanese paid no attention to air raid warnings, but at night, guards unceasingly rousted us from our sleep and herded us to the shelter.

The early summer months of 1945 were the worst times I had known as a prisoner of war in Camp 3. Most nights were spent crowded together with other prisoners in the useless air raid shelter. The constant irritation of fleas and the incessant scream of the siren grated harshly against every nerve in my body. My head roared from the reverberant pounding of my air hammer, and many times sleep nearly overtook me as I worked. Frayed nerves brought about constant bickering and many fights. Japanese guards laughed as we fought among ourselves, then beat both combatants when a fight ended.

The stress and lack of sleep drained us physically and emotionally, but through it all we remained confident ultimate victory would be ours. We doggedly persisted and somehow endured the seemingly endless days and nights.

Chapter Fifty-three

Conditions began to change as we entered summer, both for the Japanese and for us. We had no real evidence of damage being inflicted in other parts of Japan, but we suspected it. A few of the more talkative guards, and some of the civilians at the mill, referred to bombing runs which were taking a heavy toll in lives, property, and industrial capacity.

A sense of gloom hung over both the camp and the mill, and many of the guards became more brutal. Others reacted in an opposite way and became friendlier, as if trying to soften the impact of defeat. Our food ration was cut even further, we had fewer days off, and harassment in the barracks increased.

Like all the prisoners, I took a morbid pleasure in watching the apparent demise of the Japanese. I resigned myself to waiting for the end, whatever it might be. A nagging question always accompanied my thoughts of the war's end. Would the Japanese kill us? Guards had told us we would be lined up on the beach if the American Navy shelled the beachhead. We often considered the great peril we would face in the event of an invasion.

Mr. Haase began bringing stolen Japanese newspapers to the barracks where he would sit at night in the latrine searching for any pertinent war news. The task was tedious, and he worked through the night translating the Japanese language. If caught, he would have been executed. Prisoners assigned as fire guards warned Mr. Haase whenever Japanese guards entered the barracks, and we had all quietly agreed to kill any guard who found him with the newspapers. Fortunately he was never caught.

Through the Japanese newspapers, we learned the Americans had invaded Okinawa, the last stop before invading Japan. Earlier we had talked little about the war's progress, but as we sensed the war winding down, we began to talk freely. War news, scant though it was, united us as nothing else had, and we were encouraged. It also caused us to focus more on our own questionable fate. The general feeling was the Japanese were preparing for defeat and planning to take us down with them.

My crew at the mill began working on hand grenade casings which would be used against Americans during the final invasion. I wanted to resist, but was powerless to do so. It was not the first time we had been forced to work on weapons, but somehow the hand-held grenades seemed such a personal means of death, and the task was totally repugnant. According to rumor, Japanese children were being trained to carry the grenades, walk up to an American soldier, and pull the pin. Civilian adults, rumor said, would be armed with bamboo spears. Guards boasted to us about the *kamikaze* attacks on American ships. The entire Japanese population, it seemed, was ready to fight to the death.

We developed a cockiness and a resistance we had never before displayed. Winking, laughing, and making caustic replies in English became common. We no longer cared whether the supervisors understood our remarks, and we enjoyed verbally hassling both guards and civilians. Some Japanese still posed a threat, but we quickly learned which ones would not tolerate our taunts. The *Kempeitai* guards maintained their brutal attitude, and we feared execution if we pushed them too far, but many other Japanese lost their attitude of superiority and power.

We also stepped up sabotage. In the sand pit where I worked, we found great satisfaction in devising ways to break drill bits or lose equipment. The men on the cement detail where Helhowski worked threw small, irreplaceable machine parts into the cement. They weakened its strength by adding extra gravel to the mixture.

Jerb Morris, a former aircraft mechanic working at the automobile repair shop, put molasses in the gas tanks, permanently ruining the engines of several cars and trucks.

Bill Ostrander, in the electrical shop, began winding wires on electric motors backwards. Everywhere at Yawata, it seemed, prisoners were undermining the Japanese war effort. Such tactics earlier would have been extremely dangerous, but with the apparent Japanese loss of heart, our cockiness increased and we regained our courage.

Living conditions continued to grow worse. Lice and bedbugs thrived in the warmer weather. Between the constant air raid alarms, the increased harassment, and the insects, we often went the whole night with no sleep. Men fell asleep in the latrine and on the train carrying them to the mill. Lack of sleep became our most serious health problem.

The bartering, which had been an important aspect of the prison economy, gradually deteriorated, and as it did, relations between the ethnic groups in camp became more tense. Sergeant Takada was more irritable, but there were fewer beatings. The homosexual interpreter, Evelyn, did not smile anymore. All such changes fed our optimism as we sensed the end was near. Through four years of war, most of us had become conditioned to death and had been ready to accept it. Now we anticipated the end of our captivity, whatever that end might bring.

The hot July days plodded slowly past, and the nights became a dreaded ordeal as Moaning Minnie continued her futile warnings of nonexistent air raids. Sometimes guards rushed us to the bamboo shelters, sometimes they did not bother. Work in the factory did not seem important, even to the Japanese. Like Maji, Suzy Q had disappeared from her job. Only the Gunsel ran the crane now, and he never came down from the cab.

By August guards did not even bother coming into the barracks. Once proud, aggressive, and dangerous, they became sullen and noncombative. Major Rikitake began to look like a haggard old man who slept at his desk. His boots needed polish, his uniform went unwashed and unpressed. We often overslept, reporting late for our work details. The guards did not seem to care, sometimes skipping even the ritual of counting off before work. We wandered to the train, boarded, and rode in silence. Prisoners and guards alike were simply going through the motions. Even the young civilian boys ceased throwing rocks at us on our way to the mill.

It was a time of great uncertainty and peril as everyone, both American and Japanese, waited for the end.

Chapter Fifty-four

Monday, August 6, 1945, was my thirty-first birthday, and as I shaved that morning I remembered past birthdays. I had celebrated my twenty-eighth in Pampanga with a cake, I had forgotten my twenty-ninth at Cabanatuan, and had arrived in Japan the day I was thirty. Now apparently, my thirty-first would be just another day at the Yawata Steel Mill, and I wondered where I would be in another year. I finished shaving and returned to the others, wondering if they too felt a lack of recognition as their birthdays passed by, unmarked and unnoticed.

Something had marked that day, however, and although we had no way of knowing what it was, we were immediately aware the next morning of a drastic and unexplainable change in the behavior and attitude of the Japanese. They seemed almost to act in deference to the Americans, and there was a strange look of fear written across their faces.

We went to work as usual that day, but the Japanese did not seem to care if we worked or not. For the first time, I sat down in the sand pit and rolled a cigarette. Even the previous week I would have been punished for such an open act of defiance.

As I worked, a lone B-29 flew over the Yawata mills. The Japanese, hearing the plane, fled from the pit and disappeared into the bomb shelters. Ordinarily they would have ignored the single plane and continued working. Their behavior was totally uncharacteristic, and none of us understood the reason for it. We talked quietly in the barracks that evening, seeking a logical explanation for the obvious and sudden change.

The mysterious atmosphere continued through Wednesday, but there was still no explanation. Clouds were rolling in as we returned to camp that evening, and I wondered if a change in the weather would relieve the strange tension.

The morning of August 9 dawned hot and humid, and the smell of rain was in the air. We ate our breakfast of rice and tea as guards circulated nervously among us. There was a perfunctory shouting and jabbing with sticks as they urged us to hurry, but it was obvious their hearts were not in their work.

"*Tenko!*" a guard shouted, catching me by surprise. The prisoners seemed unusually preoccupied and many of them made mistakes while counting, but the guards seemed indifferent to errors. The gates of the stockade swung open, and we straggled out to board the train. Sitting on my *bento* box, I studied the tired, drawn faces of the others, wondering what each man might be thinking about the changed attitudes of the Japanese.

The train emerged from the tunnel and stopped at its usual place in front of the Yawata business office. We routinely lined up, counted off, and walked to our work stations. I glanced at the sky. Clouds were rolling in from the Tsushima Straits, and I took comfort in the possibility of a relieving rain.

I was assigned to the slag detail that morning, so I went to the building where the accumulated ash from the smelters needed to be loaded into a gondola for disposal.

I already looked forward to the 10:15 A.M. smoke break. I had a long cigarette butt in my pocket, along with the bamboo holder which would enable me to get every possible puff from it.

Just three minutes before the midmorning break, the first bomb crashed into Yawata with a shattering force. If there had been a warning, no one heard it amid the din of air hammers, high-speed drills, and other equipment. Switches were cut, shutting off all the equipment, and in the silence that followed, I could hear the drone of heavy bombers.

The guard who was overseeing my work that morning suddenly broke down. With tears streaming down his cheeks, he threw his rifle to the ground and crawled under a railroad car. I picked the rifle up and handed it back to him, but he threw it away again, then grabbed my pants leg and tried to drag me under the car too. Incendiary bombs rained down on the plant. I had been working without my shirt, but when I saw the white phosphorus spray from the exploding bombs, I grabbed my shirt before joining the guard under the car. When the incendiary bombs quit falling, I headed for the protection of the railroad tunnel.

Before I reached it, however, a second wave of bombers flew over. I could not see them through the clouds, but heavy demolition bombs began falling. I ran to the nearest shelter, found it crowded with Japanese, and ran quickly to another as bombs exploded in the immediate area. Two more times, I tried entering shelters only to find them crammed with Japanese mill workers and guards. Then I found one not completely filled and crowded inside.

I descended the crude stairs as more Japanese behind me pushed their way into the shelter, jamming it far beyond its capacity. I could not breathe in the packed shelter, and the panic-stricken Japanese were pressing harder and harder against me. I suddenly had an overwhelming sensation of being suffocated and began madly to push, shove, and kick my way out. I had never experienced such total fear and desperation and seemed driven by a life-or-death struggle to get some air. I would rather be bombed than smothered.

Outside, the air was filled with dust and smoke, and phosphorus continued to burn around the mill. The stench of cordite and powder was stifling, and the chaos around the plant was frightening. Weaponless guards, supervisors, and workers scrambled through the plant in a state of panic, a sight I had not seen before.

I spotted some other prisoners and joined them. American noncommissioned officers who could not remember the last time they had issued an order were taking over. The only adequate shelter was the railroad tunnel, and together we started toward it.

A strange quiet descended over the whole area of destruction as the last plane flew out of hearing range. It began to rain, gently at first, but rain nevertheless, and the clouds seemed to press in from every direction. Visibility decreased by the minute.

The rain continued, but for the moment, at least, we were aware only of the scene of devastation and fire. The acrid smell of phosphorous, gasoline and oil fumes, burning buildings, and even the smell of burning flesh filled the air.

Inside the tunnel, confusion reigned as we tried to determine if any prisoners had been lost. Close friends eagerly sought one another in the disorderly melee. I was relieved to find Helhowski among the safe prisoners, and we agreed to stick together. A sense of wonder and optimism began to creep through the whole group as we moved through the tunnel. One by one, then two by two, and finally in mass exodus we emerged from the Kokura end of the tunnel.

In Kokura there was no sign of war, no ugly smells or burning buildings. Only the peaceful green countryside met our smoke-filled eyes, and I sensed a release from fear and uncertainty as I trudged down the tracks with the others, knowing somehow my long ordeal was coming to an end.

It had actually been only little more than an hour since the bombing of Yawata had begun, but the sudden terror and the desperation to escape had seemed interminable. As we approached the camp, my tense nerves began to relax, and then we heard the drone of a single B-29 coming from the northern sky. Feeling safe in Kokura, I did not worry about the single plane, thinking it was probably on a reconnaissance mission. The sound of the motors died out, and all was quiet. Moments later we heard the plane approaching again from the north, but it passed and all was quiet. No one spoke as the plane made a third approach, passed over, and flew on toward Nagasaki, sixty miles south of Kokura.

Gradually I would learn about the bomb dropped from a single B-29 that day on Nagasaki and another atomic bomb that had been dropped on Hiroshima three days earlier, the cause of the unexplained change in the behavior of my captors and guards.

For now, however, my head spun only with thoughts of the future.

Chapter Fifty-five

Few guards returned to camp, and those who did seemed preoccupied with their own concerns. We sat in small groups going over the events of the day. None of us really knew what had happened, but we sensed the direction of our lives had changed. Japanese supervisors had disappeared from the kitchen, and prisoner cooks prepared large portions of rice and soup. I went to bed with a full stomach.

Too excited to sleep, my head swam with thoughts of the past four years. The melange of events seemed to tumble pell-mell through my head, and it was difficult to sort them out in any reasonable order. Thoughts of the war, my escape, Orlo's death, and life on the run mixed together in a jumbled confusion. I thought about Isabel and vowed I would find her again. I recalled my surrender to the Japanese colonel and still wondered if his promise of good treatment had kept me from being executed. I recalled the horror of watching Wendle Morgan's execution at San Fernando, the interrogations at Bilibid Prison, internment at Cabanatuan, the journey to Japan on the hell ship, and finally the endless days in the Yawata Steel Mill. Each experience was vivid in itself, yet they blended together in my mind, becoming a strange and remote montage.

The voices of prisoners talking in hushed tones woke me the next morning. There were no sounds of guards yelling or swinging their bamboo clubs. The barracks, it seemed, belonged to us. It was announced there would be a formation after breakfast, and Major Rikitake would speak.

Earlier that morning I had seen the major walking from the Japanese washroom clutching a towel. The once-proud officer looked dragged out, his head bowed. Now as he stood before us with Mr. Haase at his side to interpret he appeared as a pathetic old man. The sparkle had disappeared from his eyes.

Mr. Haase interpreted Rikitake's carefully chosen words.

"The war is over, and you have won," he said.

As the broken Japanese officer spoke to the tired, emaciated men whose nation had defeated his, I recalled the speech he had made when I arrived at Camp 3 a year earlier.

"You Americans have slipped into a lazy way of life. You do not deserve to win the war," he had said.

Major Rikitake finished speaking, and in a stoic, expressionless manner, handed his Samurai sword to Major Dorris, a symbolic act of surrender. He turned and walked into his office, avoiding the piercing eyes of the assembled men.

I had realized the war was over, but was not prepared for the emotional impact of Rikitake's words. Even as I slowly absorbed the reality of the war's end, Mr. Haase had more shocking news. He had learned from a radio broadcast of the atomic bombs dropped on Hiroshima and Nagasaki, and as I listened I remembered the single B-29 which had made three passes over the cloud-hidden city of Kokura before flying south toward Nagasaki.

It took several hours to assimilate the significance of the events of the past few days. The war was really over, and we were free.

Rumors intermingled with news, and for the next couple days it was impossible to know what to believe. Mr. Haase tried to keep us informed as events unfolded. He sent runners to each barracks whenever he heard radio news and posted news on a bulletin board in the compound. Rumors stated that Tokyo Harbor was full of American battleships and paratroopers were landing. I watched the sky, hoping to spot one of the parachutes. One rumor claimed a caravan of American Army trucks was headed for Camp 3, but it did not arrive that day or the next or the day after that.

We ate large rations of rice and soup, slept, and milled around the camp, but we grew restless waiting for something to happen. Father Curran and Major Dorris attempted to restrict us to the compound, but after years of confinement such restriction was impossible.

"Let's get the hell out of here and see what we can find," Bill Ostrander said to me on the third day.

Ostrander wanted to walk into Kokura. With the exception of the narrow, winding side streets leading to the crematorium, which we had walked together on burial detail, neither of us had seen the city beyond our prison gates.

A sense of excitement filled us as we walked unhampered through the gate and started toward town. A barbershop located at the city's outskirts attracted our attention. Looking through the window, we saw five young women barbers standing behind their chairs, waiting for customers. There were none. Morning after morning as my dull Gillette razor scraped and tore my skin, I had thought how great it would feel to shave with a good sharp razor. We decided to go inside.

After the initial shock of seeing two disheveled Americans walk in, the women smiled and bowed. Ostrander and I sat in the first two chairs, and the women went to work. They shampooed our hair, dried it with clean towels, and cut it evenly. Prison camp haircuts had been a hit-and-miss job. I reveled in the luxury of real shaving lather as the barber began to shave me with her well-honed straight razor. I realized later she could easily have cut my throat, but the thought did not occur to me as I enjoyed the luxury of a barber's shave.

After the haircuts and shaves, the girls gave us facials and topped off our visit by trimming our fingernails and toenails.

None of them spoke English, and neither Ostrander nor I knew more than a few words of Japanese. Yet as they worked they successfully conveyed messages to us through gestures and smiles. The refreshing experience was over too quickly for me, and when we left they refused our money, smiled and bowed. I felt clean for the first time in years as Ostrander and I walked back to camp.

At the gate we met an American guard who had been posted by Major Dorris to restrict travel outside the compound.

"Where in the hell have you guys been? Where are your passes?" he demanded in a southern accent.

"Get lost, hillbilly," Ostrander said. "You don't even want to know where we've been."

The guard's face reddened as he realized he had no real authority over us. He grinned sheepishly as we walked through the gate.

We knew it would be some time before we were evacuated, and though attempts were made to keep us within the camp confines, it was difficult. Bored and restless, prisoners moved in and out of camp at will.

In a mood for change I hunted up Tom Coleman who was sitting on his mat with pencil and paper, working on his Japanese vocabulary.

"Hey, Tom, let's get out of this place for a while. Why don't we try to find Vacher? He's got to be somewhere in the area."

"What the hell are we waiting for?" Coleman said. "Let's go!"

Riding the streetcar to Fukuoka on Sunday morning, Coleman and I found ourselves surrounded by thousands of people at the train station. Soldiers, laborers, young women and children were lined up everywhere. Japanese generals and privates competed for places in line. The depot was a hub of confused activity, and no matter which direction the fifteen-to-twenty-car trains went, they were full. Passengers crammed into the cars and others clung to the sides. Getting directions was difficult, not because people did not want to help us, but rather because of the confusion at the depot. We finally boarded a train heading south toward Nagasaki.

Bodies pressed against bodies as we worked our way through the packed aisles. Japanese officers and privates bowed to us, allowing us to pass through the crowded cars, and everyone was courteous. In the face of this warm acceptance, I felt embarrassed about my tattered clothing.

We found ourselves facing two Japanese colonels who stood, bowed, and offered their seats to us. When we were seated, one of them handed me his Samurai sword. I admired the beautiful jade-inlaid handle, obviously a prized family possession. Though tempted to accept the gift, I returned it to the grateful officer.

Out of courtesy, or possibly embarrassment, no one looked at us as the train began to roll. I wondered if I should be afraid, but sensed no fear as I sat surrounded by throngs of Japanese. A week earlier these people had been our sworn enemies, but now they treated us with almost reverential respect.

The beauty of Japan became more apparent as the train passed through the suburbs and entered the countryside. I marvelled at the neatness of the small farms. Countless pedestrians and bicycles moved down the roads, but there were no motorized vehicles except an occasional charcoal-powered truck that coughed, smoked, and sputtered along the narrow country roads. I found it hard to believe these gentle-appearing people were responsible for the cruel treatment I had endured.

We did not know where we were going, but hesitated to get too far from Camp 3, so when the train pulled into a station about an hour out of Fukuoka, we got off.

We found ourselves in a rural village nestled among rice paddies, trees, and gently rolling hills. With no particular plan, we examined our options. If we returned on the next train to Fukuoka, we would have had an enjoyable excursion. Still we wanted to give our attempt to find Vacher a fair chance. People on the train had generously offered us rice balls, so we were not concerned food would be a problem. In good spirits, we began walking down a gravel road.

The rattle of a Model T Ford pickup behind us drew our attention, and the elderly driver stopped and motioned for us to get in. Coleman sat with the driver, and I found a spot to sit among the watermelons, cantaloupes, and vegetables. Using his limited knowledge of Japanese, Coleman talked to the old man, trying to explain we were looking for other Americans.

We had not gone far when the driver stopped at a crossroads and pointed into the distance.

"Futasi tanko," he said several times. Finally, Coleman understood he was pointing to a coal mine where there was a prison camp.

We started to get out, but the old man insisted on driving us to the compound, not, however, before we sampled his cantaloupes. He apparently had no desire to provide for all the prisoners in the camp, but made sure we ate our fill before he stopped at the gate and let us out. He bade us *"Sayonara,"* and the old pickup rattled on down the road.

The compound was in a remote country location, unlike the metropolitan industrial area where we had spent the past year. Beyond the camp we could see coal derricks, and the smell of coal was in the air.

An American sat in the office near the gate, listening to a radio.

"My God, where did you guys come from?" he said.

He shook our hands warmly and welcomed us to Camp 10. Like Mr. Haase, he had been listening day and night to the latest news and passing information to the others in camp. The guards had fled that camp too.

Despite word to the contrary, he told us the Japanese had not officially conceded surrender, and a state of war still technically existed between our nations.

Until then Coleman and I knew little about the fateful last week of the war. He told us that eight hundred American B-29s had dropped six thousand tons of bombs on the Japanese mainland on August 1. Two days later the American Navy had completed an iron-ring blockade around Japan. On August 8, he said, the Russians had declared war on Japan. This information startled me, and I began to have second thoughts about traveling willfully around Japan, although I could not discount the friendliness of the Japanese people.

"Do you know a guy named Vacher?" I asked.

"Sure. He's here."

Following directions to Vacher's sleeping area, we found it empty, but there was an open book on his straw mat, and I smiled as I recalled Vacher's constant desire to read.

We were still nosing around the barracks when John Scott, one of the Special Prisoners at Bilibid Prison and Cabanatuan, came in. Elated to see one another, we eagerly exchanged any information either of us had about the other Special Prisoners.

Scott's continued philosophical attitude about being a prisoner of war had served him well. He had not been sick and had maintained his weight. I marveled at his good physical condition and realized the strong self-discipline he had practiced at Bilibid and Cabanatuan had been a vital factor in his health, both physical and mental.

Scott said Vacher was in the kitchen and would be back in a few minutes.

"Where's the kitchen?" I asked.

With his back toward the door, Vacher was pouring a cup of coffee as we went in.

"Hey, Vacher, how about pouring some for me?" I said.

"Well, I'll be goddamned! You never know who you're going to find under a lump of coal."

He did not seem particularly surprised, but greeted us heartily.

His demeanor demonstrated he had just naturally expected we would meet again. He got food and coffee for us.

As we talked we compared our work in the steel mill with Vacher's work in the mines over the past year. We concluded that probably one was no better or worse than the other. However, I had always had a fear of mines and was glad I had not spent the last year underground.

Coleman and I were in no hurry to leave Camp 10. The food was good, and the change in surroundings was a welcome break. We stayed two days, then took a train back to Camp 3, arriving just in time to hear Emperor Hirohito's surrender broadcast.

His high, effeminate voice seemed tragically comical, but his speech meant the war was really over.

Chapter Fifty-six

There was an ample supply of rice in the camp storehouse, and Japanese civilians brought vegetables to us. Although the variety in our diet remained limited, we no longer felt the constant pangs of hunger. With the supply room left unguarded, it was not long before some former guards and Japanese workers came back to raid the food supply.

Husky, who had defeated Hog Jaw in the bayonet competition, caught a former guard stealing a sack of rice, grabbed him in a hammerlock, and broke his arm. I watched as the defeated and humiliated guard retreated from the compound with his arm dangling. That ended thefts.

Mr. Haase heard on the radio the Americans planned a food drop. Each camp was to be marked with a POW. We hurriedly formed the identifying letters with rocks on the beach, whitewashed them, and began to wait expectantly for the promised food.

As the days passed we became skeptical, our restlessness increased, and trips outside the camp became more frequent. On one such excursion Harold Irving and Sill Herring, two of the Special Prisoners, came upon a railroad siding where Japanese laborers were unloading the contents of a boxcar into a truck. Discovering the cargo was beer, and the truck already half loaded, Irving took advantage of his fluency in Japanese and began quizzing the workers.

"Have you ever heard of General MacArthur?"

"*Ah, so.*"

The workers snapped to attention and bowed.

"I am an emissary of the general," Irving said. The workers bowed again, and Irving instructed them to finish loading the truck for the general. They obediently complied.

Promptly, Irving and Herring climbed into the truck and drove it back to Camp 3 where they were greeted with jubilation. The air of celebration did not last long, however. We learned quickly our emaciated bodies could not assimilate the alcoholic beverage. Many became violently ill.

A day or so later Helhowski and I were drinking coffee when we heard planes in the distance.

"Hey, maybe they're finally going to drop that food," he said to me.

Three B-29s were flying low over the horizon. The big bombers passed over camp and disappeared, but came back moments later in single file with their bomb bay doors opened. Yellow, green, red, blue, and white parachutes carrying barrels and boxes of various shapes and sizes began drifting toward the earth. As the brightly colored parachutes rained down on the camp, we ran excitedly from one carton to another, eagerly examining the contents.

One chute, attached to a heavy crate, failed to open, and I watched in horror as it fell toward the ground, killing a young Japanese boy as it struck. The impact broke many of the cans of peaches it held, creating a ghastly mixture of blood and fruit.

Hungry for anything from the United States, excited prisoners greedily gathered everything they could carry. Others only stared in disbelief. Helhowski, Ostrander, and I found a fifty-five gallon barrel filled with cans of bacon. I immediately anticipated a luxury I had missed since the war started. Pulling the small key off the side of a can, I eagerly inserted it in the tab and began rolling it back.

Ostrander and Helhowski, sharing the same hunger for bacon, tore the door off the latrine, chopped it up with a borrowed saber, and started a fire. I ran to the barracks for my old mess kit which would be used for a frying pan. Minutes later the smell of cooking bacon filled the air, bringing a flood of memories of breakfasts I had missed.

The prisoner of war diet had included no animal fat, and I ate my first slice of bacon with great relish, then another, and another. By the time I finished my fifth or sixth slice, my stomach vehemently rebelled against the rich, fat food. I began vomiting and went back to the barracks where I spent most of the day on my sleeping mat. Violent cramps, diarrhea, and vomiting affected most of the prisoners in Camp 3 as long-starved digestive systems reacted to the sudden abundance of rich American food.

During the past year a popular topic of conversation had been how the army would slowly reacclimate us to the American diet when the war ended. Now we realized the army would not need to manage our diets. Our own digestive systems would make the adjustment to animal fat and other foods we had gone without for so long.

In addition to food, the parachute drop included shoes, clothes, socks, underwear, and even overcoats. The overcoats, most impractical on Kyushu Island in August, were cause for much amusement.

Late that afternoon Helhowski and I, walking across the compound, were surprised to see an American flag flying from the flag pole. Huskie, the camp tailor, had created it from the colored parachutes. It was the first American flag we had seen since Bataan, and it had a profound emotional impact on us.

"Hileman, have you ever seen anything so pretty?" Helhowski asked.

"No, and I wondered if I'd ever see that flag again."

The next day planes again dropped parachute loads of food and clothing. One fifty-five gallon oil drum landed in the bay. Five men raced into the water, and the rest of us helped them pull the big drum to shore. We were exultant to find it was filled with quarter-pound Powerhouse candy bars. I grabbed one, ate what I could, and threw the rest away. My acquired habit of saving every morsel of food was already changing. Other barrels contained cigarettes and toilet articles.

Men who had painstakingly saved even the smallest cigarette butt were secure in taking a few drags, throwing them to the ground, and grinding them out with their heels. We wantonly enjoyed the freedom of abundance.

Since the war's end, Japanese civilians had been bringing vegetables and other food into camp for us. Now we had the opportunity to show our appreciation by sharing our newly acquired wealth with the people of Kokura, especially the children. Few former guards or other military personnel came into the camp, but many civilians visited daily.

Mr. Haase finally brought the long-awaited news of evacuation. We would be transported to Okinawa, and from there to the Philippines. I thrilled at the idea of returning to the Philippines, and wondered if there would be any possible opportunity to visit the Pineda's and Isabel.

Chapter Fifty-seven

On Sunday, September 16, 1945, I heard a commotion at the gate and turned to see an American Army truck, followed by a staff car, moving into the compound.

Soldiers from the liberation team jumped out and carried a portable table and typewriter to the office steps. I could not help but notice how rugged they looked compared to the skinny prisoners who stared with deep-set, glazed eyes. My excitement grew as I joined others in front of the office.

A sergeant shouted above the confusion.

"Okay, you guys, get your asses in gear so we can process you, and you can get the hell out of this hobo jungle."

He had his back to Helhowski and me, and we admired his bearing and confidence. A carbine was slung over his right shoulder, and he wore a steel helmet, combat boots, and green fatigues. The military dress was new to us. The last uniformed soldiers we had seen were in Bataan where soldiers had World War I vintage equipment. The sergeant turned and looked directly at Helhowski and me.

For a moment I stared in disbelief, and then turned to Helhowski.

"I don't believe it," he muttered in a visibly shaken voice.

The sergeant was a Japanese-American. The first order we

received from an American was issued by Sergeant Takahashi, U.S. Army. He said we would leave in a day or two. A special train would take us to Nagasaki, and from there we would go to Okinawa.

The efficiency of the processing amazed me, a striking contrast to the army's inefficiency when the Luzon Forces had withdrawn into Bataan. Then trucks had often traveled empty, orders were confusing, and no one seemed to be in charge. Now things moved rapidly as Americans were processed at one table and other nationalities at another.

The army had changed. I had witnessed the new strength of U.S. air power, and now I was seeing the well-trained efficiency of American soldiers. I realized I would be going back to a different world.

The clerks quickly completed the processing, and then Takahashi spoke.

"Cut down on your luggage before we board the train," he said.

We broke into laughter. Most of us had nothing, although a few had begun collecting souvenirs.

"I'll bet you'll be glad to get out of this shit hole," Takahashi said.

I liked the Japanese-American sergeant and noticed he spent time talking with Japanese children. He gave them food and other items which not only pleased the youngsters but helped them survive during this difficult time.

Our return home began before sunrise on Tuesday, September 18. We took streetcars to Fukuoka where we boarded a passenger train which we quickly dubbed the "Nagasaki Special." We each carried a rice ball and candy bars for lunch, the clothes we were wearing, and a few souvenirs. My only souvenir was the small silver spoon I had considered such a precious possession during my years of captivity.

Elation grew as the train moved south towards Nagasaki. We broke into song, singing, "California here I come, right back where I started from." With the emotional release of singing, our minds were freed for the first time to dwell on the reality of going home. Everyone was in a jovial mood as the train entered the outskirts of Nagasaki, but the atmosphere suddenly changed.

We fell silent as we crowded against the windows and stared numbly at the devastation. Our limited information about the atomic bomb had made it seem remote and impersonal, but now the impact of its destructive power struck forcefully. We gazed in disbelief at the city flattened by a nuclear explosion. I saw a steel building, not unlike the one where I had worked at the Yawata mills, which seemed to have literally melted. Everything was in ruins. Block after block had been completely obliterated. Yet in the midst of the ruins, restoration work had already begun. Temporary installation of power lines brought electricity and communication to the city, and railroad tracks had been repaired to handle trains like the one on which I was riding. The train reached the waterfront and stopped near an undamaged warehouse at the edge of the utterly desolate city.

We scrambled off the train and were met with a sight we had not experienced in years: American women. Red Cross workers had set up tables with cookies, doughnuts, coffee, and soft drinks. I quickly grabbed an ice-cold bottle of Coca Cola. When I had been burning with malarial fever on the Gumain River, I had dreamed of a pit filled with crushed ice and bottles of Coke, always just beyond my reach. Now, more than three years later, I actually had one of the precious bottles in my hand. I finished one and drank another. We responded readily to the women who expressed a very real interest in our experiences. Their sincerity put us at ease and encouraged us to talk freely. They were interested in the Japanese sabers and other souvenirs some men had collected, and were fascinated with the canteens and mess kits many former prisoners had engraved during their captivity. Through the long, wearisome hours in prison camp, prisoners had carefully scratched works of art in the metal, designs that included women, horses, and the American flag.

After the heartening reception we were directed into a building where we stripped down, and with an air of celebration threw our tattered clothing, including our airlift replacements, in piles. Everything would be burned as a precaution against lice.

I looked at the small piece of towel in my hand, the gift from an impoverished farmer on my last trip from Zambales to Pampanga. I wanted to keep it.

"Throw it away, Mac," someone ordered.

Reluctantly, I threw it on the pile with the rest of the clothing.

We were directed to a shower room where someone had written Kilroy Was Here on the wall. We had no way of knowing the words had become a popular slogan during the war, and I figured Kilroy was just another released prisoner. Had there been a piece of chalk at hand, I would have written Hileman Was Here.

A medic sprayed us with an insecticide before we showered and received a new issue of clothing. Each of us was fitted with shoes, underwear, and fatigues, and given two wool blankets.

Dressed in the only decent clothing we had worn in three years, we were directed to the British HMS *Speaker,* a light aircraft carrier which would take us to Okinawa. Ostrander, Helhowski, and I boarded the ship together.

"Hi, lads," a crewman said as we walked up the gangplank.

"Jolly glad to see you, Yanks," another called out.

We were directed below deck where we found bunks made up with rubber pads and blankets. The British Navy had prepared soup and crackers, but most of us had eaten so many doughnuts and cookies we were not hungry.

As the ship moved away from the dock and into the channel, we stood on deck where we could watch the Land of the Rising Sun fade into the distance. The sea breeze, the deep green water, and the endless blue sky seemed to symbolize our regained freedom as the *Speaker* cut its way towards Okinawa.

We were served British lamb stew for supper, but appetites were small. Breakfast the next morning was fried tomatoes, toast, sweet rolls, tea, and coffee. We teased the British crew about the menu.

"Good enough for us to win the war, laddies."

"Bullshit," Ostrander said. "You know who won the war. No wonder we had to help you Limeys, the way you feed your troops."

The teasing was good-natured, and in our joy over the war's end, camaraderie with the British sailors came easily.

The liberated prisoners were allowed to move freely around the ship. I found the English Spitfire planes especially interesting and spent several hours examining the fighters that had won the air battle over Britain.

Toward evening land was sighted, and what I saw offshore amazed me. Everywhere, almost as far as the eye could see, ships lay at anchor. Great aircraft carriers, cargo ships, mine sweepers, battleships, and destroyers dotted the water like hundreds of ducks on a pond. Small liberty launches were taking men to and from shore in a constant stream. The *Speaker* dropped anchor amid the vast armada.

An American liberty launch approached the ship as I gazed in fascination at what I was certain must be the most powerful naval fighting force ever assembled. The launch pulled up to the *Speaker,* and we were ordered to get our belongings.

"Hold on, you're Oki bound," the coxswain said as I climbed into the boat with the others.

Dressed in blue dungarees, a white hat, and T-shirt, the sailor who operated the small launch looked to me like Charles Atlas. Compared to the emaciated men he was transporting, he was a healthy giant whose picture belonged on a recruiting poster, and I stared at him in admiration.

On shore we boarded an olive drab bus which took us to a temporary housing area near the airstrip. The sight of the endless armada off Okinawa had overwhelmed me earlier. Now, the airstrip had the same effect. Hundreds of American aircraft, including row after row of the B-29s which were still so new to us, were lined up in seemingly endless formation. Jeeps, staff cars, and other military vehicles moved about like ants at a picnic. Everywhere, it seemed, there were piles upon piles of materiel. The final invasion of Japan would have been launched from Okinawa, and the build-up was a preparation for that invasion. It looked to me like the United States had enough materiel on Okinawa to fight the whole war all over again.

Above the temporary administration building where the bus stopped, an American flag flew in the breeze, as if in confirmation of our freedom and our never-ending faith in the United States. Speechlessly, I gazed as it gently waved in the breeze, and turning to Helhowski, I saw a tear in my friend's eye. It was a deeply emotional moment for both of us.

We were directed to the sleeping area where row upon row of World War I vintage tents had been erected on wooden floors. As Helhowski, Ostrander, and I entered one, I stared at the Army cots and realized the last time I had slept in a real bed had been December 7, 1941, the night before Clark Field was bombed.

A sergeant with a bullhorn called us for roll call and an orientation. I had assumed we would be quarantined and our diet would be restricted, but that was not the case.

"All right, you guys, we're going to start your rehabilitation right here," the sergeant said. "The mess hall will be open day and night, and the cooks are authorized to fix anything you want, anytime. If you want a steak, tell them how you want it cooked. We're going to put some meat on those bony bodies before we ship you out of here."

We were given complete freedom within the compound in Okinawa, and everyone we met seemed to treat us like royalty, a status we thoroughly enjoyed. Guards stationed around the planes on the huge airstrip allowed us, within the necessary bounds of security, to examine the aircraft. I found the vast military arsenal astounding as I ran my fingers along the steel wing of a P-38, and for the first time got a close look at a B-29. It dwarfed the B-17s I remembered at Clark Field.

Back in the tent, I picked up the October 1945 *Readers' Digest* and read "The Blasts That Shook The World." I was amazed at the secrecy which had surrounded the development of the atomic bomb and found myself in unbelieving awe of the power it contained. I had, however, seen the convincing results at Nagasaki.

The second evening we were at Okinawa a formation of Navy Corsairs came roaring in over the administration building. Their air scoops made a whistling sound when they reached their top speed of four hundred miles per hour, and I was told the Japanese had called them Whistling Death. Unlike anything I had ever seen, the Corsairs were able to dive at an eighty-five degree angle. I watched in fascination as their pilots buzzed the administration building and went on to demonstrate their prowess and skill.

In single file they dived at the flag pole high atop the building. The first passed over in a screaming dive, then a second came screeching in. I heard a pop, like a gunshot, and then a whistling noise which sounded like a bullet. The second pilot had knocked the ball off the flag pole. The pilots, and their planes, were different from any I had known before the war. Astounded by their ability, the sight of America's air power filled me with pride.

Walking back to my tent, I recalled a formation of American fighters I had seen at Kokura after the war ended. Six P-38s had flown over Camp 3 in formation, made a wide circle, peeled off, and came diving back in single file. They had flown directly toward the big powerhouse with the six smokestacks. One by one they had rolled just enough to make a vertical pass between the stacks, the wing spans being too great for a horizontal pass. All six made it through without a problem and then repeated their feat. The pilots had wagged their wings over the camp and disappeared over the horizon. The devil-may-care attitude of the young pilots, and their skill levels, had been unknown before the war.

    We enjoyed the hospitality at Okinawa for five days before rosters for departure were posted on a bulletin board. Helhowski, Ostrander, and I would fly to the Philippines with a group of Dutch Javanese. We were scheduled to leave in a few hours.

Chapter Fifty-eight

*I*t was with excited anticipation I boarded an old Army truck and headed for the airstrip. Going back to the Philippines would be like going home, and since I was away from Japan and all it stood for, I sensed no great urgency to get to the United States.

The truck stopped next to a battle-scarred B-24 bomber. One of its side windows was missing, and its fuselage bore evidence of enemy gunfire. The four motors were already coughing in an uneven rhythm as they warmed up when Helhowski, Ostrander, and I, along with twenty Javanese, climbed aboard and were directed to the temporary seats installed over the bomb bay. I had settled in for a rough, drafty flight when the flight engineer came back to make sure the weight of his twenty-three passengers was evenly distributed.

"Stay put, you guys. This runway ends at the bluff with a sheer drop into the ocean, and we've only got one shot at it," he said.

We willingly complied with the engineer's suggestion, none of us relishing the thought of surviving prison camp only to die flying home.

The old plane sped down the runway, gradually lifted off the ground, and passed safely over the bluff. The engines seemed to sputter and groan, but the plane kept climbing. The vibration and apparent laboring of the old B-24 caused no little concern in my mind, but I was assured it was normal.

The flight engineer came back again and invited the three Americans to join the crew up in the flight deck. When we entered the cabin, the navigator was dozing off, the radio operator was asleep on the floor, and the copilot slept in his seat.

"We're all so damn tired I don't know if we can stay awake long enough to get back to Clark," the engineer said. "If you'll excuse me, I think I'll take a nap too."

I sat on the floor between the pilot and the sleeping copilot, fascinated with the complexity of the instrument panel in front of me. Ostrander and Helhowski sat right behind me, and as we visited with the pilot he told us he had logged 3,500 hours air time and enough missions to be rotated back to the States. The plane, he admitted, was on its last legs.

"It should have been junked a long time ago. You guys might get a little cold. We had some of the windows shot out so we can't pressurize the cabin. Six to eight thousand feet is about our limit. Any higher and we'll all freeze to death."

The pilot began working with a set of controls.

"What are those?" I asked.

"I'm setting the automatic pilot so I can catch a nap. I'm bushed," he said. "I sure hope you guys don't mind."

I looked at Ostrander and Helhowski and shrugged my shoulders.

"What the hell difference does it make?" I whispered.

In moments the whole crew was sound asleep.

"Goddamn, I wish I'd walked," Ostrander said.

"These guys are nuts."

In a few hours small islands became visible as the plane approached the Philippines. The surf created a fluffy white halo around the perimeter of each island as though to punctuate its splendor against the deep blue ocean. I had never seen them from the air and was overwhelmed at the sight of hundreds of islands dotting the expanse of ocean as far as I could see. The awe-inspiring beauty of the tropical islands gave me a sense of peace and tranquility I had never before experienced. My years in prison camps were past. I had survived, and now I was coming home.

My mind swam with memories of Clark Field and my cherished friendships there. I thought of Sherdie Allin with whom I had ridden the horses of the 26th Cavalry. Standlee had told me Allin survived the Death March and Camp O'Donnell, but I knew nothing more about him and wondered if he was still alive. Thoughts of other friends in the 698th passed quickly through my mind as we approached the airfield where we had all spent so many carefree, happy hours. It seemed so long ago. Almost fearing to know how many had survived, I suddenly felt lonely.

The flight engineer wakened, and aroused the pilot who took over the controls. As we neared Clark I looked east toward Mt. Arayat and west toward Mt. Pinatubo and the Zambales Mountains. It had been more than two years since I had crossed those mountains after shooting at the Negritos. I had been barefoot, sick, hungry, covered with leeches, and had wanted to die. I remembered the hut along the trail and the Filipino farmer who had cared for me and given me the small towel which had somehow become a symbol of the caring and loving Filipino people.

As the old B-24 entered the traffic pattern for its landing at Clark Field I eagerly anticipated my return to familiar surroundings. When I stepped out of the plane, however, I hardly recognized the hangar line, and unfamiliar planes lined the runway. I looked for the ordnance shop, but with new construction and changes could not even determine where it had been located. Only the control tower, which had remained untouched, served as a reminder of a former time.

In a state of disappointment and confusion, I was rushed with the others to a waiting C-47 transport which flew us on to Nichols Field in Manila. From there we were taken by truck to the 29th Replacement Depot at Las Pinas, a few kilometers from Manila. Things were happening so fast I was unable to assimilate the changes I was encountering. Nothing looked as I remembered, yet there was a wonderful familiarity in the very atmosphere of the Philippines. The sergeant was yelling, "Hurry, hurry," and I wanted only to stop and drink in the reality of returning to a country I had learned to love.

It was a great relief when we entered the rehabilitation center and were met with a wholly different attitude than we had encountered since landing at Clark Field. Everyone was relaxed, and normal Army regulations, we found, were essentially nonexistent. As it had been in Okinawa, the mess hall would be open to us twenty-four hours a day with cooks to prepare whatever we wanted, and there seemed to be a limitless supply of cigarettes, coffee, candy, and soda pop. A month earlier the Japanese had controlled every aspect of my life, but now I was back to the independent, almost wasteful, way of life I had known before the war. I was glad to be back.

Helhowski, Ostrander, and I shared a tent and were kept busy for the next couple days with paperwork and searching for old friends. On our second day there, I was resting in my bunk and was startled to hear a familiar voice behind me.

"Hileman, you son of a bitch. I thought you were dead!"

I did not need to look. Recognizing the New England accent, I turned to greet the blond, curly headed man standing in the doorway. I stood and embraced my friend Sherdie Allin. In the excitement of our reunion, we both talked at once for several minutes.

"Where in the hell is that damn Vacher?" Allin asked.

"He's around here somewhere. He made it through fine."

"How about Peewee and Homer?"

Peewee Standlee had survived Camp 3, but I knew nothing about Boren.

Vacher joined us shortly, and the three of us reminisced for hours. Allin remembered the Japanese strafing attack when the surrendering army had walked towards Mariveles on April 9, 1942 and recalled some of us had disappeared right after that. He had gone on to survive the Death March, Camp O'Donnell, Cabanatuan, and a prison camp on Formosa.

Now he listened with fascination as Vacher and I related the experiences of our escape from Bataan and our fugitive life in Pampanga Province. He was eager to hear every detail of the months between our flight and our capture. When we told Allin about Orlo Heinzman's death, his face paled and he lamented the loss of a good friend. He was fascinated, however, as we extolled the loyalty of the Filipinos and the risks they had taken for us. The more he learned, the more convinced he was he had missed a unique adventure.

Allin and I were sitting on my cot the next day when Vacher came into the tent, followed by a young soldier.

"Hey, Hileman, I found a friend of yours," Vacher said.

I stared at the uniformed man for a moment, not recognizing him.

"If you can remember Arlington, California, you can remember me," the soldier said.

I looked in disbelief at Keith Johnson whose parents were close friends of my parents. The last time I had seen him he was fourteen years old. Now he was an American soldier and the first person from home I had met since the war started. The visit with young Johnson was enjoyable, but also disturbing. He was a living reminder that time had passed me by.

A couple of days later Allin came bursting excitedly into our tent.

"Hey, you guys, I've got a hell of a good idea! How would you like to take a trip back into the hills?"

Allin had met a colonel in the quartermaster who said he could arrange passes.

"Hell, Hileman, the colonels in this new army aren't any older than we are. I was telling one of them about you guys, and he wants to meet you."

Allin's eyes sparkled with excitement.

"What the hell," I said. "If the colonel wants to talk with us, let's go."

Allin had not told us he had already arranged ten-day passes for himself, Vacher, Main, Ostrander, and me. The colonel had agreed to provide an ammunition carrier for transportation, his only requirement being we take a driver with us.

"You can leave in the morning," he said.

Former prisoners who requested leave were given an authorization signed by General MacArthur, saying, in effect, the bearer had just been released from prison camp and was subject to no one but the commanding general. The letter gave us freedom to travel anywhere in the Philippines, unrestricted by normal Army regulations.

I hated to go off on a ten-day pass without Helhowski, but this trip concerned a time before I had met him, and he readily understood my desire to go.

After a restless night's sleep, thinking about all the people I hoped to see, I awoke with a sense of great excitement, eager to return to the hills of Pampanga.

Chapter Fifty-nine

We rushed through breakfast and hurried to the quartermaster office where the colonel approved our paperwork and introduced our driver, Private Sam Janke.

A new recruit from Pennsylvania, young Janke seemed excited about the trip.

Most of the combat veterans who had recaptured the Philippines had gone home and had been replaced by inexperienced recruits. The replacements brought changed attitudes toward assignment in the Philippines, looking arrogantly at the country as belonging to America. They referred to the Filipinos as *gooks,* a term which offended those of us who had spent time among them. In the short time we had been back in the Philippines, we had already come to resent the way newcomers, as we called the occupation force, regarded the native people.

Preparing to leave, we loaded ten cases of C-rations onto the truck.

"What the hell you going to do with all that food?" Janke asked.

"We're taking it to our Filipino friends," I said.

A look of disbelief came over Janke's face. Americans having Filipino friends was an alien idea to him.

"Janke, you're acting like a smart-ass draftee," Vacher said.

Each of us drew a partial pay of three fifty-dollar bills before leaving.

"How much money do you guys think you'll have when you're all paid up?" Janke asked.

We estimated our back pay would be over five thousand dollars.

"Hot damn, that's a lot of money. You guys are sure lucky."

"Shut up, kid," Vacher said in disgust. "You were hired to drive this jitney, and all you have to do is get us where we want to go. This isn't your trip."

Open friction was already developing between Janke and his passengers. In terms of experience we were worlds apart, and his naive remarks irritated us. Janke stared straight ahead, scowling, but his attitude did not matter to us. The weather was good, and we eagerly looked forward to the next ten days.

Traveling through the familiar streets of Manila, I was struck with the run-down condition of Rizal Park which had been a center of recreation and a favorite spot for picnics before the war. The old Manila Hotel on Dewey Boulevard, once the pride of the city, was in shambles, as was the U.S embassy building. Remembering former times, I was deep in my thoughts when Janke spoke.

"Where're we going?"

"Lubao, and don't stop until we get there," Vacher said.

"Where's that?"

"Just drive. We'll tell you where to turn."

Leaving Manila behind, we passed through a small barrio where pigs, chicken, and kids ran in the road. Janke slowed down, cursing the kids and commenting that the dogs looked like they were starving. He stopped when a pig defecated on the road ahead of us, and a dog ran up and ate the feces. That was a reality of life in the Philippines.

"What kind of dogs do they have over here, shit eaters?" Janke asked.

"Hell, Sam, that's why they don't need sewers over here. Nature takes care of everything," Vacher said sarcastically.

When we saw our young driver was repulsed at the sight, we broke into laughter.

"I don't see how an American could live here," Janke said.

His remark only served to punctuate our growing dislike of him.

"Son of a bitch, you're really a dumb bastard, aren't you?" Vacher said. "We're going to have to tape your goddamn mouth shut when we're around the Filipinos!"

Janke fell silent, grimly staring at the road ahead.

We decided our first stop would be to visit Bill and Martin Fassoth in Lubao.

"Who are they?" Allin ask

"They're twin brothers who have lived here for years. They set up a camp for fugitives like us," I said, "and they helped a hell of a lot of guys who would have died otherwise. I never stayed there, but I know a lot of guys who did."

"Goddamn, they sound like characters I'd like to meet," Allin said.

His interest and enthusiasm continued to amaze me. I thought again, as I had so often, how easily Allin would have fit into the kind of life we had experienced in the hills.

We stopped in Guagua and bought some San Miguel, the high-quality Philippine beer we had come to like before the war. Drinking the beer as we continued on, our conversation became more and more sprinkled with Japanese, Tagalog, and other words foreign to Janke. He remained sullen as we called and waved to Filipino girls we passed along the road.

Our devil-may-care behavior attracted the attention of some MPs who pulled the truck over and began berating us about drinking beer and yelling at the girls. Janke hunkered down behind the steering wheel while Vacher took great delight in egging the MPs into a state of frustration and anger. When they had given full vent to their authority, Vacher exhibited the copy of General MacArthur's orders. The MP sergeant gave us a mock salute and grinned.

"Okay, you guys deserve everything you can get. Have a helluva good time!" he said.

Ostrander waved a Japanese saber around in the back of the truck, and our hoots of joy became louder as we increasingly sensed the freedom of celebration. Janke was showing signs of fright and was obviously relieved when we arrived at the home of Bill Fassoth. By Filipino standards, it was a large, modern house.

The two brothers were in front of the house when the truck stopped and we jumped out. None of us had met them before, yet their greeting, when they learned we were former fugitives in the hills, was like the welcome of returning family. I was struck with the difference in their appearance. Bill was a man of considerable stature, and Martin was much smaller and more slightly built. They were alike, however, in the warmth of their joy in meeting us and inviting us to come in and visit.

Bill's wife, Catalina, a beautiful, well-groomed Filipina, came from the barrio market soon after we arrived. She was carrying a basket filled with fruits and vegetables on her head. Their teenage son Vernon was with her, and he ran excitedly to Ostrander when he spied the Japanese saber. Allowing Vernon to examine it carefully, they were soon talking as though they had known each other for years.

Fassoth brought out several bottles of corn whiskey he had stashed away for special occasions. This was one, he proclaimed.

I felt a flush of warmth go through my body as I slowly sipped the first whiskey I had tasted since before the war. In a very short time we all felt the dizzying effects of the liquor, especially Bill Main whose tolerance for strong drink had always been low.

We had planned to visit only a couple hours at the Fassoths, but the hours stretched into several days. Filipino neighbors and friends came from the barrios and the surrounding countryside to greet us, and the air of festivity continued day and night. Visitors brought meats and various dishes of prepared rice and coconut combinations. There was a seemingly endless supply of food and drink. I especially enjoyed both the pork and chicken *adobo,* meat cooked in vinegar and pepper. The spices gave it flavor, and the vinegar kept the meat from spoiling. As I sampled the *tapa,* Filipino dried meat, I remembered Malleri's deal with Vacher and me when we ended up burying the horse. I wondered if I would ever see that conniving Filipino again.

We slept intermittently for short periods, preferably under one of the temporary mosquito bars Bill had set up. Resting under the mosquito bar during the third night we were there, I determined to go to Pio in the morning. I wanted to find Isabel, and the next day would already be the fourth of my ten-day pass.

When I awoke, Vacher and Bill Fassoth were sitting at the kitchen table.

"Here, Hileman, have some coffee," Vacher said.

He handed me a cup, I took a swallow, and felt the burn of whiskey all the way to my stomach.

"Wow, I didn't expect that," I said.

Vacher handed me another cup which I carefully sipped to determine it was coffee. Holding a cup in each hand, I impulsively poured the whiskey into the coffee. Starting the day with alcohol was a new experience for me, but it seemed somehow appropriate on this excursion.

Catalina prepared a big breakfast of ham, eggs, and pancakes made from flour Main had brought from the kitchen at the replacement depot at Las Pinas. I smothered my pancakes with wild honey, a treat I had learned to enjoy at Fernando's farm.

"I'm going over to Pio this morning," I said to the others. "I'll be back in a couple of days."

"Hell, why don't we all go? Maybe we can find the Pinedas and some of the other people who helped keep us alive," Vacher said.

I would have preferred to make the trip alone, feeling strongly I wanted my reunion with Isabel to be a very personal time. Yet I knew Vacher and Main had as many friends in the area as I did.

Ostrander, not knowing anyone in Pio or Pasbul, decided to remain at the Fassoths. Janke would drive the rest of us.

Memories flooded my mind as we passed through familiar areas. I observed the people along the way and sensed they were in good spirits now that the war was over. The Japanese occupation had been tough on the Filipinos, but they were a strong people who had rebounded quickly.

The truck stopped near the big white-domed Spanish church in Barrio Pio. I got out and looked around. I could see Mt. Arayat in the distance, and remembered Pop, the old Filipino who had used the mountain to guide us, rejecting the compass I had offered him. It was a special moment for me, and I had a sense of having come home to a country and a people I loved.

I crossed the narrow, dirt street and entered the patio where Isabel and I had spent our last evening together when I returned from Zambales. I had not bothered at the time to see Vacher and Main whose shack was just across the river, and I still had not told them I had come to Pio then.

Nervously and with a lump in my throat, I knocked on the partially opened door. Inside, I heard footsteps. An old woman, a stranger to me, came to the door.

"I'm looking for Mrs. Montemayor. Is she here?"

The old woman looked at me curiously, showing her surprise in seeing an American soldier.

"No, she has not been here in many months," she said.

"Can you tell me where she is?"

"I do not know, sir. I am a cousin of Mrs. Montemayor. She has gone to Manila many months to be with Isabel."

"Where can I find Isabel in Manila?" The woman's suspicious attitude seemed to increase as I questioned her.

"Do you know Isabel?" she asked.

"Yes, we are very good friends," I said.

The woman became even more evasive, saying they were not coming back and she did not know how to contact them. It was obvious she would give me no further information, and I knew pressing her would do no good.

I was devastated as I walked dejectedly back to the truck. Main, sensing my mood, suggested visiting Mrs. Valentine, the widow of an American dobie citizen we had known during our time on the run.

The old Filipino lady greeted us warmly and told us all she could about the Montemayors. José had been killed by the Japanese while fighting with the Huks, and his death had so embittered Isabel that she had vowed never to return to Barrio Pio. I remembered the gun I had given José and wondered if he had ever told Isabel where he got it. Soon after José's death, Isabel's mother had joined her in Manila where Isabel hoped to finish her education. Not knowing what else to do, I gave Mrs. Valentine my parents' address and asked her to try to get it to Isabel.

Affected by my disappointment, my friends were unusually quiet as we climbed into the truck to go on to Pasbul.

When Janke saw the bullcart road leading to Pasbul, he wanted to go no farther. Threatened by Vacher, however, he reluctantly drove up the dirt trail. The deeper we went into the rural countryside, the more hesitant and frightened the young driver became.

We passed the hut where I had met Carmen and her Negrito husband Serappio. Now the hut was vacant and in a sad state of decomposition. Wherever I looked, I could see change, yet there was a fond familiarity about the area.

I remembered the night in June 1942 when I had first traveled this bullcart road. Heinzman had just been buried along the Gumain River and the Filipinos were moving Vacher, Main, and me out of the canyon. Dr. Pineda had heaped straw over us in the bullcart to keep us hidden from the Japanese. As I thought about that nightmarish night of dysentery, malaria, and rain, Janke resumed his complaining about the road, the country, and the *gooks*.

"Get the hell out," Main shouted. "I'll drive if you don't like the goddamn road."

Janke was out of his element and scared. He feared going on with us, but was more afraid of being left on his own in this remote area. He quickly weighed his options and continued driving.

The truck moved toward the barrio where Vacher, Main, and I had first met Dr. Pineda and his family. It all seemed so long ago, and yet our familiarity with the area seemed to close the gap of time.

Dogs began barking as the truck approached the house at the far end of the street, and curious children ran to meet us. A man with a peasant-style straw hat was cutting wood with a bolo behind the house. I was sure it was the doctor, but realized immediately the intervening years had been hard on him. He looked old and even smaller than I remembered. The doctor put his bolo in its sheath, pushed his straw hat back, and looked up at the U.S. Army truck.

I stepped out and saw a smile break slowly across Dr. Pineda's face. With tears of recognition and joy, he ran over and embraced Vacher, Main, and me. Ernie came out of the house, much taller than he was when he had carried food and medicine to us two years earlier. In stark contrast to the apparent weakening of his father, the two years had changed Ernie from a curious boy to a mature young man. The doctor and his son looked at us unbelievingly. Then as if to explain his own hesitation, he spoke to us.

"I do not believe I am seeing you. We thought you were already dead!"

Dr. Pineda had been told Vacher, Main, and I were executed at San Fernando after our surrender to the Japanese.

"You will come in now and eat with us," he said.

Janke's face turned pale at the thought of eating in a Filipino house with *gooks*. Main and I unloaded boxes of C-rations for the family, but as we did so, we told Dr. Pineda we wanted Filipino food for supper.

"I wish I hadn't come," Janke muttered.

Vacher, Main, and I were overjoyed to share a reunion meal with the Pinedas, and Allin listened intently as we reminisced, not wanting to miss even the smallest detail of our experience. Eating with my fingers, I appreciated again how good food tasted without the metallic flavor of spoons and forks. Janke, however, seemed to have trouble eating according to native custom, so Dr. Pineda got him a fork.

Gathered in the main room of the house, we visited for several hours. Dr. Pineda told us a Japanese patrol had come to the house soon after our surrender, and the sergeant had spied the binoculars I had given him on the wall. The sergeant had asked if they belonged to Mr. Vacher whose name was apparently well known to the garrison in San Fernando. The doctor had not told the Japanese where he got them, even though the sergeant had beaten him brutally with a rifle butt, seriously injuring him. I realized I could never repay the doctor and his family for all they had done, and I wondered if I would have done as much.

Even as we visited, I was suddenly overwhelmed with the sadness and disappointment of the day. All through my months of imprisonment I had looked forward to a reunion with Isabel. Now I sensed it would never happen, and in my depression, I wanted only to leave the area I had so anticipated visiting. The others, sensing my mood, reluctantly prepared to return to Lubao.

Chapter Sixty

The sun was setting when we returned to the Fassoths and found a celebration dinner waiting. They were hosting a party in our honor. There were huge platters of both pork and chicken *adobo,* banana leaves held great heaps of steaming rice, and there was roast turkey, baked ham, native vegetables, and traditional sweet puddings made with rice and coconut milk. Catalina had decorated with paper lanterns and native flowers, giving the entire house and yard a festive atmosphere in the fading twilight.

Fassoth had hired three musicians who played at the local cabaret. With a guitar, saxophone, and bass fiddle, they entertained us and the many guests who had gathered from the surrounding area. Reminiscent of the New Year's celebration at San Marcelino, native girls appeared in high heels and dresses kept only for special occasions. The unfamiliar foods and the presence of so many Filipino people put Janke in a sullen mood, but everyone else joined in the spirit of the evening. Even the sadness I had experienced earlier in the day was cast aside as I sensed the joyous mood created by music, food, liquor, and friends.

When I went outside the next morning, the truck was gone, and I supposed Janke had gone to get gas for our planned trip to Zambales. As I returned to the house Bill Main came charging into the living room.

"Some dirty bastard took my money last night!" he yelled.

Realizing Janke, the truck, and his money were all gone, Main exploded in an uncharacteristic rage.

"The little son of a bitch," he said. "He better not be around when I get back to Las Pinas. I'll wring the little bastard's neck!"

Despite the anger I felt about Main's empty wallet, I was glad Janke was gone. I knew hitching a ride would be no problem, and now the little pip-squeak would no longer put a damper on my trip.

Vacher and Ostrander went to the local cabaret that evening, while Allin, Main, and I spent the time with our host. We listened with rapt attention as he related how the war had changed their lives.

Bill Fassoth had come from Hawaii in 1913 and purchased 1,300 acres and was joined ten years later by his twin brother Martin. Together they had raised sugarcane and successfully operated a large rice mill. On December 29, 1941, the Japanese had bombed the mill and surrounding area, including their house. The family had fled, and three days later found a remote area in the foothills of Pampanga where they established a camp that would provide refuge to many American fugitives who, for one reason or another, had not withdrawn into Bataan with the main body of American forces.

The activity of the camp increased after the surrender of Bataan. With American soldiers escaping daily from the horrors of the forced march, the Fassoths sought many out, offering them refuge. It soon became apparent they would need additional facilities, and so they built a second camp deeper in the hills. At one time the Fassoths employed as many as seventy-five Filipinos and Negritos who carried supplies. Eventually the camp was raided, but not before many Americans had rested and regained their strength under the watchful eyes of the two brothers. I knew men, including Henry Patton, Earl Oatman, and Hank Winslow, who had been cared for by the Fassoths.

It was long past midnight when Vacher and Ostrander returned from the cabaret. New replacements had filled the bar where loud music and drinking created a raucous atmosphere. Two MPs had come in at 10 P.M, the curfew hour, and ordered everyone out.

"Don't give me any of your military shit," Vacher had threatened.

"Come on, soldier. You're going to the guardhouse," the MP replied.

Vacher swung, caught the MP on the chin and sent him reeling across the floor. Then he pulled the MacArthur letter from his pocket and waved it in the MP's face.

"Hell, there's no way I could tell you from the rest of the dog faces around here," he said. "Stick around until I get back. I'd like to talk with you guys."

When the bar was cleared of Army personnel, the MP sergeant joined the two former prisoners, and they sat in the bar for several hours sipping whiskey and visiting.

It was nearly daylight when I crawled under a mosquito bar to get a little sleep before leaving for Zambales to visit Fernando. Without Sam and the truck, I planned to hitch a ride. Ostrander and Allin decided to go with me, but Vacher and Main chose to stay at Fassoths. Ostrander, during his time as a fugitive, had also spent time with a family in the Zambales Mountains, and he was eager to return to the area. Allin, in his continuing zeal to experience all he could of our adventure, was excited to see where we had been.

Each of us carried a case of C-rations as we stood on the dusty roadside waiting for a ride. Our first opportunity was with two lieutenants and their driver in an Army reconnaissance vehicle. They were going to Olongapo, and we climbed in.

"How far past Olongapo?" one of the officers asked when I told them where we were going.

"Oh, about twenty or twenty-five kilometers."

"What the hell, I'd like to hear what you guys have been up to. Why don't we take you all the way?"

At San Marcelino we thanked the lieutenants, picked up the cases of C-rations, and started walking down the rural road leading to Fernando's farm. A Filipino with a bullcart offered to give us a ride. We gave him a chocolate bar, climbed into the bullcart, and rode the last eight kilometers.

"Goddamn," Allin said. "I never thought I'd see the day when I'd ride in one of these contraptions."

Fernando was sitting on the step of his bamboo house when we approached. He recognized me immediately and ran toward the bullcart. With tears in his eyes, he embraced me. He had heard nothing of me since the Negrito attack on his house more than two years earlier. He started a rapid-fire series of questions about the intervening months, wanting to know all about the prison camps where I had been.

News of our arrival spread quickly, and by afternoon local people began gathering to welcome us. Toward evening, Fernando butchered a pig and built a large fire. The pig was skewered on a bamboo spit, and as twilight fell over the Zambales Mountains, men from the barrio kept it turning steadily over the fire. It would take most of the night for the pig to roast to perfection, and the occasion proved to be a social event for the men who squatted by the fire and visited all night. I had nearly forgotten the simple, almost primitive, way of life in this remote area. I was glad I had come back to experience again the genuineness of these very humble people.

I drifted off to sleep, comforted by the peace of the Zambales foothills. As a fugitive there I had remained constantly alert to the dangers they held. Now in my freedom, I could fully appreciate the beauty that surrounded me.

When I woke, Fernando's wife, Euphemia, was already cooking rice, vegetables, and other food. She directed the women who prepared and arranged food on the long table that had been covered with giant banana leaves. The pig's heart, liver, and intestines were chopped fine and cooked in a small caldron. Women stirred it constantly, adding garlic, onions, and native herbs as it cooked. Just before removing it from the fire, the pig's blood was added and cooked until it coagulated. The mixture, called *denardaraan*, reminded me of fried liver and onions.

We would be guests of honor at a native feast. Among the many who came from nearby farms and barrios, some walking and some in bullcarts, were the Barones who I had known and the Arguillas with whom Ostrander had stayed. There were others I did not know who came simply to celebrate the return of Fernando's American friends.

I was taken by surprise when a beautiful young girl squealed with delight at seeing me. She ran to me and threw her arms around my neck as I caught her.

"Mr. Hileman, you do not remember me? I am Trudy."

During the months I had lived with Fernando, a skinny little girl who I had assumed to be a relative stayed with the family for a short time. I had paid little attention to her. Now as I looked into her shining brown eyes, I saw a beautiful, well-rounded girl who continued to smother me with kisses, another reminder that time had passed by.

Leaving the people of Zambales was difficult for both Ostrander and me. The renewing of treasured friendships, the spontaneity of the outpouring of food and love, and the peaceful surroundings made this a day we would long remember.

"What would you like me to send you when I get home?" I asked Fernando.

"I would like to have an American shotgun like the one Pamalicia had."

Pamalicia, a Negrito, had achieved fame throughout Pampanga and Zambales for killing Japanese soldiers with his Winchester twenty-gauge shotgun. He had notched the gun for each one he killed and proudly displayed the record of his marksmanship to everyone he saw.

"Okay, I'll get you one," I promised, remembering how Fernando had put his own family in peril to provide shelter for me.

Surprisingly, the visit seemed to mean nearly as much to Allin as it had to me. He had been given the opportunity to see a remote part of the Philippines he had never seen before and to experience the reality of native friendship and culture. As a result, he understood, as so few Americans did, the bond of loyalty and gratitude I felt for these simple, sincere people.

We had no difficulty hitching a ride from San Marcelino back to the Fassoth house in Lubao. By now we were all eager to get back to the 29th Replacement Depot to see if we were scheduled yet for our return to the United States. We left for Manila the next morning.

Chapter Sixty-one

Back at the 29th Replacement Depot, I went to the bulletin board to check the shipping rosters. My name, along with Sherdie Allin's and Jerry Emerick's, the rice cook at Cabanatuan, appeared on the manifest of the Dutch luxury liner *Klipfontein* which would dock in Seattle. Bill Main, Paul Vacher, and Walt Helhowski would board a ship bound for San Francisco. The *Klip,* as we soon called the ship, would sail in two days. It was with a sense of sorrow mixed with excitement that we made preparations to leave. I wondered how long it would be before I would see my friends again, especially Helhowski whose home was across the United States from mine.

On the morning of October 14 I joined others leaving on the *Klipfontein.* The truck rumbled through the streets of Manila to Pier 7, the same pier where I had disembarked from the USS *President Pierce* nearly four and one half years earlier. Vacher, Heinzman, and I had been so excited that day and so filled with wonder about what this strange land held for us. In July 1944 Pier 7 had been the embarkation point for the *Nissyo Maru,* and the nineteen days of hell that followed remained vivid in my mind. Now I would leave Pier 7 once more, this time for the trip back to the United States.

"You know, Pier Seven has been the place for some pretty damn important changes in my life," I said.

Allin and Emerick looked at me in surprise.

"Hell, it doesn't mean anything to me, except it's a place to get out of this shit hole," Emerick said.

At that moment I recognized a vast difference between myself and those who had surrendered to the Japanese on Bataan. Their time had been a period filled only with horror, hardships, and death. They tended to view the Philippines as a filthy, hostile land. In contrast, those of us who had escaped and spent time in the hills had a different view. I had experienced the beauty of the land and its people, and it had become a part of me that would remain with me all my life.

I was certain my trip to the United States would be only an interim visit, and I would return to live in the Philippines. The best and worst times in my life had been shared with friends there, but I had already begun to think of only the good times, like singing under the guava tree at the Jordan farm, falling in love with Isabel, and even the quiet life in Zambales. Yet with each step up the wooden gangplank, I became more excited about returning to the United States.

It was noon when the *Klipfontein* slid quietly away from Pier 7 and moved into Manila Bay. We stood on the deck watching Dewey Boulevard fade into the distance. The smell of the Orient disappeared in the fresh sea breezes. I remembered how soldiers often called the Pearl of the Orient the Shit Hole of the Orient, a comment on the odors I had grown accustomed to during the past four years. Those smells had bothered me, too, when I first arrived, but I had learned to separate the smell of filth from the smell of roasting pork and chicken, the smoke of cooking fires, and the ever present musty smell of the jungle in the barrios.

Sailing through Manila Bay, we passed by the silent wrecks of warships, stark sentinels still standing watch over the site of great devastation and horror. Emerick had disappeared, but Allin remained on deck with me. The rhythmic pounding of the *Klip's* engines took us quickly past the shores of Bataan.

"Hey, there's Mount Bataan," I said. "I can always say I climbed that son of a bitch."

I told Allin about the unnecessary climb up the 4700-foot peak during our trek out of Bataan, and the bullet birds we had seen.

"Bullet birds?"

"I don't know what they were, but we called them that because of the way they seemed to attack us. The little bastards would dive at us and sound just like a bullet."

Passing Corregidor where the fighting had been ferocious, I viewed the Rock with a sense of reverence. I wondered just where on the island Helhowski had been stationed during the fighting. The Polack from Pennsylvania had proved to be just the kind of friend I had needed in Japan.

We turned south in the late afternoon sun, and I felt a quiet sadness as Bataan disappeared beyond the horizon. The peninsula, although it represented a time of hardship and defeat, generated a strange sense of nostalgia.

Allin and I decided to sleep on deck, preferring the cool tropical breezes to the closed-in stuffiness of the state room. We talked for hours.

Long after sunset, Allin pulled his blanket up over his shoulders and fell asleep. I remained awake under the star-studded sky.

The ship rumbled on, and in the darkness I thought it must be moving through the San Bernardino Straits. My mind turned again to my first trip through the straits in 1941. The events of that day remained deeply etched in my memory. Sadness and guilt fell over me as I recalled standing on the fantail of the USS *President Pierce* with Paul Vacher and Orlo Heinzman.

"Orlo, where do you think we'll be a year from now?" I had asked.

"Hileman, a year from now I'll be dead. They're going to bury me here. Don't ask me how I know, but I'm never going home."

"You've got to be kidding. This trip is a great adventure."

A year later Orlo Heinzman had been buried in one of the countless unmarked graves: an anonymous casualty who had served in a forgotten army.

I had lived through the hell of war, escape, life as a fugitive, and brutal imprisonment. I had survived my great adventure.

Now, on the deck of the *Klipfontein*, I remembered my lost friend, and in the darkness, I felt alone.

Epilogue

Millard Hileman is one of only five men from the 698th Ordnance stationed at Clark Field who remains living today. The others are Homer Boren, Arthur "PeeWee" Standlee, Charlie Johnson, and Grover Bump. Separated by varied prison camp experiences, the five men were reunited in 1982, and it has been largely through the friendship and encouragement of that group that this story has been brought to completion.

The Escape:
Millard Hileman is the sole survivor of the seven men from the 698th who fled into the hills of Bataan on April 9, 1942. Paul Vacher returned to California after the war where he died in 1964. Bill Main lived in California and Oregon where he died in 1983. Orlo Heinzman died while still a fugitive in 1942. Wallace Kinder was caught by the Japanese and beheaded in 1943, and Sergeant Henderson was bayoneted by a Japanese patrol in 1943. The fate of George Wicks remains unknown.

Pasbul, Porac, and Pio:
Dr. Catalino Pineda, brutalized and in failing health, died in Porac

in 1970. Mrs. Pineda still lives in the family home there. Their son Ernie, as well as several brothers and sisters, resides in Porac and remains in close touch with Millard Hileman. Neives Jordan and her sister emigrated to the United States in 1960, and both live in San Diego, California. Joe Cheesman returned to the United States with his family in 1953. He and his wife Loring both died in Seattle where their son Roy still lives. Isabel Montemayor died in Manila in 1970. Felix and Sundai, the young Negritos who dug the grave for Orlo Heinzman, still live in Pasbul with their semi-nomadic tribe.

Zambales:
Fernando Esquibel died at his home in 1989 where his wife also died in 1982. Their youngest daughter Leonila, who was a baby when Millard Hileman was sheltered in their home, resides in Zambales and remains in close contact with the Hilemans.

Bilibid:
Twelve or thirteen of the prisoners who received red tags at Bilibid, thereby escaping execution, are yet living in areas throughout the United States. Hank Winslow and Earl Oatman who lived at the farm adjoining Esquibels both live in California. John Scott whose map attracted the interest of the Japanese has residence in California, but lives in the Philippine Islands much of the time. Harold Irving who recited poetry and brought calm to the prison cell lives in Hawaii, and Pierce Wade who parodied poetry lives in Florida. Bill Ostrander who succeeded in selling fake tooth powder to the Japanese guards lives in Virginia, and Henry Patton who became known as "the mean old man" lives in Kansas.

Ray Schletterer died in prison camp in Japan, and Mike Slish died in Indiana in 1970.

Cabanatuan:
Jerry Emerick and Monty Montgomery from the Cabanatuan kitchen crew both lived at Snoqualmie, Washington, for several years. Monty died in the late seventies, and Jerry continues to live in the Seattle area. Tom Coleman with whom Hileman had been friends before the war lives in Ohio.

Japan:

Walt Helhowski, the Polack from Pennsylvania, returned to his home state where he still lives.

Father Curran whose quiet authority brought some order out of chaos on the prison ship returned to California where he continued his priesthood until he died in 1972.

Liberation:

Sherdie Allin, who was reunited with Hileman at the 29th Replacement Depot, returned to New Hampshire where he lived until his death in 1981.

PICTURE CREDITS

Page 1, top, National Archives 127-GR-114538; bottom left, Grover Bump; bottom right, Carl Kinder. Page 2, top, Millard Hileman; bottom left, Ernie Fisk; bottom right, Ernie Pineda. Page 3, top left, Henry Patton; top right, Mrs. Robert D. Hoffman; bottom, Millard Hileman. Page 4, top, John Scott; bottom left, Department of the Army, West Point; bottom right, Leonila Esquibel. Page 5, top, Roy Cheesman; bottom left, Marvin Morgan; bottom right, John Scott. Page 6, top, UPI/Bettmann Archives 1013577; bottom left, Juanita Vacher; center, Millard Hileman; right, Henry Patton. Page 7, Dr. Paul L. Ashton. Page 8, the men pictured. Page 9, top, Charles T. Johnson; bottom left, Grover Bump; center, Tom Coleman; bottom right, *Heroes Of Bataan*, Marcus Griffin, editor. Page 10, top, National Archives 111-SC-265431; bottom, National Archives 111-SC-202644. Page 11, top, National Archives 111-SC-265430; bottom, National Archives 111SC-202646. Page 12, top, Paul Silverton and Frank Bard Young of Vanderbilt University Press; bottom left, Dr. Paul L. Ashton; bottom right, National Archives 80-G-450241. Page 13, top left, Millard Hileman; top right, Walter Helhowski; bottom, John Falconer. Page 14, top, Millard Hileman; bottom two, John Falconer. Page 15, Patrick Davie. Page 16, Donald C. Harris.